DONORS FOR LIFE

a practitioner's guide to relationship fundraising

Craig Linton and Paul Stein

The White Lion Press

The White Lion Press Limited, London, UK
www.whitelionpress.com

© 2017 The White Lion Press
All rights reserved
978-0-9553993-6-7
All rights reserved
First printed 2017

No part of this publication may reproduced, stored in a retrieval system, or transmitted, in any form or by any means, electronic, mechanical, photocopying, recording, or otherwise, without the prior permission of the author or publisher.

British Library Cataloguing-in-Publication Data.

A catalogue record for this book is available from the British Library.

Cover illustration by Thinkstock: Wavebreakmedia Ltd
Copy editor: Jane Fricker
Design and print production by Bradbury and Williams
Printed and bound in the United Kingdom by CPI Group (UK) Ltd,

Contents

Acknowledgements		5
Foreword by Ken Burnett		6
1.	How this book came about	8
2.	Fundraising and nonprofits in the twenty-first century	23
3.	Relationship fundraising: what it is	35
4.	Why people give and the importance of emotion	50
5.	Developing a relationship fundraising strategy	69
6.	Creating a culture of relationship fundraising	85
7.	Recruiting your donors	94
8.	The seven elements of successful door recruitment	106
9.	The seven elements in action: four outstanding donor recruitment campaigns	133
10	Integration: creating a seamless experience for donors. A tale of two brands	144
11	Friends for life: welcoming and keeping your doors	168
12	Community fundraising, mass participation events and peer-to-peer fundraising	210
13	Major donor fundraising: launching a twenty-first century progamme	225
14	Transformative appeals: achieving your charity's visionary goals	245
15	Techniques for specialist areas of fundraising	263
16	Legacy fundraising	283
17	How do people really make decisions? by Rob Woods	303
18	Rekindling friendships	322
19	Measurement of performance, innovation and the planning cycle	341
20	Final thoughts and further reading	366

This book is dedicated to

Grace and Tanesha.
And to Rachel and Sam.

Acknowledgements

Craig Linton

It is hard to know where to start when writing acknowledgements as so many people have influenced, supported and contributed to the experience and thinking I've shared in this book. It is impossible to thank each and every person individually.

First I'd like to thank all the teams I've worked with at Sue Ryder, the Greater London Fund for the Blind, the Royal Society for Blind Children and Amnesty International.

I'm also grateful to everyone who has allowed me to use their stories and case studies in this book and to those who read some of the draft chapters and provided constructive feedback. The book is better for their generosity in sharing.

Relationship fundraising has been a massive influence on my career so thanks go to Ken Burnett for asking us to write this book. It has been a privilege to work with Paul on it and I'd like to say a big thank you to Rob Woods for his contribution and producing such a great chapter.

My family have always been a huge source of support in my career. Once my parents got over the initial shock of me abandoning a career in law they have been fully supportive and helped financially and emotionally. Thanks mam and dad!

My wife jokes how I got more emotional on our wedding day about my family than her. The truth is I was a blubbering wreck and I would've been a bigger mess had I told her how much I love her and how wonderful she is. She has supported me during the writing of this book and given up numerous weekends and evenings to allow me to write. Thanks Grace.

If you've made it this far, then my final thank you is to you, the reader, for buying this book.

I'd love to hear your stories and feedback so please do get in touch. Wherever you are reading it, I hope it will inspire you to be the best fundraiser you can be. Enjoy.

Craig Linton, Croydon, UK, May 2017

Paul Stein

Like Craig, I would also like to thank my parents for providing me with a great education, for supporting me in my decision to enter the charity sector and my dad for ensuring my grammar and syntax were always up to scratch. I am forever grateful.

Jane Porter, Paul Anticoni and Cynthia Joyce have managed and guided me so remarkably well and demonstrated what can be achieved by hard work, integrity and commitment to the cause. I am hugely indebted to you all.

I add my thanks to Ken Burnett for so kindly giving Craig and me the opportunity to write this book and for inspiring us in our careers and our development.

I must extend my gratitude to Misty, Toffee, Cleo, Gizmo and Tabitha for providing me with a constant source of entertainment, companionship and comfort.

Sam Stein you are a wonderful son and rightly remind me to get off my emails. I grow more proud of you every day.

Rachel, thank you so much for keeping me sane, checking endless copy and for being the most wonderful and caring partner. I love you very much.

Paul Stein, London, UK, May 2017

Foreword

Some years ago I promised myself that I'd written my last fundraising book and that hasn't changed. But as experience of relationship fundraising and developing donor relationships has become clearer and public concern at inappropriate, over-aggressive fundraising methods has grown more acute, I've begun to see that a serious, donor-focused practitioner's guide to relationship fundraising would be really welcomed by, and useful for, fundraisers the world over. When by chance I bumped into Craig and Paul as they were running a conference session on relationship fundraising in practice I knew I'd found the right people to compile and write that book.

What's in here is a step-by-step, detailed guide to how you can excel in donor relationship-building and delight your donors. Helpfully, it's designed for both the fundraiser who is part of a team in a large organisation and the sole operator responsible for every part of the process in a very small charity. For all, the emphasis is on retention and relationship development, a counter-swing for a sector that for far too long has focused too heavily on donor acquisition, an obsession we've paid a heavy price for in donor attrition.

In these pages you'll find all you'll need to make relationship fundraising work for you, your cause and your donors. I've often said that I've made a career out of simply stating the bleedin' obvious – in essence, my philosophy of relationship fundraising is: if you are nice to people they'll be nice to you in return. It's not enough to fill half a page, far less a whole book. I've written three substantial tomes on the subject.

Of course, there's more to it than that, as this book shows. Particularly in the light of today's renewed focus on the all-important quality of the donor experience and how we ensure it's just as good as it can be.

But relationship fundraising does seem highly prone to over-analysis. For anyone alarmed by this, I'd say that, just like walking, sex, or cycling, it's best if you don't think too much about it at first but just do it. Your natural instincts and sense of right and wrong will be your best guide as to how to put it into practice. That said, there's no doubt that if you do your homework into what donors want and don't want and familiarise yourself with all the issues and complexities that surround the subject you will almost certainly have an edge over those that don't. What distinguishes a great relationship fundraiser from a merely good one is that the great fundraiser simply knows more.

So this book sets out for you, excellently, what you really need to know.

In the summer of 2015, just as *Donors for Life* was being put together, fundraisers in the UK found their trade and how they practice it firmly in the crosshairs of the nation's investigative reporters, who proceeded to pull professional fundraising and its worst excesses apart, exposing multiple shortcomings and shining a spotlight on the shaky fundraising foundations of many of our nation's best known, most-loved charities. The British government duly confirmed the media's assessment that British fundraising is overly persistent, aggressive and unwelcome in its asking, which served to underscore what many have considered obvious for years now – that it's about, if not past, time that the donor was put firmly at the heart of British fundraising.

That horrid summer of discontent led directly to the creation of The Commission on the Donor Experience (see www.donor-experience.com) and a new commitment among British fundraisers to put concern for their donors rather than achieving their financial targets at the centre of how fundraising should be done. The Commission, promoting many of the core values and ideas in this book and earlier books from myself and others, has set out to regain some of the lost ground by showing that fundraisers can be trusted to provide their donors with a consistently impeccable, rewarding and enjoyable donor experience.

This book reminds us, if reminding is needed, of what fundraising done well is really all about. It shows us a different, better way. And it helps us to celebrate, in all its shades and formats, the fine craft of asking properly, which my late friend and former business partner George Smith described so warmly two decades ago in his book of the same name.

> *My mother always told me to ask properly for things. I was told off if I was impolite or over-aggressive. I was reprimanded for asking in sloppy language or incomplete sentences. I was scorned for asking for the impossible. I was honoured when, on occasion, I did manage to ask properly.*
> George Smith, *Asking Properly: the art of creative fundraising*, White Lion Press, 1996.

Charitable giving is voluntary, always. As George knew well, invariably it pays to ask properly, just as it can seriously, permanently alienate donors if they think they are being sold to, pressurised, pursued, condescended to, or taken for granted.

I hope you will enjoy this book and that you and your donors will profit from it.

Ken Burnett, Suffolk, May 2017

How this book came about

Almost every fundraiser we've ever met didn't set out to become one. Most of us have stumbled into the profession from other careers or by chance, but having done so we have found one of the most rewarding and enjoyable occupations that exists.

The chance to truly make the world a better place by inspiring people to give to the good causes we work for is immensely gratifying and inspiring.

Craig's story of how he fell in love with a career in fundraising is one you may relate to:

> *Initially my fundraising career was only intended to last a year or so. After that I was meant to go back to university and get a 'proper' job in law, but I found I loved the role and have had the pleasure of being a fundraiser for over 15 years.*
>
> *The big turning point for me was when I read the second edition of* Relationship Fundraising *by Ken Burnett. It was Ken's book that got me hooked on fundraising as a career.*
>
> *I remember buying the book in 2002. At the time I'd been a community fundraising assistant for about 18 months and as much as I'd enjoyed helping out at various events and activities, it wasn't really intellectually stimulating and I couldn't see a long-term future for me.*
>
> *Then I read Ken's book.*
>
> *I remember devouring it in the course of a day, then going back through it with a fine toothcomb – making notes and jotting down ideas. By the time I'd finished the book for a second time I had about 12 pages of notes. I eagerly went and presented them to my bosses at the time and it says a lot about their attitude and leadership that they didn't tell me 'to get lost!' but encouraged me*

to introduce a number of my ideas.

From that moment on I was a professional fundraiser.

I re-vamped our thank-you letters, took responsibility for the database, looked for ways to recognise and thank donors and worked hard to implement as much of the theory and ideas in the book as possible.

The book made me proud to be a fundraiser and showed me what a fulfilling, stimulating and enjoyable career it could offer me.

I haven't always got things right, but Relationship Fundraising *and Ken's other books have been a compass pointing me in the correct fundraising direction throughout my career.*

Paul's journey is very similar:

I had been a community fundraising assistant and then a fundraiser for a couple of years. Like Craig, I enjoyed being in the charity environment and had perfected the art of dressing up in a giant Miles the Mouse costume for Macmillan Cancer Support's Miles Challenge.

It was at this point that Jane Porter, a dynamic and experienced fundraiser, joined the organisation. She became my manager and opened my eyes to the professional world of fundraising. Jane is widely read, so I asked where I should begin. 'Ken Burnett's Relationship Fundraising', *she replied, without hesitation. I read it rapidly and my approach and ambition were transformed.'*

Fast forward 10 years.

We both decided to put together a session for the annual Institute of Fundraising National Convention and chose relationship fundraising as a theme. We were both nervous, as it was the first time we'd spoken together at the conference and we wanted to make a good impression. Those nerves were magnified tenfold when Craig bumped into Ken in the corridor and he announced that he'd be in the audience.

Doing a talk based on relationship fundraising, when the author of the book of the same name is in the room is a bit of a strange experience. But the talk seemed to go well and, to cut a long story short, Ken suggested to us that if we felt inclined to work together on this book, he would help us.

Hence *Donors for Life: A Practitioner's Guide to Relationship Fundraising*. It's been a privilege to pour our experiences into this book and we hope that it can provide the same kind of inspiration to you that Ken's book gave to us and thousands of other fundraisers around the world.

ABOUT THIS BOOK

Academics, consultants and fundraising agency staff write the majority of fundraising books. There's nothing wrong with this per se, but sometimes the practising fundraiser can be left scratching his or her head thinking, 'the theory is great, but how do I do this in reality?'

Our aim is to provide a guide that is accessible, entertaining and, most importantly, useful in your day-to-day job as a fundraiser. We want to share our experiences as hands-on fundraisers who face many of the same challenges that you will in your work. We believe this book is different as it is rooted in the experiences and needs of fundraisers.

Where we are unable to go into sufficient detail, we hope to signpost where you can get more information and read deeper. We've also talked to practising fundraisers from around the world and will share with you their stories and experiences. We've learned huge amounts from them. We hope you will too.

Importantly, neither of us claims to be a perfect fundraiser and will be the first to admit we make mistakes. There are plenty of examples of where things have gone wrong and hopefully you can learn from and avoid the errors we've made during our careers.

You will see the influence of other fundraisers, marketers, scientists and business leaders throughout this book. We've tried to read extensively in our research and to bring you the best information we can find. However, the central tenet of the book is that the ideas and principles of relationship fundraising that Ken Burnett talked about more than 20 years ago still hold true.

Our view is that as a profession we haven't implemented it well enough in practice, which is why giving to charity is not the joy it should be for many people. We hope this book will help change that.

WHAT'S WRONG WITH FUNDRAISING TODAY?

We believe that the overall standard of fundraising around the world could be much higher. Don't believe us? Well, a brief look at donor attrition rates shows we have a major problem.

In the United States, the Association of Fundraising Professionals (AFP) *2017 Effectiveness Report*[1] found the following grim facts about fundraising:

- Gains of $4.893 billion in gifts generated from new, upgraded current and previously lapsed donors were offset by losses of $4.625 billion through reduced gifts and lapsed donors. This means that, while there was a positive $267 million net gain in giving, every $100 gained in 2016 was offset by $95 in losses through gift attrition.

- Gains of 4.882 million in new and previously lapsed donors were offset by losses of 4.832 million in lapsed donors. This means that there was a growth of – 49,421 – donors and every 100 donors gained in 2016 was offset by 99 lost donors through attrition.

- Overall, the median donor attrition in nonprofits was 55 per cent — that is, 55 per cent of 2015 donors did not give again in 2016 to nonprofits that they had supported in the previous year. These results are not down to one bad year. In fact only twice since 2000 have new donations exceeded attrition.

The problem of high donor attrition isn't confined to the United States. It's a sad fact that within a year of making their first gift to our causes over 50 per cent of donors stop giving in nearly every country we've found statistics for.[2]
If we are going to change the world then we need to do better.

You'll see throughout this book that there are a number of practices that we believe need to change, that aren't good enough, that frankly irritate us about fundraising today.

At the heart of this are seven major problems that exist within our profession. They start with strategic difficulties, which filter down to the operational level and cause donor apathy and attrition.

Poor fundraising leadership

Running alongside the problem of short-term thinking is a leadership deficit within our profession. There is a merry-go-round where average (or worse) fundraising directors regularly go from one charity to another, inflicting their own special breed of damage before moving on to the next victim, often with a hefty pay rise.

These people do our profession much damage and cost millions in lost revenue from our donors, yet they continue to get good jobs. As a sector we need to pay more attention to weeding out poor fundraising leaders and poor fundraisers.

This problem is compounded by boards and chief executive officers who don't fully understand fundraising. They often demand instant returns and don't understand concepts such as lifetime value and retention.

Overall, poor leadership in an organisation soon shows itself as a lack of vision, unclear decision-making and an absence of strategic planning within an organisation and means less money is raised.

The good news is that fundraising is increasingly seen as a legitimate career option. Across the world there is a growing range of university courses on the subject. The number of internships has grown and some larger charities now offer graduate schemes for aspiring fundraisers. So hopefully we will soon see a new generation of fundraising leaders.

Of course there are many examples of great fundraising leadership and we'll be studying these throughout the book.

High turnover of fundraising staff

This poor leadership manifests itself in high turnover of fundraising staff and low morale.

A 2012 survey by *Third Sector* magazine found that 50 per cent of UK fundraisers thought morale was low in their charity, 53 per cent thought they would leave in the next year and 55 per cent didn't think that their senior management was effective.[3]

In the United States, the *Chronicle of Philanthropy* reported on research that found that the average fundraiser only stays in post for 16 months.[4]

In the research report *Under Developed – A National Study of Challenges Facing Nonprofit Fundraising*[5] the authors concluded that there is a vicious cycle in play at many US nonprofits (figure 1).

The report found that development director roles were vacant for a median time of six months across all organisations. This jumped to 12 months in organisations with a turnover of under $1 million.

Short-term decision-making

Due to poor leadership and high turnover of staff, decision-making is often too focused on the short term and donor lifetime value is sacrificed to please

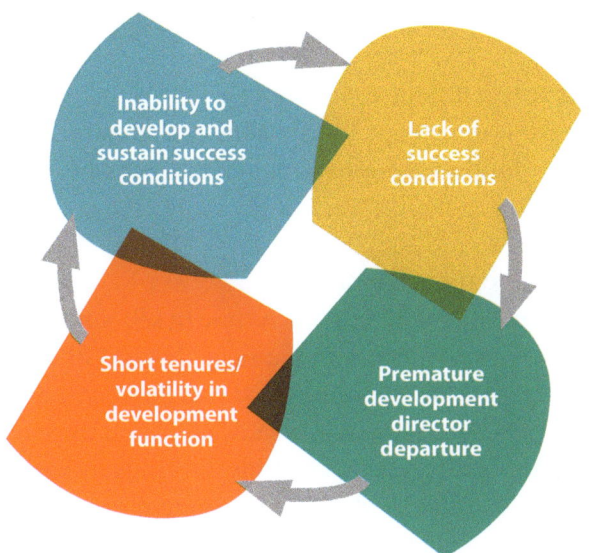

Figure 1: The vicious cycle causing high turnover of staff

the coming quarter or year's budget forecast. This results in poor long-term fundraising performance and high donor attrition.

It is no coincidence that the charities with the best fundraising performance tend to be those with low staff turnover and stable leadership. We believe fundraisers need to be in post for two to three years at least to really make a lasting impact. The best fundraising leaders we've met tend to be in post four years or more and the truly great ones for over a decade.

We need to work harder to make sure fundraisers are assessed on medium- and long-term performance, as well as the monthly/quarterly/annual goal. Should we really be sacrificing $100 today for $10,000 in the near future?

These three strategic issues cause the following everyday difficulties for fundraisers.

Fundraising lacks emotion

To paraphrase David Ogilvy: you cannot bore people into giving to your cause. Yet sadly we see too many charities trying to do this through inaccessible language, poor images and vague asks.

As we'll show in chapter 4, giving is a personal and emotional decision, yet we try to rely too much on logic and rationality to make our cases.

Many larger organisations have copied some of the worst and most annoying practices of the commercial world, such as automated call centres and outsourced response handling. This has removed the core human-to-human interaction and connection that are essential to feelings of altruism and giving. When you believe you're a number in a machine and your donation isn't making a difference, then of course you'll think twice about giving.

To revolutionise our fundraising in the coming years, we need to reconnect with our donors emotionally and make them feel a valued and important part of our mission to change the world.

Navel gazing turns donors off

Many charities spend too much time in self-congratulatory mode, like preening peacocks showing off their plumage. Instead of showing donors the difference they have made in the world, these charities boast of their own achievements and smugly give themselves a self-satisfied pat on the back.

The level of reserves that charities collectively have in the bank is symptomatic of this. Whilst the need to have a prudent reserves policy is sensible, the sector is sitting on a pile of cash that could be unleashed to great effect. In the United States alone, charities have over $4.2 trillion of assets[6] yet a cure for malaria is only estimated at $60 billion over the next 30 years.[7] This is wrong.

Too many charities have become more about self-preservation than changing the world. They've stopped being radical and have become too safe and accepting of the status quo. Donors sense this and when they don't feel that they are making a difference they stop giving.

Over the last few years, this has led to a plethora of bright new fundraising stars emerging to challenge more traditional charities. Look at Help for Heroes in the UK, Charity: Water in the United States and Movember worldwide. They haven't taken over from the big boys yet, but they are pushing them to explore new ways of raising money and are attracting many donors to their causes.

Inadequate donor service

Giving to charity should be a joyful experience. Yet often the good feeling you get by giving is lost due to a poor experience after you make a gift. This can be something such as a mistake in spelling your name, a slow response to a question, an impersonal thank-you letter, or not showing you the difference you have made.

Too often donor care is seen as a cost and not a profit centre. As we'll show, we think this is a mistake. If the key to a successful relationship and maximising lifetime value is building loyalty, commitment and trust, then we need to make sure that every interaction we have with a donor (at the very least) does no harm to the relationship.

Poor use of data and databases

Data are at the heart of successful fundraising. If you don't know who your donors are, what they give to and why, you are going to struggle. Every charity we have worked in has had a badly implemented database. This has cost the charity thousands of pounds in lost income both from donors and reduced staff productivity. Speaking to fundraisers in other organisations, we know we are not alone.

Yet having clean, accurate data that are easily manipulated and used in your fundraising is absolutely crucial and shouldn't be beyond our powers to achieve. In recent years the costs of databases and IT in general have reduced massively so there is no excuse for any charity failing in this area.

Relationship fundraising without strong data is like eating a pizza without a base. All the toppings and good bits are there, but without the base the ingredients ooze through your fingers and create an inedible mess.

Databases might not be the most glamorous area of fundraising, but they underpin your entire fundraising operation and are ignored at your peril. In our opinion, excellent data and the ability to use them to raise money are areas of significant competitive advantage. They will remain so whilst many charities struggle to make the most of the information they hold.

Good relationship fundraisers are committed to understanding their numbers and applying the lessons their data are telling them. If you aren't able to understand data, then make sure you employ someone who does and make her or him explain things in a way you can understand.

THE END RESULT OF THESE PROBLEMS? PUBLIC SUSPICION OF FUNDRAISING PRACTICES AND COSTS

In the last few years the fundraising profession in the United States has been hit by a series of exposés and scandals about the costs of fundraising.[8]

A story run by the TV channel CNN in 2012 found that out of tens of millions of dollars that had been raised for a disabled veterans charity, only a tiny percentage had ended up helping the intended beneficiaries. Instead, the majority of the funds had gone to the charity's direct marketing agency.[9]

More recently, in 2015, four cancer charities (run by the same family) were charged with scamming $187 million from donors across all 50 states. The sad tale of affairs saw the vulnerable and frail deliberately targeted to give money through aggressive and abusive fundraising tactics.[10]

In the UK there has been the sad case of Olive Cooke. Mrs Cooke was a 92-year-old lady who committed suicide. A family friend claimed it was because Mrs Cooke could not cope with the number of 'begging' letters and phone calls she was receiving from charities. The facts of the matter are somewhat different.[11] However, the damage has been done and it has given numerous commentators open season on fundraising practices. After further exposés in the press, a review into fundraising regulation was held. This has resulted in the creation of a new fundraising regulator and a proposed new 'opt-out' that any donor can use to stop receiving fundraising communications. The exact details are still being worked out at the time of printing, but there is no doubt this will change the fundraising landscape in the UK forever.

Another example comes from Australia in 2012, when a journalist attending the Fundraising Institute of Australia National Conference wrote a damning report about the conference and the way fundraisers talk about donors and legacies in particular.[12]

Whilst to the trained fundraiser, and remember your donor isn't, the comments might not seem too bad (and the journalist does seem to have had a sense of humour bypass), the public were rightly outraged that individual donors were spoken of in such disparaging terms including being described as 'mad' for supporting animal charities.

In the Republic of Ireland in 2013, a scandal broke about secret payments to the board of a leading charity in the country. The resulting backlash led to hate mail, cancelled donations and increased suspicion from donors about how their money was being spent, not just in the charity mentioned, but in all charities.[13]

These scandalous stories give all fundraisers a bad name and tar us with the same brush. There will perhaps always be rogues in every profession, but we need to do our best to ensure transparency, adherence to codes of practice and placement of the donor at the heart of our thinking and our decision-making.

A related, but different problem is that as a sector we have also promoted the myth that fundraising costs are a bad thing per se. There is a race to the bottom to announce that 100 per cent of donations go to the cause and that nothing is spent on administration. This might work for individual organisations that have the corporate support and backing to make such an offer, but it damages the sector as a whole by promoting the view that fundraising costs are bad.

We should be a lot more robust in demonstrating the need to invest in fundraising. It generates a far better return for the causes we care about than keeping money in the bank or invested in the stock market.

Save the Children puts it brilliantly when it says to donors:

> *On average, over the last five years, for every £1 you gave us, we spent 85p to benefit children and used the remaining 15p to raise the next £1.*

REASONS TO BE CHEERFUL…

However, it's not all doom and gloom.

There are numerous examples of great fundraising that inspires people to give. We'll look at some of these throughout this book.

Even as we come out of the largest global recession since the Second World War, giving to charitable causes has remained relatively static and not dropped dramatically.

Technology is giving us new tools and media to attract people to the causes we care about. It is enabling us to tell richer, more personal stories and making true relationship fundraising affordable and achievable for every charity.

Despite the scandals mentioned, people continue to give and to believe in the importance of charity. There is no evidence of donors abandoning causes in large numbers. When donors decide to stop supporting a particular charity they tend to find another to support, rather than stop giving altogether.

Finally, never forget that giving feels good and provides donors with a buzz and sense of pride. There are now numerous studies that show giving releases dopamine and serotonin (which make you happy) and also provides a number of other benefits including improved mental and physical health.[14] We'll be looking at these in much more detail later in chapter 4.

So, with all these things in our favour, imagine how much more we could raise if our donors didn't view us with suspicion and distrust.

HOW THE WORLD HAS CHANGED – AND STAYED THE SAME

When the first edition of *Relationship Fundraising* was published in 1992 the Internet as we now know it didn't exist. Mobile phones were like bricks and were the preserve of the wealthy. Likewise, when the second edition was published in 2002 Facebook, Twitter and YouTube were yet to come into existence. Smart phones and tablets were a twinkle in Steve Jobs' imagination and clouds were still things that you only found in the sky. A decade and a half later, these new technologies have given fundraisers easier ways to communicate with donors and to share their stories.

Philanthropy is growing around the world, spreading beyond the traditional Western countries. The BRIC countries – Brazil, Russia, India and China – are starting to support good causes in larger numbers than ever before and will continue to do so as their collective wealth and prosperity grows.

Acquisition of donors has continued to get tougher and more expensive in mature fundraising markets. It is rare now if an acquisition programme in the UK or the United States breaks even in year one. Donors have become wiser to our techniques and gimmicks and there are an ever-growing number of charities all chasing a relatively static number of donors.

Yet despite these changes, the basics that underpin good fundraising remain the same and people still give for broadly the same reasons they always have.

You still need to have a problem to solve, a solution that is plausible, achievable and affordable and a compelling, emotionally led story to inspire donors to want to play their part in solving it.

We'll show you how to do this throughout the book.

WHY RELATIONSHIP FUNDRAISING REMAINS THE BEST WAY TO RAISE MONEY

We'll be looking at this in greater detail in chapter 3, but we wanted to set out right at the start why we believe in relationship fundraising.

From the notes (and donations) we received after we sent personal thank-you letters to donors, to the feedback that our causes are the only ones that listen to donors and act on their wishes, our combined experience has led us to the conclusion that implementing relationship fundraising really does make a difference to the net amount you raise. This is borne out through the conversations we have had with fundraisers around the world.

But our faith in relationship fundraising is based on much more than a collection of anecdotes and misty-eyed recollections. It is backed by detailed evidence and research too.

Here are a few research examples to whet your appetite.

Professor Adrian Sargeant is a pre-eminent fundraising academic who has studied fundraising and donor behaviour for many years. One of his studies looked at why donors stopped giving.[15] His research identified six factors that are directly influenced by the quality and type of your fundraising:

- Recognition
- Personal benefits versus altruism

- Pressure
- Impact
- Relationship
- Service quality

Recent studies on donor commitment by DonorVoice showed that moving donors from low to high commitment increases their three-year giving by 131 per cent.[16] How do you increase commitment? Well, DonorVoice identified seven key drivers that influence donor commitment. We will look at them in chapter 3 but the important point here is that *all of them* can be improved by implementing good relationship fundraising practice.

In the commercial world there is increasing acceptance that customer experience is one of the most important drivers of business performance. Analysis by Forrester Research[17] shows that those companies that excel at providing excellent (or at least best in class) customer experience have a significant competitive advantage and produce greater profits than their rivals.

The key learning from all of this is that relationship fundraising isn't important because it will make your donors or even your fundraisers feel warm and fuzzy – it's important because it will help you raise more money today, tomorrow and forever.

In fact, relationship fundraising is likely to fail when charities treat it like something cosy and comforting and not as the discipline that is critical to your business: the raising of money for your valuable cause.

We'll be showing you how to build the financial case for relationship fundraising in chapter 3 and will return to the factors that make it successful throughout the book. In particular, we will be looking closely at how you can improve the quality of the donor experience you provide and how you can use this to build meaningful relationships with donors.

Relationship fundraising isn't the only way to raise money and there are other approaches you could use. Yet we vehemently believe it's the best, most rewarding (for fundraisers and donors) and most stimulating way to fundraise. If you're not a convert at the minute, then we hope this book will help to change your mind.

WHAT YOU WILL FIND INSIDE
The book is split into four sections:

The principles of relationship fundraising
- Fundraising now.
- Why people give.
- Why relationship fundraising is the best way to fundraise.
- Fundraising strategy and culture.

Recruiting your donors
- Developing your donor recruitment plan.
- The seven elements of successful donor recruitment campaigns.
- Integrated campaigns.

Developing your donors
- Managing your database.
- Community and events fundraising.
- Major donors, companies and trusts and foundations.
- Legacies.

Learning from your donors
- Behavioural economics and relationship building.
- Rekindling friendships.
- Donors for life.

A RALLYING CALL TO DO BETTER: THE RELATIONSHIP FUNDRAISING DECLARATION
In the second edition of *Relationship Fundraising* Ken Burnett ended the preface with a powerful reminder to fundraisers everywhere that their job is special and different from many trades and professions. As Ken said:

> *Fundraising is more than a job. In the right hands, it is a powerful force for change and while that change is under way it should be an inspirational beacon of hope.*[17]

This is as true today as it was then. Yet it remains a sad fact that donors often give despite fundraisers and our techniques, not because of them.

We wanted to end this first chapter with a rallying call to fundraisers everywhere. A cry to fight bad fundraising; a pledge to the donors and causes we serve. Think of it as a type of Hippocratic oath for fundraisers, where we promise to be the best we can.

THE RELATIONSHIP FUNDRAISING DECLARATION

As a fundraiser, I know that the causes I work for and represent are dependent on me to raise the money they need to change the world. It is a big responsibility and one that I take seriously and commit to do to the best of my ability.

As a fundraiser, I promise to uphold the following to the best of my ability and judgement:

1. To act ethically and professionally at all times and to adhere to codes of practice and fundraising guidelines as minimum standards.
2. To place the donor at the centre of my decision-making. To stand up for them when I think their interests are being downplayed or not represented.
3. To be proud to ask for the money my cause needs, while being aware that great fundraising is about more than asking people to give money – it is about inspiring people to see the world as I do and convincing them that my cause can overcome the problems that they care about. If I have succeeded, the money will follow.
4. To be transparent, honest and accountable for the funds donated to my cause. To report back fully to donors on the impact that they have made in the world. To be honest when things go wrong.
5. To make sure every interaction I have with a donor improves the relationship or, at the very least, does no harm.
6. To not sacrifice long-term results in place of short-term gains.
7. To commit to on-going professional development and learning so that I can do my job to the best of my abilities.
8. To challenge the status quo. To constantly question the way I do things so I am always learning and seeking to improve fundraising performance.
9. To not be afraid of making mistakes and trying new things. To apply the lessons I learn along the way.
10. To enjoy my job and approach it with a positive attitude, even when times are tough. To remember it is ok to laugh, and cry, sometimes.

NOTES
1. The Association of Fundraising Professionals, *2017 Fundraising Effectiveness Survey Report*. Available at: http://afpfep.org/wp-content/uploads/2017/04/FEP2017Report4212017.pdf Last accessed 5 June 2017.
2. See for example the Donor and Retention Survey (DARS) that is conducted in the UK. This has shown attrition from street fundraising is around 50 per cent in year one. You can read more about the survey here: http://www.civilsociety.co.uk/fundraising/news/content/15538/sector_shows_scepticism_about_attrition_monitoring Last accessed 1 May 2015.
3. http://www.thirdsector.co.uk/Management/article/1139178/Morale-plummets-among-fundraisers-survey-shows/ Last accessed 9 October 2012 – registration required.
4. http://philanthropy.com/blogs/prospecting/the-cost-of-high-turnover-in-fundraising-jobs/32752 Last accessed 9 October 2012.
5. Bell, Jeanne and Cornelius, Marla (2013) *Underdeveloped – A National Study of Challenges Facting the Nonprofit Sector*, Compass Point & the Evelyn and Walter Haas, Jr. Fund.
6. http://www.nptrust.org/philanthropic-resources/statistics/ Last accessed 12 May 2012.
7. Global Malaria Action Plan, Global Strategy part 2: section5. Available at: http://www.rbm.who.int/gmap/2-5.html Last accessed 12 May 2012.
8. The Agitator sums up some of these reports here: http://www.theagitator.net/don't-miss-these-posts/take-this-to-your-ceo-board-today. Last accessed 14 October 2012. You can also watch one of the CNN videos at: http://ac360.blogs.cnn.com/2012/09/24/fund-raising-company-faces-new-questions/ Last accessed 14 October 2012.
9. Full report available at: http://edition.cnn.com/2012/05/07/us/veterans-charity-fraud/index.html Last accessed 14 October 2012.
10. *Bad week for Brits. Worse for the Yanks. Terrible for us all*. The Agitator blog, May 2015. Available at: http://www.theagitator.net/nonprofit-management/bad-week-for-brits-worse-for-the-yanks-terrible-for-us-all/
11. Mrs Cooke had a history of depression and had recently had £250 stolen from her. Her family also said that although the letters and calls were a nuisance they were not a cause of her death.
12. Marshall, Jonathan (2012) 'Charities target the elderly and dying for bequests', *The Sunday Mail* (Queensland), 4 March 2012. Available at: http://www.couriermail.com.au/news/queensland/charities-target-the-dying-dollar/story-e6freoof-1226288261921 Last accessed 14 October 2012.
13. For a summary of the story see 'Pay scandal at CRC – Principle and society betrayed', *Irish Examiner*, 13 December 2013. Available at: http://www.irishexaminer.com/viewpoints/ourview/pay-scandal-at-crc-principle-and-society-betrayed-252526.html Last accessed 11 January 2014. For the impact on other charities see 'CRC scandal has "tarred us all with the same brush", says Bothar founder', *Irish Independent, 10 December 2013*. Available at: http://www.independent.ie/irish-news/crc-topup-scandal-has-tarred-us-all-with-the-same-brush-says-bothar-charity-founder-29825517.htm. Last accessed 11 January 2014.
14. For a comprehensive summary of some of the benefits of giving read Rico, Diane (2012) *The science og giving: Why giving feels so good*, Huffington Post, 12 January 2012. Available at: http://www.huffingtonpost.com/2012/01/11/the-gift-of-giving_n_1200238.html Last accessed 14 October 2012.
15. Sargeant, Adrian (1999) 'Why donors stop giving?', *Professional Fundraising*, September, pp. 12-14. 16. DonorVoice, *Donor Commitment Study 2011: Executive Summary*. Available at: http://www.thedonorvoice.com/
16. Manning, Harley and Bodine, Kerry (2012) *Outside In: The Power of Putting Customers at the Center of Your Business*, New Harvest Books, New York.
17. Burnett, K (2002) *Relationship Fundraising* 2nd Ed, Jossey Bass: San Francisco, at page 18.

Fundraising and nonprofits in the twenty-first century

Fundraising has been around for centuries. It's mentioned in the Bible and in the Koran. In the twelfth century an endowment was set up to build a hospital in Damascus. In the Middle Ages fundraisers raised money to build the cathedrals of Europe. And in the nineteenth century American philanthropists set up endowments that are still changing the world today.

The first charity newspaper advertisements and direct response fundraising in the UK began in the late nineteenth and early twentieth century. Fundraisers such as Charles Sumner Ward, credited with raising $100 million in one week for the American Red Cross, encouraged all of society to give and make a difference. Some of his techniques made their way across the Atlantic to influence fundraisers in the UK, particularly the YMCA and the Red Cross. Fundraising from press and poster advertising was already well developed by the end of the Victorian era, with many fine examples of effective fundraising from even earlier.

Oxfam and others were employing sophisticated direct response techniques in the 1950s and 60s and by the late 1960s and 70s several fundraising charities had begun to copy the techniques of commercial direct marketers – perhaps, with hindsight, a mixed blessing.

By the early 1980s, direct marketing techniques were beginning to transform fundraising for a large number of charities. A boom in new donor acquisition coincided with the development of off-the-page advertising, inserts and direct mail fundraising. These were aided by the appearance of commercial databases capable of managing transactions, if not yet actual relationships, and a realisation from some far-sighted fundraisers that it would pay big time to invest in donor acquisition.

All this flourished alongside a new spirit of cooperation and sharing between charities that led to the forming of the Institute of Fundraising in the UK, increased training provision in various forms and the appearance of national and international fundraising conventions, notably the annual International

Fundraising Congress in Holland. The modern fundraising paradigm had arrived.

The earliest exhibit on SOFII, the Showcase of Fundraising Innovation and Inspiration (www.sofii.org), dates back to 1500 BCE. Fundraising has come a long way and today's fundraisers are stewards of a rich, colourful and prestigious history. This chapter will explore the size of nonprofits and fundraising today, as well as looking at ethical considerations.

THE NONPROFIT WORLD IS LARGE – AND GROWING

If you were to ask a friend or relative to guess how many charities there are in your country, or how many people they employ, the vast majority of people would, massively, underestimate the size of the voluntary sector. Put simply, it is big business, just about everywhere.

Here are a few statistics from the UK to prove the point:

- There are nearly 200,000 registered charities (including trusts and foundations).
- These charities collectively employ more than 750,000 people – 2 per cent of the workforce.
- Their collective turnover is in excess of £58 billion per year.[1]

The biggest charity market is the United States, where the numbers are even greater:

- There are over a million charities and foundations.
- These account for 5.5 per cent of the USA's GDP.
- They employ nearly 14 million people – more than 10 per cent of the workforce.

To put this into perspective, that's more people than work in higher profile professions such as finance and leisure services (hotels to you and me).[2]

The rest of the world is catching up too, though reliable statistics are harder to find. However, the *Measuring Civil Society and Volunteering* report[3] has some interesting and surprising facts:

> There are over 450,000 active nonprofit organisations in India.
> In the 17 countries studied (including Brazil, Israel and Mozambique) the

nonprofit sector accounts for 7.4 per cent of the workforce.
The sector has grown by 10 per cent more than the overall growth in GDP in all of these countries.

Wherever you look the conclusion is inescapable: the nonprofit sector plays a huge role in the lives of billions of people (as beneficiaries, staff and donors) and is growing bigger, not only in the Western world, but around the globe too.

PROUD TO BE A FUNDRAISER

Although fundraising is increasingly seen as a legitimate career choice, with undergraduate courses and trainee programmes dedicated to it, many of us older fundraisers stumbled into the profession and can recall the looks and comments we received (and occasionally continue to receive) whenever we'd tell people what we do for a living.

This disdain is less than it used to be – for example, Craig's brother no longer asks him how many raffle tickets he's sold this week – but we believe fundraisers still need to do more to proclaim the wonder and uniqueness of our profession.

In 2013 Mark Astarita, director of fundraising at the British Red Cross, gave a talk on why he was proud to be a fundraiser. It's one of the best speeches we've heard on the theme so we've decided to include a small extract here:

> *We must never forget that giving help, either food, money, aid, or shelter is a basic human instinct. It is the cornerstone of civilisation. It's what sets apart the human race. The selfless act that may or may not be reciprocated is the most positive, inspiring facet of human nature.*
>
> *We as fundraisers nurture that, we cultivate it, we promote it, we give people the chance to take humanitarian actions every day. We provide the vehicle by which everyone can make a difference.*
>
> *My old boss used to say to me 'Mark, never ever ever feel guilty for asking because you're giving donors the chance to give, the chance to make a difference, and when they do give they will feel better for it, they will be grateful to us for giving them the chance to have done it'.*
>
> *The job of fundraisers is always to inspire even in the face of the worst possible catastrophes ... I give people the chance to save lives. What can be more positive*

than that? I love the fact that there are people alive today because of what I did yesterday. That's why I love my job and that's why you should all want my job.[4]

We fundraisers need to be proud of our profession, not apologetic. Donors may give to need, but they also need to give.

Fundraising is a diverse and inspiring force for good in the world. It gives the general public the chance to do something about the problems they see and care about. All fundraisers should be as bullish about our profession as Mark. We aren't 'professional beggars', we've nothing to be ashamed about in asking for money for the causes we represent and we should challenge such attitudes whenever we encounter them. One of the duties of the relationship fundraiser is to protect the name of our profession and discourage bad practice.

WHEN IS A FUNDRAISER NOT A FUNDRAISER?

When they tell people they are in business development or income generation.

It disappoints us that so many fundraisers no longer want to be called fundraisers. It's like window cleaners being called vision clearance executives and dinner ladies being known as education centre nourishment production assistants.

In our experience, fundraisers who don't want to be called fundraisers don't tend to raise much money.

Fundraising is an eclectic mix of marketing, sales, PR and advertising. It is a unique profession. Why downgrade it by copying titles from elsewhere? We should be proud of what we do and we shouldn't change job titles to try and make us sound fancier or to impress our friends and family. Phrases such as business development are borrowed from the commercial sector. They are an attempt to commoditise or rebrand fundraising into something it's not.

If as a profession we don't believe in, and stand up for, fundraising, then why would the general public?

That's not to say there's no room for improvement. There invariably is (and we will talk about it later in this chapter), or we wouldn't be writing this book. Yet, for all the bad publicity and derogatory comments about our profession, fundraisers do much more good than harm and we mustn't be shy in recognising this.

FUNDRAISING ETHICS

The relationship fundraiser is also an ethical fundraiser. This should go without saying. As Ken Burnett said in *Relationship Fundraising*:

> *We all like to believe we are essentially ethical in what we think and do, and that we wouldn't dream of setting about our fundraising jobs clad in anything less than a top-to-toe cloak of ethical certainty. More than in most jobs, the public expects fundraisers to think and act ethically. But are we really ethical and in an ethical profession? Do we make our decisions on the basis of ethics or expediency? Or is it a bit of both? And how ethical is that? And when confronted with ethical issues, just how do we decide between what's right and what's wrong?*[5]

Before answering some of these questions, let's consider some ethical dilemmas and questionable practices. Do you do any of the following? Are such actions ethical?

- Should a cancer charity accept a large donation from a tobacco company?
- Do you send back a list of all the returned mail for a cold mailing to the list provider? Do you check that they have removed the names of envelopes marked deceased and do not mail?
- Do your fundraising disclosure statements in phone calls or face-to-face fundraising use accurate figures or do they fail to mention the impact of attrition?
- Should you report donors who don't hand over sponsorship or event money to the police?
- Is it ok to make donors feel guilty so that they then feel obliged to give?
- How many times should you ask a prospect before accepting that they aren't going to give?
- Should you claim that you have no administration costs or that 100 per cent of donations are spent on frontline services?
- Should fundraisers be paid commission?
- Is it environmentally friendly to send direct mail when so much of it is instantly binned?
- When does e-mail marketing become spam?

It is likely you will instinctively have an answer to each of the above questions. But be careful of jumping to conclusions. Take the first example. Our first thought was a firm no, of course they shouldn't accept the money.

Then, in our research we came across this supposed quote from The Salvation Army's founder, General Booth. When he was asked a similar question, he is alleged to have replied:

I shall take all the money I can get, and I shall wash it clean with the grateful tears of orphans and widows.

Makes you think, doesn't it? The answers to our questions aren't always as clear-cut as they may first appear. To help you decide when you face an ethical dilemma here's a hierarchy of sources to consult:

The law – the starting point, and bare minimum, is to follow the law of the land. This is not only the law governing charities and nonprofits, but also the law covering areas such as data protection (e.g. the EU data protection directive) and e-mail (e.g. the Can-Spam Act in America).
The International Statement of Ethical Principles in Fundraising[6] – in 2006 fundraising representatives in 24 countries across the globe agreed five universal principles (honesty, respect, integrity, empathy and transparency) that should underpin fundraising standards of practice across six key areas:
a Fundraisers' responsibility regarding donations.
b Relationships with stakeholders.
c Responsibility for communications, marketing and public information.
d Management reporting, finance and fundraising costs.
e Payment and compensation.
f Compliance with national laws.
Fundraising codes of practice – following on from the ethical principles are more specific codes of practice on how they apply in individual jurisdictions. These split their guidance according to what fundraisers 'will', 'must' and 'should' do. The Institute of Fundraising UK's Codes of Practice[7] are a good example and give specific advice on 20 different areas of fundraising, including events, major donors and volunteers.
Other professional bodies' codes of practice – fundraisers also need to consider codes of practice that exist for overlapping industries. For example, FEDMA (Federation of European Direct and Interactive Marketing) has codes of practice for the use of personal data in direct marketing.[8] Similarly, ADMA (Association for Data-driven Marketing and Advertising) in Australia has a comprehensive set of codes of practice.[9]

Organisational values and beliefs – the next place to look is internally at your own nonprofit. What are your organisational values and beliefs? Are you holding true to them? Your chief executive and board should also be helping in this area and it is prudent to have a donations policy in place (outlining who you will and won't accept donations from) to help guide your decision-making. Also, if your charity is large enough to have reserves invested then you will need an ethical investment policy. For example, you would not expect a human rights charity to invest in any part of the arms industry. Boards need to ensure that their financial advisors are being rigorous in this area and are not investing in funds that hold shares in companies that go against the values, history and political stance of their charity.

Advice from fellow fundraisers – with the rise of networking sites like LinkedIn and social media such as Twitter, it is easier than ever to ask our peers for guidance and advice. Many fundraisers may have faced the same ethical problem you are facing and you can learn from their experience (both good and bad). Be aware though that not everything you read online should be taken as true.

Your own skill and judgement – once you have consulted the above and exhausted your lines of enquiry then you need to make a decision using your own skill and judgement. When doing so, think of the fundraiser's unique triple responsibility to donors, employer and beneficiaries.

Finally, if you still find yourself unsure of the course of action to take and whether you are acting ethically, then ask yourself this ultimate question: what would your mum say if you asked her? Or your granny?

SHOULD WE BAN BAD FUNDRAISERS?

What happens if a fundraiser does something unethical, or breaks one of the laws or codes we mention above? The police will take care of any action for lawbreakers, but for other offences the available sanctions are fairly limited. If we look at professions such as medicine, teaching and law the ultimate sanction is for the individual to be banned from practising. However, since there is no formal licensing or training needed before becoming a fundraiser, this would be almost impossible to introduce.

A fundraiser can be expelled from a professional association, but since it's not compulsory to join such an association before becoming a fundraiser it is a relatively toothless sanction. The Association of Fundraising Professionals (AFP) in the United States has only expelled 12 members since 1992.[10]

Then there's the issue of deciding what exactly is bad fundraising. Is it breaking one of the codes listed above? Or would someone who has consistently missed targets, or not actually raised any money, indeed might have lost the charity money, be up for sanction?

Such problems shouldn't be insurmountable though. And if we truly want to improve our professional standards then we need to find ways of solving them.

The shift to more evidence-based qualifications, such as the international CFRE (Certified Fund Raising Executive), helps and gives a proven fundraising passport of achievement. Yet these are far from standard and most boards and chief executives who hire senior fundraisers don't necessarily know about them.

As fundraising continues to grow around the world, this will become an increasingly important issue. Our preferred solution is that all fundraisers who reach a certain level of responsibility must have a qualification or demonstrable fundraising success that has been certified by a professional body. When people move into fundraising from another profession we need to make sure they get the chance to take a fundraising qualification within a year of the move.

It is only by insisting on minimum qualifications or achievements and demonstrating the damage done by unqualified fundraisers that we can raise standards across the sector.

FUNDRAISING AS ART

As well as the fundraising profession being an ethical force for good that we should be proud of, we'd also argue that great fundraising is art and the best fundraisers are artists. Not in the traditional sense of the word, but in the way Seth Godin describes art in his book *The Icarus Deception*:

> *Art is not a gene or a specific talent. Art is an attitude, culturally driven and available to anyone who chooses to adopt it. Art isn't something sold in a gallery or performed on a stage. Art is the unique work of a human being, work that touches another. Most painters, it turns out, aren't artists at all – they are safety-seeking copycats.*
>
> *Seizing new ground, making connections between people or ideas, working without a map – these are works of art, and if you do them, you are an artist, regardless of whether you wear a smock, use a computer, or work with others*

all day long.

Speaking up when there's no obvious right answer, making yourself vulnerable when it's possible to put up shields, and caring about both the process and the outcome – these are works of art that our society embraces and the economy demands.[11]

When colleagues first hear this they may be highly sceptical and think you're just being pretentious. But when you start to explain why they should aspire to be fundraising artists, then something magical happens. They start to see their role in a new light. Their pride in their profession intensifies and their motivation increases. Attitudes change and great things become possible.

When you embrace the idea that great fundraisers are artists, then you'll take risks, push boundaries, challenge the status quo and make fantastic things happen. Sure, you'll make mistakes and have some failures along the way, but if you don't embrace the idea of great fundraising as art then you risk disappearing into a vacuum of mediocrity. Our donors and beneficiaries deserve better than that.

This shift in mindset can be hard to make. One of our favourite books on the subject is *Steal Like an Artist* by Austin Kleon. He recognises some of the fears and barriers we put up that stop us being creative and reaching our potential.
One of the interesting things he talks about is imposter syndrome. This is something we've both experienced (writing this book for example!) and Kleon describes it as follows:

There's this very real thing that runs rampant in educated people. It's called imposter syndrome. The clinical definition is a 'psychological phenomenon in which people are unable to internalize their accomplishments'. It means that you feel like a phony, like you're just winging it, that you really don't have any idea what you're doing.

Guess what? None of us do. Ask any real artist, and they'll tell you the truth: they don't know where the good stuff comes from. They just show up to do their thing. Every day.[12]

We've had this feeling many times in our careers and, although sometimes it was justified, the majority of the time it was our inner voice stopping us appreciating our results. Often it is only when you look back at achievements at a later date that you truly realise the difference you made.

When we interviewed people for this book, we found that many of the best fundraisers in the world have experienced this same feeling – it's amazing how much self-confidence you gain when you realise this. Of course, the more you read, observe and learn from others, the quicker your own judgement and confidence will improve and the sooner you can recognise impostor syndrome and overcome it. By doing so you'll be on the path to becoming a truly great relationship fundraiser.

DEMAND THE BEST – WHY WE NEED TO DRAG OURSELVES AWAY FROM A RACE TO THE BOTTOM

The biggest disappointment in terms of relationship fundraising over the last decade is the failure of fundraising teams to implement its principles. The phrase may be an oft-repeated buzzword heard at conferences and training sessions everywhere, but the reality is that very few charities have truly embraced and applied its teachings on a consistent basis.

Instead, charities have engaged increasingly in a race to the bottom to cut costs and maximise short-term returns with no thought to the long-term consequences.

Former NSPCC director of appeals and fundraising legend, Giles Pegram CBE, explains the situation as he sees it:

> *A regular giver has declined to upgrade 10 times in a row. She will soon receive her eleventh ask. Have we learned no insight into this donor?*
>
> *The typical telephone fundraiser who asks her is likely to be inexperienced and much younger than the donor he is speaking to. He couldn't hold a conversation with a 50-year-old woman, he can merely read from a script, and bring the donor back to the script when she wants to wander. Why? Because the charities have negotiated so hard with the telephone fundraising company that they can't afford to pay for good quality callers. Do they do that with 'their fundraiser' pay? Yet the best telephone fundraisers are likely to have had hundreds, if not thousands, more conversations with donors than the so-called 'professional' fundraiser. We need to ensure we recognise and reward the abilities of these fundraisers and not race to the bottom.*

> The appeal that goes out has three 'thank yous' in the letter before the ask. But does any donor feel thanked?
>
> These 'irritations' are now so commonplace, we, and the donor, have come to accept them. But I sometimes think donors give despite the fundraisers, not because of them.

Instead of taking a customer-centric approach to the opportunities the Internet, social media and other technology have given us, fundraisers have generally taken the Ryanair (a low-cost European airline that consistently comes bottom in customer satisfaction surveys) strategy – cut costs, forget the customer and maximise short-term income.

In classic strategy terms (something we'll look at in chapter 5), rather than trying to develop a differentiated strategy, fundraisers have consistently sought the low-cost option, where there is a constant drive to lower costs, to standardise our approaches and to sacrifice donors who don't neatly fit into pre-defined boxes. If you're like us, then you will know from your own experience that 'lowest cost' is rarely best. As the old saying goes: you can't afford to buy cheap.

AN EASY WAY TO FUNDRAISING RICHES

Behold! The amazing, magical, fundraising serum – guaranteed to make donors give you all their cash, or your money back.

Like the nineteenth century snake oil salesmen who sold their wares from town to town in the Wild West, there are fundraisers (we know, we've met a few) who believe there is an easy remedy that will lead to fundraising riches.

To our knowledge no such fundraising solution exists and, despite the efforts of some people to try and convince us of easy, raise-money-quick schemes, we've yet to discover any that work on a long-term, sustained basis. If something sounds too good to be true, it usually is.

The truth is, good relationship fundraising now is extremely hard work. It requires the whole organisation's dedication over a long time to reap the rewards. That's why we understand (though it saddens us) why much of our profession has taken the low-cost, short-term, much easier approach to fundraising, outlined above. Walmart and Primark seem to be the commercial models we've followed rather than Whole Foods or Zappos.

The rest of this book will be about promoting the harder but, we believe, more successful and more rewarding way of fundraising. By the end of the book we hope you'll be convinced of the urgency and importance of moving from this low-cost model to one that is based on long-term thinking, insight and truly putting the donor at the centre of your work.

This will entail a huge shift in thinking and behaviour, but it's only by demanding the best for our donors on a repeated basis that we will be able to overcome the issues that we face.

NOTES
1. Charity Commission, Information for Charities, MP Fact Sheet and Charity Facts and Figures. Available at: http://www.charity-commission.gov.uk/About_us/Contacting_us/mp_factsheet2.aspx and http://www.charity-commission.gov.uk/About_us/About_charities/factfigures.aspx Last accessed 11 January 2013.
2. Independent Sector (2013) The sector's economic impact.Available at: http://www.independentsector.org/economic_role Last accessed 11 January 2013.
3. Salamon, Lester, Wojciech Sokolowski, S and Haddock, Megan (2012) *Measuring Civil Society and Volunteering: New Findings from Implementation of the UN Nonprofit Handbook,* John Hopkins Center for Civil Society Studies, Baltimore. Available at: http://ccss.jhu.edu/wp-content/uploads/downloads/2012/09/ISTR_Handbook-Results_7.2012.pdf Last accessed 20 February 2013.
4. Quote taken from http://www.civilsociety.co.uk/fundraising/news/content/13601/clayton_stop_apologising_for_fundraising Last accessed 12 January 2013.
5. Burnett, Ken (2002) *Relationship Fundraising,* second edition, Jossey-Bass, San Francisco, p.303.
6. The Statement is available at: http://www.afpnet.org/Ethics/IntlArticleDetail.cfm?ItemNumber=3681 Last accessed 24 February 2013.
7. The Institute of Fundraising Codes of Practice are available at: http://www.institute-of-fundraising.org.uk/guidance/code-of-fundraising-practice/ Last accessed 24 February 2013.
8. Available at: http://www.fedma.org/index.php?id=56 Last accessed 24 February 2013.
9. Available for viewing at: http://www.adma.com.au/comply/overview/ Last accessed 24 February 2013.
10. A full list of the 12 people is available at: http://www.afpnet.org/Ethics/content.cfm?ItemNumber=3095&navItemNumber=541 Last accessed 24 February 2013.
11. Godin, Seth (2012) *The Icarus Deception,* Penguin, New York, p.6.
12 Kleon, L Austin (2011) *Steal Like an Artis*t, Workman Publishing Group, New York.

Relationship fundraising: what it is and why it matters

Relationship fundraising is not something you can dip in and out of. It requires sustained total focus and commitment if you are to truly reap the benefits of the approach. In fact, we believe that relationship fundraising is about adopting a mindset and philosophy that puts donors at the core of your decision-making.

Craig was once accused of being a 'disciple of the cult of relationship fundraising'. And whilst relationship fundraising is simply an approach to fundraising and not a religion or theology, he took the insult as a bit of a compliment. The comment came on a LinkedIn discussion about the merits of relationship fundraising and whether it has actually helped charities raise more money.

It's an important point, because if it doesn't raise more money then why bother? The good news is we know it does and will provide the evidence in this chapter. We'll also consider why many fundraisers and charities claim to be advocates of relationship fundraising, but don't always practise what they preach.

WHAT IS RELATIONSHIP FUNDRAISING?
At the core of relationship fundraising is a simple principle.

If you treat people with respect, listen to their needs, respond appropriately, show gratitude and give them great feedback on what their donation is achieving, then people will give you more time and money in the long run.

Underpinning this is a complex blend of contemporary and traditional marketing theory that proves why such an approach is the best way to fundraise.

Ken Burnett's definition is as relevant today as it was in 1992:

> *Relationship fundraising is an approach to the marketing of a cause that centres on the unique and special relationship between a nonprofit and each supporter. Its overriding consideration is to care for and develop that bond and to do nothing that might damage or jeopardise it. Every activity is therefore geared toward making sure donors know they are important, valued, and considered,*

*which has the effect of maximising funds per donor in the long term.*¹

A BRIEF HISTORY OF RELATIONSHIP MARKETING AND FUNDRAISING THEORY
Although charities have been using direct marketing for over 150 years, it was Philip Kotler (named by the American Marketing Association as the most influential marketer of all time) who was one of the first to recognise the importance of modern marketing techniques to charities. In 1969 he said:

> [M]arketing is a pervasive societal activity that goes considerably beyond the selling of toothpaste, soap and steel.

He urged all organisations to embrace the techniques and warned:

> *The choice facing those who manage non-business organisations is not whether to market or not to market, for no organisation can avoid marketing. The choice is whether to do it well or poorly, and on this necessity the case for organisational marketing is basically founded.*²

In the 1980s and 90s traditional marketing theory (such as the four Ps of place, price, product and promotion) was found wanting for many products and services where a transactional approach (focused on securing one off rather than repeat sales) was no longer good enough.

This paradigm shift was driven by the growth of the service economy, rapid improvements in technology and recognition that customer retention was as important as customer recruitment.

In many ways, the first edition of *Relationship Fundraising* was ahead of its time. Although relationship marketing was being increasingly cited in business marketing literature, it wasn't until the mid-1990s and the publication of books such as the *One to One Future: Building Relationships One Customer at a Time* by Peppers and Rogers (Currency Doubleday, USA, 1993) that it became a mainstream marketing concept.

Since the late 1990s then, relationship fundraising is the lens through which the majority of academic research on donor loyalty has been viewed. Similarly, many of the most popular fundraising books of the last two decades have quoted *Relationship Fundraising* and Ken's work extensively.

In recent years, relationship marketing and fundraising have evolved and new concepts such as customer experience, donor commitment and experiential marketing have built on the earlier body of work. Yet, at the heart of all these theories is the basic premise that you need to go beyond a transactional approach to your fundraising if you are to build the lifetime value of your donor base. It is important to note that Ken did not have relationship marketing in mind when he first wrote *Relationship Fundraising*. It just happened to be an in-fashion word at the time. As he states in the introduction to *Friends for Life*:

> *Relationship fundraising is, after all, just a currently fashionable piece of jargon … I wish I'd paid more attention to its subtitle: A donor-based approach to the business of raising money. Those 10 words, I believe, are ultimately much more important than the two words that precede them.*

PROVING THE CASE FOR RELATIONSHIP FUNDRAISING

It's not enough to say 'relationship fundraising is great, just go do it'. We need to offer some proof that it works and is the best approach to raising money. Fortunately, there is now a large body of research that demonstrates the value of relationship fundraising.

Professor Adrian Sargeant is (at the time of writing, professor of fundraising at the University of Plymouth Business School and director of the new Centre for Sustainable Philanthropy) the most respected fundraising academic in the world. Adrian and his colleagues have demonstrated in numerous studies over the years the importance of improving donor retention. We quoted Adrian in our opening chapter and want to look at more of his research here. Back in 2001[3] he outlined the four main reasons why donors lapse:

- Attraction by competition – a pressing appeal, e.g. the tsunami in 2005, or communications from another charity that the donor finds inherently more appealing.
- Poor quality of service – not responding to communications, incorrectly addressing mail, not providing feedback.
- Poor relationship quality – not taking into account the wishes of the donor, asking for inappropriate amounts, communications at the wrong time of year, etc.
- Lost to market – natural attrition through death, moving away, or change in financial circumstances.

The first three can be directly influenced by applying relationship fundraising techniques.

Sargeant's further research with Lee (2004)[4], Jay (2004)[5] and Woodliffe (2005)[6] demonstrates the link between trust, commitment, loyalty and giving behaviour. Sargeant and his co-authors showed that there are 10 key drivers of commitment to a charity. Seven of these are clearly influenced by the quality of relationship fundraising and marketing employed by the charity. Those seven determinants are:

- Shared beliefs – showing in your communications that your charity shares similar values to the donor.
- Organisation's performance – communicating the difference the donor is making and how the organisation is spending the donor's money.
- Tangible link to beneficiaries – making donors feel part of the charity and connecting them directly with beneficiaries through stories and pictures.
- Labelling – by using words such as *kind, helpful* and *generous* to describe donors and their behaviour.
- Multiple engagements – asking donors to take other actions, e.g. campaigning as well as donating.
- Choice in communications – donors who are offered choice in communication are less likely to lapse than other donors.
- Quality of communication – donors indicating they were 'very satisfied' with the quality of fundraising service provided were twice as likely to offer a second or subsequent gift than those who identified themselves as merely satisfied.

What's the value of this? Well, Sargeant and Jay demonstrate that reducing your attrition rate by 10 per cent can lead to as much as a 200 per cent increase in the lifetime value of your supporter base.

Furthermore, research by Bennett and Barkensjo in 2005 found that:

> *Relationship marketing activities ... are likely to generate valuable payoffs in terms of supporter retention and longevity, willingness to engage in positive word-of-mouth, and the frequency and levels of supporter's donations.*[7]

In recent times, these results have been confirmed by research from donor retention experts DonorVoice in 2011 and 2012.[8] In a national survey of donors and an e-mail survey among donors from participating charities in the USA and UK, they showed how commitment is a key indicator of donor value. Over a three-year period highly committed donors in the USA gave 131 per cent more than donors with low commitment. In the UK, it was 105 per cent.

In other words, for every 1,000 donors you can move from low to high commitment you can expect an increase of $200,000 in their three-year value in the USA and an increase of £83,000 in the UK.[9]

And what influences commitment?

DonorVoice looked at 32 possible options and found seven key drivers that were statistically the most influential on donor commitment. These were:

1   Donor perceives your organisation to be effective in trying to achieve its mission.
2   Donor knows what to expect from your organisation with each interaction.
3   Donor receives timely 'thank yous'.
4   Donor receives opportunities to make his or her views known.
5   Donor is given the feeling that he or she is part of an important cause.
6   Donor feels his or her involvement is appreciated.
7   Donor receives information showing who is being helped.

These were broadly the same themes identified in the research we discussed earlier by Sargeant et al. Most importantly, applying the fundamentals of relationship fundraising can positively influence the seven factors.

MYSTERY SHOPPING: PAINTING A SORRY PICTURE ABOUT STANDARDS OF DONOR CARE

With such overwhelming evidence of the increased income relationship fundraising can bring to your nonprofit, you might assume that it is the bedrock of every fundraising strategy. Yet, every fundraising mystery shopping report we've ever read shows the inadequate state of donor care. Ken Burnett's *Friends for Life* (The White Lion Press, UK, 1996) details several mystery shopping tests that he undertook in the USA and UK. The results were consistently poor. It appears nothing has changed. Here are some examples from three reports over the last decade:

Pell & Bales benchmarking report, 2007[10]

Forty household name charities in the UK were contacted by phone, mail and e-mail to try and set up direct debit gifts:

- Half of the attempts to set up the gift failed.
- It took some of the charities up to 62 days to respond to letters.
- Thirty-six per cent of charities sent no thank you or direct debit confirmation.
- Only three charities sent a welcome pack.

John Grain – failing to hit the (bench) mark, 2008[11]
This was a study of the responses received to a £10 donation made over the phone to 25 overseas development charities of various sizes:

- Only 56 per cent of charities asked for gift aid on a credit card donation made over the phone.
- Fifty-two per cent of charities failed to acknowledge the gift.
- Only 12 per cent sent a welcome pack (though two contained an appeal).
- Fifty-six per cent of charities made at least one mistake in capturing the data.

Bluefrog and Ask Direct – mystery shopping, 2011[12]
This report documented a wide-ranging study that made in-memoriam, postal and online donations to 15 charities in six countries: Australia, Canada, New Zealand, Republic of Ireland, the USA and the UK:

- Australian charities took on average at least three weeks to respond, across all three donation methods. An honourable mention was given to Irish and New Zealand charities who responded to the in-memoriam donations in under a week.
- Only two UK charities sent a proper e-mail welcome to the online gift.
- Only six out of 15 American charities sent a tailored in-memoriam thank you.
- Only 27 per cent of Canadian charities sent any postal thank you.

What are the consequences of this poor service?
Increased attrition, rising cost of acquiring new donors and overall donor fatigue.
It's worth mentioning the results from the 2017 AFP *Effectiveness Report* again:

- Every 100 new donors gained in 2016 were offset by 95 recent donors lost through attrition – a net gain of just five donors at very

considerable expense.
- Overall median donor attrition in 2016 was 55 per cent – that is, 55 per cent of 2015 donors did not give again to participating nonprofits in 2015. These findings aren't just confined to the USA. In 2013 UK telephone agency Pell & Bales reported the following results from their analysis of client data:

In 2000, fewer than one in 10 people who signed up for monthly giving, stopped making donations within a year... By 2005, nearly one third stopped within a year, by 2011, the proportion had risen to nearly half – 41 per cent. Attrition is at an all-time high.[13]

Over the last few pages we've shown the state of the problem our profession faces and how relationship fundraising techniques can help solve it. If you're still not convinced, then consider this quote from Adrian Sargeant back in 2004:

The consequences of failing to embrace these relationship marketing techniques for the sector appear all too evident. Donors are likely to increasingly complain that they are over-mailed and inundated with requests for inappropriate sums of money...charities should be actively demonstrating that they care for their supporters and that giving to charity can be a pleasant and rewarding experience.[14]

Overall, the examples we've used highlight that the quality of donor care simply isn't good enough. It is a sign of the untreated malaise in our midst. We have to tackle the problem otherwise we risk permanently alienating donors. We need to get the professional bodies and top fundraising charities to work together to tackle the poor customer service that is endemic in our profession.

For those who buck the trend, heed Sargeant's warning and embrace relationship fundraising, the rewards are huge.

LESSONS FROM THE COMMERCIAL SECTOR

It's worth taking a moment to look at the commercial sector and how they consider issues of loyalty, satisfaction and commitment – all the things that build (or destroy) relationships with customers.

As Sargeant notes:

> *Corporates have known for over 30 years that the single biggest driver of customer loyalty is their satisfaction with the quality of service provided. This is why customer satisfaction surveys are now so ubiquitous. Managers are hungry for the data and want to use them to inform their strategy.*[15]

Take a minute to think about some of the companies you buy from and how they try to convince you to become a long-term customer:

- The supermarket loyalty card that records your purchases and then uses the data to send you relevant and personalised offers for future shopping.
- The department store that offers a 100 per cent no quibble refund on any item you buy from them, regardless of whether it is damaged or not.
- The online retailer who makes it so easy to purchase that you can do it in one click.
- The footwear company that offers new staff $1,000 to leave if they don't like working there, so they are sure they get employees committed to providing great service to their customers.
- The bank that texts you after contacting customer services to ask you to rate their performance.

They don't do this just because they are nice people. They do it because they know it leads to customer loyalty and, in turn, greater sales and profits.

Forrester[16] is a research company that specialises in customer experience. Each year the company conducts a survey of consumers about their experiences with leading brands across 13 industries. In 2012 they assessed 160 USA brands on customer experience – only 3 per cent were rated excellent and just 34 per cent were rated good. This means that mediocre customer experience is the norm, that great customer experience is rare and is a powerful differentiator for the few companies that do it well.

Why does this matter? Well, customer experience correlates with customer loyalty, meaning companies with high customer experience scores are more likely to get repeat custom, benefit from word-of-mouth recommendation and won't lose customers.

Given the lack of a tangible product, then, charities might expect that loyalty and polite service are even more important to donors than for customers of organisations whose purpose is to sell commercial products.

This, in turn, has an impact on the bottom line. In the same research, Forrester

Figure 3.1: Revenue impact of improving the Industry's Average CX Index™ Score by one point.
The Revenue Impact of Customer Experience, 2015

Industry	Annual incremental revenue per customer*	×	Average number of customers per company†	=	Annual impact per company
Wireless providers	$2.13	×	82 million	=	$175 million
Luxury auto	$337.10	×	350,000	=	$118 million
Upscale hotels	$6.52	×	10 million	=	$65 million
TV providers	$3.56	×	17 million	=	$61 million
Retail banks	$3.92	×	15 million	=	$59 million
Insurance firms (home and auto)	$3.25	×	15 million	=	$49 million
Internet providers	$3.09	×	16 million	=	$49 million
PCs manufacturers‡ (excluding Apple)	$2.07	×	10 million	=	$21 million
Credit cards	$0.25	×	61 million	=	$15 million

Base: 28,823 US online adult customers (ages 18+) of these industries who interacted with at least one brand within the past 12 months (bases vary by industry)

Source: Forrester's Customer Experience Index Online Survey, US Consumers Q1 2015

*This analysis shows the effect on revenue potential of increasing CX Index scores by one point from the industry average CX score. Curves for individual brands differ from this industry curve. For brands that don't have a linear relationship between CX and revenue, the revenue effect of improving CX by one point will vary greatly depending on the CX score that serves as the starting point for this analysis.
†Number of customers represents number of customers of a big player in the industry based on inputs that include Forrester's Consumer Technographics®, Forrester's analysts, and publicly available industry data.
‡Excluding Apple due to the high difference in price points

Source: Forrester Research, Inc. Unauthorized reproduction, citation, or distribution prohibited.

modelled the financial impact of moving customer experience scores from below average, in a specific sector, to above average.

They measured the increase in revenue due to increased purchase, lower attrition (churn) and sales from word-of-mouth recommendations. Their findings are shown in figure 3.1.

Though some of these industries are actually smaller than the nonprofit sector in the USA, the impact of customer service runs to huge sums of money. It raises the question, how much of our donors' precious money are we wasting by not getting this right?

So what does customer experience look like in some of the excellent customer experience organisations? Here Manning and Bodine share some of the secrets of USAA:

> *USAA is a diversified financial services company that has the highest customer experience index score in three industries: banking, credit cards and insurance. This translates into strong financial performance in both good times and bad. As Wayne Peacock, executive vice president of member experience, points out, USAA retains 97 per cent to 98 per cent of its members year after year. It also had one of its best years ever in 2008— when most of the financial services industry tanked.*
>
> *In January 2010, USAA reorganised and placed all nine thousand of its customer-facing employees into a single organisation under Wayne. This helps the firm execute on its vision of going to market based on customer journeys, not internal business silos. For example, USAA offers auto insurance, auto loans, and a car-buying service to its members. If it took a typical approach it would let each of those lines of business sell its product in whatever way it saw fit probably without sharing customer data across silos. Instead, in 2010 USAA launched Auto Circle, an integrated offering that supports members' journey of finding the right vehicle, paying for it, and insuring it. That move drove a 15 per cent year-over-year increase in completed auto loans and a 23 per cent increase in vehicles sold through its car-buying service.[17]*

While we may not like or even understand some of the jargon in this commentary its overall message is clear: if a bank is capable of providing such a great customer experience why can't fundraisers? There should be no good reason yet, as the DonorVoice survey we discussed earlier showed, few charities would rate as excellent or even good on donor experience. Those that do score highly are no doubt those charities experiencing the greatest fundraising growth and lowest donor attrition.

Relationship fundraising: what it is and why it matters

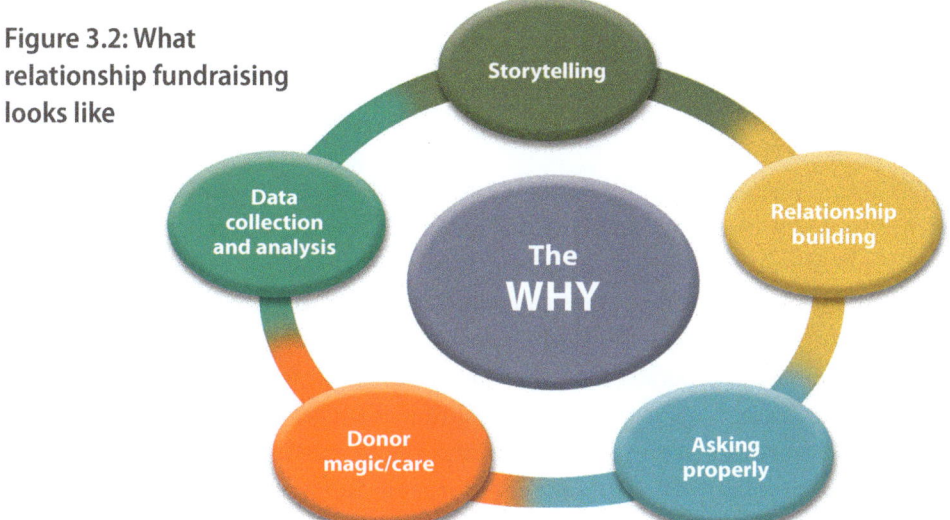

Figure 3.2: What relationship fundraising looks like

WHAT RELATIONSHIP FUNDRAISING LOOKS LIKE TODAY

So putting this altogether, what does relationship fundraising look like currently?

We propose that relationship fundraising comprises six elements, which can be represented in the model shown in figure 3.2.

Throughout the rest of the book we will show you how to put these six elements into action in your organisation.

It won't be easy, but if you and your nonprofit can put all the elements together, then you will be on your way to raising more money for your cause.

You may wonder why the 'why' is in the middle? It was a very deliberate decision, which we will discuss at length in the next chapter. The 'why' is about putting yourself in a donor's shoes and understanding the values, beliefs and world view that the donor holds so you can show how supporting your cause meets his or her needs.

If you don't understand and articulate why potential donors would want to give to your cause, then fundraising will be difficult. By putting the other five elements in place you will consistently remind donors why your cause is important to them and why they should give.

Throughout the rest of the book we will refer back to this model and explain how you can apply the six elements in practical terms.

CRITICISMS OF RELATIONSHIP FUNDRAISING (AND WHY THEY'RE WRONG)

That's not to say relationship fundraising is without criticism. It's not. But it's our view that the criticisms are either due to a misunderstanding of what relationship fundraising is, or down to the poor application of the theory.

Here are the three main arguments we've heard against relationship fundraising:

1 Not everyone wants a relationship/you can't treat everyone the same.
The argument that not everyone wants a relationship with a nonprofit would be a valid one if you take too literal a definition of 'relationship' and compare it to that of husband and wife, brother and sister, etc. Similarly, some people take relationship fundraising to mean that you treat all donors the same and give everyone the same levels of service and personalisation regardless of their level of giving.

Let us be clear. Nowhere in the literature is it suggested, or even implied, that this is the sort of relationship you should try to nurture with all your donors. Likewise, it doesn't say that you should treat a donor who gives £5 once a year the same as a donor who donates £1 million.

The definition of relationship we use is much looser. A relationship exists (whether you like it or not) from the moment a donor or potential donor interacts with your nonprofit. Your job is to make sure that the interaction leaves a good impression and makes the donor want to continue to support your cause or takes him or her a step closer to making a first donation.

If someone says they don't want to hear from you again, respect it.

If someone says they don't want phone calls, respect it.

If someone only ever gives to a certain aspect of your work, respect it.

A relationship is a two-way thing and respecting each other's wishes and listening to one another is what builds trust and loyalty over time. Sure, some donors will say they don't want thank-you letters or they only want to hear from you once a year, that's fine and you can manage your relationship with them accordingly. Similarly, some donors will want to come to every donor event, volunteer for you and will become your biggest fans and advocates.

Different donors deserve different levels and types of relationship depending on their own personal values, needs, wants and desires. The good relationship fundraiser will be aware of this, will act accordingly and do nothing that will harm the donor's support for her or his cause.

2 Relationship fundraising is too soft and woolly.

Another argument we often hear is that relationship fundraising is used as an excuse for not asking for donations, or it takes too long to see the results so is not worth the effort.

Again, let us be clear, relationship fundraising without asking is like a Formula 1 car without petrol. They both look the part, but fail as the key component of their success is missing.

Telephone fundraising expert Rich Fox explains why asking is the fuel that drives relationship fundraising success:

> *For relationship fundraising to work, you must take financial advantage of the relationship you are building. You can't just cultivate and cultivate without ever getting a payback. It's far too expensive. So you need to have an effective upgrade strategy in place at the start. You need a definite plan to move people to larger gifts, to monthly giving, to open-ended giving and to wills, bequests and legacies. If you don't have such a strategy in place, you are wasting your money on building the relationship.*[18]

It's also crucial that you measure and record the impact of your relationship fundraising efforts. This means you can demonstrate the improvement on lifetime value and return on investment to your chief executive and board. If you don't do this, then short-term decisions can be taken that damage the relationship but boost immediate returns.

Don't be afraid to stop your relationship with unprofitable donors. The best relationship fundraisers know when not to pursue a relationship and are willing to stop an unprofitable donor relationship in order to put that time and money into an alternative. The importance of this is brought home in the most widely quoted and accepted definition of relationship marketing. It comes from a 1994 study by Professor Christian Grönroos:

> *Relationship marketing is to identify and establish, maintain and enhance and when necessary also to terminate relationships with customers and other stakeholders, at a profit, so that the objectives of all parties are met, and that this is done by a mutual exchange and fulfilment of promises.*[19]

The notion of maximising income in the long run by having mutually beneficial relationships with customers is at the heart of relationship marketing. Fundraisers need to apply the same rigour to their fundraising to ensure that income is maximised in the long run.

In our experience, this is one of the areas where many fundraising teams fall short. Here are a few examples of where charities should have stopped the relationship with 'donors':

- Craig once gave £5 to a hospice then received nearly 30 mailings from them over four years before he moved house. His successor might still be receiving mail from them addressed to him, for all he knows.
- After sponsoring a friend online Craig received multiple mailings from a large national charity. Not one of the letters referred to his sponsorship or reason for giving. These mailings continue to this day and have included invitations to events, appeal letters, newsletters and even a legacy request. Craig has never responded to any of these further requests.
- One charity Craig worked for used the same mailing criteria for over 15 years. This resulted in people who hadn't given for over a decade receiving appeals. The worst example he found was one donor (though she can hardly be called that) who gave a £1 gift once and had received over 50 mailings over the subsequent 16 years without ever giving again.

We've heard this kind of activity excused by the claim that some people may go on to become legacy donors. This may be correct, but there are much more cost-effective ways to pursue legacies. Even basic selection criteria based on the recency, frequency and value of gifts donors have given would have saved significant funds for all three of the charities mentioned above. The money saved could have been invested in more profitable activities and produced far greater legacy income.

Remember, relationship fundraising is only worth doing if it raises more money than pursuing alternative strategies.

3. Relationship fundraising is great in theory, but hard in practice.

There is no doubting that relationship fundraising is challenging to implement. It requires hard work, focus and a commitment to create a fundraising team culture where long-term results outweigh short-term priorities.

We also recognise that there are other ways to raise money. Some of these can undoubtedly be successful. For example, we know of many charities that have raised millions of pounds by pursuing a very transactional, incentive-led direct marketing programme.

When donor recruitment costs are low there is also little incentive to improve the lifetime value of supporters and build long-lasting relationships. You can simply treat donors like a commodity and get some new supporters in to replace those who stop giving. Although effective, it is, perhaps, not very satisfying.

It's our steadfast belief that soon charities won't have a choice about whether to improve the donor experience and service. As donors stop giving in larger numbers and the costs of donor recruitment become ever higher, then the only way to fundraise cost-effectively will be by retaining donors for longer periods and maximising their lifetime value.

Quite possibly, relationship fundraising isn't for everyone. Yet, as we'll show in chapter 5, those fundraisers who can put together and implement an effective relationship fundraising strategy, over time, will, be well ahead of the competition.

NOTES
1. Burnett, Ken (2002) *Relationship Fundraising*, 2nd edition, Jossey-Bass, San Francisco, p.38.
2. Kotler, Philip and Levy, Sidney J (1969) 'Broadening the concept of marketing', *Journal of Marketing*, January: 10-15.
3. Sargeant, Adrian (2001) 'Relationship fundraising: How to keep donors loyal', *Nonprofit Management and Leadership*, 12(2): 177-192.
4. Sargeant, Adrian and Lee, Stephen (2004) 'Trust and relationship commitment in the United Kingdom voluntary sector: Determinants of donor behaviour', *Journal of Psychology & Marketing*, 21 (8): 613–635.
5. Sargeant,, Adrian and Jay, Elaine (2004) *Building Donor Loyalty: The Fundraiser's Guide to Increasing Lifetime Value*, Jossey-Bass, San Francisco.
6. Sargeant, Adrian and Woodliffe, Lucy (2005) 'The antecedents of donor commitment to voluntary organizations', *Nonprofit Management and Leadership*, 16(1): 61-78.
7. Bennett, Roger and Barkensjo, Ann (2005) 'Relationship quality, relationship marketing, and client perceptions of the levels of service quality of charitable organizations', *International Journal of Service Industry Management*, 16 (Iss:) 81-106.
8. DonorVoice (2011) *Donor Commitment Study 2011 Executive Summary* and DonorVoice (2012) *UK Donor Commitment*. Both available at: www.thedonorvoice.com Last accessed 30 September 2013.
9. Ibid.
10. Pell & Bales' annual mystery shopping exercise. As reported in *Third Sector* on 10 July 2007. Available at: http://www.thirdsector.co.uk/Fundraising/article/670543/Half-top-charities-fail-mystery-shopping-challenge/ Last accessed 30 September 2013.
11. Grain, John (2008) *Failing to hit the (bench) mark*. Available at: http://johngrainassociates.com/index.php/free-stuff-downloads/. Last accessed 7 September 2013.
12. Information taken from a talk at the 2012 Institute of Fundraising Scotland Conference by Damian O'Broin of Ask Direct. Slides available at: http://www.slideshare.net/damianob/do-you-care-about-your-donors-and-do-your-donors-care. Last accessed 7 September 2013.
13. Holloway, Bethan (2013) 'Using the phone to reduce donor attrition and drive loyalty', *International Journal of Nonprofit and Voluntary Sector Marketing*, 18(1) 31-35.
14 Adrian Sargeant and Elaine Jay (2004) *Fundraising Management: analysis planning and practice*, Routledge, London, p.156.
15. Sargeant, Adrian (2010) *Tiny Essentials of Donor Loyalty*, The White Lion Press, London.
16. Manning, Harely and Bodine, Kerry (2012*) Outside In: The Power of Putting Customers at the Center of Your Business*, New Harvest Books, New York.
17. Ibid., (pp.323).
18. Fox, Rich (1996) The future of relationship fundraising: What goes wrong. Available at: http://www.tgci.com/magazine/The%20Future%20of%20Relationship%20Fundraising.pdf Last accessed 28 September 2013.
19. Groonroos C. (1994) From Marketing Mix to Relationship Marketing. Towards a Paradigm Shift in Marketing. Management Decisions. 32(2) Pp. 4 – 20.

Why people give and the importance of emotion

So many experiences of giving can be disappointing. That's why we thought we'd start with a story to show that providing a memorable experience is possible for charities of all shapes and sizes. Craig describes the best donor experience he's encountered:

> *Grace and I spent our honeymoon touring China. While we were in Xi'An we were invited to visit a charity that looks after children with learning difficulties. We had an amazing time and at the end of the experience giving seemed a natural thing to do.*
>
> *Here's the textbook way they got us to give our biggest ever one-off donation.*
>
> *First of all we were welcomed and served refreshments by some of the children. The children then sang a number of songs and performed dance routines. It's fair to say there wasn't a dry eye in the house. It was very touching.*
>
> *Then there was an interesting talk about the ethos of the children's home (which would put many Western institutions to shame), the need for funds and a quick tour of some of the classrooms and other facilities.*
>
> *After that were invited to join in a special song and dance with the children – doing the birdie song in Chinese is one of the more surreal experiences of my life!*
>
> *Finally, came the fundraising. We were told we were getting an exclusive look at some of the art and crafts the children had made. We were welcome to buy these and contribute to the upkeep of the home.*

Best of all, the children showed us the fundraising wall where individual kids had designed posters and asked for donations for specific items. There was Mei who loved going to the cinema and Ning who wanted to buy a new camera so he could send pictures of what he'd been doing to his family. Just 500 yuan could achieve so much. How could anyone say no to such a bargain?

After buying some art (a picture proudly hangs in our study at home), buying a virtual gift and making a further donation we left. On our departure we were sincerely thanked, given a final song, so while we were poorer in wallet we had big smiles on our faces and a warm glow of satisfaction that we'd done some good. Later we were sent a follow-up by e-mail and made to feel really appreciated.

Craig's experience followed a classic process for successful relationship fundraising that fits with the model we discussed in chapter 3:

1. Make the donor feel at home, welcome and needed (relationship building).
2. Lead with a strong emotional story/experience (storytelling, the why).
3. Back up the emotional case with rational reasoning that demonstrates the need (the why).
4. Involve the donors and show them how they can help (relationship building, asking properly).
5. Make a specific, tangible and non-aggressive ask (asking properly).
6. Thank, report back and make the donor feel good about giving (data collection, donor magic).
7. Repeat.

This chapter is going to look at the theory about why this process works and how you can apply it to your own fundraising. We'll begin by taking a closer look at why people give.

WHY DONORS GIVE – UNDERSTANDING THEIR MOTIVATIONS

The TV programme *Secret Millionaire*[1] is one of our favourites. The premise of the show is brilliantly simple. Every episode a really rich person is sent undercover, with a film crew and a made-up story to a deprived community. We're sure some of the recipients must have an inkling by now when they get someone volunteering accompanied by a TV crew, but don't let our cynicism spoil the fun.

The millionaire volunteers for local good causes, gets to know the people and the projects and at the end of the show gives away a substantial amount of money to the featured charities and individuals.

As well as being a life-affirming and uplifting hour of television (barely an episode goes by without the tissues coming out to wipe away the tears), it is also a brilliant training video for fundraisers who want to understand why people give.

Here are just some of the numerous reasons we've seen on the show for people donating to charity:

- Access to services
- Altruism
- Because they were asked
- Compassion
- Duty
- Empathy
- Fit with self-image
- Forgiveness for sins
- Giving back
- Guilt
- In-memoriam
- It feels good
- Reciprocity
- Recognition
- Religion
- Self-esteem
- Self-preservation
- Social justice
- Social norms
- Support of friend or colleague
- Sympathy
- Tax breaks
- Value for money

What's fascinating about the *Secret Millionaire* is that every donor is different and all have varying reasons for giving. It is very rare that people's decisions aren't a mix of at least three or four of the above list.

However there are five reasons for giving that consistently feature and are worth looking at in closer detail.

1. It feels good

It becomes clear after watching a few episodes of the show that the people giving away the money get just as much out of giving, if not more, as the beneficiaries get from receiving the money. When the cameras return a few months later, nearly all the participants report feeling happier in their lives and are grateful that they were able to help.

Thanks to advances in neuroscience and how the brain works we now understand why this response is not surprising.

In *Brainfluence*,[2] author Roger Dooley highlights a number of research studies that demonstrate that giving activates the same part of the brain (the medial orbitofrontal-subgenual and lateral orbitofrontal area for those interested) as the satisfaction you get from food or sex. The 'joy of giving' isn't a warm and fuzzy feeling that has no basis in fact. It is hard-wired into our core.

Fundraisers forget this at their peril. When donors give it feels good to them and doesn't induce pain, as many people assume. The pain sometimes comes later through bad fundraising, such as when we fail to thank and report back to our donors on the impact their gift has made.

GIVING FEELS GOOD – JUST ASK LONDON'S *BIG ISSUE* SELLERS

One of the big fundraising traditions in the UK is flag days. These are days when volunteers from a charity take to the streets and collect money from the general public. I've taken part in many of these over the years, but one that sticks in my mind is the first time I ever collected on the streets of London.

At 6.30 in the morning I arrived at Waterloo station, took up position on the route towards the South Bank and asked passers-by to help blind people by sparing some loose change. Thousands of people streamed by me. Not many gave. After a few hours, as the rush hour subsided, I was approached by a *Big Issue* seller (*The Big Issue* is a UK magazine sold on the street by homeless people and gives them an opportunity to earn a wage).

I was worried he was going to criticise me for being on his patch, but instead he put some loose change in my bucket, said he knew what a tough business it was and wished me a successful day. I was bowled over.

Probably the poorest person I'd encountered all morning not only stopped and had a chat, but he also gave as well. It restored my faith in humanity.

By lunchtime I'd moved north of the river and was outside a supermarket, hoping to collect people's small change as they left after buying lunch. Again, people streamed past with few of them giving. As before, I was approached by another *Big Issue* seller and again he stopped for a chat, put some loose change in my bucket, told me how The *Big Issue* was helping him turn his life around and even asked about volunteering for my charity.

I ended the day in Soho, hoping to catch the after-work crowd in a good mood as they headed to the pubs and bars. You can guess what happens next. Yet another *Big Issue* seller stopped, donated a few pence and wished me luck.

I was stunned and humbled. Here were three people, all down on their luck, with not much to give, but they wanted to help anyway. They probably empathised about standing all day soliciting and being so frequently ignored, but they also probably knew the pleasure of someone stopping, having a chat and buying a copy from them, so they wanted to share that with me.

As you can imagine, I've bought a lot more copies of *The Big Issue* since then.

2. Recognition

The more individualistic a culture the more important recognition becomes to a donor.

Work by Dutch psychologist Geert Hofstede[3] ranked 66 countries by their individualistic versus collective attitudes. Individualistic countries emphasise achievement over group goals, resulting in a strong sense of competition. Collectivist countries put emphasis on family and group goals at work over individual targets or desires.

The top five individualistic countries are:

1 United States
2 Australia
3 United Kingdom
4 The Netherlands

5 New Zealand

And the bottom five (most collective cultures) are:

62 Colombia
63 Venezuela
64 Panama
65 Ecuador
66 Guatemala

It's no surprise then that recognition is a big influence to donors in the United States and most donors in the Western world. The desire for the approval and respect of your family, peers, community and colleagues is an extremely important motivation for giving.

If you're fundraising in Guatemala (and also China or other South-East Asian countries, which also score low on individualism) then you may need to think twice about how you recognise donors. Naming a library or hospital wing after a donor may not have the same social status at it does in the Western world.

Giving appropriate recognition to donors is crucial and we will be taking a closer look at this in chapters 11 and 13 on stewardship and major giving.

3. Closeness to cause and in-memoriam

Proximity to cause is also extremely important. If you know someone who has fought cancer or has heart disease then you are more likely to support causes related to this. Perhaps the most visible example of this is in-memoriam giving.

The memory of loved ones is a powerful reason for giving. On the *Secret Millionaire* show many of the millionaires give to causes that have had an impact on their lives. It may be that a parent had cancer or a sibling had cerebral palsy, but the motivation to do something in another's memory is always very strong.

From personal experience we know this is true and both of us have direct debits to charities that have helped members of our friends and family in some way. Most likely you have too.

In the UK, the CAF (Charities Aid Foundation) *UK Giving 2012*[4] survey reports that the biggest area of giving is to medical research, followed by giving to hospitals and hospices. A big part of this giving is based on gifts in memory of loved ones.

4. Religion

The CAF reported in 2012[5] that people in the UK who are religious donate over twice as much to charity as those without a faith. The good news for charities that aren't faith based is that only 31 per cent gave to religious causes.

Similarly in the United States, the *Chronicle of Philanthropy*'s How America Gives[6] research shows that people living in more religious states give more of their disposable income to charity. However, unlike the UK, most of this giving is directed to their church. When you take out religious giving, the more secular states give more to non-church causes.

Whatever your faith, there is no doubt that many of your donors will be religious and the relationship fundraiser needs to be aware of this. All the major faiths have elements of giving – the tithe in Christianity, *sadaqah jariyah* in Islam and the obligation of *tzedakah* in Judaism.

However, there is a balance to be had here. If your organisation is non-religious, then it would be insincere and hypocritical to suddenly start dropping in lines from the Bible, Koran, or Torah – you shouldn't try to be something you're not.

Yet having an understanding of your donor's religious beliefs and the impact it has on their giving is both sensible and good practice.

5. Being asked

It's an old fundraising truism that 'if you don't ask, you don't get' and many fundraisers miss the opportunity to raise money by not making a clear ask to donors. The donor may have lots of reasons to give, but if we never get round to making the right request, at the right time to the right donor, we won't be able to turn those reasons into a tangible gift.

We'll be looking in part 2 of the book on how to make a successful fundraising ask to donors.

HOW DONORS CHOOSE CHARITIES THEY SUPPORT – THE IMPORTANCE OF EMOTION

Deciding which charity to support is an emotion-led decision. As much as we like to think of ourselves as rational, well-informed individuals, the simple truth is that we are emotional creatures. If, as relationship fundraisers, we are unable to provoke or release the right emotions in our donors then we are unlikely to raise much money.

Websites like Charity Navigator and GuideStar in the United States and the now defunct Intelligent Giving in the UK have tried to bring a more rational approach to giving with only limited success.

GuideStar's own research published in the *Money for Good II*[72] study shows that only 35 per cent of donors ever do any research into the charities they give to and of those 35 per cent only 16 per cent spend more than two hours on the research. Perhaps the killer statistic for those who think that donors choose charities in a rational way is that only 6 per cent of total individual donors actually use research to decide between different causes.

These findings echo Dr Beth Breeze's analysis in *How Donors Choose Charities*,[8] a UK study that looked at how donors choose charity beneficiaries and how much 'need' plays a part in the decision process.

Beth discovered that people don't necessarily give to the most urgent need, but support causes that mean the most to them. The study found the following four non-needs-based reasons for why people give:

1   Donors' tastes, preferences and passions, acquired as a result of an individual's social experiences. These motivate many decisions to give, even among those who perceive themselves to be motivated by meeting needs.
2   Donors' personal and professional backgrounds, which shape their 'philanthropic autobiographies' and influence their choice of beneficiaries.
3   Donors' perceptions of charity competence, notably the efficiency with which they are believed to use their money, often judged on the basis of the quality and quantity of direct mail.
4   Donors' desire to have a personal impact, such that their contribution makes a difference and is not 'drowned out' by other donors and government funding.[3]

The study also found that people find it difficult to make decisions about donating and so use strategies to help them in their choices. These include:

- Constructing self-made classifications and 'mental maps' to help cope with the complexity of the charity sector.
- Using heuristics, or 'rules of thumb', to filter potential charitable recipients.
- Pre-assigning value judgements to certain causes as intrinsically 'worthy' or 'unworthy' of support. For instance, depending on your personal values, you might instinctively decide whether an animal charity is something you would or would not support (for the record Craig is a 'no' and Paul a 'yes')

and therefore automatically filter any fundraising offer from such a cause.

Similarly, in the business world the *Journal of Advertising Research* reported in 2002 that:

> ... *emotions are twice as important as 'facts' in the process by which people make buying decisions.*[11]

This may be a massive understatement. If we look again at neuroscience and studies of the brain it quickly becomes apparent why these findings shouldn't surprise us.

A SHORT TOUR OF THE BRAIN – WHY EMOTIONS TRUMP REASON

Just as the 'joy of giving' is hard-wired into us as humans, so is the fact that we make decisions through the emotional part of the brain, which evolved long before the rational part of the human brain. To conceptualise this, it can help to visualise the brain as three interlinked, but separate parts.

The oldest part, in evolution terms, supports our senses. It is often referred to as the 'lizard brain' and described as the part of brain that controls 'fight or flight' and the survival instinct in us.

It is our 'lizard brain' that can make us conservative, procrastinate and avoid difficult decisions.

The second part of the brain is the limbic system. This is our emotional centre. It turns the things we sense in the world around us into emotional and physical responses.

We like to imagine that the third part, the rational part of the brain (the neocortex), is the one in charge. Descartes 'I think, therefore I am' sums it up perfectly. Yet it is a deception. The rational part of the brain is constantly playing catch up to our emotional core and looks for ways to validate the emotional decision that has already been made.

According to Dan Hill in his book *Emotionomics*,[12] the hard-wiring of our brain has a number of implications:

- It makes us more primitive than we might think.
- Emotions are central, not peripheral, because they drive reason more than the other way round.
- Feelings happen before thought and they happen with great speed.

- Emotion leads to action, while reason leads to conclusions.
- Recall is emotion based – we have gut reactions in 3 seconds or less. Why? Ninety per cent of serotonin, known as the happiness hormone, is formed in our stomachs. So the term gut feeling is no exaggeration.
- Conscious thought is the tip of the iceberg. A host of other processes and synapses constantly happen in our brain that we are not aware of and which influence us without us knowing it.
- Visual imagery and other non-verbal forms of communication predominate, i.e. 'a picture really does paint a thousand words'.
- We perceive matters in ways that emotionally protect our habits and biases.

WHAT THIS MEANS FOR FUNDRAISING

All this has profound impact for fundraisers, who need to understand the importance of emotion.

In fact, if you take just one point from this book then we hope it is this: if your fundraising doesn't resonate emotionally with your audience then it will fail.

Ken Burnett described the importance of emotion in fundraising in an article on SOFII in 2012:

Can fundraising really be so predictably easy? Well, yes, it can, if we understand our donors' emotional brains and find ways to consistently and indelibly print powerful, emotional, appropriate memories there, to be reactivated later.

First impressions last. Sure they do.

This is a transformational insight, the single biggest realisation of all. It explains things that many fundraisers often feel intuitively but mostly haven't quite rationalised and that others miss altogether.

Such as the surge of emotion when we see a child in distress, the appeal in the direct gaze of a child's eyes that means all we have to say is, 'sponsor me'; no more explanation is needed. Or the sweating palms and lump in the throat conjured by the mere image of those soldiers in first world war trenches, waiting for that pre-dawn whistle. Or the recall of time, place and feelings prompted by a piece of music from our past, or by the smell of perfume, or the taste of an exotic fruit. Think Amnesty's long copy ads, children running from exploding shells, or waiting in food queues at times of famine, or the tired, shocked, dripping lifeboat

> man just washed in from the sea.
>
> How powerful are the emotions conjured by images such as these? How useful would it be to consistently harness them to your cause? Well, the emotional scenes are already there or they can be planted there to be called upon later, if only we get better at emotional storytelling, at presenting our emotional case with power and passion that will burn the memory of our story so deep that it will last and last long term, to be called upon again and again, whenever needed.
>
> We should study the brain to learn how we can skilfully, sensitively and carefully exploit its potential to store emotional memories that we can access, later, when we have use for them.[13]

More recently, Ken told us about the two main lessons he learned from studying the role of emotion in fundraising:

> It's no surprise that emotion trumps logic every time, but a key realisation – and it runs somewhat contrary to our increased professionalism of recent years – is that we should keep the logical, rational part of our case for support very simple, very short and very good, so that it's unchallengeable even, and the donor can simply take it as read. Then, with the pause for logical justification comfortably dealt with, the fundraiser has to connect the donor very quickly indeed with the emotional reward that should follow on as close to instantly as possible after the gift that resulted from the initial emotional need. That emotional reward will most likely come in the form of feedback that says, yes, you did make a difference. But the key is, the feedback – the brilliant emotional reward – should come very quickly indeed – hours, not days. This is the need and reward cycle, of course. But dramatically speeded up.

So how can you put this into practice and make sure emotions are at the core of your fundraising?

In *Emotionomics*,[14] Dan Hill argues there are six key emotions that drive an action, such as writing a cheque or signing a petition. These key emotions are:

- Anger
- Disgust

- Fear
- Happiness
- Sadness
- Surprise

It's easy to see how the six primary emotions apply to relationship fundraising:

Anger: how could someone abuse a vulnerable child? It makes me furious.

Disgust: how can some parents allow their daughters to be cut by a tradition such as female genital mutilation? It disgusts me that society turns a blind eye.

Fear: global warming, deforestation, animal extinction. What sort of world are we leaving for our grandchildren?

Happiness: after slowly nursing Rover back to health, it was a joy to see him running round the field with his tail wagging and tongue lolling.

Sadness: a tear rolled down the nurse's face. There was nothing more she could do. The child was going to die.

Surprise: wow! It only costs £10 to solve the problem? Who'd have thought it could be such a bargain?

Each of these primary emotions has a scale of intensities. Happiness ranges from satisfaction to joy, and anger goes from mild annoyance to rage. Similarly, you can break down these base emotions further and map them out to produce a set of secondary emotions as outlined in table 4.1.

At its most basic level fundraising is simply a case of triggering a negative emotion and then offering donors a solution that provokes a positive emotion. Need, then reward.

Let's look at a part of an appeal showcased on SOFII from Make-A-Wish® Canada to see how this works in action.

It is the first two pages of a direct mail letter from Make-a-Wish® Canada and it takes readers on a rollercoaster ride of emotion.

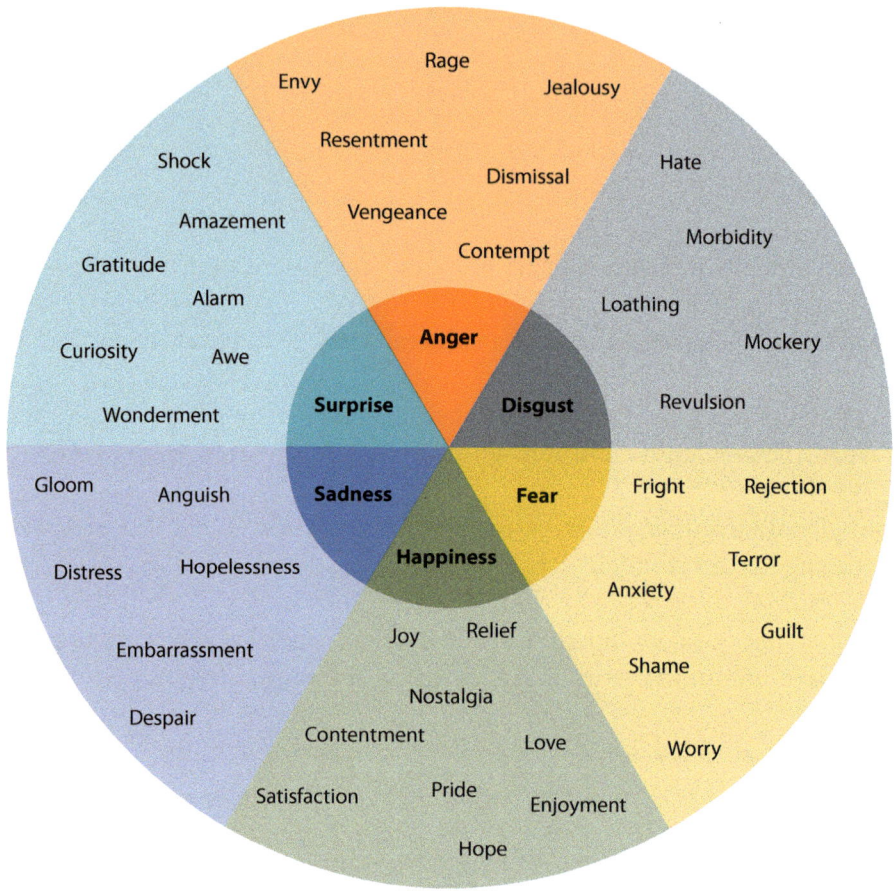

Figure 4.1: Primary and secondary emotions

It starts with:

> There is absolutely nothing worse than watching your three-year-old child die.

Emotions: sadness, worry, outrage, despair, distress.

> And there is nothing better than stealing her back from heaven.
> My daughter came back from certain death thanks to people like you.
> I hope you'll give me one moment of your time because I'm not a fundraiser, I'm a parent. And when I tell you my story I think you'll realize you can make miracles happen.

Why people give and the importance of emotion

Emotions: hope, delight, relief, surprise, happiness.

> *My daughter Carlie was a perfectly healthy child. Then one day she got a bad fever. We took her to the hospital only to discover every parent's nightmare. Carlie had cancer.*
> *We started the treatment, and we prayed.*
> *Then, when Carlie was near the end of 10 months of chemotherapy, her grandmother gave us a wonderful surprise. She gave Carlie's name to Make-a-Wish Foundation and asked that her dream wish be granted.*
> *But three weeks before Carlie got her dream wish (she wished to go to Sea World), she came down with pneumonia and influenza. Six days later Carlie was in a coma.*
> *The doctors told us she had a 20% chance to live. Then it got worse.*
> *By Carlie's 17th day in a coma she had lost 98% of her lung capacity. She had 13 tubes in her tiny body. She was paralysed.*
> *The doctors told us she would not live through the weekend. I don't know if you can imagine how horrible it was to hear this news. Our baby was dying.*

Emotions: guilt, despair, distress, sadness, fear, anger, disgust.

> *But a miracle happened.*
> *Carlie regained consciousness. She had lost half her body weight – but she was alive.*
> *Just 12 days later, Carlie was carried on to a plane to fly to Sea World. She was going to get her wish to swim with dolphins.*
> *When Carlie returned two weeks later, she had the strength to run into her grandmother's arms. Carlie's recovery was amazing.*
> *You may, or may not believe this, but I'm convinced that Carlie came back from certain death because of her dream wish.*
> *When you're as sick as Carlie was, the only thing that could get you out of bed is a <u>dream</u> – something you desperately wish for.*

Emotions: delight, relief, surprise, happiness, hope, awe.

You can see the emotional journey that the reader of the letter is taken on. By the end of the second page you're almost screaming 'I want to help – what can I do?' and the letter goes on to make a compelling offer and fundraising ask.

Managing the emotional content of your fundraising is an important task. For example, if you go too high on the disgust, then you may turn donors off before you get to the solution and offer.

GUILT AND NEGATIVE EMOTIONS – A CAREFUL BALANCE FOR RELATIONSHIP FUNDRAISERS

Guilt is a very powerful emotion and can be extremely effective. However, we believe it is a dangerous emotion for the relationship fundraiser so should only be used with great care. It is negative and you need to avoid exploiting this emotion in unethical ways.

The Institute of Fundraising Code of Practice in the UK now outlaws the practice of sending money or unwanted gifts, such as tea towels, in direct mail packs that rely on reciprocation and guilt to get people to donate. The relationship fundraiser should avoid them (we will look at what makes a good incentive and involvement device in chapter 8). In general, we think the banning of such 'phoney' gifts is a good thing.

Fundraisers need to be careful not to confuse guilt with a sense of injustice or feeling over-advantaged compared to others (i.e. my children are much better off than children in poor countries). Charities have a duty to report on the problems of the world. We shouldn't try to sanitise the reality of the work we do. If pictures of starving children, tortured animals and devastating disasters are genuine, or representative of the truth, then we shouldn't shy away from using them.

The fact that these images provoke strong negative emotions isn't a bad thing. In fact, it is almost essential. Giving is a simple way that people can channel that negative emotion and so experience all the joys of giving that we talked about earlier.

There can be a fine line between highlighting a specific problem that provokes a strong negative emotion (disgust, sadness, fear) and overtly using guilt to make donors feel the problems are their own fault, thereby guilt tripping them into giving.

There is no easy way to decide

when that line is crossed. Every person will have their own tipping point when something goes too far. Adverts like this one [shown on the previous page] from Save the Children in the 1970s wouldn't be socially acceptable now as we believe it relies too much on guilt to provoke a response.[15]

Compare this approach to the emotional power of their current No Child Born to Die campaign. This took the long over-rationalised case to reduce poverty and made it a hyper-emotional imperative.

Ultimately, the best relationship fundraisers will be those who understand the power of emotion and use it sensibly, wisely and carefully in their fundraising. We need to recognise the sense of injustice, fear and sadness and combine it with more positive emotions, such as hope, joy, achievement and happiness to take donors on a journey where, ultimately, they feel good about giving and the difference they are making.

THE IMPORTANCE OF IMAGERY

The phrase 'a picture paints a thousand words' is a cliché, but, as explained earlier, we now know it is also neurologically true. Getting the right imagery in your fundraising can make the difference between success and failure.

We have a section on choosing the right imagery in your fundraising in chapter 8, but we wanted to explain the biology of why imagery is so important here.

Dan Hill, author of *Emotionomics*, gives us the answer:

> A battle between pictures and words is like one between Mike Tyson and Tiny Tim: the picture throws the bigger punch. Consider the following:
>
> Two thirds of all stimuli reaching the brain are visual
> Over 50 per cent of the brain is devoted to processing visual images.

> *80 per cent of learning is visually based.*
> *Business people, take note. Humans are extremely visual: we think largely in images, not words.*

He continues:
> *For anyone who wants to 'get back to basics', remember that nothing is more basic than non-verbal communication. Human beings have existed for over 500,000 years, but we've had the benefit of language for less than a quarter of that time.*
>
> *Moreover, because the rational and sensory parts of the brain aren't adjacent neighbours, we're not very good at verbally describing the details our senses detect. Ironically, that's true despite the fact that our gut-level perceptions are largely based on sensory impressions.*[16]

All of this means that if we want to elicit emotion and response in our donors, then understanding the imagery that supports and underpins our fundraising message is crucial.

In practical terms, think of the last time you cried or got emotional.

Take a second to recall the experience. What springs to mind? Do you paint a mental image or do you remember the words that were written or spoken? Having asked hundreds of people this question, we're willing to bet it is an image that comes to mind first.

MEASURING EMOTIONS IN YOUR FUNDRAISING

How do you know if your appeal or campaign has enough emotion in it? How can you measure emotion?

Most research methods, such as focus groups or online panels (we'll look at research methods in chapter 19) are based in rational thought. They give people time to think and respond in a thought-through way. Yet, as we've demonstrated earlier, it is the instant, emotional response that we need to measure.

The simple fact is that there is no easy, cheap way to measure the types and strength of emotion in your fundraising. In fact, measuring emotion is an emerging scientific field and is currently prohibitively expensive for all but the largest charities, and maybe even for them too.

There are currently two ways to measure real time emotion and reactions.[17] Both use complicated science and advanced technology to measure minute changes in your body. These include temperature, sweat, heartbeat, micro-spasms and eye movement.

The first involves selecting suitably willing and representative candidates who match your donor profile, then attaching super sensitive sensors that fit to their skin so you can measure micro-changes in their skin temperature and conductance. These have been used in medicine to help understand the emotional reactions of non-communicative autistic children to various stimuli.

The second is through using facial coding technology to record a person's facial expressions. This records micro-changes in the facial muscles (human beings have more facial muscles than any other species on the planet) to map out the type and intensity of emotions you are feeling in real time.

Not convinced? Take a second to think of the face of someone who is very happy. What characteristics does it have? Contrast this with the face of someone who is extremely angry. You'd know instinctively which person is which.

Alternatively, think of a time you have laughed politely at a joke versus when you have been crying with laughter. Again, the difference in facial expressions is something you would identify instantly.

The business world is beginning to catch on to the importance of testing for emotion in advertising. For example, Forbes magazine[18] got people to watch commercials online and measured their happiness via their facial expressions on webcams. The one that made most people smile was Volkswagen's 'The Force' commercial, which parodied *Star Wars* and is worth watching if you have a couple of minutes to spare.

We predict that in the next five to 10 years the costs of the technology will tumble, so it will be accessible to every relationship fundraiser, not just big companies. It will become the norm to test for the emotional response of appeals before launching them. This should, in theory, revolutionise fundraising and reduce the number of dull, emotion-free fundraising failures that currently exist.

CONCLUSION

Fundraising is full of truisms and basic principles that have been passed from generation to generation of fundraisers. One of the most quoted, usually attributed to Harold Sumption, is:

> Open hearts, open minds, open wallets.

We've heard this in many conferences and read it (in various guises) in numerous books over the years. The best fundraisers instinctively know this is true and understand how important emotions are in soliciting gifts.

As we have shown, we now have the scientific knowledge to prove what previous generations instinctively knew was correct. Giving is good for us and is an emotionally led decision.

Fundraisers can develop and execute the most sophisticated and brilliant campaign in the world. In fact, we'll try and show you how to do this later in the book. However, even the best-planned appeals will fail if they lack emotion and don't connect in a way that makes potential donors want to give. That's why we've dedicated a chapter of the book to emotion and motivations for giving. Quite simply, they underpin every aspect of fundraising and need to be understood by every fundraiser who wants to change the world.

NOTES
1. The show originated in the UK, but there are now American, Australian and Irish versions. You can find out more on the Wikipedia page: http://en.wikipedia.org/wiki/Secret_Millionaire Last accessed 11 November 2012.
2. Dooley, Roger (2011) – *Braininfluence*, Wiley, New York.
3. See *Indivualism*, Clearly Cultural blog at www.clearlycultural.com/geert-hofstede-cultural-dimensions/individualism/, which lists all the countries and has a colour coded map for the countries where the research has been conducted. For a fascinating account of how one Hofstede's cultural dimensions (power distance) was responsible for a number of plane crashes, read Malcom Gladwell's *Outliers* (2008) Little, Brown and Company, Boston.
4. CAF *UK Giving 2012*, p. 13. Available: https://www.cafonline.org/publications/2012-publications/uk-giving-2012.aspx Last accessed 10 December 2012.
5. *Religious donors give more than double those of no faith*, CAF press release, 2012. Available at: https://www.cafonline.org/media-office/press-releases/2012/religious-donors-give-more.aspx Last accessed 11 November 2012.
6. 'How America gives: Faith and giving', *Chronicle of Philanthropy*, 19 August 2012. Available at: http://philanthropy.com/article/FaithGiving/133611/ Last accessed 11 November 2012.
7. Hope Consulting (2011) *Money for Good II*. Full report available at: http://www.guidestar.org/ViewCmsFile.aspx?ContentID=4038 Last accessed 11 November 2012. For a summary press release see http://www.guidestar.org/rxa/news/articles/2011/results-of-money-for-good-2.aspx
8. Breeze, Beth (2010) *How Donors Choose Charities*, Alliance Publishing Trust, London. Available for free at: http://www.kent.ac.uk/sspssr/cphsj/documents/How%20Donors%20Choose%20Charities%2018%20June%202010.pdf Last accessed 11 November 2012.
9. Ibid, p.9.
10. Ibid., p. 10.
11. Morris, Jon et al (2002) 'The power of affect: Predicting intention', *Journal of Advertising Research*, May/June.
12. Hill, Dan (2010) *Emotionomics: Leveraging Emotions for Business Success*, 2nd edition, Kogan Page, Philadelphia.
13. Burnett, Ken, *The emotional brain*, SOFII website, 2012. Available at: http://www.sofii.org/node/1004 Last accessed 11 November 2011.
14. Hill, Emotionomics, op.cit.
15. Taken from the Old Charity Ads Pinterest board founded by Mark Phillips of Bluefrog: http://pinterest.com/markphillips/old-charity-ads/ Last accessed 9 December 2012.
16. Hill, *Emotionomics, op. it., pp.* 20 and 21.
17. Angelica, Amara D *How to measure emotions*, Kurzweil blog, 2011. Available at: http://www.kurzweilai.net/how-to-measure-emotions Last accessed 16 December 2012.
18. McDuff, D, (2011) *Interactive: Analyze Your Smile*, Forbes.com. Available at: http://www.forbes.com/2011/02/28/detect-smile-webcam-affectiva-mit-media-lab.html

Developing a relationship fundraising strategy

For many years the donor pyramid has been used to demonstrate, in a simple format, how donors might come into contact with a charity, engage with it and progress through various levels of support until, ultimately, they might leave it a legacy.

The humble pyramid has attracted much comment, hypothesis and debate over the years with trapezoids, inverted pyramids and vortexes all being proposed in its place.

Such over-analysis seems to miss the point of what the pyramid was designed to do – demonstrate, simply, how donors might interact with your nonprofit.

In truth no model or diagram is ever going to be able to represent the myriad motivations, emotions and reasons why people give. Similarly, people rarely act in predictable, linear ways. Indeed, life would be boring if they did.

However, the pyramid does give a starting point for you to consider how donors behave and there is evidence to suggest (when large enough volumes of donors are involved) that the pyramid is indicative of donor behaviour. In 2010 *The Agitator* fundraising blog ran a series of posts on the donor pyramid and its usefulness.[11] They reported on research from Lawrence Henze, managing director of Target Analytics, who found:

> … *research shows that $1,000 gifts to organizations occur most frequently when that donor has already been giving to the organization for about seven years. Many years of research with successful nonprofits also shows that those very same donors are approximately 900 per cent more likely to make a major gift in their lifetime than individuals without that progressive history.*

So if you don't take the pyramid as gospel and are kind enough to allow donors to enter it at places other than at the bottom, it can help you visualise how you might build a relationship.

This brings us to a pyramid of our own. We want to introduce you to the relationship fundraising pyramid (figure 5.1). This shows the three elements you need to put in place to create a culture of relationship fundraising in your organisation.

Figure 5.1: The relationship fundraising pyramid

The three parts of the pyramid are:

1 Meeting the basic needs of donors – when a donor first interacts with your charity do you get the basics right? Things such as getting the donor's details correct, or sending a prompt acknowledgement that reinforces to the donor that he or she has made a good decision.

2 Ease of continuing relationship – when a donor has given once do you make it easy for him or her to give again? How much effort is involved in continuing to support your cause? If you make it hard to give many people are likely to abandon the process. For example, online donation forms have a non-completion rate of between 50 and 70 per cent.[2] Conversely, this is what makes recurring gifts (such as direct debits) so great and why donating by SMS has grown so much. Both make it simple for donors to give.

3 Donor magic – getting the basics right and making it easy to give aren't enough by themselves. You need to create what we call 'donor magic' to recruit donors for life. This can range from great thank-you letters and outstanding customer service to involving your donors in your work and providing meaningful feedback about their gifts.

Sadly, many charities find themselves in the desert of donor apathy and attrition as they struggle to engage donors sufficiently, don't make it easy for donors to support them and even get basic details wrong.

Here are two real stories that show how bad some charities are at the basics.

The first comes via US-based fundraising consultant, blogger and author

Pamela Grow. It is about a dysfunctional organisation she used to work for. The charity had very many problems, but their approach to fundraising was summed up by this story:

> *At one point, a gift arrived in the mail. The shaky handwriting alerted me that this was an elderly woman. The gift she sent in, a small donation of less than $100, was designated specifically for a memorial program honouring her daughter. I set out to ensure that our donor's gift was directed as intended … only to learn that there was no record whatsoever of any such memorial program. It took days of research to learn that this donor's daughter had passed away at one of our facilities years earlier. A plaque had been placed on the wall of one of the camp cabins honoring the young woman and a scholarship had been established in her name. Amidst all the organisational changes throughout the years, the plaque had been lost and the scholarship long forgotten.*[3]

Another donor horror story was shared by British innovation expert Lucy Gower on the 101fundraising blog (www.101fundraising.org). Just after she graduated Lucy had set up a £3.00 per month gift to this particular cause by direct debit. She had given to them for more than 12 years, but was fed up by the lack of communication and feedback on her gift so she decided to cancel the direct debit.

When she rang she spoke to a helpful woman in the supporter care team and was persuaded not to cancel. It was at this point that things started to go wrong. The woman explained it would take a few months to 'get back in the system', which is never good to hear, and there was no immediate thank-you letter or e-mail to acknowledge Lucy's decision not to cancel her gift.

Five months later Lucy hadn't heard anything so telephoned again to cancel. The caller relayed the fact she had a duplicate record and hadn't made the last batch for the quarterly mailing. Language that is really donor unfriendly – who wants to be a 'duplicate' or 'in a batch'? The final straw came when two months after cancelling Lucy finally received the newsletter for her batch – her cancellation hadn't worked its way through the system yet.

We've heard many other donor horror stories and whilst you may think that could never happen at your own nonprofit, are you 100 per cent sure?

We'll take a closer look at these examples later in the book and give you the tools to ensure you won't make the same mistakes.

THE ESSENTIAL ELEMENTS OF RELATIONSHIP FUNDRAISING

We showed you our model of relationship fundraising in chapter 3. We believe that chart demonstrates the elements that go into creating donor magic on a sustainable basis. Here it is again.

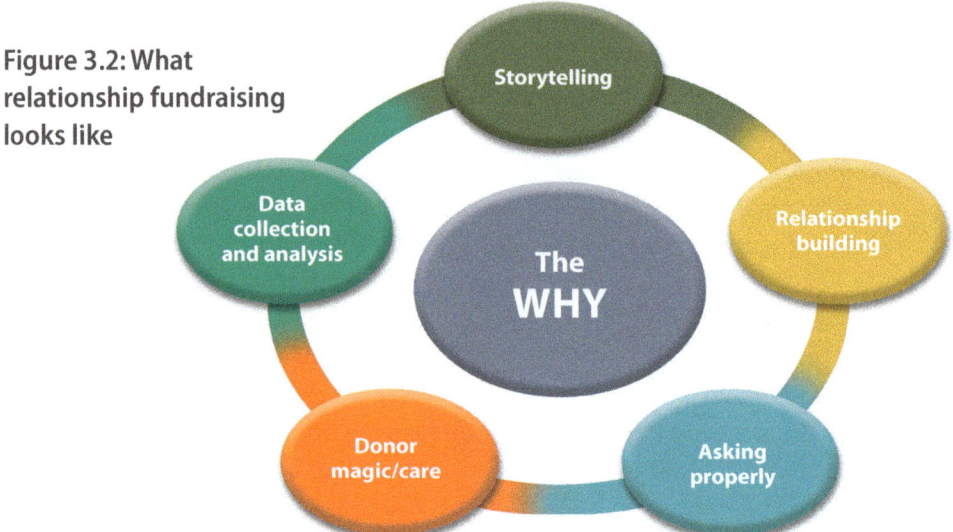

Figure 3.2: What relationship fundraising looks like

In part 3 of this book we will look at how you can implement the operational elements to create relationship fundraising in your organisation.

However, before you can do this you need to have two things in place:

- An overall fundraising strategy.
- A relationship fundraising culture to ensure the strategy is followed.

We will look at strategy in the rest of this chapter. Chapter 6 is about creating a relationship fundraising culture in your charity.

CREATING A RELATIONSHIP FUNDRAISING STRATEGY

Great relationship fundraising doesn't happen by accident. It requires a roadmap and a vision so that every fundraiser in a charity knows what is expected of them on a daily basis. This is your relationship fundraising strategy and it sets out the guiding principles of how you build strong relationships with your donors.

You need to make sure this aligns with your resources and overall charity strategy. When Paul worked at Macmillan Cancer Support they referred to this as the 'golden thread' that ran from corporate strategy to fundraising strategy to team objectives and finally individual objectives.

A common mistake we've both made is to try to follow the same fundraising strategy being implemented by a much bigger charity that we admire, without taking the time to consider how this fits with our own team and budgets. For example, Craig was a fan of the NSPCC fundraising team in the early 2000s and tried to copy some of their fundraising techniques. This didn't work because the organisation he was working for didn't have the same culture, resources, or mass appeal as the NSPCC.

We're not alone in doing this. We've heard people say 'we want to be the Apple of fundraising', which sounds great but if you think through what that actually means – leading edge design, fantastic innovation, products that appeal to younger people – then it won't work for the vast majority of charities. In fact, the only charity we know that could reasonably have this mantra is Charity: Water. This is a fantastic organisation, which has done some amazing relationship fundraising, but whose approach wouldn't work for many nonprofits that couldn't replicate their quality of video production, celebrity supporter base and focus on one single problem and its solution.

It is essential that your relationship fundraising strategy supports your overall charity strategy and brand. For example, an overseas development charity that relies on child sponsorship for the bulk of its fundraising income will have a very different relationship fundraising strategy to a hospice, which gets most of its income from the local community and in-memoriam fundraising.

There are hundreds of strategic models and ways of setting out your vision. One we've used, which we think works well for fundraisers, is set out in *Playing to Win: How Strategy Really Works* by Lafley and Martin. They say:

> *Strategy is about making specific choices to win in the marketplace. According to Mike Porter, author of* Competitive Strategy, *perhaps the most widely respected book on strategy ever written, a firm creates a sustainable competitive advantage over its rivals by 'deliberately choosing a different set of activities to deliver unique value.'*
>
> *Strategy therefore requires making explicit choices – to do some things and not others—and building a business around those choices.*

> *In short, strategy is choice. More specifically, strategy is an integrated set of choices that uniquely positions the firm in its industry so as to create sustainable advantage and superior value relative to the competition.*[4]

This view is backed up by *Great Fundraising*, a 2013 report by Adrian Sargeant and Jen Shang in conjunction with fundraising consultancy Clayton Burnett (now Revolutionise) that focuses on what it is that makes fundraising truly great.

The report found that exceptional fundraising directors:

> *(… m)anage their teams and achieve desired change through a combination of will and personal humility. We also found that they devote considerable attention to what they regard as the critical building blocks of success, namely building an exceptional team, structure(s) and culture …*

> *In our view, however, what seemed to us to elevate good fundraising to outstanding fundraising was the quality of the thinking that each leader was able to generate. Neither the ideas nor the considerable experience of our directors alone could have given rise to the fundraising success they created. The real difference these leaders were able to make occurred as a consequence of the way in which they understood and coped with the complexities of everyday decision-making.*[5]

So if great fundraising is about decision-making, how do you go about making an integrated set of choices?

The authors of *Playing to Win* propose a five-step system:

1 A winning aspiration – this sets out the frame for all the other choices. How does your charity 'win'? What is the end goal you are aiming for in your fundraising? This should be aspirational. It's not enough to say you want to grow your fundraising from £x million to £y million inside a certain time. Why do you need to do this in reference to your beneficiaries and mission? By framing it this way you can quickly evaluate the choices you make in the other steps – are those choices helping you to achieve your winning aspiration?

2 Where to play – you have lots of choice of where and how to fundraise so (2) and (3) are intertwined. They set out the specific activities you will undertake to achieve your winning aspiration. Where to play narrows down which market you will compete in for which donors. You will have to make choices about your target donors, your channels, your products and your geography. Take a few seconds to consider the plethora of cancer charities that exist. Some fundraise in the mass market with multiple products for different audiences (for example, CRUK in the UK and ACS in the US); some are single cause but have international reach with one product (Movember); some are smaller niche charities that fundraise for one specific type of cancer or patient (such as blood cancers or children); finally, there are local charities, such as hospices, that raise funds in and for the communities where they operate. All of these have to make different decisions on where to play for their fundraising.

It is almost as important to define where not to play. It can be tempting to try to do too many things and spread yourself too thinly (especially in smaller charities). That is why, for example, in one of the places where Craig worked he made the decision not to pursue affiliate marketing fundraising opportunities. With a small donor base and low brand recognition his charity wasn't then in a position to raise substantial funds from this type of fundraising partnership. This made it easy for him and his colleagues to say no to sales calls and opportunities, as they had made a strategic decision to concentrate on, and become better at, other types of fundraising.

3 How to win – this defines the choices you need to make for winning in your chosen place to play. To paraphrase Lafley and Martin, in order to win a charity must decide what will allow it to create unique value and then sustainably deliver that value to donors in a way that is distinct from the charities' competitors.[6]

For example, in the early 2000s the NSPCC won with its Full Stop campaign. They created a powerful fundraising story and structured their offers and products to appeal to both small and large givers. NSPCC was one of the early adopters of large scale, low value monthly giving via direct debit (EFT, electronic funds transfer), as well as securing numerous seven-figure gifts through the appeal.

Similarly, Charity: Water is winning in its chosen online market by delivering high quality digital storytelling and superior service and feedback, all online.

'Winning' isn't confined to large charities and high profile campaigns. All fundraising teams can find a winning proposition. For example, at a fundraising conference we heard a case study about a small, regional US charity that fundraises only from donors capable of giving over $10,000. This strategy works perfectly for them, enabling them to secure the funds they need while enjoying an incredible retention rate among their donors.

What distinguishes a winning choice is that it is hard for other charities to replicate your strategy and you can use your strengths to create competitive advantage in your chosen marketplace

4 Core capabilities – what activities and competences need to be in place to make sure you can deliver your 'where to play' and 'how to win' choices? It is no good deciding on a strategy if you are not capable of delivering it.

For example, if your 'where' and 'how' to win choices are based on having great donor insight then you'd better make sure your database is up to the job.

For large charities a big part of this might be working with the right partners who can help build your capability. For small organisations it might be important to respond quickly to opportunities and to get to market as fast as possible. Whatever core capabilities you decide on in your strategy you need to make sure they complement each other, so you can win.

5 Management systems – Lafley and Martin say:
These are the systems that foster, support, and measure the strategy. To be truly effective, they must be purposefully designed to support the choices and capabilities outlined in the strategy. The types of systems and measures will vary from choice to choice, capability to capability and company to company. In general, though, the systems need to ensure that choices are communicated to the whole company, employees are trained to deliver on choices and leverage capabilities, plans are made to invest in and sustain capabilities over time, and the efficacy of the choices and progress toward aspirations are measured.[7]

In other words, do all your team know and buy in to the strategy and do you have the information and insight you need to deliver your plans?

For example, if your how and where to win choice is based around corporate fundraising, then you need to make sure you have a robust leads management system in place, that your team is highly trained in how to write and deliver pitches and you have a plan on how to measure your account management capabilities.

So how does this all work in practice? To answer this, here's a two-page strategy that Craig produced in a previous job:

What is our fundraising team's aspiration?
To raise the money needed to make London and the south east of England the best place in the world for vision impaired young people to grow up.

How will we do this?
By becoming the favourite charity of individuals, corporates, community groups and trusts.

To do this we need to constantly look for ways to:

- Increase donor loyalty.
- Surprise and delight donors.
- Build our brand.
- Improve our current offering and develop new fundraising ideas.
- Integrate our ideas across fundraising and marketing.
- Recruit and retain outstanding fundraising talent.

We will not:
- Compete on price.
- Slavishly copy other fundraisers – although some tactical plagiarism is encouraged.
- Use affiliate marketing schemes.

Where and how will we fundraise?
We will use the following questions and principles when doing our fundraising planning:
What will make us stand out from other fundraisers?
- How can we do this better than anybody else?
- Focus on lifetime value of supporters and prioritise long-term growth over short-term (temporary) success.
- Be cost effective.
- Fail fast, fail often – have a pipeline of new fundraising ideas and initiatives to test, although the aim is to get it right first time.

What values do we need to make this happen?
The team have discussed values and as well as the overall charity values, we all felt the following were crucial to the team success:

- Teamwork
- Hard work and determination
- Integrity

What capabilities do we need to make this happen?
- A high quality customer relationship management (CRM) system.
- Excellent customer service and account management.
- Outstanding storytelling.
- Making donors our heroes and making our success their success.

From the master document, every team then has its own departmental two-page strategy and individual objectives and responsibilities naturally flow from this. This is the 'golden thread' we referred to earlier. The two-page strategy is supported by a rolling operational plan on what a team needs to deliver in the short and medium term, backed up by a more in-depth document that discusses some of the choices in greater detail and sets out the three- to five-year plan.

In many ways setting the strategy is the easiest bit. It is implementing and then monitoring its success that takes the time and skill. The rest of this chapter will look at how you can do that. We'll start by taking a closer look at some of the strategic tools you may find useful.

THE RELATIONSHIP FUNDRAISER'S STRATEGIC TOOLBOX
The following questions and tools are all useful in helping you plan your relationship fundraising strategy and assess the environment in which you are operating.

How does your strategy fit into the organisation's wider objectives?
The 'golden thread' for fundraising should be influenced by your organisation's overall corporate strategy and must be the starting point in any decision-making process. What exactly is the organisation's approach, not just now but over the next five years too? Are you planning for rapid growth in your service delivery, or are you embarking on a period of consolidation? If it's the former then you are going to be seeking shorter-term gain, if it's the latter, then this will provide

you with more breathing space to take a longer-term, possibly more considered approach.

And what is the wider health status of the organisation? Is it enjoying a purple patch or has it encountered a few lean years? Also, is there appetite for investment or do you have a conservative board reluctant to release further funding for new initiatives until certain criteria can be met? (It is always worth checking in advance of taking on a new role, by the way, the position of your prospective organisation and the funding that may, or may not, be available to you.)

Strengths, weaknesses, opportunities and threats (SWOT) analysis
Charities vary enormously in their composition, their infrastructure and their positioning in the sector. Size, in terms of staff, budget and voluntary income, might be the most obvious variable – the opportunities and challenges facing small and big charities may be very different. But often what holds back one benefits another and vice versa. For example, a large charity may have the reach and finances to flood a market at any given point in time, but a small organisation may well be open to riskier, more creative initiatives. It may also lack the red tape that often hinders a large organisation and prevents it from moving quickly to test innovative ideas. Smaller charities might also be better placed to synchronise more effectively and build a fundraising portfolio that is not rooted in silos.

More simply, the personnel involved, in terms of your board, staff and volunteers, can affect what you try and take on. As with any business, it's often best to play to your strengths and not to undertake an activity about which you know little. You may not have the skills to manage it in-house or have the budget to recruit those who do, or be able to employ an agency to assist you along the way.

A SWOT analysis is one of the most common strategic tools used to assess an organisation's plans. It stands for strengths, weaknesses, opportunities and threats. It provides a framework for assessing the characteristics of your organisation that give it an advantage or disadvantage over others. It also considers elements that could give you an advantage and factors in the environment that could cause trouble for you.

The SWOT is usually one of the first bits of analysis you do for any strategy or project as it helps you later in the planning process when you define your objectives.

Reviewing external factors including political, economic, social and technology (PEST) analysis

Fundraising does not take place in a vacuum. You can know your organisation inside out but still not have all the facts to hand for a full and thorough evaluation of the opportunities. The wider economic climate clearly has a bearing on your fundraising, though one must be careful not to use this as an excuse either to be unambitious or to cite it as the primary reason for the ineffectiveness of any of your initiatives.

Don't be afraid if taking the initiative it might not work. There is absolutely nothing wrong in making mistakes or the odd lapse in judgement, as long as you are able to recognise the error as soon as possible, take responsibility where appropriate, gain a clear and detailed understanding of what went wrong and, perhaps most importantly, ensure that you don't make the same mistake twice. Then, and only then, are calculated risks and errors acceptable.

Challenges may also present opportunities. Many organisations that have invested during a downturn have reaped the benefits later when the good times returned. As Cathy Pharoah, co-director of the Centre for Charitable Giving, points out:

> *This has been the experience in previous economic cycles, when donations have even seen a spurt in growth after recession.*[8]

The Center on Philanthropy at the University of Indiana, USA, predicts that it takes on average about three years after the conclusion of a downturn for giving levels to return to their pre-recession levels. They go on to advise that during the recession fundraising professionals should be planning for a period of recovery, when donors again feel a sense of financial security and willingness to make commitments.

> *In any year, some nonprofit organisations see increases in the amounts they receive in charitable contributions. By using the best practices known for fundraising your organisation will be prepared.*[9]

And certain elements of the fundraising portfolio, such as charity shops, have been proven to flourish and take advantage of the cut-back culture that can pervade these periods of financial gloom.

Indeed, many nonprofit organisations thrive in periods of recession, as we saw during the 'great recession' of 2007 – 2011. Many organisations with robust fundraising programmes have survived reasonably well, while most of those who cut back their fundraising investment because times were hard will now be finding times even harder still.

The most useful strategic tool to help you in your external analysis is called a PEST analysis. PEST stands for political, economic, social and technological. Often prepared in conjunction with your SWOT analysis, where the analysis dovetails with your opportunities and threats, this tool takes a big picture view of those things outside your organisation that could have an influence on it.

Political – are there political factors that might have an impact on your fundraising? For example, regulation might be on the horizon for a particular channel, such as face-to-face or telemarketing.

Economic – how does the state of the economy, and the direction it is heading, affect your fundraising? Does it impact on some of your target audience more than others and should you change your plans accordingly?

Social – what are the social and demographic trends that will have an impact on you? These could be an ageing population, public opinion on fundraising, or other changing social norms.

Technology – is there technology that will make a difference to your fundraising? How does the rise of smart phones influence what you do? How can you use social media to involve donors? What developments are on the horizon that might have an effect on how you fundraise?

Sometimes environmental and legal factors are also included in the analysis, which, if you feel it appropriate, would change the acronym to PESTEL.

Assessing your competitors

'Competitor' research is a must in our sector. It pays to keep your head up constantly, to ensure that you don't become bogged down in the daily routine of your role and become institutionalised by your charity's way of doing things. Regular competitor research will ensure you remain strategic and don't just focus on the minutiae. It will also show you what is proving effective for others in the sector.

One of the biggest advantages of working in the charity world is that the vast majority of activity takes place in the public domain and, even it isn't, fundraisers generally are very willing to share their knowledge and best practice. And we should certainly not see donations as a zero sum game. Exceptional events, such as emergency appeals and periods of national grief and celebration, prove that the cake can get bigger and we should not be obsessed with merely increasing our market share. For example, in 2013, the typhoon Haiyan emergency appeals for the Philippines drove up disaster relief donations by 0.7 per cent, but not at the expense of other areas, with donations as a whole rising by 4.4 per cent. Hence, the term *competitors* should remain firmly italicised.[3]

As we show in chapter 19, it is highly advisable to ingrain a culture of sector monitoring and evaluation both within your strategy and possibly in individual objectives. Only systematic sourcing of best practice ensures it remains always on the agenda, otherwise it tends to get de-prioritised, wrongly, behind seemingly more pressing daily activities.

To best inform your portfolio it is advisable to select a range of charities to monitor, some of which are of similar size, some which share a similar cause and others which are known to be market leaders in their areas of operation. And this research should certainly not be confined to the public sector. Many fundraising marketing activities are also used in the commercial sector and, more often than not, such companies are further ahead in their implementation. Finally, it is important to ensure you are not simply focused on activities in your own country. With the aid of the Internet and social media, it has never been easier to gain access to best practice occurring all over the world.

When he was working with a charity for blind people Craig kept a file of direct marketing from other charities working in the same field (known as a swipe file, because when you're searching for ideas there will be several that you might want to swipe). He used this to look for ideas and to assess propositions that were working in the marketplace. With this approach you can identify the banker packs that rival charities are using (those that are repeated multiple times with small variations) then analyse them for ideas and propositions you could potentially adapt for your own use. Similarly, if an ad only appears once in one channel it can be assumed it hasn't worked very well; if it appears often it's probably a success.

Measuring your strategic performance

It is important that you put in place a system to measure how you are doing against your strategic plan and identify areas for improvement. Your strategy should be re-visited regularly and not be allowed to gather dust on the shelf, ready for the next strategic review.

To help you overcome this problem, we'd recommend measuring where you are at least twice a year and developing a plan for your strategic priorities in the coming period.

We like the MARS tool discussed in *Playing to Win*. For each part of the strategy you need to assess what is:

Missing – we don't do this.
Ad hoc – we do this sometimes.
Repeatable – we have a process that defines what to do and we follow it most of the time.
Systematic – we have a process that defines when to do this and we follow it all the time in our current fundraising.

Once you've made this assessment then you can set your relationship fundraising priorities based on the resources available to you.

For example, it might be quick and easy to turn a current repeatable action into one that becomes systematic. Similarly, it might take a huge amount of time and capital investment to turn an ad hoc process into a systematic one.

By undertaking this process you will be able to set a relationship fundraising roadmap for success and detail the things you need to do, in the order you need to do them and the associated costs and benefits.

It's important to remember that putting the building blocks of successful relationship fundraising in place is not a discrete project. Instead, it should be viewed as a journey of continuous improvement and progression towards your stated aims.

CONCLUSION

Putting together a strategy is an essential part of fundraising success. However, it is not enough on its own. Too often months of hard work are put into creating a huge strategic document that is then left to gather dust on the shelf. We believe the best strategies provide clarity to the whole organisation and act as a guiding hand in all decision-making. That's why we've recommended the simple two-page approach outlined in this chapter. You might still need to do all the analysis that goes into a bigger document, but by distilling it down you will be able to help your team do great fundraising and raise more money.

As we said earlier in the chapter, a strategy is only a starting point. If you don't have the people, culture and operational planning in place to make it a reality then the strategy won't be worth the paper it is written on.

NOTES
1. Dead wrong, and dead right, a five-part series of post on the donor pyramid, The Agitator blog, 2010. First part available at: http://www.theagitator.net/don't-miss-these-posts/dead-wrong-and-deadright/Last accessed 11 January 2013.
2. As quoted by NP Engage (2013) *You've been abandoned*. Available at: http://www.npengage.com/online-fundraising/you-have-been-abandoned/Last accessed 11 January 2013.
3. Grow, Pamela (2013) *I cried for the donor*. Available at: http://www.pamelagrow.com/3699/i-cried-donor/ Last accessed 21 October, 2013 .
4. Lafley, Alan G and Martin, Roger L (2013) *Playing to Win: How Strategy Really Works*, Harvard Business Review Press, Boston, locations 114 and 115 (Kindle edition).
5. Sargeant, Adrian and Shang, Jen (2013) *Great Fundraising (full report)*. Clayton Burnett, Fort Augustus, Scotland, p. 2. Availabile at: https://revolutionise.wufoo.com/forms/pzot01b0yr3qqv/Last accessed 6 January 2015.
6. Lafley and Martin, *Playing to Win*, op. cit., location 418.
7. Ibid., location 492.
8. Pharaoh, Cathy, *Trends in giving during economic downturns*, Centre for Charitable Giving and Philanthropy date?
9. Miller, Melanie, Schaefer, Sarah and Wagner, Corinne (2009) *Giving Recovery After Economic Depression or Recession*, Giving USA Spotlight, Center on Philanthropy at Indiana University, Indianopolis.
10. Giving USA, The Annual Report on Philanthropy for the year 2013.

Creating a culture of relationship fundraising

Management guru Peter Drucker once famously said 'culture eats strategy for breakfast'.

Having the best strategy and plan in the world isn't enough by itself. If you don't create a culture that guides employees' decisions and how they work with others, then the strategy will ultimately fail.

Culture is about the way you do things and the values your organisation holds dear. It guides decision-making and underpins your strategic choices.

If your strategic choice is to pursue relationship fundraising you need to make sure you implement a culture that makes this possible. You will struggle to create donor magic if you don't have the staff, board members and volunteers who buy into the importance of donor experience and being brilliant at the basics.

One of our favourite stories about the importance of culture comes from Zappos, the online shoe retailer. All new recruits to their customer service team go through a paid, intensive, four-week training period when employees are immersed in the company's culture, strategy and obsession with customer service.

At the end of the training all recruits are made 'the offer'. You can walk away now with your full pay and an additional month's salary (it started at $100, then went up to $500 and on to its current level, $1,000) with no strings attached.

The theory behind this is simple. If you take the offer you probably don't have what it takes to become a star Zappos employee. Therefore a month's salary is a small price to pay to protect the culture. It also means that everyone who decides to stay has made a conscious decision not to leave. Consequently, he or she is much more likely to be committed to the company and embrace the Zappos culture.

SO HOW DO YOU CREATE A RELATIONSHIP FUNDRAISING CULTURE IN YOUR ORGANISATION?

We believe creating the right culture starts with leadership.

Even if you're not the most senior fundraiser in your organisation you can take personal responsibility for your specific area of fundraising and make sure you are applying relationship fundraising techniques.

Here are our top 10 tips for embedding a relationship fundraising culture in your organisation:

1. Make people accountable for donor experiences and the donor journey.

If no one has ultimate responsibility and accountability for donor magic then it won't happen. As it will be a key part of your strategy, you'll need to make sure it's in every fundraiser's objectives to be donor focused and to deliver outstanding experiences.

2. Prevent donor problems from happening in the first place.

It sounds obvious, but do all you can to prevent problems happening in the first place and pre-empt where issues might arise. If you can identify problems before donors (or potential donors) do you have a much better chance of providing a good experience.

This is why a good database system and basic processes are so important. They make sure thanking, follow-ups and reminders are consistently delivered.

3. Deliver the right experience for each donor.

If a donor gives to one aspect of your work, don't try and promote different aspects unless you are willing to risk losing their support. This is especially true in larger organisations where silos may 'compete' for the right to communicate with the donor.

This often happens to donors to overseas aid charities when they give to a specific project or appeal in one country (where they might have a particular interest) but then receive requests for support to other countries without any coherent story about why the country they originally gave to does not need any further help.

A former colleague of Craig's tells a similar story. She loved orang-utans and gave to support a wildlife organisation working with them, but kept getting requests to help other animals that she didn't feel as strongly about. Eventually she decided to move her giving to a charity that specialised in conservation for orang-utans.

The 90-degree shift: your fundraising structure should reflect this too. Do you design your team around your internal needs, or the donor needs? In our experience, most large fundraising teams are organised in a linear and functional way. Is this really the best way to create donor magic?

In his books Ken Burnett talks about the '90-degree shift', which puts the entire fundraising department in our donors' shoes so that they see everything that is done through the donors' eyes. It's a difficult shift to make, but achieving this change will be one of the best ways to build mutually beneficial relationships with donors. As Ken says:

> *Imagine – instead of giving donors what we want them to have, when we make the 90-degree shift we can be sure to offer them only what they want to receive!*[1]

4. Be brilliant at the basics.

Does everyone in your office answer the phone in the same way? Are enquiries passed to the relevant person quickly? Do you answer donors' e-mails within an hour? Setting basic standards and making sure you are brilliant at the simple things will put you on the road to success.

5. Make sure your team values reflect the importance of relationship fundraising.

Your organisation and team values should recognise the importance of great donor and supporter experiences. This should be embedded in your performance management system so that every employee is assessed against these values when their performance is reviewed.

6. Let go and trust your staff to deliver donor magic.

Trust your team to get things right rather than constantly monitoring them. Give staff who are in direct contact with donors the tools and freedom to do the right thing and then watch them flourish.

Business author Dan Pink, in *Drive: The Surprising Truth about What Motivates Us*, explains that giving staff autonomy over their time, tasks, technique and teams is an essential building block to create highly motivated and performing individuals.

By making sure everyone knows the importance of donor magic you can empower people to go the extra mile for donors without fear of being told off. For example, the charity Send a Cow regularly send thank-you cards round the whole office for each member of the team to sign and say thank you to donors for their support. A simple practice, but one that makes them stand out from other charities.

Another example comes from a colleague of Craig's. She received a phone call from a donor asking about services in her local area, which the charity didn't offer. Craig's colleague could have just explained the situation and left it at that. However, she went out of her way to do some research and sent the donor a letter with the information she was looking for. The donor was overjoyed and sent a heartfelt letter in return explaining how much trouble she'd had finding the information. As well as sending a sizeable cheque, the donor also promised to include the charity in her will.

7. Hire relationship fundraisers.

Fundraisers in direct contact with donors need to be good with people and have the right attitude towards relationship fundraising. Are you assessing this in your hiring processes? Do you ask people to give you examples of when they have exceeded customer expectations?

They might have all the academic qualifications in the world, but if they don't like interacting with people then do you want them talking to your donors?

It is relatively straightforward to test this in interviews either through role playing or carefully worded questions. Listen carefully to the answers and ask for specific examples from candidates to back up their answers.

You also want fundraisers who care about your cause and are committed to your aims. Passion is an over-used word in our profession and is often employed as a substitute for competence. We don't believe the two things are mutually exclusive. You should aim to recruit technically competent people, who are also able to demonstrate passion for what you are trying to achieve.

8. Share and embed donor magic stories and rituals.

How do you share stories of donor magic in your organisation? Do you make it easy for your teams to share anecdotes about great service that has become part of your organisation's culture?

One of the most famous stories about customer experience comes from Nordstrom, an upmarket American department store famous for its great customer service and its 'no-quibble' refund policy. One day a customer went into a Nordstrom store with two tyres and asked for a refund. Nordstrom has never sold tyres, yet the clerk issued a 'no-questions asked' refund to the customer.

The story has become part of the Nordstrom culture and is told at staff conferences and training sessions. It is the ultimate story about how Nordstrom wants its employees to treat their customers. Whether it is true or not, the story acts like a compass in guiding staff on how they should interact with and treat customers.

9. Reward outstanding relationship fundraising.

It's also a good idea to make sure your rewards and recognition scheme recognise great relationship fundraising. Most people equate rewards with money and say their nonprofit can't afford to offer them. Yet there are other, non-financial and low-cost ways to recognise and say thank you to fundraisers who create donor magic. Here are a couple of ideas to get you started:

Send a personal, handwritten thank-you note to employees when they exceed expectations. This can come from you or another senior person, such as the chief executive or chair of your board.

Allow everyone to nominate colleagues when they see great donor service happening. Hold monthly/quarterly/annual competitions to recognise this and offer tongue-in-cheek awards or small tokens of appreciation to the winners.

At one organisation we had a 'shark of the month' award that travelled around the country to the different fundraising teams. The toy shark had been found in a vacated office and we adopted it for our award. Teams took great delight in photographing the shark in their offices in compromising situations! If you don't have a shark of your own available, vouchers, chocolate, or alcohol (depending on your workplace) can all make excellent, low-cost rewards.

10. Training of internal and external fundraisers.

If you outsource any aspect of your fundraising, such as telemarketing or face-to-face fundraising, do you provide the same level of training to these fundraisers as your in-house team? Do you expect the same standards from these fundraisers and do they feel part of your organisation too?

Speaking to the suppliers of services, the general answer appears to be 'no'. Few charities spend quality time talking, engaging and inspiring their external fundraisers before a campaign starts. Too many charities go through the motions when training suppliers, often reducing it to a dull 20-minute PowerPoint presentation. This is a huge missed opportunity and the few charities that do spend quality time on this see large increases in their results.

It is not a one-off exercise to tick off your to-do list. Make sure you see your suppliers as equal partners and constantly push them to provide great donor experiences. Regularly mystery shop and benchmark them to make sure they are consistently delivering the standards your supporters deserve.

CASE STUDY: HOW ANTHONY NOLAN HAVE CREATED A RELATIONSHIP FUNDRAISING CULTURE AND TREBLED THEIR FUNDRAISING INCOME

We interviewed Catherine Miles, ex-fundraising director, and Mary Campbell, head of events, at Anthony Nolan, the UK's blood cancer charity and bone marrow register. Here they explain how they have established a culture of relationship fundraising that has transformed their fundraising.

How did you achieve this?
'We've embedded this culture in a number of ways. We have buy-in at a senior level from Anthony Nolan's trustees, CEO and senior management team, not just the fundraisers, to move to a relationship approach with all supporters.

'A key element of securing this buy-in was demonstrating the potential power of Anthony Nolan's 600,000 supporter base, over 500,000 of whom are on the bone marrow register. We conducted independent focus groups, which established that supporters who had entered the charity through different first points of engagement (fundraising, joining the bone marrow register, volunteering) were remarkably consistent in their emotional commitment to us, their desire to help more, willingness to consider a range of other types of support and their desire to be communicated with more frequently.

'Another important stage of securing internal buy-in for a relationship approach came in 2010 when we were given approval to test a regular giving telephone appeal to the bone marrow register. This proved extremely successful and we now have over 12,000 regular givers who are also on the bone marrow register, giving over £500,000 pa. The phone calls strengthened relationships with those supporters, allowing us to thank them for being on the bone marrow register, update them on our work and keep their contact details up to date too (vital when someone comes up as a transplant match for a patient and we need to contact them quickly).

'For the past two years we've been running a cross-organisational "many ways" project, which aims to enable all Anthony Nolan supporters to help save lives in a range of ways, founded on insight and reflecting our strategic goals. This programme works across our fundraising, marketing communications and operations departments, bringing together the teams responsible for financial supporters, potential stem cell donors on our register, volunteers, campaigners, patients and their families and our digital audiences. The goal is to understand supporters' motivations then test the best way to communicate with them so they become long-term supporters.

'In fundraising we have an extensive and evolving programme of training, sharing of best practice, testing and analysis. This includes attending conferences, networking with other fundraisers, running a wide range of bespoke internal training courses, sharing sector insight at team meetings, sharing learning across the division including a monthly "supporter development of the month", when each team nominates a practical example of best practice and then votes for a winner. We focus on the supporters, discussing what we think they want to achieve by working with Anthony Nolan and how by being relationship-focused we enable them to achieve this.'

What has been the impact on your fundraising from this shift in approach?
'We started moving to a relationship fundraising model about four years ago, with the strategic shift really picking up pace when we restructured our community fundraising to a central account management model.

'In 2008/09 Anthony Nolan's voluntary income was £4.6m; in 2014/15 we will raise £12m. Since moving to a relationship fundraising approach in our community team our net income has grown from £175k in 11/12 to over £1m in 2014/15 (a return of over 5:1) and we expect it to continue to grow significantly.

'The divisional growth has been fuelled both by a relationship fundraising approach and by a significant investment in regular giving acquisition, but relationship fundraising principles are also reflected in the individual giving programme.

'We focus on thanking and reporting on impact in our regular giving retention and development communications and we run upgrade campaigns less frequently than other charities, though we still see better results.'

What tips would you give to other fundraising teams who want to follow a similar approach?
'The key things we've learned are to use really practical examples to help gain buy-in from both fundraisers and other colleagues. So we've illustrated supporter journeys with real-life case studies and arranged for staff across the organisation to attend supporter focus groups so they can hear directly from supporters themselves. We've also run sessions where staff take a practical example and try to map out a supporter journey based on his or her knowledge and insight of that particular supporter.

'We have also taken a test and roll-out approach: each new supporter journey is tested, evaluated and learned from before it's rolled out to a larger group. This reduces our risk of getting anything wrong.

'Telephone and face-to-face contact is vital in building relationships with supporters. E-mail and social media can be great channels to communicate too, but there is no substitute for talking to donors at key stages in their supporter journey.

'Finally, we've found it vital both to recruit fundraisers who want to work in this way and to continually invest time and resources in their training and professional development. We are very clear at interview that we work in an integrated way, without silos and that we follow relationship fundraising principles. We have a varied and continual programme of training, in order to constantly develop our skills.

'Effectively we are applying significant elements of major donor cultivation and solicitation theory to groups of supporters across the fundraising division, who would not generally be classed as major donors in most charities. So having a good understanding of best practice in major donor cultivation, and which elements are relevant, is a great advantage.'

CONCLUSION
You can have the best fundraising strategy in the world, but if it doesn't fit your

organisational culture then it is doomed to failure. If, as we hope, you make the strategic choice to implement relationship fundraising then it is crucial that you spend time to nurture the culture to support this.

As we noted in chapter 1, many of the problems our profession faces are due to many charities having a culture that rewards volume and hard-selling over donor experience and care.

Establishing a relationship fundraising culture is not easy, but as Anthony Nolan show, it can reap big rewards if you do so.

NOTE
1   Burnett, Ken (2006) *The Zen of Fundraising*, Jossey-Bass, San Francisco.
2   Pink, Dan (2009) *Drive: the surprising truth about what motivates us*, Riverhead, New York

Recruiting your donors

Take a few seconds to think about what you have already done today – read the newspaper, watched some television, travelled to work? Whatever you've been doing you've probably already been exposed to hundreds, possibly even thousands, of advertisements and marketing messages.

Now ask yourself: how many of those adverts do you remember?

If it's only a couple, then don't worry. You're not alone. In fact, research shows that 99 per cent of adverts make little or no impact.[1]

Our brains have evolved an amazing capacity to 'delete' those things that aren't important to us and only store information that might be useful in the future. This means that as a fundraiser you have to work hard to cut through the clutter and create memorable messages that potential donors will respond to.

The vast majority of people ignore even the greatest fundraising campaigns. Your job is to make your campaign as relevant and compelling as you can. One of the best ways to get your message across to large numbers of people is direct marketing.

WHAT IS DIRECT MARKETING?

Direct marketing is any advertising or promotional activity that creates and maintains a direct relationship between you and your prospect, or donor. In fundraising terms, direct marketing provides the bedrock for most charities' individual giving programmes. A well-run programme creates opportunities for regular gifts, builds donor loyalty and, ultimately, leads to significant legacy income.

However, juggling between acquiring new donors, welcoming them and then keeping them engaged, loyal and committed is a tricky business and the sad fact is most donors only give to a charity once before leaving.

ABOUT THIS SECTION

This section will look at how you can put together a direct marketing programme that will produce happy, satisfied and committed donors; donors who will give to your organisation over many years. In these chapters we will look at:

How to develop your donor acquisition plan.

We'll then consider:

Writing a creative brief and working with agencies and freelancers.

The seven elements that go into producing successful fundraising direct marketing to acquire new donors.

The importance of integration.

How you can use direct marketing to welcome new donors.

How to apply direct marketing principles to keep and engage the donors you already have.

Fortunately, direct marketing has been used in fundraising for a long time. That means there are well-established rules and techniques that you can learn and then apply to recruit new donors.

DEVELOPING YOUR DONOR ACQUISITION PLAN – PORTFOLIO ANALYSIS USING BOSTON AND ANSOFF MATRICES

These tools help you to plot the current effectiveness of your fundraising products and inform your growth strategy. We're going to talk through how you can use the models in relation to your fundraising portfolio and donor acquisition plans.

Figure 7.1: The Boston Matrix

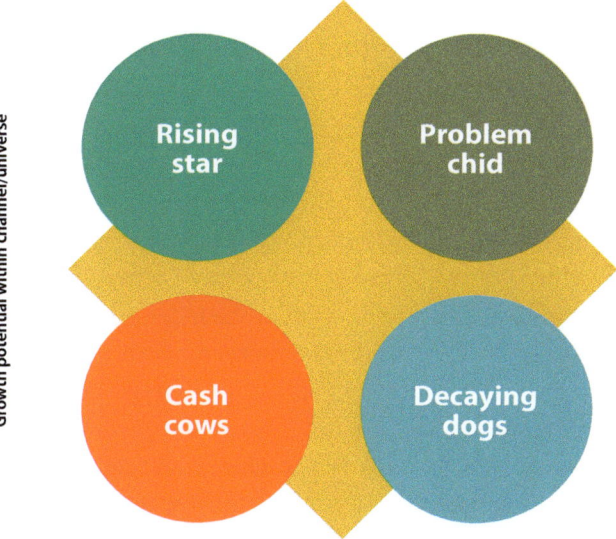

Current success of channel/proposition to recruit new donors

Each of your current ways of fundraising will fit into one of the four following areas:

Cash cow: is an established steady earner. You need to milk this for as long as you productively can, but be aware that the potential for growth is limited.

Rising star: is a good area to invest in as it has room for growth and you already know it is a proposition/channel that is working well.

Problem child: you are unsure how this will pan out. There may be encouraging signs, but you need to keep testing and refining the target audience, channel, or product.

Decaying dog: this may be a past rising star or cash cow that is coming to the end of its product life. Don't get so hung up on products/channels/target groups that you keep pursuing them long after they've ceased to be cost effective. You will want to move away from your decaying dogs, though you might never fully abandon them. There could be an opportunity in the future to resurrect and recreate their previous success.

By plotting your fundraising acquisition methods and products in this matrix you can identify which areas to increase investment, which to stop spending money on and which to re-evaluate and refine. It is likely that at any one time you will have fundraising products in all four areas. Your job is to use this analysis to identify gaps, make decisions on investment areas and then implement your acquisition strategy.

HOW THE BRITISH HEART FOUNDATION STREAMLINED THEIR EVENTS PORTFOLIO AND INCREASED NET INCOME

The British Heart Foundation, one of the largest charities in the UK, recently scrutinised its existing portfolio in this manner. On the surface BHF had a highly successful events programme with income totalling nearly £10 million, including 94 BHF running events raising £6.8 million. However, a handful of very successful initiatives were masking a poor general return on investment; 70 per cent of the income was generated by 5 per cent of the events. Additionally, the events were developed in isolation, often regionally, with a distinct lack of strategic coordination or any long-term planning. Instead, fundraising and event managers were caught in a highly labour-intensive cycle and were unable to analyse properly the portfolio and plot a more cost-effective course. And, from a supporter's perspective, their experience of these events and associated communications was fragmented and, at times, negative.

Louise Parkes, BHF's director of fundraising, coordinated a review of the entire income stream. Each event was assessed on the Boston Matrix, rated according to its market share and potential for growth. Those that scored highly were classed as 'stars' and those that rated poorly on both axes were labelled 'dogs'. The charity quickly established that a lot of its events fell into the latter category, with a lack of insight and excessive nostalgia preventing their being abandoned.

So they set about rapidly reducing the portfolio, weeding out the events that produced less than £30,000 of net income. With a strict focus on the mantra of 'fewer, bigger, better', greater emphasis and resources were placed on those activities with a high return on investment and strong medium- to long-term prospects. A cultural shift ensued: five swimming events were reduced to one, with two waves to maximise entrant numbers cost-effectively. Higher yielding cycle events were expanded. Added to BHF's well-established and lucrative London to Brighton Bike Ride were a night ride, off-road cycle and a trek.

Overall, the number of events was more than halved to 40 in total. Despite opposition from many supporters and volunteers with vested interests, the move proved to be worthwhile. The charity experienced a significant growth in event net income in 2014/15 with valuable time and resources saved in the process.

After doing this exercise you will be left with one of four strategic choices to make for recruiting donors and growing your fundraising (see figure 7.2).

In most cases the easiest strategy to follow is to try to recruit new donors with a similar profile to those who are already giving to an existing fundraising product. The logic behind this is simple: you know that the current offer is working with that audience and so can be confident that if you get your profiling right the same offer will appeal to prospects of a similar nature.

However, it is likely you will need to adopt a variety of recruitment strategies, so you can try to create a balanced portfolio. Your final decisions will be dependent on the recruitment objectives that you have set to meet your organisation's requirements. These can be basic, such as to recruit X new donors for Y cost, but the relationship fundraiser should take a more sophisticated approach.

For example, it is important to consider the quality of donors recruited, as well as the quantity. The phrase 'rubbish in, rubbish out' should never be far from your mind when you are considering your acquisition plan.

Consider the following: for a £15,000 investment would you prefer 5,000 donors who give £5 once or 50 donors who give £100 and are interested in

Figure 7.2: The Ansoff Matrix for fundraising growth

Acquisition choice	When to pursue
Recruiting donors of a similar profile to your current supporters via an existing channel, using a current proven product.	When you have a successful fundraising programme and donor journey that provides good donor lifetime value to the charity. For example, the Royal National Lifeboat Institution (RNLI) has used the same approach to donor recruitment for many years. In loose inserts placed in magazines and newspapers they feature the picture of the brave, heroic, bearded lifeboat man above a direct request for funds.[2]
Recruiting donors of a similar profile to your current supporters to a new product or via a new channel.	You may need money for a new service, or want to increase donation values by offering a new product to a current donor. For example, child sponsorship is a useful product for moving people from one-off support to a regular monthly gift.
Recruiting donors of a new profile to an existing product via an existing channel.	Your research might find that an existing product appeals to a market you hadn't previously considered. For example, Guide Dogs discovered that their Sponsor a Puppy proposition appeals as much to dog lovers as it does to people who want to help people with sight loss.
Recruiting donors of a new profile to a new product or via a new channel.	If costs of acquisition are increasing, or if you need to achieve large growth in income then you may – even though it is risky and difficult – find it advisable to look at a completely new type of audience and product. Greenpeace revolutionised their fundraising and changed the profile of their supporters when, in Austria in the 1990s, they developed monthly giving via face-to-face recruitment.

learning and hearing more about your cause?

The first scenario results in a quick profit raised, of £10,000, the other loses you £10,000 at the point of recruitment. However, apart from in an emergency, the relationship fundraiser would choose the second scenario almost every time, because by putting in place a welcome programme and having an on-going, engaging communications plan he or she will have the chance to raise many times the initial £15,000 over the donor's lifetime of giving.

THE CREATIVE BRIEF

At the start of every major campaign and fundraising project we recommend that the relationship fundraiser should write a creative brief. Whether working with an agency or doing the project yourself, it pays to get into the discipline of preparing a creative brief as it helps the campaign get off on a good footing.

As David Oglivy once said, 'give me the freedom of a tight brief'.

If you leave your brief too open then it can be interpreted in many ways, which can lead to endless revisions going back and forth, resulting in delays, woolly thinking and a loss of focus.

T S Eliot observed,

> *When forced to work within a strict framework the imagination is taxed to its utmost – and will produce its richest ideas. Given total freedom the work is likely to sprawl.*

At its best, a strong creative brief is a road map guiding you to fundraising success.

So what should a good brief include?

There are two parts. The first is setting out the essential information such as the name of the project, the deadline, the approval process, method and budget. The second is a list of questions that require thought and detail to help you achieve your aims. We've looked at lots of different creative brief templates and come up with 10 essential questions that your brief could contain.

Of course if you are using an agency and the people working on your account are very familiar with your cause and your audience, it is possible to short circuit this process considerably. So please adapt this list to your circumstances.

1   What do you want the project to achieve? What specific action do you

want the donor to take? How will you measure success? For example: is it cash donations, regular giving, increasing their existing gift, money for a specific project?
2   What is the offer?
3   Who is the audience?
    • Describe a member of your typical target audience: use the demographic, lifestyle and geographic data you have to paint a picture.
    • Are they new, existing (how long, what level), or past donors (when did they last support, what level) to your cause?
    • How much do they know about your work?
    • Is there any other background information that will help the creative team to understand them better?
    • What is the size of the audience?
4   What segmentation do you plan to use? Date of last gift, amount of last gift, total given, regular versus one-off giving, etc? What, if anything, makes the project urgent? If you plan to follow up, how?
5   What are the key details about the project?
    • What problem will it solve?
    • What are the features?
    • What is the fundraising target?
    • Are there any taboo words or phrases?
6   What is the tone of voice? Who is telling the story? Is it a service user, CEO, service staff? What imagery should be used to engage them?
7   Do you have any real-life stories and case studies on this project? How can they be accessed? Do you have/want to use any credibility boosters? Donor testimonials, third party endorsements, outside ratings, etc.
8   Can you personalise the approach? If yes, how?
9   Are you testing any elements? What and how? If not, why not?
10 How will this project inspire donors? What are the benefits of giving? What won't happen if they don't give?

WORKING WITH AN AGENCY OR FREELANCE

No fundraiser or fundraising team is ever going to be expert at every aspect of fundraising and sometimes you are going to need help in putting together your fundraising programme.

Depending on the size of your team, this may range from using the occasional freelance to help you with design or copywriting, to retaining a full service agency to help with all aspects of your strategy, planning and creative work.

Here is a list of some of the ways freelances and agencies can help you with your direct marketing programme:

- Data analysis
- Planning
- Creative work
- Product development
- Design
- Copywriting
- Market research

Deciding when to use an agency or freelance
Calculate whether the value they will add is more than the fees they charge.

Here is a simple example, based on a real-life experience.

You are a small charity and have a database of 10,000 donors that you can mail. Your appeals typically get a 10 per cent response rate and an average gift of £20. Including staff time, it costs £7,000 to produce and send a mailing. This means your mailing produces £20,000 of income and a net profit of £13,000.

You approach Brilliant Agency and they claim that they can improve your response rates by 20 per cent and average gifts by 10 per cent. Fantastic you say.

Total income improves from £20,000 to £26,400. Then the bill comes in. The costs have jumped from £7,000 to £15,000, leaving you with a net profit of £11,400.

You're £1,600 worse off than when you did everything yourself.

The best agencies will be honest with you and tell you when this is likely to happen and decline your business. But be aware. There are agencies that will gladly take your business and leave you in a worse position than if you did it yourself.

Judging this is hard, but generally the larger your charity, the more likely an effective agency is to add value to your fundraising. Smaller charities may find more value in employing freelances with specific skills as and when they need them.

In the above example, it wouldn't take much of a shift to make using an agency or freelances cost-effective. Here are two ways:

- Employ a copywriter and designer only. In this scenario the response

rate would increase by 20 per cent, but average gift stays at £20. The costs would reduce from £15,000 to around £8,000, leaving you with £16,000 net income.
- If the file was larger and you were able to achieve economies of scale, then working with an agency would quickly become a good option. At a marginal cost of 50p per pack, a mailing volume of around 12,500 would make the agency the better choice.

As we've said it's unlikely that you'll have experts in every aspect of fundraising and direct marketing in your team – and if you do, then we're jealous! Recognising your weaknesses and buying in the expertise of an agency or freelance is a good use of money.

We've had the pleasure of working with some great agencies and freelances over the years, but also had a couple of disasters too. The disasters were often as much our fault as the agency's.

Here are some tips from SOFII, together with our own observations on how to get the best out of working with agencies.[4]

Choosing an agency or freelance

First of all, it is worth asking for recommendations from people you trust and who have completed similar projects. If this isn't forthcoming and the budget is sufficiently substantial then you can put the work out to pitch.

Make sure the pitch process is clear. What *exactly* do you want? If you aren't certain, then you risk setting yourself up for failure before you begin.

Ask the agency or freelance about their working style. Does their culture fit with your organisation? Will you be able to work together? The best agencies and freelances we've worked with are those we've got along with, could have a robust discussion – argument – with (but not hold grudges) and who we trust.

Look at their past results and recent work. Do you want someone who has worked in your sector or are you looking for a fresh approach? What is their area of expertise? Ask them for specific results. If they aren't willing to share them you should be wary.

Get testimonials, both formally and informally. Speak to current clients, but also try to find a few ex-clients. Why did they stop working with them? Were there any specific issues or was it just time for a change?

Not every agency is going to be great at every aspect of fundraising. Some will be brilliant at planning, others produce fantastic creative work and some are data experts. Look where your main weaknesses are and go from there.

Meet the account team. Those who pitch aren't necessarily the same people you will be working with. We've been wowed a few times by the figurehead of an agency, only to discover on appointment that we'll never see or hear from him or her after the appointment. Specifically, ask who will be working on your account and meet them.

Paul learned this the hard way with his first marketing agency at World Jewish Relief (WJR). The CEO pitched and was fabulous. But Paul should have been suspicious when no one else participated in this process. Once the agency was hired, the CEO was rarely evident and the team proved to be wholly unsuitable for his charity.

Project considerations

Make sure that in your creative brief you have outlined the extent of the help you require from the agency. Is it tactical, strategic, or both?

Agree the budget upfront. Don't neglect this: you must get an itemised breakdown at the start. This protects both parties and prevents any nasty surprises. Make sure you don't make too many changes once your project is underway as this can prove both frustrating and expensive. It is invariably costly to make major changes once the project has started.

Agree the deadlines and sign-off process in advance i.e. what is the number of revisions needed for a piece of copywriting?

Address any problems early. Not happy about something? Don't let it fester. Raise it at the earliest opportunity and try and find a solution.

The approval process

We've put this as a separate entry as, in our experience, this can take lots of time and be the most frustrating part of direct marketing. It doesn't necessarily involve the freelance or agency, but at some point you are going to have to get sign-off from within your organisation and this can be painful, annoying and lead to intense arguments.

In his book *Asking Properly* George Smith summed this up brilliantly:

> Most clients agonise over creative work. They feel a responsibility to worry about every nuance of the mailing pack or the ad, to declaim a point of view lest their clienthood is seen to be less than virile. The psychology of a meeting is such that people start agreeing with meaningless points of view. A whole negative

and useless momentum starts. It is rarely productive or helpful. It goes like this.

Senior client: I like it a lot, but I'm not quite comfortable with this headline. And I think the pictures could be larger.

Less-than-senior client: I think I agree with that. Actually I think we could have chosen better pictures.

Really smart junior client: And there's no mention of our new policy on community development. Was this deliberate on the part of the agency?

Agency hacker: … er...

Senior client: I certainly think that community development should be in. And we should make more of GiftAid as well. Come to think of it, it's very big isn't it?

Less-than-senior client: Just what I was going to say. I think it's too big, much too big. And do we really need the second colour?

And so it goes. The client would be more helpful if he or she just said, 'I don't like it. Do it again'. Posturing and role-playing rarely make a positive contribution to good creative work. I think of the long lost client who would narrow his eyes every time he was presented with a visual and say, 'Now, what is this envelope really saying to me?' It was the sort of thing he thought he ought to say. In fact it marked him out as a complete prat.

Anyone approving creative work has only three questions to answer,
1. Is it accurate?
2. Is it on brief?
3. Does it coincide with the budget for the job?

All the rest is subjectivity. And there is little point in trading subjectivity with people you have hired to do a specialist job.[5]

Now, Craig has a confession to make here. On more than one occasion, he has solicited internal feedback (because he's had to) and then completely ignored it. This is especially true of subjective feedback. As long as what you are doing isn't factually incorrect or totally against what your charity stands for, this can often be a wise decision. The funny thing is, once the work is out in the public domain he has never had a member of the fundraising, marketing, or service team come up to him and say, 'You didn't make the changes I asked for'. Often people seem to feel they need to say something and then forget about it soon as they've said it.

We're not advocating this as a default position, but sometimes it is best to sin first and repent later – hopefully when the results are good...

American copywriter and donor communications expert Tom Ahern takes a novel approach to problems surrounding the approval process. He has what he calls the 'verbatim rule', where clients accept they will only correct his factual mistakes. He reckons this saves a lot of time and means the copy he produces is much more effective and raises more money. It's an approach worth considering.

Now we've got a plan in place, we can look at the seven elements that go into making a successful donor recruitment campaign.

NOTES
1. Shopper's eye view of ads that pass us by http://www.guardian.co.uk/media/2005/nov/19/advertising.marketingandpr
2. Apparently RNLI have tested numerous types of images over the years, but a man with a beard always delivers the best results.
3. These include: Sargent, Lisa, A creative brief for fundraisers: Why it matters, and how it can help you raise more money. Available at: http://www.sofii.org/node/731 Last accessed 21 October 2012. Schwartz, Nancy, This creative brief template helps ensure powerful design and copy. Available at: http://gettingattention.org/articles/197/planning-budgets/nonprofit-creative-brief-template.html Last accessed 21 October 2012. Ahern Tom, Your creative brief: Don't leave home without it. Available: http://www.aherncomm.com/ss_plugins/content/content.php?content.5014 Last accessed 21 October 2012.
4. Resources on SOFII about working with consultants and agencies include: Gill McLellan series, Top tips to get the best from your agency, http://www.sofii.org/node/755 Humphries, Derek, Have I told you lately that I love you? http://www.sofii.org/node/761 Smith, George, Working with suppliers http://www.sofii.org/node/819 McCants, Alison, A sector divided http://akmccants.blogspot.com/2011/01/sector-divided.html Also see Clients and consultants punchbowl survey results The Agitator. Available at: http://www.theagitator.net/dont-miss-these-posts/clients-consultants-punch-bowl-survey-results/ Last accessed 4 March 2012.
5. Smith, George (1966) Asking Properly, The White Lion Press, London, p.183.

8

The seven elements of successful donor recruitment

To get people to respond to your donor recruitment campaigns you will need:

- Data and media channel
- Emotion
- Story
- Narrative and copy
- Offer and involvement
- Pictures and layout
- Response mechanism

The initial letters of each element can be re-arranged into an easy to remember mnemonic – RESPOND. As we'll show, mnemonics are a powerful tool to get people to recall information.

We'll begin by considering how you need to use data to choose the correct media channel to reach your target audience.

DATA AND MEDIA CHANNEL

Using data to inform your media channel selection gives you the best chance for your message to achieve cut-through.

In chapter 19 we look at how to conduct donor research and create personas to help develop your target audiences. You can use these to develop your acquisition plan.

For example, if your target audience is 60+ year-old churchgoers, then advertising on MTV is unlikely to work.

Here are our top 10 ways to use direct marketing to recruit new donors to your cause:

1   Face-to-face – including street, door-to-door and private site fundraising.

In its purest form, fundraisers talk directly to donors and ask them to sign up to a regular monthly gift.
2   Direct mail and door drops – mailing packs, addressed and unaddressed – are delivered directly to prospective donors' homes, asking for a donation.
3   Direct response television (DRTV) – short appeal commercials are shown on television during advertisement breaks.
4   Inserts – loose appeal leaflets or even unaddressed direct marketing packs are included in publications read by your target audience.
5   Off-the-page advertisements – appear in newspapers and magazines. In the recent past a stalwart of donor recruitment in some markets, nowadays these are used most successfully in emergencies.
6   Billboards and advertising panels – these can appear on anything from trains and buses to cinemas and the walls of washrooms.
7   Telephone – phone calls to potential donors asking them to give. Tends to work better with warm audiences rather than cold, although it is increasingly used to 'convert' donors after undertaking a non-financial activity, such as signing a petition or requesting information.
8   Radio – typically 30- or 60-second spots during ad breaks.
9   E-mail – similar to direct mail but delivered electronically, thus saving the costs of production and delivery, i.e. postage.
10 Online banner ads and videos – the modern day equivalent of off-the-page advertising. Ads appear on websites visited by your target audience.

In the chapter there are examples of successful campaigns using various media channels. We will show how they incorporate all the elements of RESPOND.

With all these options available to you, how do you decide which is most suitable for your organisation?

As we said at the start of this section, the donor personas you developed as part of your strategy will guide your decision-making.

- Which media do they use?
- What interests do they have?
- What commonalities, such as geography and demographics, do they have?
- When are they most likely to take in and respond to your message?

A good starting point is often age. As a general rule of thumb, direct mail works best for the over 65s and face-to-face fundraising works best for the under 35s. You can decide for yourself which of these groups has most potential to be a serious long-term donor. Older people have more disposable income, of course, but younger donors can live and give longer.

The options available to you will also depend on your budget. If you've only got £10,000 to spend then DRTV and face-to-face fundraising through an agency are going to be out of your price range.

Similarly, if you have a six- or even seven-figure sum to invest then your options increase. With investment adequate to the task you are likely to use a mix of techniques to reach your target audience. Integrated campaigns are often the most effective ways to fundraise as they give donors and potential donors multiple ways to engage with your cause. This cumulative impact can increase overall response rates and effectiveness. We think integration is so important that we're devoting a whole chapter to it (see chapter 10).

EMOTION AND STORY

A large part of chapter 4 explains why emotion is so important. Yet we want to stress it again. *If your fundraising doesn't emotionally resonate with your audience then it will fail.*

That's why choosing the story that will most appeal to your target audience is so important.

Often the best story for recruiting donors might represent only a small part of your work. This can be frustrating. Instinctively you (and your colleagues) will want to show off the complexity and nuances of all that you do. However it can be expensive to do so.

The best and smartest fundraisers know it costs more money if you try to educate donors and move them to where you want them to be than for you to move to where donors are emotionally. Remember – emotion trumps logic nearly every time. It is not your job to *educate donors*. It is your job *to move them to give.*

This means it can be difficult to find the story that works best for your fundraising. The easiest way is to test your stories in the real world. Ideally this should be done scientifically with split testing in your chosen media, however budgets and time often don't allow this. One shortcut to get you to the right ballpark is to spend time meeting with, and chatting to, donors. You can also test stories at presentations and talks and see which ones elicit the most interest and response. Focus groups and online panels are useful too, but can lead to people giving answers based too much on rational thinking and not enough on emotion, i.e. they over-think and say what they think they will do, which is often different to how they behave in the real world.

Once you have a rough idea of the stories that might work for your fundraising, you can start thinking about how the story will translate into your chosen recruitment method. Even the most simple poster campaign needs to have a story that people can relate and respond to.

Ernest Hemingway was famously challenged to write a story using just six words. He came up with 'For sale. Baby shoes, never worn' and claimed it was his best ever work. (This story may be apocryphal.)

Choosing a storytelling style

Christopher Booker's epic bestselling book *The Seven Basic Plots: Why We Tell Stories* (Continuum, UK and USA, 2004) provides a framework for storytelling and details the seven plots that all literature follows. You can use one or more of these plots in your fundraising, so we've summarised them below, along with examples of how your nonprofit can use them.

1. The quest (Watership Down) – the heroes set out on an epic journey and meet many problems (such as monsters, temptations, etc) on the way before finally succeeding. What journey are you asking your donors to join you on? The NSPCC's Full Stop campaign is an example of a quest.
2. Voyage and return (Alice in Wonderland) – the main protagonists go on a voyage, meet difficulties, before returning triumphant. It differs from a quest as it has a clear destination and return point, while on a quest you never quite know where you are going. People giving to missionary causes might respond well to this sort of story.
3. Rebirth (the Frog Prince) – it looks like the dark power has won before the miraculous redemption of the hero. Many human rights charities use this approach, as their wins may be spread out over time.
4. Comedy – there are lots of subplots in comedy and it is probably the hardest to use in your storytelling for fundraising. The best examples we've seen are from some of the prostate and breast cancer charities, who use humour to get their message across. See the success of Movember, 'Coppa Feel' and the 'Balls to Cancer' campaigns. However, you need to be very careful when using comedy in fundraising. Humour is a very personal thing and might change with your donors as they age. What makes

one person laugh can cause another to be bemused, indifferent or even offended.
5   Tragedy (Anna Karenina) – there are no happy endings in tragic stories. You use fear and anger to persuade the donor to give. Some animal welfare charities use this (think of some of the sad photos of injured animals you've seen in fundraising appeals) successfully in all their communications. The work is never done and, sadly, there will always be another animal to save.
6   Overcoming the monster (Star Wars) – the hero is faced with an apparently insurmountable problem and overcomes the odds to defeat the monster. Think research causes, battling the monster disease and the brave scientists fighting to defeat it.
7   Rags to riches – the original Cinderella story. You can use it to show your donors how their donation helped an individual person overcome the odds to become successful. For example, micro-financing sites such as Kiva give loans to people in developing countries. The people use the loans to start their own business and break the cycle of poverty.

Many charities will use a mix of the basic plots in their storytelling, but whatever blend you use, you need to make it consistent. Often you see charities use one type of story in their recruitment campaigns only to switch to another type of story in their ongoing communications. This can confuse donors and the lack of consistency can then make securing the second gift even more difficult than usual.

Similar problems can occur when a charity changes its director of fundraising. The new leader might decide that the cause's appeals need an update or change of style and a new approach to storytelling is necessary. Craig recalls an animal charity that changed their storytelling style from one of tragedy to a more positive rebirth and overcoming the monster message. Donations plummeted. Their donors were so familiar and used to giving to the tragedy story that a new approach just didn't work for them. Fortunately, the charity quickly recognised this and switched back, so they only lost tens rather than hundreds of thousands of pounds worth of donations.

Beware the curse of knowledge

As you know your nonprofit inside out you might easily assume that other people will have similar knowledge, which might prevent you from simplifying your story into something that donors can instantly understand. You assume that something will be obvious or that the reader will have some prior knowledge. This is a well-known cognitive bias called the *curse of knowledge*. Also known as the *curse of assumption*: knowledge is a good thing, assumption about that knowledge is not.

In a *Harvard Business Review* article, authors Chip and Dan Heath (who we will meet again later) describe a famous experiment that demonstrates the curse in action:

> *In 1990, a Stanford University graduate student in psychology named Elizabeth Newton illustrated the curse of knowledge by studying a simple game in which she assigned people to one of two roles: 'tapper' or 'listener'. Each tapper was asked to pick a well-known song, such as Happy Birthday, and tap out the rhythm on a table. The listener's job was to guess the song.*
>
> *Over the course of Newton's experiment, 120 songs were tapped out. Listeners guessed only three of the songs correctly: a success ratio of 2.5%. But before they guessed, Newton asked the tappers to predict the probability that listeners would guess correctly. They predicted 50%. The tappers got their message across one time in 40, but they thought they would get it across one time in two. Why?*
>
> *When a tapper taps, it is impossible for her to avoid hearing the tune playing along to her taps. Meanwhile, all the listener can hear is a kind of bizarre Morse code. Yet the tappers were flabbergasted by how hard the listeners had to work to pick up the tune.*
>
> *The problem is that once we know something—say, the melody of a song—we find it hard to imagine not knowing it. Our knowledge has 'cursed' us. We have difficulty sharing it with others, because we can't readily re-create their state of mind.[1]*

When you tell your nonprofit story you need to make sure you are tapping a simple tune that the potential donor will understand. You cannot assume that it will be the case. The curse of knowledge, or assumption, is powerful and fundraisers need to be conscious of when it is making your fundraising story more complicated than it needs to be.

It can be easy to show off and proudly tell people about every aspect of the amazing work your organisation does. However the best stories are simple, reflect donors' values and beliefs and make them feel strongly enough to do something about the problem you have described.

NARRATIVE AND COPY

Once you know which story you want to tell you need to put it into a narrative that will inspire donors to give. If you are unable to write coherently and with emotion then your story will be lost in the maelstrom of messages we described at the start of the previous chapter.

Most people think they are good copywriters and have an opinion on what makes strong writing. Craig recalls his first experience of this:

> *When I first started in fundraising one of my responsibilities was to write thank-you letters to donors. I was proud of the long sentences, grammatically correct prose and formal tone I adopted. It was only when I started reading books on the subject that I realised that I had to change the style of writing I'd used at university and school. When I made my writing easier to read, warmer and less formal I instantly saw an increase in positive feedback and comments on the thank-you letters I was sending.*

Top 10 tips for fundraising copywriting

To help you write effective fundraising copy here are the top tips that we have gathered over the years:

1. You are writing for results, not a Pulitzer prize.

    This headline from Mal Warwick's book *How to Write Successful Fundraising Letters* (Jossey-Bass, USA, 2013) is a phrase that has stuck with us. As much as we might like to show off with long words and sentences that contain more clauses than an insurance contract, the reality is that we need to make our copy simple and easy to read.
    Fortunately, there are some great free tools to help with this.
    The best online app is called Hemingway (after *Baby shoes* author Ernest Hemingway). The app colour codes your writing to show where it is hard to read and how it can be improved.
    In Microsoft Word, you can turn on readability statistics in the spelling and grammar section. Then when you spell check a document you will be

presented with some statistics at the end of the process. Two of these – the Flesch reading ease and Flesch-Kincaid grade level – tell you how easy or difficult your writing is to read.

You want to get the grade level as low as possible (think Dr Seuss and aim for under 10!) and the reading ease as high as possible so donors can quickly read and comprehend the message you are trying to get across. This is not about dumbing down. It is about making your message easy to understand and absorb. This will increase the likelihood of your message getting a response.

2   Make your copy stick – SUCCESs principles.

One of our favourite books on creating effective ideas and messages is *Made to Stick*.[2] Authors Chip and Dan Heath developed six principles to help readers develop stories that people remember. They looked at why some ideas, such as those found in urban myths and fables, were so memorable, yet other ideas were almost instantly forgotten. They use the mnemonic 'SUCCESs' to outline what makes an idea sticky:

Simple: how do you find the essential core of your idea? You need to create ideas that are simple *and* profound.
Unexpected: does your idea create interest and curiosity?
Concrete: you must avoid abstract language and be clear about what you are saying. Avoid woolly and ambiguous language.
Credibility: You need to make sure the idea/story you are selling is credible or your readers simply won't believe you.
Emotions: we keep banging on about this key point! For now it is sufficient to reiterate that the reader needs to feel moved, not bored or indifferent, when they read your copy.
Stories: we get people to act on our ideas by telling stories that people can learn from and relate to.

If coming up with ways to promote your charity's ideas is a big part of your job, then *Made to Stick* is essential reading and goes into much more detail about each of the SUCCESs factors.

3   It's all about 'you' and 'me'.

Your copy is meant to be from one individual to another. Avoid the royal 'we' as much as possible – it makes your writing impersonal. Much nonprofit copywriting slips into this trap and ends up being more about the organisation than the donor. The easy way to test this is to count up the number of times you use 'you' or 'I' and how many times you use 'we'. The use of 'you' should substantially outnumber that of 'I' and 'we'.
You also need to relate the copy to your donor. Saying you need to give because your grandparents have a one in four chance of losing their sight is much better than saying one in four over 65s loses their sight.

4   Use short sentences and paragraphs.

As a general rule you should use short sentences. They are easier to read and comprehend. Don't over do it though. It can become boring. See? Good.
The same goes for paragraphs. There is nothing wrong with single-sentence paragraphs, but don't abuse this as it can become clichéd and lose its power. The danger of long paragraphs (and anything over seven lines should be considered long) is that the reader loses interest half way through.

5   Use emotion over statistics.

It is often tempting to try to convince people to support you by using statistics and to win donors over by making a rational case. Yet all the research[3] seems to show that people respond best to emotion and stories. Giving isn't a rational decision and the fundraiser's first job is to open hearts and minds. The wallets will then follow...
As we outlined in chapter 4, in *Emotionomics*[4] Dan Hill argues there are six key emotions that drive an action, such as writing a cheque or signing a petition. Your copy should ooze with a combination of these key emotions:
- Anger
- Disgust
- Fear
- Happiness
- Sadness
- Surprise

6   Make the copy as long as it needs to be.

Service staff and trustees often complain that letters we've written are too long. 'Surely, no one will read all that?' 'Can't we make it a bit shorter?' Again, all the research suggests otherwise and, all other things being equal, a long letter will outperform a short letter.
This shouldn't be taken as an excuse for boring letters and waffle. You still need to make your writing interesting and stimulating. Yet if you need to take four (or even six) pages to get your message across then don't be afraid to do so. We're not saying every person who receives the letter will read every word, but by taking the time to tell an amazing story, re-stating your case for support and asking for money throughout you will give your copy the best chance of success.

7   Make donors feel good.

Sell the benefits of giving. What is the donor going to achieve? How are you going to make her feel? If you're using incentives, then sell the tangible benefits of giving.

8   Use active verbs and avoid unnecessary adjectives, adverbs and jargon.

Avoid the passive voice and use active verbs. Compare and contrast.
Your malaria net will be sent to Africa as a matter of urgency.
With
We must send those malaria nets to Africa urgently.
The second example makes the donor part of the story and solution. It is clear, direct and inspires action. The first sentence is weak, stilted and puts the donor outside the action.
It is also tempting to litter your copy with adjectives and adverbs. You may think these add to the story. The truth is they can clutter up your writing and distract the donor from the point you are trying to convey.
Finally, one of our pet hates: copy that is full of jargon and acronyms. The Plain English campaign has an annual awards ceremony that 'celebrates' the worst examples of jargon.
Here's a recent favourite:

Your enquiry about the use of the entrance area at the library for the purpose of displaying posters and leaflets about Welfare and Supplementary Benefit rights, gives rise to the question of the provenance and authoritativeness of the material to be displayed. Posters and leaflets issued by the Central Office of Information, the Department of Health and Social Security and other authoritative bodies are usually displayed in libraries, but items of a disputatious or polemic kind, whilst not necessarily excluded, are considered individually.[5]

They were trying to say: 'Thanks for asking about putting up a poster in the library. Before we answer we will need to see the poster to make sure it won't offend anyone.'
If it makes you angry to read such inaccessible tosh it is likely to do the same to your donors. Don't do it!

9 Read it out loud.

Once you've prepared your copy it's worth reading it out loud. How does it sound? Does it flow correctly? Does it sound interesting and get your point across? If it sounds stilted or different from how you would converse with someone, then you need to change it.

10 Focus on the individual.

Many nonprofits fall into the following trap:
One million people are starving. Please give.
Your donation will help the 5,000 homeless people in the New York area.
It seems logical to want to express the need to donate in such a way. Surely the more people who need help, the more likely donors are to give? Unfortunately, the human brain doesn't work in this way.
This was demonstrated by a study conducted by marketing professor Deborah Small and her colleagues for Save the Children.[61]

THE POWER OF ONE: ROKIA'S STORY
Participants were given a small sum of money and asked how much they would donate to an international development charity. One group received general information about the need, including statements such as 'Food shortages in Malawi are affecting more than three million children.'

A second group was shown the photo of a young Malawian girl named Rokia and told that she was very poor and that their gift could change her life for the better.

The group receiving information about Rokia gave significantly more than the group getting general and statistical information. A third group was given the general information, the photo and information about Rokia. Its members gave more than the general information group, but not as much as the Rokia only group. The researchers found that even adding only one more child to the appeal lessened the donation amount.[7]

This 'power of one' is what makes child sponsorship such a great fundraising offer (as we'll show below). It is much harder to stop giving to a single child rather than to a village, or to a vague statistic such as 5,000 homeless people. It is especially true when you know that child by name, have seen photographs and received correspondence from him or her. That's why child sponsorship attrition is much lower than other forms of regular giving.

When to break the rules
There are occasions when you may need to break these rules, for example if it is a genuine emergency then you might abandon the long copy and focus on the immediate need and not the donor benefits. Yet the majority of the time if you make sure your copy follows these principles then you will be well on the way to creating a successful piece of direct marketing.

OFFER AND INVOLVEMENT
Even with the best story in the world, if you forget to ask the donor for money then you are going to miss the opportunity for fundraising. So you need a fundraising offer to accompany your story.

The best fundraising offers stick long in the memory. You probably have your own personal favourite and a story to go alongside it. Craig remembers his school taking part in Comic Relief, who were promoting oral hydrating sachets. His teacher explained how they cost only a few pence each yet could save a child's

life. Craig recalls, 'Wow, we all thought, what a bargain! Our class raised enough money for hundreds of the sachets and we all felt great about it.'
Here are three of our favourite fundraising offers:

£3 to buy a mosquito net.
$15 to make a blind man see.
€20 to sponsor a child.

All good fundraising offers have the following characteristics:

- They ask for money, not resources or help.
- They create urgency. Why should the donor give today?
- They offer value for money. The offer should be so compelling that no reasonable person could refuse it.
- They quote a specific, affordable cost and show what that sum will achieve.

This sounds straightforward, but for many fundraisers developing a really strong fundraising offer for their cause is one of the hardest things to do. Every charity Craig has worked for has struggled with developing a strong fundraising offer. In some cases they have spent tens of thousands of pounds trying to develop one.
Why is that?
It is a question fundraisers have struggled with for many years. Here are just some of the reasons we've seen for fundraising offers failing or being stopped from seeing the light of day:

- Service or marketing colleagues accuse you of 'dumbing down' and not doing justice to the nuances and complexity of the work done by your organisation. They want a more technical solution.
- You are told your offer makes your beneficiaries look like victims, or is degrading to those you serve. In our experience, comments like this rarely come from the people you are helping – instead they're normally from the marketing team or from service colleagues. In fact most beneficiaries are often happy to help. For example, a hospice patient once jokingly asked Craig, 'Is that detailed enough? I want to make sure I get a few tears from people when I'm gone!'
- It is too vague or abstract? Asking for £5 for empowerment or nondescript services won't make an impression on the donor.

A recent epiphany came after reading *The Money-Raising Nonprofit Brand* by Jeff Brooks. The author talks about the importance of selling the solution and not the process to get to the solution. This was a real light-bulb moment. We could see we had been guilty of this in the past when trying to develop a tangible fundraising offer. Jeff Brooks explains:

> ... it's one of the most elusive things in fundraising: sell the solution, not the process that produces the solution. Someone who wants a cup of coffee wants the morning fog to clear from his head. He doesn't care about what it takes to move that caffeine from coffee beans growing on a mountainside into his cup and then into his brain.

He goes on to explain what this means in donor terms:

> To keep your solution in the donor's realm, you must show the clear connection between the problem and the solution. It must not be the complex process that sets your organisation apart from Brand X Charity, but a simple and obvious connection. Simplicity is everything.
> If the problem is hunger, then the solution should be food. Even if the way you solve the hunger problem is through a complex process of economic empowerment, civil society, training trainers, or whatever it is. I'm not criticising your processes. They're good, I'm sure. But they are outside the donor's experience.[8]

Too many times we see fundraising offers that fall into this trap. Here is an example from Oxfam:

> Will you lift a life today? When you lift one person, you give them the power to lift others. It's the start of a chain reaction that will lift lives – now and for good.[9]

This is too abstract. What does 'lift' mean? The webpage this is taken from has pictures of children in school. So why not say '£5 will pay for books for children to learn to read and write. The first step to breaking the cycle of poverty.'
Here are two other examples of fundraising offers that don't hit the mark:

> *Please make a difference by giving.*

Give what? What difference am I making?

> *We desperately need extra resources to help the children in our care.*

Vague, long, not donor-focused.

In the next chapter we share a number of fundraising appeals with strong offers you can learn from.

Involvement devices

Involvement devices are often included in direct marketing to connect donors with the cause. They can increase the response to your offer by offering an immediate tangible reward for doing so.

Perhaps the most famous fundraising involvement device of all time is the direct mail pen packs where appeals would include a 'free' pen to encourage you to give. If you delve a bit deeper then you actually find the first use of this idea was inspirational and highly connected to the cause.

In the UK, sending pens was pioneered by Amnesty International UK in 1995. They needed a powerful and effective way to recruit new donors.

The pack used graphic images and a compelling story about human rights abuses across the world. All the examples had one thing in common. They involved a pen.

Here's an example of the power of emotive copy:

> *In Seoul at the Korean Central Intelligence Agency, a 60 year-old man, Sok Tal-Yun, was tortured with a pen like the one you are holding. His interrogators inserted the inner plastic ink tube into the urinary canal of his penis.*

What emotions does this provoke in you? For most people it is anger, disgust, fear and surprise. You then want to know what you can do to help.

Fortunately there was a great fundraising offer to follow.

> *What you hold in your hand is an instrument of torture. It's also an instrument of change. Don't put the pen down until you've made a choice.*

It then gives a number of compelling reasons why you should give urgently and join Amnesty International UK.

The pen was integral to the story and the pack was a huge success and used around the world by other sections of Amnesty International.

This inspired numerous imitation packs, which all sent a pen as a premium (see below) without having any regard of how it connected with the cause they were promoting.

At its best an involvement device will engage donors and boost response, particularly where there is a clear connection between the cause and the device. Here are some other examples that we really like:

St John Ambulance ran a successful integrated campaign by SMS, e-mail and mail to get people to request a free first aid guide. They then used the data they gathered to go back to those who'd requested a guide to ask them to become donors. By sending something of value and then taking part in a conversation they were able to recruit thousands of new donors.

Sense, a charity working with deaf and blind children, used props in its street fundraising to give potential donors recruited face to face an idea of what it might be like to be in that situation. First they asked people they stopped to close their eyes, then pressed into their hand a short length of chain. The fundraisers asked their prospect then to imagine it was the upright chain of a children's swing. Then into the other hand the fundraiser would press a piece of cloth that, he or she explained, represented a mother's sleeve and the open-armed greeting that for these children symbolises love.

The aim of such devices is to invoke emotion and bring to life the difference a donor can make.

The relationship fundraiser should always be seeking opportunities to involve donors and bring them closer to the work of his or her organisation. This famous quote from Benjamin Franklin springs to mind:

> Tell me and I forget, teach me and I may remember, involve me and I learn.

Involvement devices used well are a powerful tool to connect with donors and make them engage emotionally with your cause. You should always be on the look out for ways to do this.

Premiums

Many fundraising appeals and campaigns often use the lure of free gifts or include an incentive for people to give. The idea behind these is simple and based on the theory of reciprocation. When you give someone something you are likely to receive something back in return. In fundraising even a token gift can make the recipient more likely to respond.

Premiums are slightly different to involvement devices as they are usually a free gift by way of an advance thank you for giving. They aren't necessarily connected to the cause. Fundraising premiums can range from address labels and cards to ethically questionable gifts such as umbrellas (which don't have anything to do with the charity) and small denomination coins. At their worst, premiums can appear tacky, exploitative and use guilt to induce response and some think that they give fundraisers a bad name. Prospective donors might despair and wonder why fundraisers can't persuade people to give based on the good work we do, rather than on a cheap and irrelevant inducement.

Why you might consider using premiums: they tend to boost response rates (more than enough to pay the increased costs). People recruited this way tend to be loyal donors if you keep sending them premiums.

Why you might choose not to use premiums: they tend to lower average gift levels. Donors get 'hooked' on premiums and so you need to include one with every pack. People give to the premium and not necessarily the cause.

The popularity of premiums and their impact on fundraising response vary from country to country. Sean Triner of Pareto Fundraising in Australia analysed data from a number of organisations around the world on the impact of premiums and found that in mature markets, such as the USA, premium donors don't respond well at all to non-premium mailings. However, in newer fundraising markets, such as Australia, New Zealand and Belgium, the difference was much less marked.[10]

There is no doubt that premiums can be an effective way of engaging donors and many charities use them consistently. We believe the harder, but more rewarding way to fundraise is through emotion, donor involvement and appropriate engagement devices. These provide a stronger basis for building more meaningful relationships.

One piece of research that might help to settle the argument about premiums would be an analysis of the volume and value of legacies left to charities by premium-only donors. We believe that such research would show that non-premium donors would give more to causes that have emotionally resonated with them than premium donors do because their relationship is far more transactional.

The seven elements of successful donor recruitment

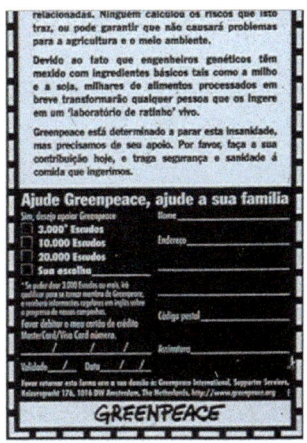

PICTURES AND LAYOUT

Even the best fundraising offer and the most emotive story can be lost if the design is poor, the copy is hard to read and you make it difficult to respond.

Yet it is sad to see so many fundraising campaigns fail this final hurdle. SOFII features an example, left, from Greenpeace in Portugal, which is probably the worst response form we've seen – unless you have a pen that writes with white ink.

In general there are four frequent fundamental design mistakes that fundraisers should avoid:

1. The type is too difficult or small to read, so donors ignore it.
2. The call to action is unclear or hard to read making it hard for donors to respond.
3. The design tries to get the message across in an abstract way.
4. The poster, advertisement, or whatever is too busy and the donor becomes distracted.

The temptation when designing a poster, direct mail piece, web banner, etc is to try and make it as eye-catching and decorative as possible. Yet all the research suggests that keeping it simple, uncluttered and without gimmickry is the most effective way to communicate.

This is particularly important in direct mail. The best letters generally have lots of **bold**, <u>underlining</u> and *italicised* sentences and words. This is quite deliberate. These act as cues for the eyes and draw the reader to the most important parts of the letter.

Similarly, adding a PS (postscript) can seem like a cliché. Yet eye motion studies show that this is often the first part of a letter that is read (usually followed by the headline, sub-heads and highlighted text). That's why it is so important you use it to reiterate your key message and call to action.

Three research reasons why you should keep design simple
1. Researchers at Berkeley University in California found that the older people get the less ability they have to suppress distracting information. This is

why older people often have memory problems. The Neuromarketing blog looked at the impact of this research for marketing to older people (aged 60+). They recommend keeping design simple, uncluttered and including white space around the message.[12]

2. It might seem tempting to use reversed out type, i.e. white on black, or lots of different colour fonts to make your marketing look prettier. However by doing so you are making it much harder to read and comprehend. Studies by Colin Wheildon[13] show that readers reported good comprehension 70 per cent of the time when black type on white background is used. This dropped to 0 per cent when white text on a black background was used. On a similar vein, when asked what colour font people prefer, 90 per cent said they found black type boring compared to other colours. Yet when tested in laboratory conditions, 70 per cent of people found the black text easy to comprehend compared to 11 per cent for blue text.[14]

3. Finally, if you look at newspapers and books you will notice that nearly all of them use a serif font, like Times New Roman (the letters have little hooks on them). Yet, look at most fundraising materials and they are often using sans serif, such as Arial (no hooks). Wheildon's research into serif versus sans serif type again produced some surprising results. Text set in a serif font such as Times New Roman was five times easier for average readers to comprehend than text set in a sans serif font like Arial. Brain scans also found that instructions set out in simple to comprehend fonts were twice as easy to follow as instructions set out in harder to comprehend fonts, despite containing exactly the same information. This research was for printed materials. For online materials read on a monitor or tablet the difference may be much less pronounced.

Using images in your fundraising

You'll often use photos within your fundraising campaigns. When images are used well they powerfully enhance your proposition.

Good fundraising photography has some of the following characteristics:

1. It makes a clear connection between the words and the image. It doesn't try and water down the proposition. For example, a disaster appeal should show photos of the need and not smiling faces. Use a strong caption that describes the photo and connects it to the rest of the material.

2. Where possible you should use a colour close-up of one person (or animal),

The seven elements of successful donor recruitment

looking sad[17] and ideally making eye contact with the camera. Eye contact is a powerful thing, even on paper. For example, one famous experiment found that an honesty box had less theft when a poster of a picture of eyes was placed near it.[18] If you can include a picture of a baby, then you really have hit the jackpot, as there is evidence that photos of babies boost altruistic behaviour.[19]

3 You should use genuine images and avoid stock photography.
4 Your image should be sharp and uncluttered.
5 It should illustrate an unmet need.

Like all rules, these aren't definitive and there will always be exceptions. However, if you use them as a starting point you won't go too far wrong.

https://flic.kr/p/9eopJm © Kevin Dooley.

www.sofii.org

https://flic.kr/p/fz42ES © Sascha Kohlmann

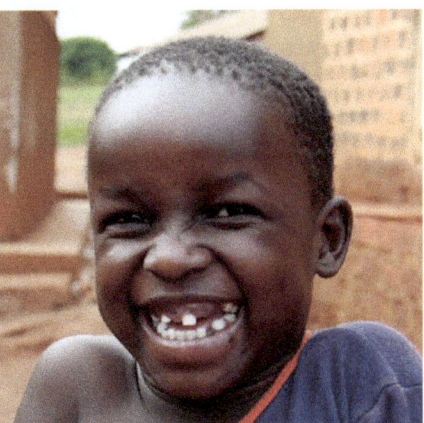
https://flic.kr/p/2bvSB1 © hdptcar

Finding your fundraising icon

Many charities have distinct fundraising images.

Look at the images on the preceding page. Which type of charity would you associate with each one?

Jeff Brooks describes such images as fundraising icons. According to Brooks:

> *A fundraising icon is an image that employs a visual language to capture the essence of your cause in the minds of your donors. It instantly reminds them what you do and why they care.*[20]

From experience we know how hard it can be to find the right image for your fundraising campaign. Get it wrong and it can have disastrous results. For example, Craig once used a picture of a distressed baby on an insert. We know babies are a good choice for an image, but the insert bombed. Why? Subsequent research found that the image was too distressing and turned readers off before they'd even got to reading the text and the story inside.

So how do you find your fundraising icon? Brooks suggests a simple three-step process:

1. Develop a hypothesis – use the checklist on what makes good fundraising photography in the previous section and ask what this means in your organisation's context. Match your existing photos with the checklist until you have a range of photos (if you can't find enough images then you can use Google images or stock photos for now).
2. Put aside your preferences and start narrowing down your choice of images – you need to put yourself in your donors' shoes and think of the images that they will respond to. Sometimes this might be at odds with your own preferences and how your service colleagues want to portray your work. Stick to your guns, because matching the donors' preferences will work best.
3. Use direct-response testing – once you've narrowed down your potential icons into a shortlist then you need to test them in a meaningful way. You should make the photo the only variable in a direct marketing split test.

Once you've identified your icon then you need to use it – again and again. Don't be tempted to change it too often. According to Brooks:[3]

Over time, your icon will become stronger as donors recognise it and form an attachment to it. That's when your icon will serve as a powerful and emotional reminder of who you are and what you make possible for them to do.[21]

RESPONSE MECHANISM

As we showed in chapter 5 making it easy to give is an essential building block of relationship fundraising.

You can have the greatest story and fundraising offer in the world, but if you make it hard to respond then you are going to lose donors.

Here are the five most popular ways for donors to respond to your direct marketing.

Response coupon /reply device

You will most likely use a response coupon that the donor returns to you along with his or her gift for direct mail, door drops, inserts and newspaper adverts.

Fortunately, response coupons have been used in direct marketing for over a hundred years. So there is a body of well-tested research on what makes a strong response form. The key elements of an effective response coupon are:

- They restate the offer and gist of the appeal in an active way. For example, 'Yes, I want to help distressed animals. Here is my gift of...'
- Information flows in a clear and logical way.
- There is enough space to write in the required details.
- The form captures key information such as name, address, payment details and tax status.

A problem you face with response forms and coupons in unaddressed direct marketing is that a high percentage of people will respond anonymously. Whilst the gift is greatly appreciated, an anonymous gift means that you can't thank the donor and you can't contact them again in the future.

It is not unknown for up to a third of responses to an insert or newspaper advert to be anonymous. So what can you do about it?

This is where incentives can come into their own. You can offer a free gift if the donor completes his or her name and address. The extra value you get from capturing a donor's details more than compensates for the cost of the gift.

You neglect response forms at your peril. They are often an untapped opportunity to gain richer data and feedback from donors.

DONORS FOR LIFE

In the first edition of *Relationship Fundraising*, Ken Burnett showed the example of Botton Village, part of the Camphill Family. Burnett highlighted their response forms that gave donors choices. They are still using a version of the same form (see above) that they've used for over 20 years. It works brilliantly for them and they still receive better response rates for their mailings than any other fundraiser we are aware of.

It is amazing that more charities haven't copied their approach. The Camphill

Family remains one of the best exponents of relationship fundraising in the world.

Another simple way to engage donors is by leaving an open box asking for comments and feedback from donors on your response form. You need to test to make sure it doesn't suppress response and must commit to read the comments and act upon them. But if you do, you can get some amazing stories and feedback from your supporters.

Website/online forms
Much of the advice for response coupons applies for online donations as well. Increasingly direct marketing includes an URL where you can donate, as well as offering more traditional ways to give. This means you need to make it easy for donors to give online. Sadly, this is often not the case.

Nomensa, a digital marketing company based in the UK, estimated that 47 per cent of attempts to make a donation are abandoned before payment is made. This is often due to frustrating user experiences and badly designed donation pages. Here are some tips to consider when designing a donation form:

- Keep it simple – the more information you ask for and the longer it takes to complete the donation process, the more likely someone is to abandon the process.
- Provide tangible examples of what the donor's gift could buy.
- Make sure to reassure donors that the process is secure and their data are safe.

It is also important to make your appeal easy to find from your website home page. Every appeal should have a prominent position on your home page and reiterate the story and call to action. You shouldn't be relying on donors to click on your 'donate' button and then tell you why they are giving. Ideally, you should use a bespoke landing page, e.g. www.nonprofit.com/craigsappeal, in your direct marketing so you can measure your visits and conversion rates. If you are using multimedia channels then you should have a different landing page for each one. This will help you distinguish between acquisition methods and to test their effectiveness.

Another important part of the online donation process is the thank you. At the end of the donation process you should direct donors to a bespoke landing page with information on the appeal they have given to and how their gift will make a difference.

Telephone

Another popular way for donors to respond is by telephoning your nonprofit and making a credit card donation. This is relatively straightforward, but there are a couple of important points to consider:

- Choose the phone number carefully that you will publicise. If you use your main switchboard number, make sure everyone who is answering the calls is properly briefed. If you use a direct line then make sure it is manned during office hours and that colleagues who may answer the phone are also briefed.
- Have a plan in place for donors who call during the evening or weekend. Do they get a message or do you re-direct their calls? Craig has previously had calls forwarded to his or colleagues' mobiles during important times when an appeal has launched. At World Jewish Relief, when conducting a large-scale emergency appeal, the charity would man the office at the weekend with volunteers and staff. We didn't feel it was right for donors not to be able to donate straight away and to be thanked personally by a charity representative.

Don't miss the opportunity provided by donors who call you. As well as the transactional process of taking the donation, you can have a conversation with the donors and find out more about them and why they give. The best fundraisers use this opportunity to build the relationship and provide a memorable experience for the donor. You can often make a thank-you letter more personal based on the conversation that you've had and add a little note addressing a comment the donor has made, or simply saying, 'It was lovely to speak to you today'.

Mobile phone

There are now more mobile phones and handheld devices than people on the planet. They are unavoidable and you ignore them at your peril. The good news is that they make it easier than ever for donors to respond to your direct marketing and other communications.

Perhaps the biggest influence has been the ability to respond to appeals by SMS. This has opened up new channels that were rarely profitable for donor recruitment. For example, SMS has made radio viable for many organisations. Similarly, you cannot get on a train in the London area without seeing a charity poster with a call to action via mobile phone.

Most commonly SMS campaigns seek a one-off text with a financial or non-financial call to action (request your free guide or sign our petition) and then follow up the donor by phone (usually to ask for a regular gift), although SMS giving changes the dynamic of the relationship between donor and fundraiser. If the only information you know about donors is their phone number, then how do you build engagement with them? Similarly, how do you record their data and giving history? It is still early days for mobile giving, but the signs are that it will be a growing (and lucrative) revenue stream for charities that adapt their fundraising appropriately.

The mobile has also led to innovation in fundraising and campaigning. In Sweden, Amnesty International used the slide feature on iPads and iPhones to encourage people to sign a petition to free prisoners at Guantanamo Bay. In the centre of Stockholm they set up a giant electronic billboard. When someone on the street signed the petition, the jail bars on the sign high above were instantly removed and the prisoner could be seen walking free as the person's signature appeared. It's brilliant use of technology for engaging passers-by.

The rise of the mobile phone and the fact you have it with you at all times make it a powerful response tool. The rise of mobile wallets and apps will mean that an increasing percentage of donations will be made via mobile devices in the future.

So you need to ensure your website is mobile responsive and renders correctly on tablets and mobiles phones. You could be putting off donors from giving if it doesn't.

Face-to-face fundraising

When face-to-face fundraising was first introduced the donor's bank details and contact information had to be handwritten on a paper form. This could lead to mistakes in data entry and wrong information being captured, which might mean the gift would be lost.

Technology now enables tablets to instantly verify name, address and bank details. Initially, the only option for giving via face-to-face fundraising was regular donations from your bank. Now people are being asked to sign a petition or send an SMS and are followed up later by phone. Some charities now ask people to give a monthly gift via their phone, cutting out the need for bank details and giving donors the chance to skip one month's payment when money is tight.

Whatever response mechanism you are using for your donor recruitment campaign, make sure you spend time thinking through how you can make it easy for donors to respond.

RESULTS

Using the RESPOND formula should allow you to create strong fundraising messages and campaigns that raise large sums of money for your cause. By putting the seven aspects into action you can create great relationship fundraising in your organisation.

NOTES
1. Heath, Chip and Heath, Dan (2006) *'The curse of knowledge'*, Harvard Business Review, December 2006. Available at: http://hbr.org/2006/12/the-curse-of-knowledge/ar/1 Last accessed 10 May 2016.
2. Heath, Chip and Heath, Dan (2007) *Made to Stick*, RH Books, London.
3. See for example the report at: http://www.nonprofitmarketingblog.com/comments/the_freakonomics_of_fundraising/ Last accessed 26 March 2012
4. Hill, Dan (2010) *Emotionomics: Leveraging Emotions for Business Success*, 2nd edition, Kogan Page, Philadelphia.
5. The Plain English Campaign, Before and After examples. Available at: http://www.plainenglish.co.uk/campaigning/examples/before-and-after.html Last accessed 31 May 2014.
6. Small, Deborah A, Loewenstein, George and Slovic, Paul (2007) 'Sympathy and callousness: The impact of deliberative thought on donations to identifiable and statistical victims', Organizational Behavior and Human Decision Processes 102: 143–14-5.
7. Small, Deborah (2007) Sympathy and callousness: The impact of deliberative thought on donations to identifiable and statistical victims, Organizational Behavior and Human Decision Processes. Volume 102, Issue 2, March 2007, Pages 143–153.
8. Brooks, Jeff (2014) The Money-Raising Nonprofit Brand, Wiley, Hoboken, NJ, p.71.
9. Taken from www.oxfam.org.uk/donate/lift-lives-for-good Last accessed 2 May 2014.
10. Triner, Sean, 'Premium v non-premium donors'. Two connected articles can be found at: http://seantriner.blogspot.co.uk/2012/03/premium-v-non-premium-donors.html and http://seantriner.blogspot.co.uk/2012/04/premium-v-non-premium-mailings.html Last accessed 19 May 2012.
11. As reported at http://news.bbc.co.uk/1/hi/health/4229372.stm Last accessed 30 May 2014.
12. Keep it simple for boomers, Neuroscience blog, http://www.neurosciencemarketing.com/blog/articles/boomers-simple.htm Last accessed 19 May 2012.
13. Wheildon, Colin (1995) *Type & Layout: How Typography and Design Can Get Your Message Across Or Get in the Way*, Strathmoor Press, Berkeley, CA.
14. For a good summary of Wheildon's research in a fundraising context, read Tom Ahern's Colin Wheildon investigates readability. Available at: http://www.aherncomm.com/ss_plugins/content/content.php?content.306, Last accessed 17 May 2012.
15. Convince with simple fonts, Neuromarketing blog. Available at: http://www.neurosciencemarketing.com/blog/articles/simple-fonts.htm Last accessed 19 May 2012.
16. Though many aid agencies do have guidelines that state showing people in distress is undignified and disempowering. This is another debate. For fundraising purposes the photo of people in need will do better than the smiling faces photo.
17. Small, Deborah and Verrochi, Nicole (2009) 'The face of need: Facial emotion expression on charity advertisements' Journal of Marketing Research vol/issue and pages
18. As reported in the Daily Telegraph in 2006: Teabreak Freeloaders Turn Over a new leaf when faced with a picture of staring eyes Available at: http://www.telegraph.co.uk/news/uknews/1522502/Teabreak-freeloaders-turn-over-new-leaf-when-faced-with-a-picture-of-staring-eyes.html Last accessed 8 August 2016. Need to reference this. Seen it plenty of places.
19. Baby pics boost altruism, Neuromarketing blog, April 2010. Available at: http://www.neurosciencemarketing.com/blog/articles/baby-pics-boost-altruism.htm Last accessed 13 May 2012.
20. Brooks, Jeff The Money-Raising Nonprofit Brand, op.cit., p.114.
21. Ibid., p.140.
22. Nomensa (2011) Creating the perfect donation experience Available for download at: https://www.nomensa.com/insights/creating-perfect-donation-experience/

The seven elements in action: four outstanding donor recruitment campaigns

This chapter comprises four examples of successful donor recruitment campaigns that show how well RESPOND works.

THE OXFAM STREET FUNDRAISING CAMPAIGN
After criticising Oxfam's 'Life' campaign in the previous chapter, we wanted to share one of our favourite street fundraising campaigns in recent years. Here is how it fits with RESPOND:

Figure 9.1 The bucket Oxfam's street fundraisers used to start conversations with potential donors.

Response mechanism
An instant text from your mobile.

Emotion and story
Oxfam had developed a bucket with a tap for use in emergency situations around the world. The bucket has a lid to keep out dirt and a tap to stop contamination. This gave the street fundraisers a great story to tell to prospective donors.

Pictures and layout
Although this was a street fundraising campaign, the supporting materials and bucket design were all easy to read and explained the offer clearly.

Offer and involvement
Donors were cleverly offered three

options to give. You could give £2 to fill the bucket, £3 to pay for a bucket, or £5 to buy it and fill it. Donors who sent a text were then followed up with a phone call to ask them to take out a regular gift.

The bucket is a great conversation starter, offering a tangible image of what the donor's money might buy. Using this involvement device sparked the potential donor's interest, as he or she invariably wanted to know more.

Narrative and copy

The street fundraisers were trained to tell the story of the bucket in an engaging and emotional way. Similarly, the follow-up calls used a powerful story to ask for a regular gift.

Data

The data from the SMS messages were then used to call people back and ask them for a regular gift. The phone call also asked for the donor's name and address, so even those who didn't sign up for a regular gift could still be kept informed.

Results

The campaign was developed in conjunction with fundraising agency Open Fundraising. During an e-mail conversation, Paul de Gregorio, head of mobile at Open, shared his thoughts with me on the campaign:

> *I love this campaign because it provided a way for the potential donor to really see what their money could do. It created a genuine moment of engagement between fundraiser and donor on the street, something that could then be referred to in the follow-up phone call. We called it 'street theatre' and its introduction in this campaign resulted in average SMS donations that were higher than we'd previously seen.*

SOI DOG FOUNDATION – RECRUITING REGULAR DONORS VIA FACEBOOK[1]

Many fundraisers struggle to raise money via Facebook and other social media. The Soi Dog Foundation has bucked this trend and acquired the bulk of its 20,000+ regular donors this way. The Foundation has done this through building a page with over 1 million 'likes' and constantly engaging potential donors with great stories and strong calls to action.

Additionally, the Foundation has made significant investment in Facebook advertising using a two-step strategy. The first captures high probability candidate donors and subsequently targets these warm audiences with financial asks.

Response mechanism

When potential donors click on the Facebook post or ads they are taken to a landing page with strong images, a compelling story and a clear ask with the following donation form embedded.

Emotion and story

Soi Dog Foundation combine powerful images of abused dogs and intriguing headlines and stories to make an emotional impact on donors. By telling stories about individual dogs and the difference donors have made, Soi Dog are able to use emotions effectively to move donors and raise money.

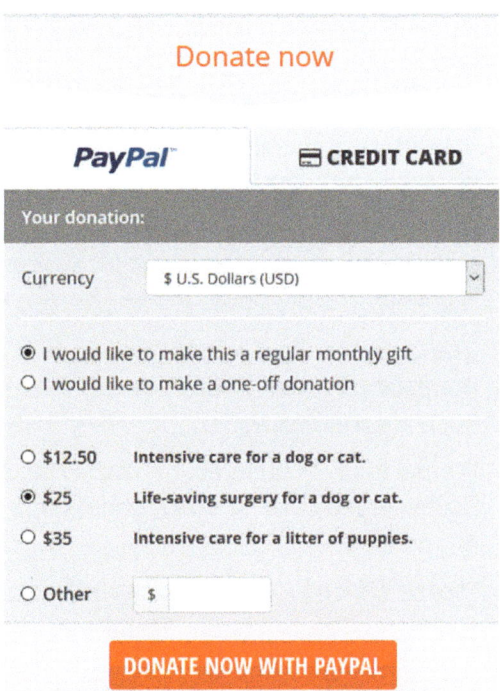

Figure 9.2 With two clicks (if you are logged into PayPal) the donation is complete.

Pictures and layout

All the Facebook ads are tested consistently and amended to ensure the layout maximises click through rates and response.

As the example overleaf shows, imagery is very important in Soi Dog's fundraising. The injured dog is their icon and features in most of the ads. However, the 'after' is also shown with images of how donor's money has helped rehabilitate the dog.

Soi Dog Foundation use a mix of styles of posts on Facebook to build donor engagement. Each post can be 'liked', 'shared', or commented on, which increases the audience that sees the ad and gives an opportunity for instant feedback and comments from donors.

Cheerio was just a tiny puppy when he arrived at our shelter over a year ago.

A shocking injury ran the length of his back, which our vets diagnosed as some sort of chemical burn. It is heartbreaking to imagine the agony this poor little boy was in.

Thanks to people like YOU, we were able to take Cheerio in and provide him with the medical care and love he needed. And after a few months at our shelter, lucky Cheerio was adopted by Prisca in Switzerland!

The picture on the right is Cheerio in his new home, looking extremely handsome for the holiday season! Thank you Prisca for giving this boy such a wonderful home.

Please think of vulnerable animals like Cheerio this holiday season. With no owners to care for them, street dogs and cats desperately need your support.

Please click on Cheerio's pictures to learn more about how you can help save dogs like him today. Thank you.

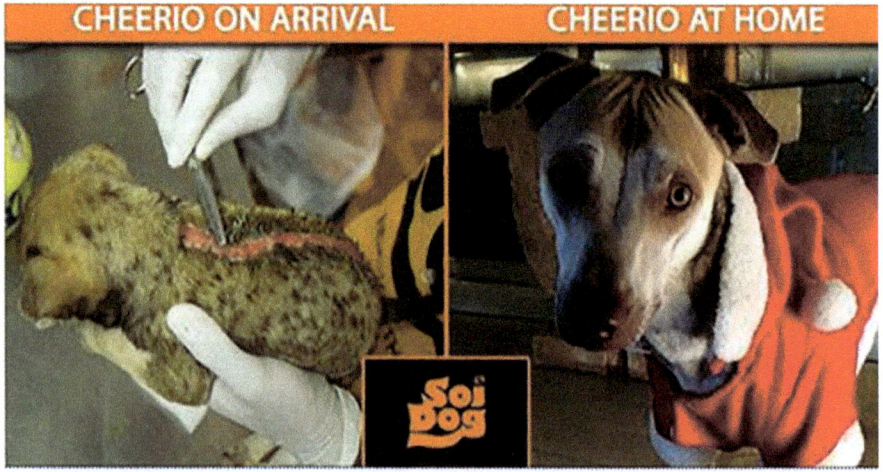

CLICK HERE TO SAVE MORE DOGS LIKE CHEERIO

Every day, Soi Dog Foundation picks up sick and injured animals in desperate need of medical treatment. With no government funding, we urgently need YOUR support to save them.

Figure 9.3 Soi Dog Foundation's donation page: powerful narrative, emotional images and a simple offer.

Offer and involvement

Soi Dog Foundation make a simple offer when you click on the ad: you can give monthly or a one-off donation to help. For example, give $12.50 a month to pay for 'surgery for a dog' or one gift of $45 to pay for a 'physical therapy for an injured animal'. For example, one post made the following offer:

**PLEASE HELP THESE DOGS –
FOR JUST $12.50 A MONTH YOU CAN KEEP ONE ALIVE**

Soi Dog Foundation use a mix of styles of posts on Facebook to build donor engagement. Each post can be 'liked', or 'shared', or commented on, which increases the audience that sees the ad and gives an opportunity for instant feedback and comments from donors.

It's also worth noting that Soi Dog also have a separate 'Sponsor a dog and rescue it from the street' fundraising product. This gives a choice of dogs and uses a different donation page to the one above.

Narrative and copy

Soi Dog Foundation use copy that is sprinkled with 'you' and shows the role the donor can play in helping the dogs. The writing is punchy and to the point, so the ads make an impact in as few words as possible. The consequences of not giving are clear and the urgency of the situation is apparent.

Data

According to SOFII:

> Part of the Soi Dog Foundation's success lies in using Facebook for targeted advertising and they made the choice to target only women. By pinning down the charity's ideal donor profile and marketing directly to people who fitted that profile, then testing the response by age, gender, relationship status, location, education, workplace and any other relevant categories they were able to hone the success of the response.[2]

ADOPT TODAY AND YOU'LL RECEIVE...

A cuddly tiger toy

My Tigers and *Wild World* magazine three times a year

Factbook, certificate, bookmarks, stickers and more

Figure 9.4 The tiger adoption pack, as shown on WWF UK website: www.wwf.org.uk/adoption/tiger.

WWF – DIRECT RESPONSE TELEVISION

WWF's direct response television advertisements have recruited hundreds of thousands of supporters globally. The simplicity of sponsoring an endangered species of animal and the accompanying rewards has proved universally popular. There are lots of animals donors can adopt, but we will comment on one of the tiger adoption videos from the UK.[3]

Response mechanism
A phone number and a text number are displayed prominently throughout the advert and announced clearly by the narrator. A website address is also given.

Emotion and story
The tiger adoption video uses close-up footage of Kamrita, a female tiger, to create an emotional connection with the viewer. The narrator issues a grave warning that there are as few as 3,200 tigers left in the wild. The viewer is warned that without their donations tigers face extinction. This is followed by the sponsorship offer and gratitude for 'the tigers that survive thanks to you'.

Picture and layout
As we said above, the video uses close-up footage of Kamrita throughout the advertisement. The video also uses captioning to give the website address and telephone number during the ad.

Offer
WWF uses a sponsorship offer in its ads. For just £3 per month (or equivalent in your country) you can protect your chosen species. When you sign up you receive a cuddly toy and a sponsorship pack that includes engaging and interesting items such as pictures, fact sheets and a certificate of adoption.

Narrative and copy
The ads starts with a close up of a tiger and the following words:

> What do you see? A rug? Bones and teeth to be used as medicine? That's how poachers see her.

The personal approach is used throughout the 60-second video. The video also describes the benefits of adoption and what you will receive. It uses short sentences to describe the situation and how to sponsor a tiger.

Data
Good media buying is essential to successful DRTV. Using data analysis to track times of response and where the donor saw the ad allow for improved targeting over time. Also, the data from split testing are used to hone the effectiveness of the ads by trying variations in images, narrative and asks and monitoring the results.

HUMBER RIVER HOSPITAL FOUNDATION – HUMBERT'S HEARTS DIRECT MAIL PACK

This series of direct mail packs was created by fundraising agency Agents of Good (http://agentsofgood.org/) from Canada. They use classic direct mail techniques to obtain impressive fundraising results for the hospital. The appeal stands out from other conventional direct mail packs by featuring Humbert – a cartoon character who represents the 'heart of the hospital'.

The results have been impressive. The autumn 2015 appeal to existing donors, which we describe below, has achieved a 19.1 per cent response rate and an average gift of $64.90.

Importantly, and often overlooked, an inspiring thank-you letter, which also features Humbert, was created at the same time as the appeal.

Response mechanism

The appeal pack uses a well-designed response form. It is personalised with the

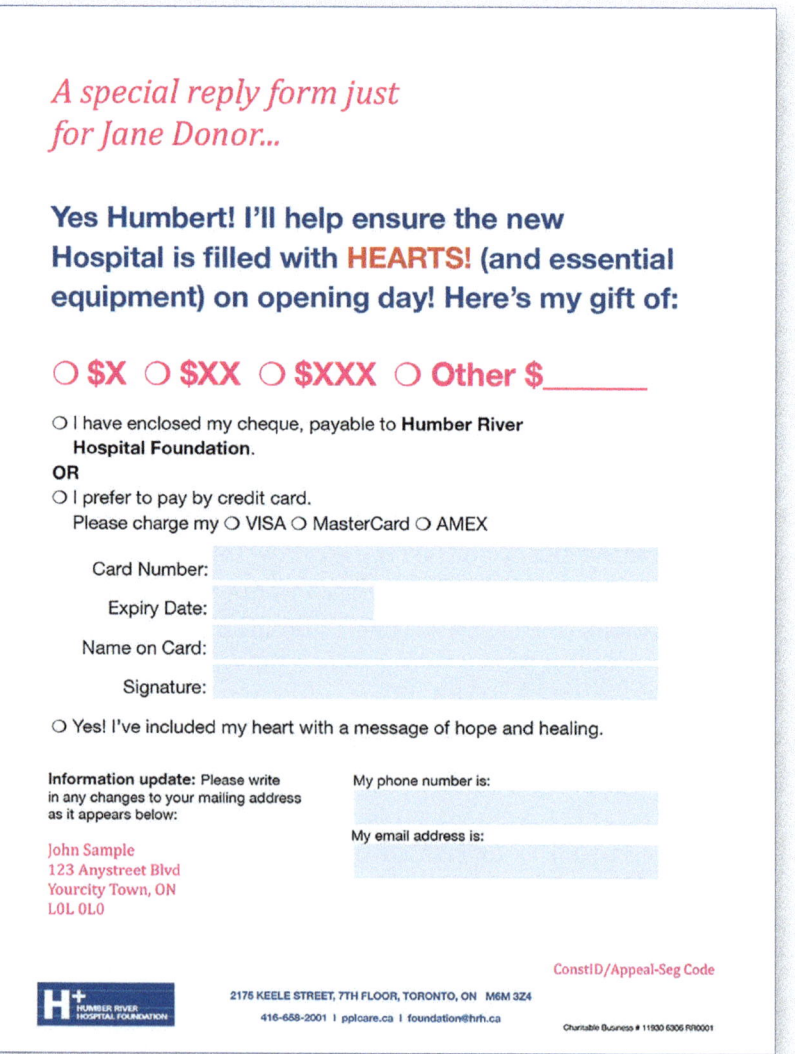

Figure 9.5 The Humber River Hospital reply coupon is exceptionally donor-friendly.

donor's name and gives three potential donation amounts. It asks if the donor has included a 'heart' message and has plenty of space for the donor to write credit card details.

Emotion and story

This letter uses lots of positive emotion to make donors feel good about giving and to celebrate their role in opening the new hospital. There is a focus on generating feelings of pride, happiness and joy.

There is also a short, emotive paragraph when the donor is asked to imagine being a child visiting the hospital. The story is designed to promote empathy and connection to the hospital and give a strong emotional reason to make a further gift to the hospital:

> *Can you imagine being a little child, walking into that big, brand and shiny-new Hospital for the first time? You'd probably feel a bunch of tiny butterflies fluttering around in your tummy!*
> *Now imagine the smile on that young girl's face when she sees a wall filled with your hearts. And, when that girl's mom reads out the special message written on your heart … the butterflies settle down just a bit. <u>She feels brave enough to go on.</u>*
> *Because you and I know that little girl is going to receive excellent care at this brand new Hospital. She's going to be seen by a world-class health care team, in an area of emergency designed for our littlest patients. She'll get tested and treated with the very latest in digital equipment.*
> ***But it's important for her to know there are people like you out there.***
> *People who care enough to support this exceptional health care. You're the reason this new Hospital is here to give her the care she needs. You are the HEART of this new hospital.*

Pictures and layout

The pack uses the Humbert character as the main emotion image. The layout of the pack is excellent. It uses lots of short paragraphs, indentation and bold, italic and underlined sections of text to emphasise key messages.

This is all designed to make the pack easy to read and digestible for the reader. The Response form is also well designed. It is laid out logically in a way that is easy for the reader to follow and leaves plenty of room to write any details.

Offer and involvement

The offer is simple: give today to help buy the final pieces of equipment needed for the new hospital.

It could potentially be made stronger by giving some examples of the equipment still needed and the cost. However, the pack uses involvement brilliantly to engage the donor.

In the letter Humbert invites donors to join in and celebrate the opening of the new hospital by sending a message of 'hope or healing' on a specially designed heart. Donors are then promised that these will be displayed in the hospital in time for its opening.

Narrative and copy

The appeal letter makes copious use of 'I' and 'you' to acknowledge the donors' role in opening the hospital. It positions the donors as heroes and makes them feel good about giving. The following paragraph shows this donor-focused narrative in action:

> *I may be heart shaped … but YOU are the true heart of Humber River Hospital! You are the reason that I even exist. I exist to celebrate YOU and all that you help to achieve with your generosity!*

Another interesting aspect is that it is written from Humbert – the custodian of donor love for the hospital. By using an unusual emotional voice to tell the story of the hospital opening in a conversational style, the copy was memorable and easy to read.

Data

Personalisation is used throughout the letter. The response form uses previous giving history to present the donor with three levels of 'ask'. The response form also tries to capture phone numbers and e-mail addresses, as well as asking donors for any change in their address.

NOTES
1. Information from SOFII at: http//sofii.org/case-study/the-soi-dog-foundation-acquiring-regular-donors-through-facebook and Sean Triner at: https://prezi.com/71hqbq38z2te/dne-who-let-the-thai-dogs-out/and http://www.seantriner.com/2015/08/what-works-on-facebook-old-fashioned.html Last accessed 10 December 2015.
2. Ibid.
3. You can watch the tiger adoption video at: https://www.youtube.com/watch?v=qZFD_C7-RfY Last accessed: 9 August 2016

The seven elements in action: four outstanding donor recruitment campaigns

Figure 9.6 A donor's special message to Humber River Hospital.

Figure 9.7 The display of 'hope or healing' messages from donors to Humber River Hospital.

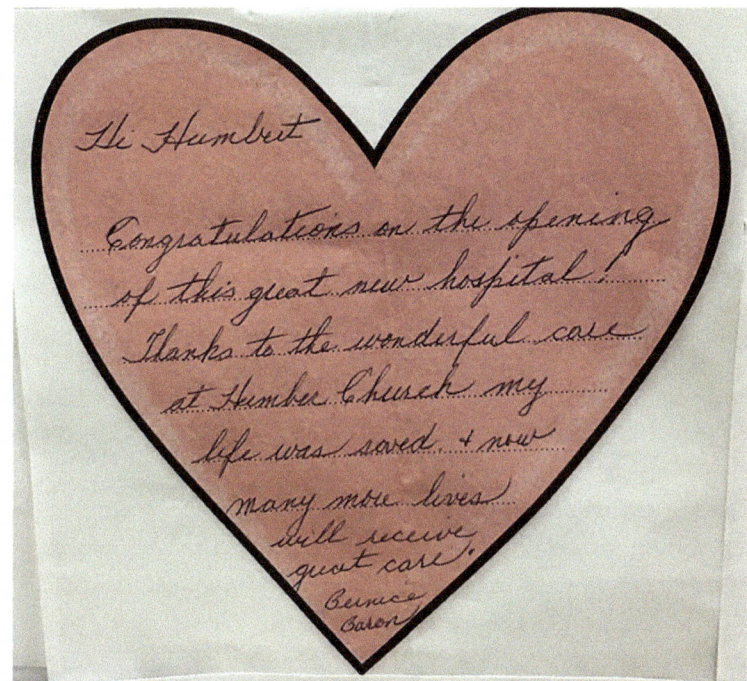

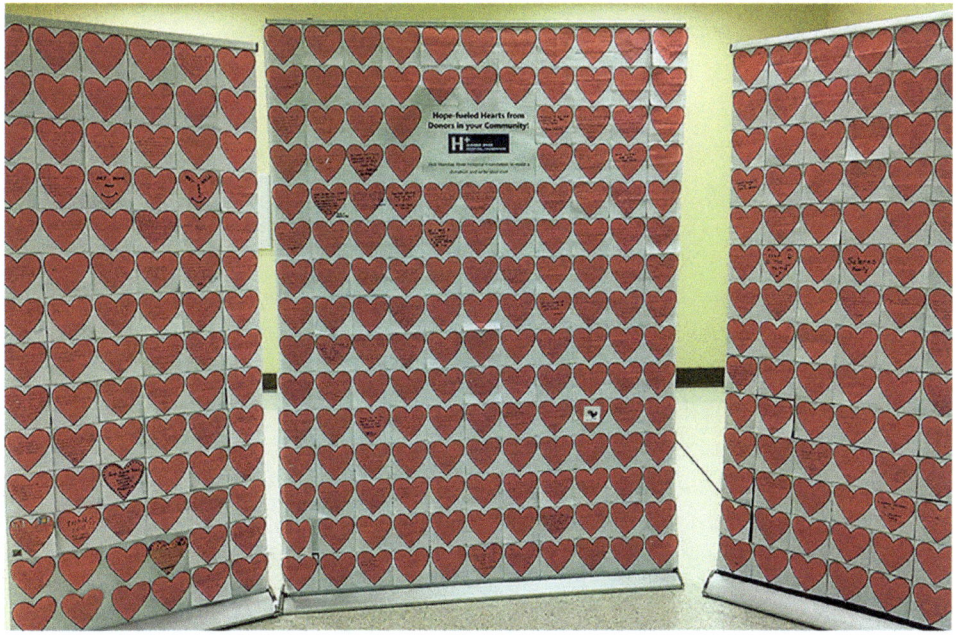

Integration: creating a seamless experience for donors
A tale of two brands

Craig recently had to set up a new bank account. It was a tortuous experience and he ended up giving up with one bank and taking his custom elsewhere. Here he explains why:

> My research showed me that bank A was offering the best deal and I went on their website and did a pre-eligibility test. The website was well designed and user friendly. I was impressed and pleased to pass the first stage.
> It was all down hill from there though.
> I was asked to fill in a full online application form. It wasn't particularly user friendly, but after half an hour I completed the form and hit send.
> I was sent an automated e-mail saying my application had been received and a customer service representative would be in touch shortly.
> Two days later I received a second e-mail asking me to call the bank, which I duly did.
> After navigating through five or six menus on the phone I finally got to speak to someone. I was told that I had to resubmit the form via post and they would e-mail a copy for me to print and complete at home. I asked what was the point of completing the online application then? I received a sheepish and apologetic response. Surprisingly I wasn't the first person to raise this issue. 'They' had raised it with 'them' and the gentleman I was speaking to agreed that it was a stupid system. He was very nice, but it was a classic computer says 'no' moment!
> I received the forms by e-mail an hour or so later and duly filled them in by hand as you couldn't type into the form they sent – it was a very good deal so I persevered – and sent them off.
> A week later I got another phone call. I'd been given the wrong information. I had to take the forms to my local branch and show some ID.
> Again, I followed the instructions and went to my local branch. It was

empty and I explained why I was there. The lady gave me a knowing smile. 'Do you have an appointment sir?' I didn't. No one told me I had to book one. I explained my situation and said all I wanted to do was submit my application form and show ID. The lady shook her head and explained that wasn't possible. I protested that no one was in the branch, surely they had five minutes to spare. The lady wearily said again that wasn't possible. I finally gave up. I'd like to say I flounced out and made a big show of my anger and frustration. I didn't. I took the more British route of shrugging, thanking her for her time and then vowing never to darken that particular bank's door again.

I want to compare that experience with my favourite brand of ice cream – Häagen-Dazs (though Ben & Jerry's is always an acceptable substitute). I love my food and wherever I am in the world I always like to sample the local cuisine. One of my favourite things is ice cream and the quality can vary remarkably from country to country.

That's why if I can't find a great local ice-cream emporium I will seek out the local Häagen-Dazs or Ben & Jerry's. From Burlington[1] to Beijing, Mombasa to Madrid I know I will get a consistent service and my favourite flavour; for the record that is dulce de leche in Häagen-Dazs and Phish Food in Ben & Jerry's. I trust both brands to fulfil my ice-cream needs and I've never been disappointed.

What's this got to do with fundraising? Well, think back to the seven drivers of donor commitment in chapter 3. Number two is the 'donor knows what to expect from your organisation with each interaction'.

Is your fundraising like the bank – dysfunctional and infuriating to deal with or like Häagen-Dazs and Ben & Jerry's – consistent and with expectations always being met or exceeded?

This chapter is about how you provide a consistent, integrated experience for your donors by making sure you have a joined-up approach to every interaction you have with them.

WHAT IS INTEGRATION?

Integration has been an industry buzzword in recent years. There have been numerous conferences devoted to the subject and it is a popular topic on blogs and social media. We believe it is a term that has been over-used and under-delivered on. This chapter will help you change that.

Why has it become so popular a term? The rise of digital and social media and the fragmentation of traditional media mean it is increasingly difficult to reach potential donors and make them interested in what you have to say.

Integrated fundraising is meant to be our weapon to combat the abundance of ways we can now communicate with, and listen to, our supporters. Yet although integration sounds appealing it remains elusive to many fundraising teams.

When trying to understand why many nonprofits have failed to embrace integration, we believe it is worth splitting integration into two parts:

Everyday integration – how you give donors a consistent experience across your organisation.

Internal integration – how you organise across different teams.

The first is externally focused. How do you make sure that supporters get a consistent experience when they interact with your nonprofit? This means your message and branding is seamless across traditional, digital and social media.

The second is internally focused. How do you organise and plan within your team and wider organisation to produce inspiring fundraising appeals and campaigns that work across multiple channels?

Both types of integration apply to recruiting new donors and keeping their support.

Understanding both is crucial if you want to reap the rewards that integration can bring to your fundraising.

And what are those rewards?

Well, we've already shown how increased commitment and loyalty lead to increased lifetime value. Integrated fundraising helps you improve both of these by providing a consistent experience and an opportunity for donors to interact with your organisation.

Trent Dunham, senior vice-president of fundraising agency Dunham+Company, describes how putting everyday integration into action had an instant impact at two nonprofits he worked with:

> *One organization did the hard work to make sure their annual summer campaign had alignment across all channels (direct mail, homepage, email, landing pages, social media, etc.) and saw a 10% increase in total income, recorded a 16% increase in number of gifts given to the campaign, and realized a 68% increase in the number of new donors acquired through the campaign over the previous year.*

> Another organization made sure that their website homepage reflected the messaging in their direct mail letter and had a strong connection between their email and the donation landing page, and saw a 94% increase in total income attributed to the campaign, realizing a 57% increase in new donors acquired.[2]

Another example of successful integration comes from Operation Smile. This charity provides reconstructive surgery and related healthcare worldwide to more than 150,000 children suffering from facial deformities. In 2011 they launched a fundraising campaign with an inspiring phone message from the charity's founder, Dr William Magee. This alerted donors about an appeal letter they would be receiving. Supporters then received the appeal and follow-up mailings, along with two e-mails, which were followed by calls from telephone fundraisers to offer the donor more information and solicit a gift. Ask levels were based on each supporter's giving history. This final communication on the phone was critical to the campaign's success. Pledgers then received another recorded phone message from Dr Magee, expressing gratitude for their continuing support. This boosted the fulfilment of the pledges made on the phone.

Operation Smile's campaign far exceeded projections, raising twice the forecast gross and three times the net revenue compared with previous campaigns. The phone campaign alone generated 30 per cent of total revenue and the organisation raised $9 for every $1 invested in telephoning its donors – far more than what had been achieved in previous telephone campaigns. However, as Jann Schultz, Operation Smile's director of donor relations, highlights:

> *The key to this hugely successful campaign was expansion of channels to include the phone with tight integration of messaging and the timing across every contact with the donor.*[3]

Further evidence comes from a 2007 paper prepared by software company Convio and their analytics partner StrategicOne. The paper showed that donors who had previously only given offline gave more than twice as much when communications were combined with electronic messages ($694 versus $314). And those that gave through both channels had a higher lifetime value indicating that the online channel does not cannibalise revenue from direct mail.[4]

Even simple things like having branded donation pages for giving can have a big impact on fundraising results. The 2015 Network for Good *Online Fundraising, Report*[5] found that branded nonprofit web-pages raised 20 – 30 per cent more than generic ones.

This tallies with Paul's experience at a medium-sized, UK-based NGO, World Jewish Relief (WJR), where conversion rates from third party fundraising sites were poor. This was because donors landed on a page that had hardly any charity branding and information. Additionally, donors had to opt in to receive any further communications from the charity. This meant most donations were given anonymously and couldn't even be thanked properly.

WJR saw the opportunity for improved donor acquisition and engagement, especially given the fact that challenge events formed a central part of their fundraising strategy. A proposal was put to a major donor to fund a tailor-made fundraising micro site, employing the same technology as the market leaders. Instead of being generic in its look and feel, however, the site, myWJR, was dedicated for sole use by the charity and, critically, donors had to opt out of receiving future communications. Accordingly, the charity has been able to acquire 2,677 new supporters over four years resulting in an increase in their active database of 25 per cent. Through a welcome and conversion plan, 13 per cent of these donors then went on to make at least one further gift, totalling nearly £47,000 during this period. Combined with the direct savings made on cutting out the transactional fees paid to a third party provider, the charity generated a total of nearly £60,000. Given the limited target market and new challenge events programme, this was considered a success.

BARRIERS TO EVERYDAY INTEGRATION – ACHIEVING INTERNAL INTEGRATION TO OVERCOME THEM

So if the results of everyday integration are so impressive, why do so many charities struggle with it?

Perhaps the biggest problem is a silo mentality that exists in many charities. In our experience, the larger the organisation the more likely you are to have this problem.

As Jeff Brooks explains in his blog article, *Your silos are going to kill you*:

> Non-profit organizations are still extremely siloed organizations. The people doing direct mail want credit for this behavior– since their efforts are triggering online gifts. But generally speaking, the digital department does not report to development but to marketing. So the digital departments get to make statements like 'online revenue is up 50 percent,' when they should be saying, 'online revenue cannibalized direct mail revenue by 20 percent.'[6]

Silos can exist in many shapes and forms. Here are some that we've experienced in our careers:

- Fundraising department silos happen when different fundraising teams don't share their ideas and plans: the phrase 'the left hand doesn't know what the right hand is doing' springs to mind.
- Donor silos, when people argue over who 'owns' a donor. A typical phrase you might hear is 'this is a digital donor, he gave online first, of course you can't mail him.'
- Financial silos are related to the first two. Teams can argue over who gets the budgetary credit for a particular donation. If this exists in your charity then be very careful, it can be highly destructive and hugely de-motivating for staff.
- Departmental silos go beyond the fundraising team and occur when services, marketing, HR, finance, etc all operate in their own little worlds.
- Cultural or external silos, when people in a team refuse to look at outside benchmarks and best practice. We've been in this position many times. You suggest a new idea or point out another fundraising team's success and colleagues answer along the following lines: 'Sure, that sounds great. But it wouldn't work here. Our donors are different.'

These negative silos can seriously hamper your fundraising ability. Most importantly, silos don't exist in donors' minds. They don't care how we are organised. They only care about the impact we have made and the donor experience they receive. Steve MacLaughlin from Blackbaud Inc., describes the situation:

> Donors are multichannel. They receive messages across multiple channels and they give across multiple channels. They don't care about your organisation chart or who gets credit for the donation.
> The problem is that many nonprofits are still organised around single channels each doing their own thing, with their own strategies, their own data, their own donors and their own systems. That's broken and really costly.[7]

One final point to remember: silos aren't always necessarily bad. We need centres of expertise that focus on specific aspects of fundraising. We can't be jacks of all trades, masters of none, the challenge is to keep the benefits that expert teams can bring and mitigate the problems they can cause.

So how do you stop negative silos forming in your organisation? Let's look at some overarching things to consider.

First of all, senior management need to show leadership and create a team culture and environment where negative silos can't thrive. If you manage a department then make sure your team see you making the effort to engage and work with other teams. Building trust and credibility is crucial. You need to build a reputation as someone who gets things done, is accountable and shares praise and recognition across teams and departments.

Secondly, consider how the layout and set up of your office impacts on the creation of negative silos. Apple founder Steve Jobs was adamant about the importance of office design to help break down silos. He thought it was crucial to encourage encounters between staff from different parts of the business. The design of the Pixar headquarters is testament to this:

> *If a building doesn't encourage [collaboration], you'll lose a lot of innovation and the magic that's sparked by serendipity. So we designed the building to make people get out of their offices and mingle in the central atrium with people they might not otherwise see.*[8]

Finally, don't forget your 'why'. When you are struggling to overcome the problems silos can cause take a step back and remember why you are fundraising in the first place.

Remind people of the duty they have to the cause they serve and to the donors they represent. Ask people questions like 'how does this help us reach more beneficiaries?' or 'what would our donors say if they could hear us talking like this?'

By reframing your issues in the language of beneficiaries and donors you can get people to see you are all on the same side and not competing against each other.

Now let's look at some specific ideas to combat negative silos.

Fundraising department silos

It is crucial that different teams are informed about each other's work. This can be through formal and informal routes. You might have a weekly or monthly inter-department team meeting, e-mail updates, use project management tools, such as Basecamp, or hold informal stand-up meetings.

Too often our default mode of communication is e-mail. Even when we are sharing the same office, the temptation can be to send an e-mail rather than talk to the person we want to communicate with. Think about how you can encourage people to send fewer e-mails and to pick up the phone or, even better, get up and go and speak to colleagues.

Richard Taylor, former director of fundraising and marketing at Cancer Research UK, takes a radical approach to the problem of fundraising silos. At the 2014 Revolutionise Annual Lectures he told the audience how he moves his senior management team around every couple of years. He believes that getting someone to switch departments brings numerous benefits to overall fundraising and marketing performance. It reduces negative silos as it helps identify cross-team opportunities and keeps senior management engaged and highly motivated.

One development from the world of technology is to bring cross-departmental teams together to work intensely on product development or software updates. These are known as 'scrums' and 'sprints'. This flips the traditional sequential approach on its head and brings teams closer together to work on a problem.

Organisations from outside the world of technology are starting to use this technique to solve their own business problems and develop products.

Try giving permission and autonomy to your staff to work together on a problem or project they are interested in. This can be a great motivator and produce high-quality work and solutions, even in a short, intense period of time.

Donor silos

We have heard horror stories from some fundraisers where they won't ask a donor for more money as they will 'lose them' to another team. This is clearly a major issue. So what's the answer?

For too long we have organised and structured fundraising teams in a way that is convenient for us and not around what suits the donor. However, there are signs of this changing.

Donor-focused nonprofits have created entire departments with trained professionals focused on donor care and the donor experience. Examples include the Humane Society of the United States, Operation Smile, Child Fund International, American Cancer Society and St Jude. Some even have, by whatever title, created the position of 'chief donor officer', to coordinate fully their activities across all departments and truly put the supporter at the heart of all their activities. This role includes establishing and monitoring metrics for defining customer relationships, cross-departmental influence to deliver the greatest value to supporters and driving an integrated agenda throughout the organisation. They actively seek to destroy negative silos.

Financial silos

Targets are important in fundraising, but they need to be used wisely. You don't want to make them counterproductive by pitting team against team. If multiple teams are involved in a successful event, major donor ask, corporate pitch, etc, then share the (budgetary) credit. Don't create a 'winner takes all' mentality that rewards selfish behaviour and only one team receives the credit for a fundraising success.

As he explains, ex-NSPCC appeal director Giles Pegram took a pragmatic approach to this problem during the NSPCC Full Stop appeal:

> The problem of crediting had become a major pre-occupation for staff and volunteers. It was stopping them getting on with the task of raising more money because they were bogged down in allocating the money from last month's event. First we tried methods like agreeing in advance how the money would be allocated, but these were not solving the problem.
>
> I came up with the following:
>
> 1. We created a classic matrix.
> 2. We filled in the horizontal axis with the names of our fundraising groups.
> 3. We listed the activities that involved two or more groups down the vertical axis.
> 4. When a joint event was organised, the total sum raised was put in the relevant boxes, two, three, or whatever.
> 5. We also put the total figure for the event in the final column.
> 6. So a £200k event would have £200k allocated to board c, say, and board f, and in the final box in the row.
> 7. When you looked at the columns, each board could see that they had been 'credited' with the total figure.
> 8. If you added up the columns, you would get a figure that was made part of the £250m target.
> 9. If you added up the final column, you would get a lesser figure, the actual

totals from all the activities where there were two (or more) boards involved.
10. *So you put in a final box in the bottom right-hand corner saying 'balancing figure'. This was the difference between 8 and 9.*
11. *So 8 was used to keep the volunteers and staff motivated; 9 was the figure that fed into the accounts and kept the financial director happy.*
12. *Nobody questioned the practice. All arguments about joint events and activities disappeared. The total figure at the end of the appeal showed the real figure, which was a few hundred thousand pounds less than the credited figure. Insignificant in the scale of the appeal. Really big events would be allocated according to an agreed formula, but they were very rare.*

Put simply: credit twice, count once.

It would be difficult to make this approach work for 'business as usual' fundraising, as the difference between the real and credited figure may become too large. This would cause problems for your finance team. Yet we believe the principle can be useful in helping you overcome the problem of financial silos.

Departmental silos
These are problematic when trying to get stories and information for your fundraising.

In one of the organisations he worked for Craig was told there was a huge problem with silos between teams. This created a culture where there was little trust and respect for each other. It quickly became apparent that it was seriously harming the organisation's fundraising ability. Working with his team, Craig set out to bring down the barriers. Through little steps such as purposely eating in the same dining room, organising job swaps and inviting other teams to fundraising social events the problem soon started to recede. Trust was built, stories shared and they were able to enjoy their mutual successes.

One of the simplest ideas was sending a thank-you card to staff he worked with on a project when it was finished. This small token of gratitude worked wonders. One colleague told him, 'I've worked here for nearly 10 years and it is the first time anyone has done anything like this. We need to do more of this kind of thing.'

Gradually people wanted to work with the fundraising team and began to understand why we needed certain information.

Rather than Craig's team constantly chasing for stories and images they could use in their fundraising, colleagues started approaching them – it was a huge transformation.

Fundraisers need to understand the motivation of other teams in the charity. When trying to motivate people to help fundraising, it is important to show 'what's in it for me?'

One final idea to break down departmental silos is to organise fundraising weeks for your own cause. Get all staff, volunteers and trustees involved in fundraising. This can range from teams helping at community events such as flag days to taking part in fundraising challenge events. At one organisation Craig worked at nearly 90 per cent of staff took part in the fundraising challenge he set his colleagues. Overall, they raised approximately £200 for every staff member in the charity. As well as producing a great fundraising result, it had a huge positive impact on internal morale and building stronger inter-departmental links.

Cultural/external silos

These can be the hardest to deal with as, frankly, encountering this sort of mindset can be extremely de-motivating. People who defend the status quo, are reluctant to change and believe the old ways are best can be described as 'drains'. They are people whose negativity and pessimism drain away any positive energy and strangle new ideas.

To combat this you need to try and become a 'radiator' and exude energy and warmth to your colleagues. Be the person who is known for your generosity of support to others.

One way to tackle cultural silos is to hold a 'sacred cow barbeque'. This is a technique described by nonprofit consultants Bernard Ross and Clare Segal in *Breakthrough Thinking for Nonprofit Organizations*.[9]

The idea here is to think the unthinkable and challenge mindsets. It is a straightforward technique. Write down things you wouldn't or couldn't do as an organisation; stick the ideas on a wall or flipchart to be discussed and debated. The sacred cows could be things such as 'we should cancel our longstanding event', or 'we need to invest more in retention than acquisition'. Use the opportunity to think beyond the norm. To help challenge mindsets, Ross and Segal propose four rules:[10]

- Anyone can say anything.
- No one is to make personal attacks and no challenges will be taken personally.

- No challenging remarks will be repeated outside the meeting.
- Only things the group has agreed to take forward will be recorded. Everything else will be forgotten.

So now we've looked at negative silos, what are the other barriers to internal integration?

Quality of data and investment

Once again one of the big barriers we face as fundraisers is the quality of our data and investment in our systems and processes.

Convio's *Integrated Multi-Channel Marketing* study[11] looked at barriers to integration. As well as the silo problem, the study identified a lack of commitment on the part of an organisation's leaders to integrate. Consequently, there is low investment in the mechanics – business processes, staff, measurement and software – that are required to make it happen. Fewer than half the organisations surveyed measure lifetime value by channel, or tracked the migration of donors from one channel to another.

Too often organisations only track metrics associated with a single channel. For example, we look at how many donors mailed in a cheque in response to a direct mail appeal, but not necessarily whether we experienced an increase in online donations when the letter arrived at the donor's home.

Greater focus is needed on how people move from one channel to another, as well as more detailed examination of retention rates by channels of engagement.

Finally, achieving everyday integration is hard work. Battling negative silos and not having the necessary processes and data to hand can make integration seem more hassle than it's worth. We'd urge you to stick with it though. As we showed at the beginning of the chapter, the rewards for getting it right can be excellent. And as the way we consume media continues to change, there is no doubt that integration will be essential to fundraising success.

Here are some tools and tips that can help you improve your everyday integration.

MYSTERY SHOPPING

Perhaps the easiest way to assess your efforts at integration is to conduct a mystery shopping exercise. Ask friends or family to make a donation through a range of channels – mail, over the phone, online, via a mobile device – and see what happens.

We would bet that there is likely to be significant differences in the giving experiences by channel.

Here are just some of the things you might want to compare:

- Ease of donating: was the online donation page easy to find, was the telephonist polite?
- Timeliness of thank you: how long does it take for the donor to get a thank you?
- Quality of thank you: do online donors get an offline thank you?
- Feedback on gift: how do you show people the difference their gift has made?
- What happens next: do people get put in the fundraising machine or get a bespoke welcome?
- Satisfaction of experience: do you measure how people feel about donating?
- Data capture: are you capturing the same data in all channels?

Once the mystery shopping exercise is over you can tabulate results and look at problem areas: some may have simple fixes, others may require more work. You can consider the problems by ease of solving, cost to solve and impact of solution. From this you can develop an action plan to improve the donor experience and make it consistent.

The *Australian Online Fundraising Scorecard*[1] study by Dunham+ Company highlighted a number of opportunities nonprofits are missing to improve their integration and online experience.

Here are some examples from the report:

- *Nearly two thirds (63%) of organisations did not send a single email to new subscribers within the first 30 days of signing up.*
- *96% of organisations did not send a welcome email let alone a welcome series.*
- *51% of organisations did not make a single ask in the first 90 days.*
- *Only 20% have a landing page design that matches the email.*
- *70% were not optimised for mobile viewing.*[12]

These results appear to show a lack of integration within Australian charities.

Take the first finding. We can guess that the web teams at most organisations have been asked to include a newsletter sign-up on their website. Yet no person or team has then been tasked with what to do with those data and to create an engaging experience for anyone who signs up. It is a huge missed opportunity.

CHECKLISTS

Checklists prevent professional fundraisers from making stupid mistakes. As we'll see, Craig has learned the hard way why they are so useful.

From the point of view of integration, a checklist makes sure you don't miss anything that will spoil the donor's experience with your cause.

Marketing guru Denny Hatch provides a 69-point direct marketing checklist in his book *Career Changing Takeaways!* As Denny says, '… checklists in this complex, high-tech world are indispensable'.[13]

Here are some sample questions you might want to think about when you are planning an integrated appeal:

- Has the receptionist been briefed and knows where to pass calls to?
- Is the appeal on the front page of the website?
- Has a bespoke landing page been made for donors to give through?
- Have you arranged for the landing date of your mailing, pre-appeal e-mail and telephone calls to flow in a logical sequence?
- Have you prepared appeal content for social media?
- Have you produced 'thank yous' by channel?
- Do you have a plan for donor feedback after the appeal?

These may all sound obvious, but it is amazing how often mistakes are made. We have heard of a DRTV advert being launched, but no one had told the call centre so it had closed, meaning no one could respond.

Maybe a new online appeal has been launched, but someone has forgotten to change the default e-mail message for donating. You might have your own personal disaster. Craig certainly does. A checklist would have stopped him from making one of the biggest mistakes of his career. Although not directly related to integration, it shows how checklists can help to make sure you don't miss anything when working on a project.

> *We had an appeal going out to thousands of supporters featuring a touching story about a young mum who had received end of life care by our charity. My*

colleague and I both assumed the other had sought the necessary permission from the family. We were wrong. Worse still we sent the appeal to the family of the deceased lady. As you can imagine, the family was distraught and extremely angry.

Fortunately, the local fundraising team did an amazing job to rectify the damage with the family. But I was horrified at the error and offered to resign over such an awful mistake (my resignation was refused). It was a huge lesson on never assuming anything and to check that everything needed was in place. Needless to say, I have never made such a grave error again.

TAILORING CONTENT

Just as you speak differently to your parents, colleagues, wife, friends and children (at least we hope you do), you need to tailor your content to the channel it is being promoted on.

In *Jab, Jab, Jab, Right Hook*, entrepreneur and social media guru Gary Vaynerchuk describes the importance of doing this:

> *Today, getting people to hear your story on social media, and then act on it, requires using a platform's native language, paying attention to context, understanding the nuances and subtle differences that make each platform unique, and adapting your content to match.*[14]

Think about Craig's love of ice cream and how he'd use different media to let people know:
Twitter: I love #icecream.
Facebook: I had an ice cream.
Instagram: look at my ice cream.
Four Square: this is where I ate my ice cream.
YouTube: watch me eat my ice cream.
Direct mail: here's a postcard of where I ate an ice cream

Although the differences are subtle they are important. You are missing out if you put a copy of your direct mail letter on your website and then link to it on your Twitter and Facebook page. Think about how your supporters interact with each medium and tailor your content appropriately. What will make someone 'share' or 'like' a post on Facebook (normally the image is important) or 'retweet' it on Twitter? It is going to be different to what inspires someone to write a cheque after reading a four-page letter.

The temptation with the opportunities that digital and social media offer is for us to try to reinvent the wheel. Often less is more: concentrate on getting the basics right. Digital and online fundraising expert Bryan Miller had this to say on his blog:

> Fundraising is all about inspiring people to help change the world for the better by funding your organisation's work. Online fundraising simply adds digital to the donor engagement mix. So, don't start by thinking about doing new things online. First look at the fundraising that is working for you already and consider how online activity might make it work even better...
>
> Focus first on the basics that will help you deliver more income before investing in innovation...ensuring your donation pages are really effective is likely to deliver you far more income than trialling innovative new ways to fundraise online or tinkering with your Twitter feed. The clarity that you'll gain from such focus will also mean you're far better prepared to brief your organisation's digital folks (who are often in a different silo) on the key things you need them to do to help you raise more money.[15]

APPEALS AND CAMPAIGNS

This last section is about bringing teams together to plan and execute major fundraising appeals and campaigns.

The barriers are similar to everyday integration, but the stakes are higher. If you are able to pull off large-scale integrated appeals then they can deliver transformational sums of money for your organisation.

Paul de Gregorio, from UK fundraising agency Open, has this to say about integration and fundraising campaigns:

> I think integration for campaigns means...
> Having a clear and single-minded proposition; one that can be articulated in many ways in many places to many people.
> Integration is not: a logo, a visual identity, a strap line.
> If you are integrating well you're communicating the same thing across multiple channels to multiple audiences in a variety of executions. And everyone gets it.
> If you're integrating well all your colleagues and all your agencies get it and are producing work that effortlessly feels part of your campaign. Most importantly it doesn't need to be explained.

We agree with Paul. Yet not many charities are able to pull it off in practice. This appeal and campaign integration is crucial for charities that have one main fundraising event. Think Movember (worldwide), Stand up to Cancer (USA and UK), Comic Relief (USA and UK) and telethons in individual countries around the world (the largest of which, in terms of funds raised per capita, is the Norwegian National Telethon).

These campaigns all focus brilliantly on a single fundraising message and then integrate it over as many channels as possible (they also happen to be fun to take part in).

Comic Relief

Whilst you may never be able to afford to take over a TV station in your country or attract major celebrity support, there are still some important lessons you can learn about integration by observing these campaigns.

For instance, Comic Relief in the UK has evolved since it began in 1985 and increasingly integrated its fundraising efforts. Originally, it relied principally on extensive cause-related marketing, the widespread sale of red noses, as well as their biennial Friday evening telethon, all of which prompted donations across the country. But just as the red noses have evolved over the years, so too has Comic Relief's marketing effort.

In 2007, they introduced social media into the mix and used it effectively with their partner organisations, such as the now-defunct social networking website Bebo.[16] Together, they ran a 'Big Bebo Takeover' that encouraged users to design a red home page for the site to coincide with the event. The same year, a promotion by Walkers Crisps called 'WalkEARS' invited people to purchase a pair of comedy ears. Customers visited the site in droves. With over 7 per cent of traffic coming from Bebo, the ears website became the number one charity and community destination in the UK in March 2007.

In 2009 Comic Relief's reach broadened to include digital marketing. Advances in broadband meant that, for the first time, the campaign could unfold online. A groundbreaking £65.7 million was raised by the end of the Comic Relief 'evening' in 2009, which owed a great deal to the success of the online campaign. The official website grew from 27,000 unique users on launch day to a peak of 580,000. BBC Online included daily coverage of the 'BT Red Nose Climb' up Kilimanjaro undertaken by celebrities, with video diaries beamed back to the UK. BBC iPlayer featured content from the main TV event and the CBBC site was subject to a complete Red Nose takeover that included game sharing features. Corporate partners, such as Sainsbury's, TK Maxx, BT and Subway, also had their own integrated campaigns, linked into viral social networking activity.

From this point onwards mobile phones, and the development of smart phones especially, also contributed significantly to the campaign's success. iTunes turned the singles chart red for 48 hours with 20p from any top 40 download going directly to Comic Relief, and iPhone noses and apps were made available for the first time.

Users were able to 'gift' red noses on the day via Facebook and nearly 250,000 users chose to interact with comedian and host Lenny Henry via this medium. Additionally, 175,000 people followed the Kilimanjaro climb on Twitter. E-mails, video content and digital red noses were also integrated with other communications, resulting in Comic Relief's most successful year to date.

In 2011 records were again broken as a staggering £74.3 million was raised. By this point Twitter was taking centre stage, reflecting its growing influence on society. 'Twitrelief' allowed tweeters to bid on a famous person, with the winning bidder gaining a following from their chosen celebrity. Auctions could be followed on eBay with links from celebrities through to their Twitter page. This raised £287,000.

On the radio too, presenters Chris Moyles and Comedy Dave attempted to break the 37-hours non-stop radio show record on BBC Radio 1. The stunt raised over £2.4 million, set a new world record by broadcasting for 52 hours and trended worldwide (#R1MoreMoyles) on Twitter. Facebook was central to this success, with the official site gaining over 325,000 fans.

DMS, a UK-based charity marketing agency, estimates that as much as 50 per cent of the income could have been due to social media's contribution to the integrated campaign. Similarly, market research conducted by Target Group Index found that Comic Relief and Sport Relief are the top two charities of people using social networking sites. Forty-five per cent of donors to Comic Relief are users of social networks, compared to 34 per cent for Cancer Research UK. By taking advantage of the rise in broadband connections and ensuring all digital activity is participative, Comic Relief has used this edge to tap in to the nation's conscience and make it easier for them to get involved.[17]

Bee Cause campaign

So what about charities that aren't focused on a single day or event?

One of our favourite examples of a big, bold, integrated campaign that has raised incredible amounts of money is Friends of the Earth's Bee Cause campaign.

The campaign was launched in 2012 and at the time of writing is still running. There are four main reasons we think this is a great integrated campaign:

1. 'Save Britain's bees' is a simple to understand call to action. From previous research, Friends of the Earth knew that many people were put off donating by the sense of helplessness they felt about global environmental problems. A common sentiment is: 'how could I possibly make a difference?' This campaign brings an important environmental issue right to your back garden. It is clear how you, the donor, can make a difference. Overall, it's an attention-grabbing fundraising proposition that will have introduced Friends of the Earth to audiences beyond its typical supporter base.

2. There's a clear offer that works across multiple channels, target audiences and price points. From texting in to get a 'bee saver' kit to a high-value direct mail pack, which asks for £1,000 to help set up a 'bee world', there's something for everyone to give to. Friends of the Earth have adapted the creative and made it work well across mail, inserts, tube/train panels, DRTV, social media and online petitions.

3. It's integrated across fundraising and campaigning. You can sign a petition to send to the 'bees minister' and Friends of the Earth have hosted a 'bee tea' at Westminster that attracted a record attendance from MPs for a Friends of the Earth event.

4. The bright yellow and black design gives the campaign a distinct look and stands out from other more mundane creative. When combined with the strong offer, it is a winning combination.

Since the launch of the campaign Friends of the Earth have received 43,000 donations, generated 63,000 individual actions for follow-up and recruited over 6,200 committed givers.

Joe Jenkins, director of fundraising, communications and activism at Friends of the Earth, writes about how he got the whole organisation together to work on the campaign:

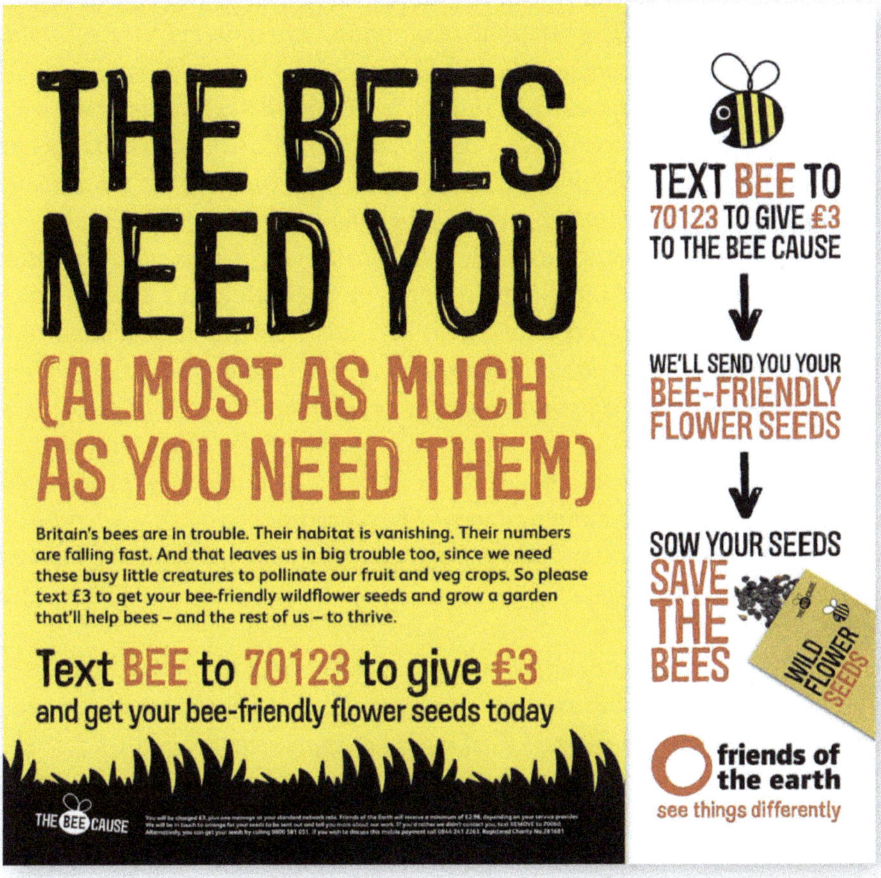
THE BEES NEED YOU
(ALMOST AS MUCH AS YOU NEED THEM)
Britain's bees are in trouble. Their habitat is vanishing. Their numbers are falling fast. And that leaves us in big trouble too, since we need these busy little creatures to pollinate our fruit and veg crops. So please text £3 to get your bee-friendly wildflower seeds and grow a garden that'll help bees – and the rest of us – to thrive.
Text BEE to 70123 to give £3
and get your bee-friendly flower seeds today
THE BEE CAUSE
TEXT BEE TO 70123 TO GIVE £3 TO THE BEE CAUSE
WE'LL SEND YOU YOUR BEE-FRIENDLY FLOWER SEEDS
SOW YOUR SEEDS
SAVE THE BEES
WILD FLOWER SEEDS
friends of the earth
see things differently

THE BEES NEED YOU
(ALMOST AS MUCH AS YOU NEED THEM)
Text BEE to 70444 to give £3
and get your bee-friendly flower seeds today
friends of the earth
see things differently

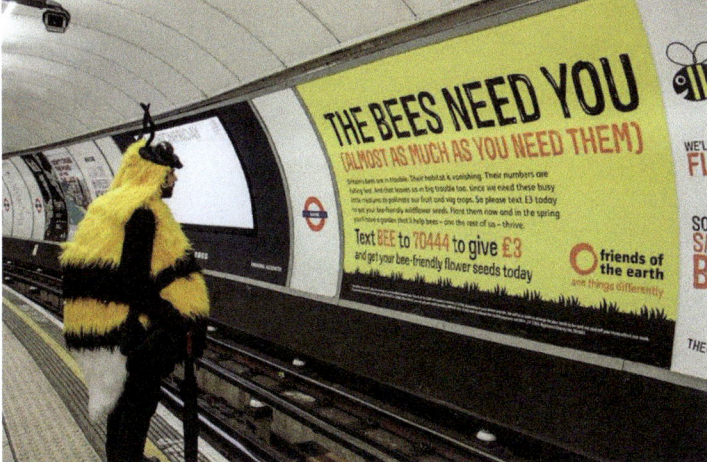

Friends of the Earth's attention-grabbing Bee Cause campaign – a winning example of integrated fundraising.

There were three key elements that really made the difference: integration, innovation and involvement.

Let's take those three 'i' words in that order. From the very outset, we were clear that the Bee Cause would not be 'owned', led, or accountable to any one team at Friends of the Earth. It would not be a policy campaign, a fundraising campaign, a brand campaign, a campaign for mobilising activists, or for recruiting new supporters. Instead, it had to be all of those things – and planned to achieve all those things from the beginning. We established a cross-organisational project team, with co-leads from the engagement and campaign areas, and set about creating a strategy and plan that could deliver real world change in a way that would involve as many people as possible in our cause.

Nothing that followed would have been possible without that clear expectation from the start that this campaign would be co-created – internally, and also with people outside the staff body; from activists to agencies, we've worked closely with a wide range of different people who have all made its success possible.

As non-negotiable as integration was our commitment to innovation. Every aspect of the campaign, from the working model to individual tactics, would require new ideas, new ways of working, new approaches and attitudes. The activity team and everyone involved in the campaign were given permission to try stuff out. We knew lots of things wouldn't work, and that was OK; the key was to back the stuff that did. For example, no one predicted in advance how popular free wildflower seeds might be; the success was to recognise they were working, and quickly scale up then roll out.

In many ways though, it's the last 'i' that I feel mattered the most. The purpose of the campaign was always to achieve a bigger job than 'just' saving the bee. We know that if we're to turn around the destruction of our environment we need people to start reconnecting with nature. Not just intellectually, but emotionally. The Bee Cause had to stir up the heart, as well as the mind, which meant finding ways for people to get directly involved in the campaign. So for two years, we've been trying different means for anyone to do something personally to save bees, as well as call on government to do likewise. From bee breakfast events to bee walks to bee worlds – and a lot of wildflower seeds in between – we've found the campaign really capturing people's imagination. It wouldn't have worked if it hadn't.

To date, tens of thousands of people have got involved with the campaign, practically, politically and emotionally. As a direct result, the government has agreed to our call for a bee action plan, and we now believe we really could be the generation that saves the bee.

But the point is that the campaign hasn't been successful (just) because people like bees. I believe the same outcomes can be achieved with any issue; as long as you build a campaign upon those same three elements. Join up from the start, create the space for new creativity and above all, find the emotional connection with your audience.[18]

Emergency appeals

When an emergency strikes then charities need to act quickly, both in terms of service response and the fundraising required to pay for it.

This means they need to integrate their fundraising efforts to make sure they are reaching as many potential donors as possible.

The earthquake in Nepal in 2015 showed how quickly the biggest charities now respond (from a fundraising perspective) when a disaster hits.

Despite it happening early on a Saturday morning UK time, we received our first e-mail asking for donations from a charity within 12 hours. An impressive response time and a sign of excellent emergency procedures being in place.

A colleague of Craig's tracked the response of a dozen or so NGOs and all had been in touch with a relevant fundraising ask within 48 hours of the disaster.

Paul knew the importance of a speedy, integrated response when working at WJR. WJR mobilises the resources of the UK Jewish community to assist those affected by disasters around the globe, regardless of race, religion, or ethnicity.

WJR has been refining its emergency appeal procedures for a number of years, testing and incorporating new media at every opportunity to build a more effectively coordinated response each time. Their results demonstrate the potential of integrated campaigns from a medium sized organisation on a tight timeframe and a limited budget.

The charity grades its appeals based on the severity, scale and profile of the disaster or emergency. The highest, level one, is reserved for the most significant natural or human catastrophes. In these instances, the charity would utilise the greatest number of media channels and invest the largest sums in advertising. For example, the Haiti earthquake of 2010 and the Philippines typhoon of 2013 both had devastating effects on their local populations and gained widespread and prolonged media coverage. The charity responded accordingly, investing time and resources into each appeal for several weeks, whilst working to maintain its core activities and meet its designated targets.

Rapid responses are critical to emergency appeals and their immediacy and effective co-ordination are essential factors in maximising income and acquisition. Delays of just a single day can have a hugely detrimental effect on both revenue and the charity's ability to attract new supporters.

In the case of both disasters, the charity constructed a formal appeal within 24 hours and promoted a single, unified appeal message across a range of media. This included direct mail, digital and offline advertising, social media and mobile. They also activated all their networks, employing a 'top down, bottom up' approach of engaging the main communal bodies, as well as grassroots synagogues, social groups and individual volunteers.

The results were impressive. After the Haiti earthquake the charity acquired nearly 1,000 new supporters, expanding its active database by nearly 10 per cent. Similarly, following the Philippines typhoon, WJR gained more than 600 new supporters and reactivated a further 900 donors. The income raised was also substantial.

The charity used the size of its target audience, the UK Jewish community, as a benchmark. Numbering 250,000, this represents roughly 0.35 per cent of the national population. Yet the charity managed to raise over £520,000 for the victims of the Haiti earthquake and over £600,000 for those affected by typhoon Haiyan in the Philippines. This represented 0.49 per cent and 0.70 per cent respectively of the funds generated by the UK population as a whole.

So WJR's integrated appeals ensured a positively disproportionate response from the community. And both campaigns were executed with limited resources and spend, each one costing around £15,000.

Significantly, on lower level appeals, when the charity invested less and did not employ a fully integrated approach, returns were far lower. The Burma cyclone appeal of 2008, for example, generated £75,000. This was 0.38 per cent of the funds generated by UK contributions as a whole and proportionate to the UK Jewish population.

CONCLUSION: INTEGRATION IS MORE IMPORTANT THAN EVER

There is no lack of guidance available on integration but the sector still has a long way to go to get this right. Many organisations still work in silos and are not being bold enough in their attempts to integrate their resources and engagement activities effectively. Whilst the challenges are great, in terms of the practical considerations and the investment required, the opportunities are clear.

Those charities that are able to achieve everyday integration and develop transformative integrated appeals and campaigns will be on the road to fundraising success.

Relationship fundraisers needs to be brave and to do everything in their power to make integrated fundraising and campaigns the norm in their organisation.

NOTES
1. The home of Ben & Jerry's. And, yes, I have visited the original shop!
2. Dunham, Trent (2015) *The imperative of integrated fundraising*. Available at: http://www.givinginstitute.org/news/222095/The-Imperative-of-Integrated-Fundraising.htm Last accessed 7 June 2015.
3. Belford, Tom *Telemarketing success…and more*, The Agitator URL http://www.theagitator.net/nonprofit-management/more-telemarketing-success/ Last accessed 18 March 2017
4. Convio and StrategicOne (2007) *Integrating Online Marketing (eCRM) with Direct Mail Fundraising*, Austin, Texas.
5. Network for Good, *The 2015 Online Fundraising Report*. Available at: http://learn.networkforgood.org/2015-online-fundraising-report.html accessed?
6. Brooks, Jeff (2011) *Your silos are going to kill you*, Future Fundraising Now blog, December 2011. Available at: http://www.futurefundraisingnow.com/future-fundraising/2011/12/your-silos-are-going-to-kill-you.html Last accessed 27 October 2016..
7. MacLaughlin, Steve (2011) commenting on *Online 'fundraising' a misnomer*, The Agitator, December 2011. Available at: http://www.theagitator.net/online-fundraising/online-fundraising-a-misnomer/#comment-128187 Last accessed 13 June 2015.
8. As quoted in *Pixar headquarters and the legacy of Steve Jobs*, Office Snapshots, July 2012. Available at: http://officesnapshots.com/2012/07/16/pixar-headquarters-and-the-legacy-of-steve-jobs/ Last accessed 14 June 2015.
9. Ross, Bernard and Segal, Clare (2002) *Breakthrough Thinking for Nonprofit Organizations*, Jossey-Bass, San Francisco.
10. Ibid, p. 185.
11. Bhagat, Vinay (2011) *Integrated Multi-Channel Marketing*, Convio, Austin, Texas.
12. Dunham+Company (2014) *The Australian Online Fundraising Scorecard: A national study analysing online fundraising habits and donor experience*, December 2014. Available at: http://www.dunhamandcompany.com/2014/12/australian-online-fundraising-scorecard/#sthash.MhRYXk7C.taQXAoav.dpbs Last accessed 14 June 2015.
13. Hatch, Denny (2011) *Career Changing Takeaways!* Direct Marketing IQ, Philadelphia p. 32.
14. Vaynerchuk, Gary (2013) *Jab, Jab, Jab, Right Hook* Harper Collins, New York.
15. Miller, Bryan(2014) *Are organisational silos blocking your online fundraising growth?* Giving in a Digital World, March 2014. Available at: http://givinginadigitalworld.org/2014/03/13/charity-silos-blocking-online-fundraising-growth/ Last accessed 25 June 2015.
16. Bebo was bigger than Facebook in the UK for a number of years in the mid-00s. It is no longer a social network, but creates social apps.
17. Taylor, Rachael (2011) *How Comic Relief has benefited from social media*, Red C, https://fundraising.co.uk/2009/05/07/red-nose-day-09-digital-campaign/#.WKxev4XluQR https://en.wikipedia.org/wiki/Red_Nose_Day_2011 http://fundraising.co.uk/2011/03/18/half-today039s-red-nose-day-donations-expected-come-social-network-sites-says-agency/#.WBZyuIXXIcA
18. De Gregorio, Paul (2015) More than matching collars and cuffs Available at: http://degregoriopaul.blogspot.co.uk/2015/05/more-than-matching-collars-and-cuffs.html Last accessed 7 August 2016.
19. As featured on the Institute of Fundraising blog. Available at: http://www.institute-of-fundraising.org.uk/blog/behind-the-bee-cause-more-than-just-bees/

Friends for life: welcoming and keeping your donors

The hard work really begins after you have persuaded and inspired someone to give to your cause for the first time. As we discussed in chapter 1 in mature fundraising markets around 30–60 per cent of regular givers will stop giving in their first year of donating. For cash givers around 50-70 per cent will only give once.

This is a huge problem that demands a solution.

However before we give you some answers, it is important to remind ourselves why donors stop giving.

Let's rewind to chapter 3 and the four factors there that Professor Adrian Sargeant and his colleagues identified in 2001 as reasons donors stop giving:

- Attraction by competition – a pressing appeal e.g. the tsunami in 2005, or communications from another charity that the donor finds inherently more appealing.

- Poor quality of service – not responding to communications, incorrectly addressing mail, not providing feedback.

- Poor relationship quality – not taking into account the wishes of the donor, asking for inappropriate amounts, communications at the wrong time of year, etc.

- Lost to market – natural attrition through death, moving away, or change in financial circumstances.

Let's take a closer look at the numbers behind this summary:

Reasons why donors terminate their support in the USA and UK[1]

Reason	UK (%)	USA (%)
I can no longer afford to offer my support	22.3	54.0
I feel that other causes are more deserving	26.5	36.2
Death/relocation	23.1	16.0
No memory of ever supporting	11.4	18.4
X did not acknowledge my support	0.9	13.2
X did not inform me how my money has been used	1.7	8.1
X no longer needs my support	1.2	5.6
The quality of support provided by X was poor	0.9	5.1
X asked for inappropriate sums	3.1	4.3
I found X's communications inappropriate	3.6	3.8
X did not take account of my wishes	0.7	2.6
Staff were unhelpful	0.5	2.1

Note: People could give more than one answer to the survey, which is why the total is more than 100 per cent.

Whilst we can't do much about death, every other factor can be influenced by the quality of the relationship we build with the donor.

You might think that there isn't much you can do about 'can no longer afford'. However, if a donor gives to 10 charities your job as fundraiser is to make sure that your cause is the last one to be cut from his or her list when times are hard.

Think about your own behaviour. If you've ever had to tighten your belt financially, then think about how you approached the task. Did you cancel all your donations and luxury items, or did you find a way to keep those things that mattered most to you emotionally? When Craig had to undergo such a task to save for his wedding he cut out three and three remained. Which three stayed? Those that meant the most to him emotionally and who had inspired him to stay through their communications and feedback.

The same goes for people who relocate. Do you make it easy for them to get in touch? Does your cause mean so much to them that they let you know they have moved (as they would with a friend)? If they do let you know, do you record this on your database? Someone who actively tells you about moving is likely to be a loyal and committed donor. On a more practical level, there are data services that may be able to screen your gone-away list and find new addresses for donors. This can often be a cost-effective way to improve your retention rates.

PREVENTION NOT CURE

One of the big mistakes we make as fundraisers is that we only respond to the problem of loss once a donor stops giving. Like a spurned lover, we make pleading phone calls, send heartfelt letters and e-mails, urge the donor to give us another chance and to give again so that we can show we've changed. We will discuss the best way to approach reactivating donors in chapter 18.

It would be much better to start our retention efforts long before a donor stops his or her giving. In fact, retention starts from the moment a donor first gives.

Let's take a look at a couple of models that help us understand this.

According to management consultancy company Bain & Company, 'churn' (attrition in the commercial world and the sort of jargon that customers, or more particularly donors, might not find encouraging) is caused by the cumulative experiences of a customer over a number of interactions. They use the following model (see figure 11.1) to demonstrate why 'churn' happens.[2]

The churn model: Churn results from the cumulative experience of many episodes
Source: Bain & Company.

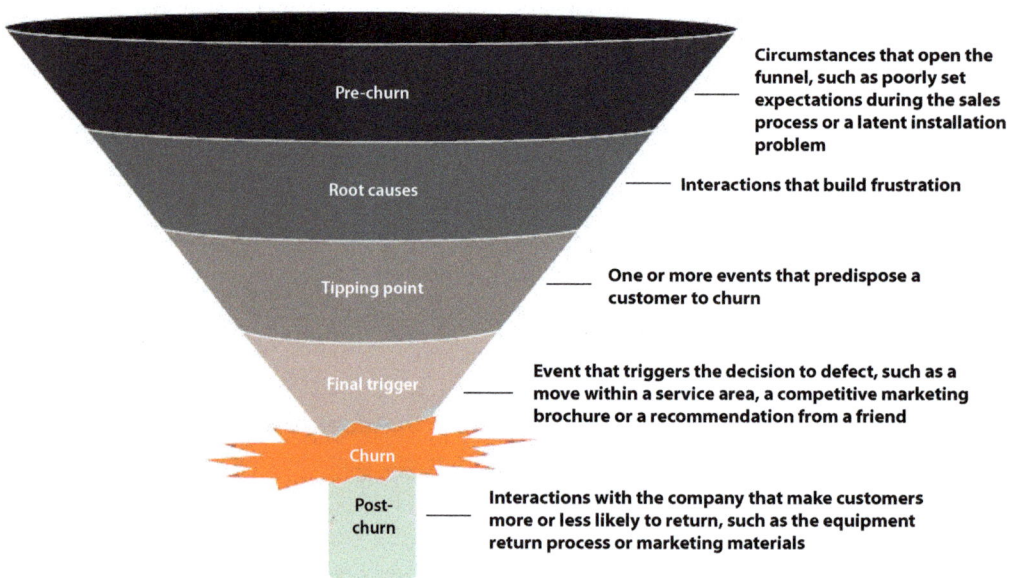

They explain how this churn model applies in the communication services sector (TV, internet, phone providers, etc) in the US:

> *When we ask communications executives what causes their customers to defect, they often point to the last thing that happened before the customer left. Often, that's a competitor's promotional offer. Competitive offers do sometimes lure customers to switch, but typically after a long period of eroding trust that results from a series of misadventures ranging from a poor installation to spotty network performance to a faulty bill. These customers have already been primed to leave by the time an attractive offer arrives, so that any change in their lives, such as moving to a new house, can bring that decision to a head. The episodes that condition a customer to dislike his or her provider and the actual decision to leave can be years apart.*
> *Treating only the last episode or two rarely leads to a complete solution that addresses the customer's discontent.[3]*

The report goes on to explain five fallacies that derail churn reduction efforts:[4]

1. One or two poor episodes cause churn.
2. Intervention at any point can save the day.
3. One silver bullet will stop churn.
4. Satisfying customers is good enough.
5. Success hinges on installing the right technology and processes.

We believe these five fallacies also apply in the fundraising world. Let's take a look at a hypothetical (but sadly all too common) experience that a donor may have with a nonprofit (figure 11.1).

Typically, when a donor has stopped giving he or she is put into a 'lapsed' file whilst efforts are made to encourage the donor to start giving again. Often this is via the phone (although in the following example the donor has told the charity not to call her) and fundraisers are usually happy if 10-15 per cent of the donors they call will give the charity a second chance.

We are lucky that donors are often so benevolent and forgiving. If a commercial company treated customers the way many charities treat their donors they would be soon out of business.

This doesn't need to be the case though. There are so many opportunities along the way to remind the donor why she signed up in the first place and make her

Figure 11.1: A journey that leads to attrition

feel good about giving.

Let's look at another model to help us understand why retention starts from the first interaction that a donor has with your organisation.

This model comes from the work Kevin Schulman from DonorVoice has done on donor loyalty and commitment[5].

Schulman argues that a donor's commitment and loyalty is the sum result of all the experiences the donor has with a charity. These experiences connect on a functional and personal level and influence overall commitment.

Roger Craver defines functional and personal connection in his book *Retention Fundraising* as follows:

> **Functional Connection.** *The journey begins with the desire on the part of the donor to establish a basic (what social scientists call 'functional') connection with your organization.*

The main characteristics of a successful functional connection are reliability and consistency. The donor comes to know what he or she can reliably expect from you, and that experiences with your organization are consistent.

Personal Connection. *This is the more emotional part of the relationship. Personal connections are actions you take to make the donor feel an important part of the cause – things like giving recognition, seeking the donor's opinion, sending timely and relevant communications, and offering other forms of involvement. In the vernacular of the social scientists, personal connection is the 'fidelity' part of a relationship. The bond saying there's a two-way street of give and take, of mutual respect, with the donor believing the organization knows him or her and truly cares.[6]*

Putting this together means we have the following model to understand donor commitment and behaviour (figure 11.2).

As we showed in chapter 3, highly committed donors give more in the long term than those with low commitment. Therefore, we have to make sure that

Figure 11.2: Donor Commitment model
Adapted from DonorVoice's Commitment Model'

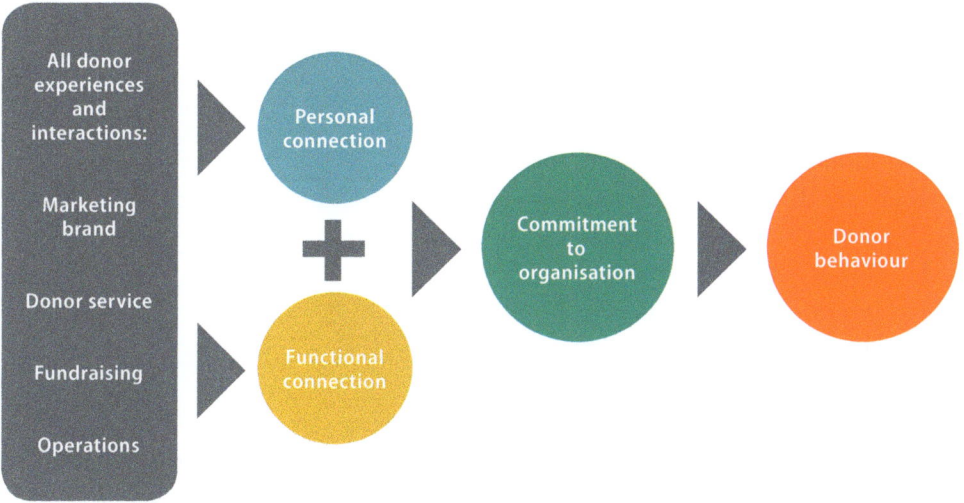

everything we do improves the personal and functional connection people feel towards our cause.

DRIVERS OF DONOR COMMITMENT AND HOW TO MEASURE IT

Every relationship fundraiser needs to know what influences these two connections. It is crucial to long-term fundraising success and making friends for life.

In *Retention Fundraising*, Roger Craver explains how DonorVoice narrowed down 32 possible criteria to the following seven most influential factors on commitment. We list them again here:

- Donor perceives your organisation to be effective in trying to achieve its mission.
- Donor knows what to expect from your organisation with each interaction.
- Donor receives timely 'thank yous'.
- Donor receives opportunities to make his or her views known.
- Donor is given the feeling that he or she is part of an important cause.
- Donor feels his or her involvement is appreciated.
- Donor receives information showing who she, or he, is helping.

By constantly referring to these seven factors and trying to apply them in your fundraising you will raise more money. Of course, you can spend your charity's money on finding out what the most influential factors are for your donor base, but we'd guess the findings won't be too different from the above.

Next we'd like to help you put in place the tools to measure donor loyalty and retention.

Measuring donor loyalty

There are three measures that every relationship fundraiser needs to know:

1. Donor retention rate
2. Donor commitment
3. Lifetime value (LTV)

Donor retention rate

Your donor retention rate is the number of people who give from one year to the next. If 100 people give in year one and then 63 give the following year then your retention rate would be 63 per cent.

The table 11.2 demonstrates the difference having a high retention rate can make to your income.

Table 11.2: The effect on income of low donor retention

Year	High retention donor numbers	Low retention donor numbers
0	1,000	1,000
1	600	500
2	540	400
3	486	320
4	437	256
5	394	205
Total donations	3,457	2,681
Total income	£69,141	£53,616
Difference	£15,525	29%

In this example, the high retention charity has a first year retention rate of 60 per cent and a subsequent retention rate of 90 per cent. The low retention charity has a first year retention of 50 per cent and a subsequent retention rate of 80 per cent. With an average gift of £20, the high retention charity has nearly double the donors and 29 per cent more income after five years. This is a huge difference.

As well as considering donor retention, you can also measure income retention, which is done in a similar way. You look at how much money the 1,000 donors donated in the subsequent year instead of how many donors remain. When used in conjunction with donor retention, income retention shows if you have increased the value of donations per donor. The theory being that a good communications programme will not only keep a donor loyal but inspire him or her to give more.

Measuring donor commitment

According to *Retention Fundraising* this is easier than you might imagine. You just need to ask donors how much they agree (on a scale of 1 to 10, where 10 is strongly agree) to the following three statements:

1   I am a committed (insert your organisation name) donor.
2   I feel a sense of loyalty to (insert your organisation name).
3   (Insert your organisation name) is my favourite charitable organisation.

Work out the mean of the three answers and you have your commitment score. Donors scoring between 8 to and 10 are high commitment and those under 5 are low commitment.

You can gather the scores through online surveys, telephone and in surveys in direct mail packs.

It is hard to get scores for everyone on your database, so you can use modelling to help you work out segments of donors with high and low commitment.

Retention Fundraising then explains the three ways you can use the score and other feedback to inform your fundraising:

> **Resource allocation.** *Shifting time and spending away from experiences and activities that don't matter. For example, you may find your organization's expensive magazine really doesn't matter to your donors, or that they couldn't care less about institutional messages declaring you have 10 regional offices or are the largest organization in your sector.*
> **Optimizing the experience.** *After identifying experiences that do matter, you want to offer them in the best way you can. For example, you may find that improvements in your 'thank you' and 'welcoming' process lead to higher commitment.*
> **Target.** *Commitment scores, whether collected on a survey or through questions on all other communications (online, offline), can be used to better focus time and money on those donors most likely to be responsive—the highly committed.*[7]

We will provide a framework for building your retention and commitment plan later in the chapter. This will help you employ the three ways to use the score in a systematic and strategic way.

Lifetime value

Lifetime value (LTV) is a longstanding and important concept. It is simply the net income a donor will give over the entirety of their time supporting your cause. Using LTV lets you calculate an acceptable donor acquisition cost and allows you to compare the long-term impact of different recruitment methods.

It can be used retrospectively or predicatively to look at how much a particular donor, segment, or acquisition campaign has or could raise.

One of the mistakes many charities make is focusing on the short term and making decisions that may impact negatively on long-term income. We believe trustees and chief executives should be using lifetime value as a key indicator of fundraising performance.

Calculating lifetime vale is relatively straightforward:

LTV = all income received/predicted from the donor – all costs associated with maintaining the relationship.

If you want to add a level of sophistication then you can also add in a 'discount rate'. This discounts the future value of the donation to reflect the uncertainty involved, inflation and interest that could be earned from investing the money elsewhere. It is also normal to limit the calculation to a certain period of time.

You can use the calculation for individual donors. However, it is most commonly used to look at discrete donor segments. For example, direct mail may have a donor recruitment cost that is 30 per cent lower than street fundraising. However, if attrition and the costs of maintaining the relationship are high then street fundraising may prove a better investment over a five-year period.

Craig used LTV to build a business case for further investment in donor acquisition at one charity he worked with. Using 15 years of data he was able to demonstrate that investing in fundraising raised significantly larger sums than investing in the stock or bond market. For example, he was able to show that for every 10,000 donors recruited by mail, the charity could expect between 50 and 100 legacies over a 20-year period. This was worth millions of pounds and helped win the debate with trustees.

A word about recency, frequency, value (RFV)
For many years, RFV has been used effectively by fundraising teams to segment their database. Here we explain the theory and give an example of why it remains useful, but also describe some of its shortcomings.
First of all, this is what we mean by RFV:

- Recency: the length of time that has elapsed since the donor last made a gift.
- Frequency: how often donations are made within a given period.
- Value: the size of the gift, either of the last donation, or, more typically,

the largest contribution the donor has made either as a one-off gift, or cumulatively in a given period.

Note: it is also known as RFM, where the 'M' stands for monetary value.

World Jewish Relief used RFV successfully to evaluate the state of their database. The results, which can be seen in table 11.3, were very revealing. They highlighted a number of gaps in the development of donors. Many of the gaps are common in one form or another to most charities.

The key findings were as follows:

- A large number of new supporters only ever made one gift.

- The charity was failing to take account of supporter habits and preferences. This meant they were mailing them more often than was necessary, or at times when they traditionally had never supported the organisation. Apart from wasting funds, this was in effect employing a *churn and burn* approach, flooding supporters with excessive requests, causing them to lapse, presumably as a result of disenchantment.

- World Jewish Relief had a significant number of mid-value supporters below its major giving threshold that it was not treating in an appropriate fashion. Therefore they failed to maximise returns from this segment.

Using these findings the charity was able to improve its targeting, provide a more-tailored donor experience and make a renewed effort to secure second gifts. In particular, see chapter 15, for how they capitalised on the large number of mid-value donors and prospects on their database.

However, although RFV can be a useful barometer of the state of your database, it should not be the only way you look at donors.

Perhaps the biggest issue with using RFV is that it takes no account of how the donor may feel about you. It's also entirely retrospective in its approach and tells us little about how donors may behave in the future.

Fundraising copywriter and consultant Tom Gaffny spoke about this problem at Blackbaud's npNEXT conference in the USA in 2015.[8]

He gave the example of two donors with the same income profile who would

Table 11.3 - World Jewish Relief RFV analysis

ACTIVE Segment	Total value of all gifts in the last 12 months	Number of supporters
First donation in the last 12 months (single gift)	£48,680.11	957
MID VALUE A Committed Givers (given cumulatively £50 - £149.99 in last 12 months)	£48,495.44	443
CORE Multiple gifts of £1 - £49.99 donated in last 12 months	£74,367.67	1316
MID VALUE A Single gift of £50 - £149.99 donated in last 12 months	£87,966.24	1189
MID VALUE B Single gift of £150 - £499.99 donated in last 12 months	£80,933.36	433

STATIC	Total value of all gifts during the period	Number of supporters
New to database in last year - no gift		575
Gave over 12 - 24 months ago - CORE Multiple gifts (£1 - £49.99 donated accumatively INCLUDING direct debits now cancelled)	£15,819.46	335
Gave over 12 - 24 months ago - MID VALUE A Single gift (£50 - £149.99)	£59,800.67	827
Gave over 12 - 24 months ago - MID VALUE B Single gift (£150 - £499.99)	£42,366.86	224

LAPSED	Total value of all gifts during the period	Number of supporters
Gave once 2 to 4 years ago CORE value	£29,124.26	1320
Gave once 2 to 4 years ago MID VALUE A	£83,182.18	1102
Gave more than once, last gift 2 to 4 years ago CORE value	£17,949.26	337
Gave more than once, last gift 2 to 4 years ago MID VALUE A	£32,669.75	200

be treated exactly the same under RFV.

Mrs Smith	Mrs Jones
Started giving in 2012	Gave $250 in 2012
Gives twice a year ($200 total)	Gives twice a year ($200 total)
Doesn't volunteer	Doesn't volunteer
Attended a special event	Attended a special event

Both donors currently look identical from a transactional point of view. However when you add some relational and loyalty data the picture looks different:

Mrs Smith	Mrs Jones
Gives to only two to three charities	Gives to lots of organisations
Gives you twice as much as she gives to others	Gives more to others than to you

Which donor would you predict to have higher commitment to the charity?

If you can identify those donors who have high passion for your cause then it gives a whole new approach to segmentation and might make you reallocate where you put your time and effort.

Rather than only using RFV to rank our donors, Gaffny encouraged us to flip the problem on its head and consider how to measure how donors rank you. This is the problem the commitment and loyalty questions outlined earlier try to address.

Gaffny describes how one organisation had used this relational data to target a segment previously neglected by RFV analysis. By selecting high passion donors for a planned giving campaign (and who would have been ignored by their traditional RFV selection criteria) they achieved a 300 per cent increase in the response rate.

A LOYALTY AND RELATIONSHIP FUNDRAISING FRAMEWORK TO CREATE FRIENDS FOR LIFE

So far in this chapter we have looked at why donors stop giving, what influences donor loyalty and commitment; and what measurements you need to have in place to assess your fundraising.

The next part provides a framework you can use to plan how to implement relationship fundraising in your organisation. To do this we have combined the seven key drivers of loyalty with the six elements of relationship fundraising. This creates the following matrix:

	Why	Storytelling	Relationship building	Asking and thanking properly	Donor care/magic	Data
Donor perceives your organisation to be effective in trying to achieve its mission						
Donor knows what to expect from your organisation with each interaction						
Donor receives timely 'thank yous'						
Donor receives opportunities to make his or her views known						
Donor is given the feeling that he or she is part of an important cause						
Donor feels his or her involvement is appreciated						
Donor receives information showing who is being helped						

Using the matrix is straightforward. Think how you can use the six elements of relationship fundraising to improve each of the seven drivers of loyalty.

For example, you may want to improve your retention of donors who donate by SMS. You can look at each of the seven factors from the point of view of the six elements of relationship fundraising. So you might see how you could use data better (more personalisation, recording first names, etc) to make the donor feel that he or she is part of an important cause. Not every element will be relevant for every situation, but approaching the task in a systematic manner will help you improve your retention efforts.

When undertaking this task you need to think about fundraising channels and messages and put yourself in the donor's shoes. Ask yourself: what would you like/dislike/feel indifferent about the current giving experience in your organisation?

To try and do this for your entire fundraising programme may seem a bit daunting. That's why we recommend you use the framework to look at one aspect of your fundraising at a time. To help you further we are going to provide some more tools and ideas on how to use the framework and give you some examples across every area of fundraising.

Mapping your current processes and supporter journeys

The framework works well in partnership with the following process mapping exercise. It may sound a bit daunting, but it's actually just a fancy way of looking at how everything in your charity inter-relates, and it highlights places where you can improve your donor's experience. It's particularly useful in large organisations where decisions made in one department can have unintended consequences on other parts of the organisation.

Think back to the examples in chapter 5. Would Pamela's nonprofit have been so awful at tracking memorial gifts if they'd mapped out a process for it? We think not. Would Lucy's charity have been more likely to do something about the language they used and the frustration their processes caused if they had systematically mapped out the way to do certain things? Yes, it probably would have.

On a related note, we know of one charity where the finance department was in charge of banking donations and thanking donors. They took (in their eyes) the logical decision to stop sending thank-you letters, believing it would save money. From their point of view it was a sensible decision, but from the fundraisers' and donors' point of view it was a disaster. Donors never received feedback on their gift and no commitment was built. So what happened when the next solicitation arrived? The donor ignored it and didn't give again.

Using our matrix the charity had failed in 'donor receives timely thank yous' and 'donor feels his or her involvement is appreciated' by not using the why, storytelling, thanking properly and donor magic to create a good experience.

Here, adapted from the book *Outside In* by Manning and Bodine,[9] is the five-step process we have used and recommend for mapping out your donor 'ecosystem' and highlighting problems within it:

First step: pick an important target donor and think of a problematic journey for that donor. For example, what happens if she cancels her direct debit, or how do you thank a donor after her first gift and then encourage her to make a second gift to your charity? Make sure you understand the current process well before starting.

Second step: write down the series of actions the donor takes as part of the problematic journey. For example, a welcome process might have the following actions:
- 'Receives standard thank-you letter', 'wonders why it has taken a month'.
- 'Receives an appeal six weeks later', 'asks what the charity has done with his original gift', 'decides not to give until he receives feedback'.
- 'Receives a phone call asking him to give', 'decides not to give again as thinks charity "too pushy" and not sure he is making a difference'.

Write these on post-it notes and put them across the top of a big sheet of paper.

Third step: write down all the people and groups your donor interacts with at each step – fundraiser, telephone operator, receptionist, etc. Do the same thing for the objects or systems the donor touches – such as letter, telephone, website. Again, put these on post-it notes (ideally of differing colours) and add them to your piece of paper.

Fourth step: draw a line across the paper under the notes placed so far. This is the 'line of visibility' – below this line are all the things the donor can't see. Your database system, internal processes, etc. Repeat step three for all the actions, people, groups, objects and systems that support the above the line parts of the 'ecosystem'.

Fifth step: next rate how you do at each step of the process from the perspective of the person (donor and staff) interacting with it. What is going well (green), what not so well (amber) and what is causing unhappiness (red). What nearly always happens is the donor interactions go red first and often the internal interactions might be amber or even green, meaning people internally are oblivious to the problems their processes are causing the donor.

Once you've done this, you can then start taking actions to turn the red dots green and so improve the donor experience.

Similar to this is the concept of donor journeys, which map out the interactions you have with a donor when they sign up to a fundraising product, such as child sponsorship, or when they make a donation for the first time.

Here are some examples of possible supporter journeys you can map out:

- First cash gift, thank you and welcome process (online and offline)
- Regular giver, thank you and welcome process
- Running/challenge event participant
- Sponsor of running/challenge event participant
- In-memoriam giver
- When someone pledges to leave a legacy
- Charity shop donor
- Event organiser
- Special event (e.g. gala dinner) donor
- Volunteer fundraiser
- Upgrade and retention journey for cash givers
- Upgrade and retention journey for regular givers
- Re-engagement journey for people who have stopped giving
- Major donor
- Mid-value donor
- Corporate supporter

Craig used the process to revamp the donor journey for people who donate on his charity's website using the same process. Figure 11.4 shows what the journey looked like beforehand.

The process was too basic, didn't properly thank donors and tended to cast them adrift on a sea of apathy. It failed in all seven elements of building donor loyalty. Figure 11.5 shows how the process looked like afterwards.

Implementing this process increased the number of second gifts by over 20 per cent and provided a much improved donor experience.
Let's take a closer look at how this new process increased donor commitment:

- We used storytelling during the phone call to make an appropriate thank you.
- We improved the quality of the data to make donors feel important.

Friends for life: welcoming and keeping your donors

Figure 11.4 The initial RLSB website donor supporter journey

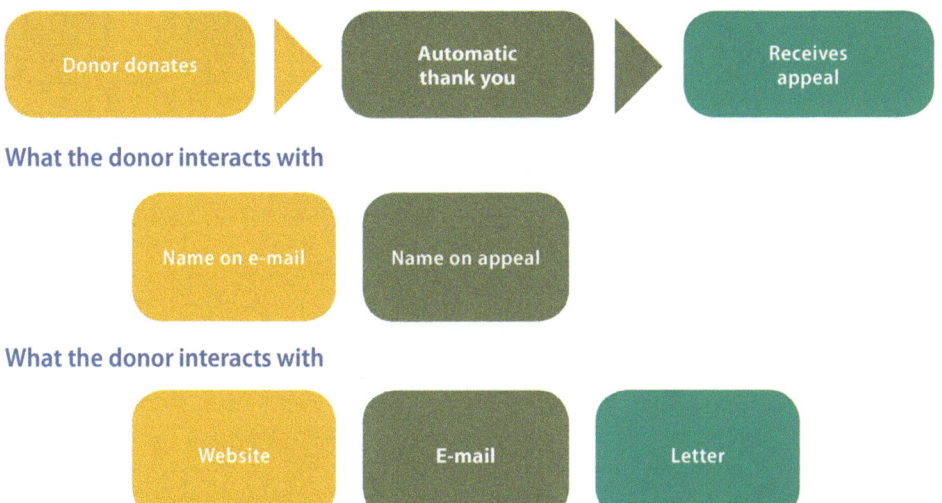

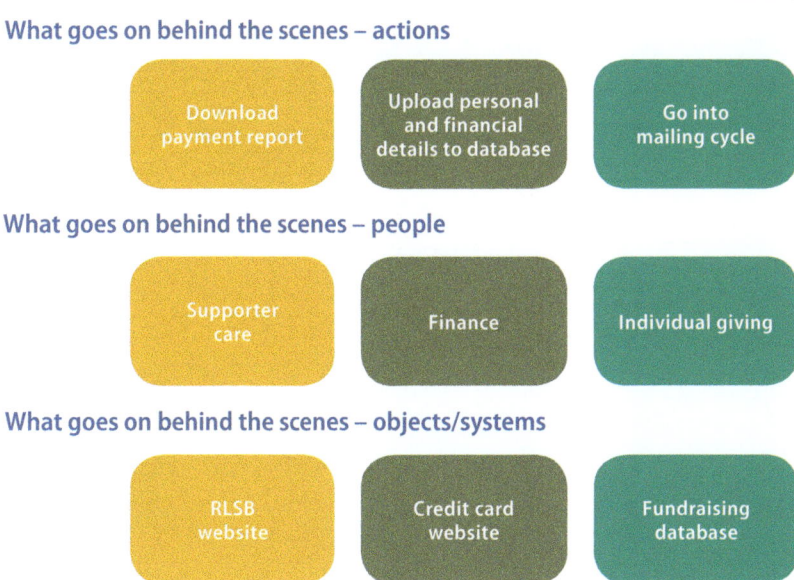

Figure 11.5 Revised RLSB website donor supporter journey

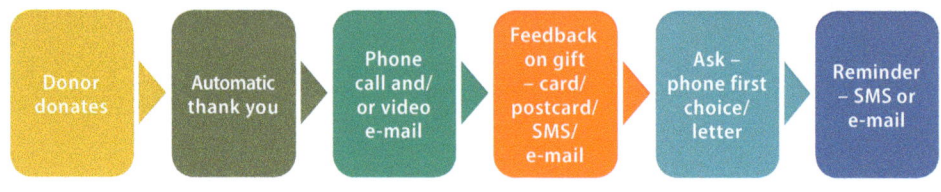

- We put in some donor magic to surprise and delight donors by asking for feedback and making donors feel their interaction was important.
- We reminded people of our 'why' to demonstrate the donor was part of an important cause.
- Finally, we asked properly, at the right time, for a further gift.

Supporter journeys: a warning
'Supporter journey' is another fundraising buzzword that needs to be approached with caution. We have heard of horror stories of charities spending hundreds of thousands of pounds on fancy welcome programmes that didn't improve retention; mainly because the charity and agency involved hadn't taken the time to understand what experiences were important to the donor. Instead, the fundraiser's own view was imposed on the donors and the seven drivers of loyalty were not considered.

When embarking on any changes, we would urge you to put in place measures so you can assess the impact they have on your retention.

THANKING AND WELCOMING NEW DONORS
You only get one chance to make a first impression. That's why how you thank and welcome donors to your organisation is so important. If you don't inspire them from the beginning and build a level of trust, loyalty and commitment then your future retention efforts are likely to be futile.

As we showed earlier in the chapter, somewhat surprisingly, the speed of thank you is more important than the quality; although we are big believers in achieving both.

So how quickly should you get thank-you letters out?

It should be quite possible for most organisations to turn them around in a maximum of 48 hours. Craig has been told many times that this is 'impossible' and been given a long list of reasons why. Yet with a change of priorities, processes and hard work, this has been achievable in every organisation he has worked at. Indeed, one team managed to get over 80 per cent of letters out on the same day the gift arrived.

Of course, not all thank yous come by the post these days. In fact, the fundraiser's best retention friend when it comes to thanking is the telephone.

In an interview with SOFII, Chuck Longfield, chief scientist at database vendor Blackbaud, revealed that:

> *...simply calling and thanking your new donors increases both renewals and average gifts. Even leaving a thank-you message on a new donor's answering machine increases giving. Though not by much, so…it's worth calling back at least once before leaving a message.*[10]

This confirmed findings by respected fundraising author Penelope Burk, in her classic book *Donor Centred Fundraising*.[11] This research showed that a call from a board member within 24 hours of a gift increased gift income to the next appeal by 39 per cent. Fourteen months later donors who received the call had given 42 per cent more than donors who weren't called.

The hard part of this is getting board members to participate! However, a call from any member of staff as soon as possible after the gift will boost retention and subsequent donations.

This is demonstrated by analysis from UK telephone agency Pell & Bales. They have made hundreds of thousands of calls to donors and analysed the impact thank-you calls have on retention.

Figures 11.6 and 11.7 show the short-term impact of a call and the long-term difference (over 16 months) that calling donors early in the relationship can make.[12]

So what are the ingredients of a good thank-you call? Pell & Bales share the following secrets:[13]

- Design a call that is about the donor, not about the charity and definitely not about fundraising or the charity needs. The aim is to make giving feel good, rewarding, involving and impactful.

- Allow yourself a budget, time and resources to have a real conversation with supporters.

- It's not so much about what you say, more about how you make donors feel: listen to what they have to say, let them visualise and contextualise the impact of their gift, inspire them. Make them feel part of the bigger picture and the solution. Reinforce the belief that their vision is your vision and that you will deliver on your promises, on your joint mission.

- Create a checklist of known drivers in loyalty and commitment and address them through conversation.

Friends for life: welcoming and keeping your donors

Figure 11.6 Impact on attrition of 'Welcome' loyalty call to new recruits giving within 0-4 weeks of signing-up.

TM = telemarketing.   Source: Pell & Bales

11.7 Cumulative impact of loyalty call by month

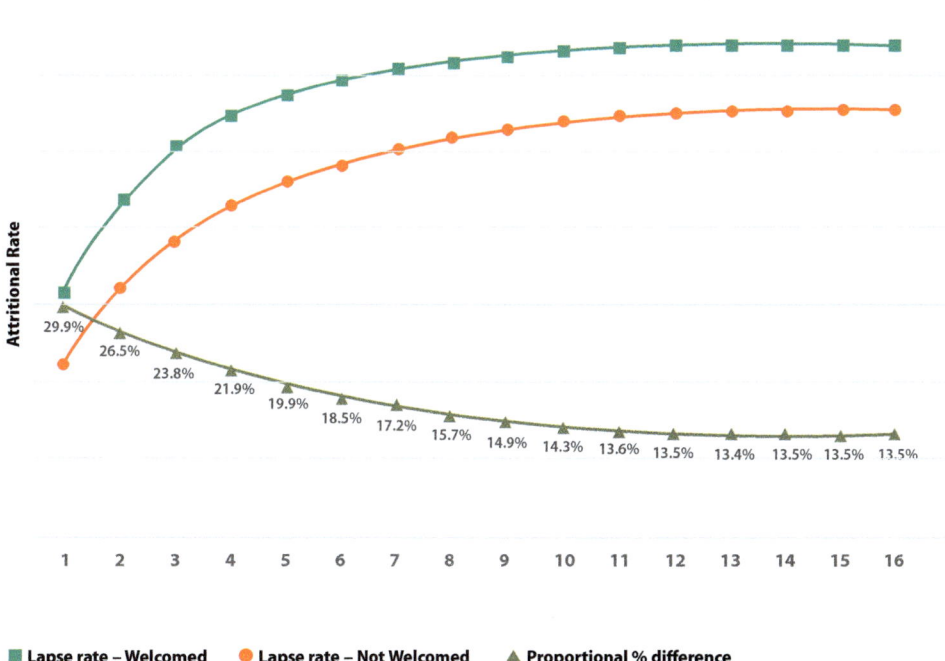

189

- Weave anti-attrition messaging into the conversation: be flexible and accommodating – offer payment holidays (one or two months when no donation is made), or even downgrades where appropriate.

- Encourage multiple relationships and a greater involvement and increased interaction in the cause (but don't ask them for more financial support).

You can see how closely these ideas match with our relationship fundraising matrix. They should be included in your retention plan.

Another, often neglected, form of thank you is an email. Sometimes the response you receive when you donate online is automated, cold and uninspiring. An international mystery shopping exercise by UK fundraising agency Bluefrog[14] and Irish fundraising agency Ask Direct revealed the sender's name under which 'thank yous' were sent out in Ireland and the UK (see opposite).

List of e-mail addresses that charities used in their thank-you communications.
How valued would you feel to receive an e-mail from 'no-reply' or 'Internet'? It might seem a small point, but such details matter. Rather than the name of a person or the organisation, most charities use the default 'from' name in the payment gateway they use. This gets things off to a bad start. Do you want to hear from 'no-reply' or the name of the actual charity you are giving to, or, better still, an individual there whose name you know?

There is no excuse for not providing an engaging, interesting and inspiring thank you when someone gives online. In many ways it should be easier than by the post or telephone as it can be automated.

E-mail is a great way to capture people's thoughts (what inspired your gift today?) and to tell stories through video that will help boost loyalty.

THE RECIPE FOR A GREAT FUNDRAISING THANK YOU
First of all, you need to make donors know their money is being put to good use and helping to solve the 'why'. The best way to do this is through storytelling. Make sure you tell a story about the area of your work that the donor has given to. This may seem obvious, but it is amazing how many generic responses we've received to donations made to specific appeals and projects.

One of the big mistakes we see fundraisers make with fundraising letters is to start with all the admin information. These are usually polite openings, but do nothing to inspire donors. We would encourage you to open with your strongest

Ireland	UK
info	NetBanx
Irish Heart Foundation	UNICEF UK
info	shopper
shopper	onlinesupport
fundraise	Amnesty Int UK CT
no-reply	noreply
Fiona Griffin	supportercare
Irish Heart Foundation	Secure Trading
PayPoint.net	donations
no-reply	webmanager
web	shopper
Barnardos	Internet
order1	Internet
Trócaire	shopper
Concern Worldwide	Supporter Care - NC
	creditcardprocessing
	supporter.services

story about the difference the donor's gift will make.

Further on in the letter you can then express your gratitude. We use 'gratitude' rather than 'thanks' because as the nineteenth century philosopher and poet Henri-Frédéric Amiel said:

Thankfulness is the beginning of gratitude. Gratitude is the completion of thankfulness. Thankfulness may consist merely of words. Gratitude is shown in acts.

With this in mind, think about how you can sprinkle some donor magic into your letter. How about writing it by hand? Producing a special thank-you card, or getting the chief executive or chair of trustees to send the letter?

Data is also important. Have you included the right amount? Is the donor's name and address spelled correctly? Getting this wrong can be the first step to a donor never giving again.

Additionally, do you make it easy for donors to get in touch if they have any questions? You should always name a person and provide his or her phone number/e-mail in case the donor wants to know more.

Finally, we would encourage you to sign your thank-you letters by hand and add a comment.

It is only a little thing, but demonstrates to the donor that they are more than just a number in your database. This helps build the relationship with the donor. If you don't believe you have time to do this, then think again about your priorities. If doing so improves your retention and the donor experience, it is worth the effort.

Based on this, always look for reasons to make the donor feel special and important. It may be the donor's fifth donation that year, the donor might have reached a milestone of cumulative donations (£500, £1,000, etc.) or you might notice the donor has been giving for a certain number of years.

Lisa Sargent is one of the leading experts on fundraising thank-you letters. On SOFII she has shared a number of 'before and after' letters, which have implemented some of the ideas discussed here. We've shared one of our favourites on the next page, along with commentary from Lisa on the changes she has made .

FEEDBACK TO DONORS AND SECURING THE SECOND GIFT

Once you've thanked your donor for her or his first gift (or for setting up a regular gift) you need to work on how you will tell the donor what her or his gift has accomplished. Doing this well addresses five of the seven key drivers of donor loyalty.

Again, this comes back to reminding donors about the emotional 'why' and telling them a story about what has been achieved thanks to the gift. It is worth repeating again: this should be related to the aspect of work the donor gave to in the first place.

For cash givers you need to feed back on what you did with the donation before asking again. This fulfils the bargain you made with your donors when they first gave: you donate and we'll thank you and let you know what we did with your money. Once we have fulfilled our promise, then the donor is likely to be in a position to want to help again when we ask.

Regular givers are slightly different in that donations will arrive consistently until the donor decides to stop the gift. One of the key times is between the initial sign-up and the first gift. There is a psychological condition known as 'buyer's remorse'. This is a sense of regret after making a purchase. If the buyer (in our case donor) feels that he or she has made a mistake or was unduly pressured into signing up then he or she could cancel. This is especially true when the rational part of the brain has more time to think about the decision. In the cold light of day, the rational mind could override the emotional decision to sign up.

That's why it is a good idea to build the relationship between thanking and the first gift. This could be through an SMS, e-mail, telephone call, or welcome brochure with more information on how the gift will make a difference. The aim

Friends for life: welcoming and keeping your donors

Before

Date

«addressee»
«street»
«city», «state»   «zipcode»

> **Lisa Comments:**
> **1.) Use an engaging lead.** Just like a good fundraising appeal, you want to draw the reader into your thank you. A great way to accomplish this is to start with something other than "thank you" or "on behalf of."
> **2.) Great use of "you" and "your."** This is where nonprofits commonly shift into "we-speak" - so by making this "you-based" and focused on benefits (vs. activities), you're on the right track. Well done.
> **3.) Make sense.** "At-risk" always makes me wonder, at risk of what? It's best to avoid jargon. And clarify how I help others enjoy the Centre.
> (more comments below...)

Dear «formalsalu»,

(1) Thank you so much for your gift of $«trcptamt» in support of the Ontario Science Centre.

(2) Science and technology enriches our lives, and a single visit to the Science Centre can plant a seed and provide the tools for a lifetime of exploration and discovery. Thanks to your support, young people and their families from Toronto's at risk communities will experience the inspiration and excitement that you and your family enjoy each time you visit.   (3)

(4) We're thrilled to announce top-notch exhibitions and IMAX films in honour of our 40th anniversary. Come and experience our upcoming features The Science of Spying, followed by Lizards and Snakes, Alive! and our summer food programming. Watch for news on our anniversary celebration in September.

(5) In recognition of your donation, we'd like to acknowledge your support by including your name in our Annual Report and on our Donor Wall. Your donation receipt, in the form of a letter, is enclosed. If you have any questions or need any assistance, please contact Matt Wiesenfeld, Head of Annual Giving at (416) 696-3233.

I hope you visit us soon, to see the impact you are making when you chose to donate to the Science Centre.

Yours sincerely,

Lesley Lewis
CEO (6)

Encl.

> **Comments, continued...**
> **4.) Great programs and excitement, but we-focused.** Note difference between you-based paragraph #2 and this one, so all you need to do here is shift the focus.
> **5.) Is donor informed of this ahead of time?** Many don't want that sort of recognition. Also, you can eliminate "in the form of a letter" phrase: If you label receipt clearly, simply tell donor it's enclosed.
> **6.) Bravo for signing w/ CEO!** Great that signer comes from highest ranks of your nonprofit.

DONORS FOR LIFE

After

Date

«addressee»
«street»
«city», «state»   «zipcode»

Dear «formalsalu»,

> **Lisa Comments:**
> **1.) For inspiration, I looked to your website.** The Science Centre has a terrific video online from which I was able to create a new lead paragraph for the letter. (This also "unifies" your theme and language across channels.)
> **2.) Here I aim to show donor how gift is already working.** To keep copy donor-centric, I use more "you" than "we."
> **3.) I kept the contacts paragraph**... and played down the tax receipt reference. (And online, Recognition Wall is noted, so I left this part.)
> **4.) Also added a P.S.** Once you get a "base" thank you letter down, you can keep the copy fresh for longer by updating postscript. (Although you should be updating thank yous, too – every 6 months should do the trick, or even quarterly.) Note: this P.S. also serves to let donors know when you'll update them next.

(1) Robots whir. Comets streak. Tide pools gurgle. When science comes to life, anything is possible... and all because of you.

Thank you for your contribution of $«trcptamt» in support of the Ontario Science Centre! Your gift is already inspiring a generation of future scientists and their families who, without you, might not have the means to visit our Science Centre.

(2) You provide the tools for a lifetime of exploration, too — illuminating the comets, giving tide pools their gurgle, and much more — sharing with others from Toronto's communities the same excitement that you and your family enjoy each time you visit.

(3) In recognition of your kind gift, we'll add your name to our Annual Report and our Donor Wall. (And you'll find your donation receipt enclosed.) If you have any questions, please contact Matt Wiesenfeld at (416) 696-3233. We'd love to hear from you.

Thank you so very much for sowing the seeds of discovery,

Lesley Lewis
CEO

P.S. (4) There's lots going on for our 40th anniversary — from The Science of Spying to Lizards and Snakes, Alive! — so I hope you'll visit us soon. Stay tuned for updates in our upcoming [newsletter?] and at www.ontariosciencecentre.ca. Thanks again.

is simple: remind the donor that he or she has made a good choice in donating and make them feel good about their decision.

It is worth investing heavily at the start of a regular giving relationship to build loyalty and satisfaction quickly, which will reduce the chance of the donor cancelling his or her gift.

RELATIONSHIP BUILDING

What would you think about a friend who only got in touch when he needed something? Probably not a lot; he would inevitably be the subject of groans and disquiet. You might end up trying to avoid him and may even give up on the friendship (although you'd always be there if it was a real emergency).

The same goes for charities. We don't want to be the friend who only gets in touch when we need something (the something usually being more money). If we are that friend, the danger is that people will quickly be turned off helping us.

That is why we need to look for ways to build relationships in-between any requests for money.

When you think about it, there are only three things that can happen when we get in touch with someone:

1   The relationship improves.
2   The relationship stays the same.
3   The relationship deteriorates.

We need to make sure that all our communications improve or at least don't damage the relationship. When you think of things this way, you can decide on whether your proposed activity is a good idea or not.

One of the best examples of relationship building on a mass scale comes from Tom Gaffny in the video we mentioned earlier in the chapter.

Gaffny, a Massachusetts resident, describes how after the Boston Marathon bombing in 2013 the fundraising team at Food for the Poor rang to check that he and his wife were ok. Just the sort of thing a concerned friend would do.

This would be impressive enough in itself, but two days later a hand-signed card arrived wishing them well.

It is one of many examples of how Food for the Poor consistently reach out to donors on a personal level. After Hurricane Sandy they called more than 11,000 donors, and after the shootings at Sandy Hook School they contacted 25,000 donors in the area.

However, it is not just when disaster strikes that they get in touch. Gaffny's wife was talking on the phone to Food for the Poor and mentioned she was going to be a grandmother. You can probably guess what happened next? Two days later a hand-signed congratulations card arrived from the entire office (also enclosed was a card for the daughter as well).

The result? Gaffny describes how he and his wife have gone from being occasional, small supporters of the cause to real advocates (and donors) to the organisation. At the end of the year, guess which charity is in line for an additional gift? As Gaffny says with a smile, 'these people are costing me a fortune!'

Another great way to build relationships with your donors is through feedback events. These invitations to come and see or hear about the work that your organisation is doing are always well received. In fact, merely inviting donors to attend (most will politely decline) can strengthen the relationship.

Craig has always been a big fan of donor events as a way of strengthening relationships. When he worked in a hospice there was nothing more inspiring for a donor than to get a personal tour from a nurse or doctor.

Similarly, showing donors round the nursery for blind children he worked at and explaining how donations had paid for equipment was always well received.

When we looked at the impact of a visit on retention we found that we had 100 per cent retention for regular donors in the first year. Although the numbers were small (fewer than 100), it shows the difference donor events can have.

Even if your charity doesn't have somewhere to visit you can get creative. If you're a research charity, why not hold an event with a scientist as a guest speaker. Work overseas? Show footage live from the field, or let donors know when workers are back in the country and invite them to meet them.

Donor events don't always need to be face to face either. Tele-conferences and webinars are low-cost and interactive ways of reporting back to donors.

One final way to build donor relationships is through surveys. We will talk about designing effective surveys in chapter 19. In this context, you are looking for ways to gather information to provide a more personal and effective experience for the donor. This might be about understanding why the donor supports your organisation, what areas of work they are most interested in, or about any communication preferences the donor may have.

ASKING PROPERLY

There is an old truism that says effective major donor fundraising is about asking the right person, for the right amount, at the right time.

We believe the same goes for all donors. Asking properly for another donation, an increase in a regular gift or to take part in an event is all part of the fundraising process.

However, get this wrong and it could be the moment a donor decides to stop giving.

Here are some examples of how fundraisers don't ask properly:

- Asking again before the donor has been thanked and received feedback on their gift.

- Assuming future support just because someone has given before.

- Not making a compelling fundraising offer.

- Asking for something totally different to what the donor is interested in.

- Asking for too much or little and failing to take into account the donor's previous giving.

- Asking too soon or too late for an additional gift (too soon and you can look greedy and ungrateful, too long and it might appear that you don't need the help).

Much of what we discussed about recruiting donors applies to asking for further donations from previous donors.

George Smith outlined a seven-point checklist in *Asking Properly* that helps you when the time comes to ask for a further gift:

1 *Who am I talking to?*
2 *What precisely am I asking them to do?*
3 *Why?*
4 *Have I made the message sound important (or evocative, passionate, crucial, urgent... select your own epithets but you'll need most of them)?*
5 *Have I made the point as simply or as powerfully as possible?*
6 *Have I made it as easy as possible to respond to what I am saying?*
7 *Have I done something that has never quite been done before?*[15]

Of course, it is a sad fact that most people will say 'no' or ignore your request for further help. However, if you follow the checklist above and acknowledge the difference the donor has made previously, then even those who say 'no' should not begrudge you asking.

DONOR CARE AND MAGIC

We use the phrase 'donor care and magic' deliberately. We see donor care as getting the basics right: of correct names, being polite and respectful.

That will only get you so far. You need to go beyond the basics if you want to become your donors' favourite charity. You should be aiming to create 'wow' moments on a regular basis that donors will tell other people about.

Sadly not many charities are good at this. The reason? Donor care is seen as a cost and not an investment in future income. That's why we are going to look to the commercial sector for examples of companies built on outstanding service.

Perhaps our favourite company for creating customer magic is Zappos – an American online shoe company.

You'd be forgiven for thinking that people couldn't fall in love with a shoe company, but you'd be wrong. Zappos built a $1 billion business in just over a decade through outstanding customer service and word-of-mouth recommendations.

As Zappos founder Tony Hseih explains in his book, *Delivering Happiness: A Path to Profits, Passion, and Purpose*:

> *Our philosophy has been to take most of the money we would have spent on paid advertising and invest it into customer service and the customer experience instead, letting our customers do the marketing for us through word of mouth.*[16]

Hseih explains this philosophy in a greater detail:

> *We're trying to build a lifelong relationship with each customer, one phone call at a time. A lot of people may think it's strange that an Internet company is so focused on the telephone, when only about 5 percent of our sales happen through the telephone. In fact, most of our phone calls don't even result in sales. But what we've found is that on average, every customer contacts us at least once sometime during his or her lifetime, and we just need to make sure that we use that opportunity to create a lasting memory. The majority of phone calls don't result in an immediate order. Sometimes a customer may be calling because it's her first time returning an item, and she just wants a little help*

stepping through the process. Other times, a customer may call because there's a wedding coming up this weekend and he wants a little fashion advice. And sometimes, we get customers who call simply because they're a little lonely and want someone to talk to.[17]

How refreshing would it be to hear a fundraising director talk about donors in such a way? Imagine if our fundraising call centre staff were empowered in the same way? How would it improve our retention?

There are lots of legendary stories about Zappos's customer service. Here's one of our favourites from Hseih, along with why he sees customer service as so important:

I'm reminded of a time when I was in Santa Monica, California, a few years ago at a Skechers sales conference. After a long night of bar-hopping, a small group of us headed up to someone's hotel room to order some food. My friend from Skechers tried to order a pepperoni pizza from the room-service menu, but was disappointed to learn that the hotel we were staying at did not deliver hot food after 11:00 PM. We had missed the deadline by several hours. In our inebriated state, a few of us cajoled her into calling Zappos to try to order a pizza. She took us up on our dare, turned on the speakerphone, and explained to the (very) patient Zappos rep that she was staying in a Santa Monica hotel and really craving a pepperoni pizza, that room service was no longer delivering hot food, and that she wanted to know if there was anything Zappos could do to help. The Zappos rep was initially a bit confused by the request, but she quickly recovered and put us on hold. She returned two minutes later, listing the five closest places in the Santa Monica area that were still open and delivering pizzas at that time. Now, truth be told, I was a little hesitant to include this story because I don't actually want everyone who reads this book to start calling Zappos and ordering pizza. But I just think it's a fun story to illustrate the power of not having scripts in your call center and empowering your employees to do what's right for your brand, no matter how unusual or bizarre the situation. As for my friend from Skechers? After that phone call, she's now a customer for life.[18]

Finally Hseih describes 10 ways to create a customer service culture in your company:

1 *Make customer service a priority for the whole company, not just a*

department. A customer service attitude needs to come from the top.
2. Make WOW a verb that is part of your company's everyday vocabulary.
3. Empower and trust your customer service reps. Trust that they want to provide great service ... because they actually do. Escalations to a supervisor should be rare.
4. Realize that it's okay to fire customers who are insatiable or abuse your employees.
5. Don't measure call times, don't force employees to up-sell and don't use scripts.
6. Don't hide your 1-800 number. It's a message not just to your customers, but to your employees as well.
7. View each call as an investment in building a customer service brand, not as an expense you're seeking to minimize.
8. Have the entire company celebrate great service. Tell stories of WOW experiences to everyone in the company.
9. Find and hire people who are already passionate about customer service.
10. Give great service to everyone: customers, employees, and vendors.[19]

OPPORTUNITIES TO CREATE DONOR MAGIC

As you can tell, we are big fans of Zappos and believe there is a lot fundraisers can learn from their success. That's not to say that there aren't any charities creating 'wow' moments for their donors. We wanted to share some examples of outstanding customer care and give you some ideas of how you can create donor magic.

For their 'Million Miracles' appeal, Sightsavers live-streamed a cataract operation from Malawi and invited donors to watch. What amazing and immediate feedback! It is something you would definitely tell friends about. The offer in the newspaper advertisement and direct mail appeal was powerfully simple. Donate £30 and then a couple of days later watch a blind person see for the first time in years. It is no surprise the appeal was a huge success and a multiple award winner.

Charity: Water understand the importance of surprising donors. Hardly a fundraising conference goes by when they aren't name checked for doing something special for their donors. Our favourite is the videos[20] they create once a year to thank specific donors for fundraising. Not only do the videos make the donors feel special, they also get shared on social media and create a swell of free publicity. As well as expressing gratitude, they also happen to be amusing.

Anniversaries and birthdays are also a great opportunity to create donor magic.

Do you do something special when a donor has given for 5, 10, 15, etc, years? This should be really easy to set up on your database, but so many charities miss this opportunity. A handwritten card, a phone call, personalised letter, or e-mail are all ways to let donors know they are special and important to the cause.

Setting up automatic e-mail anniversary thanks for regular givers reduced second year attrition by over 10 per cent in one charity Craig worked at. It took a couple of hours to set up and then automatically sent an e-mail on the anniversary of the donor's first gift – a really simple and low cost way to say thank you and show donors the difference their gift has made. As well as improving retention, a number of donors got in touch and asked to increase their gift without being asked.

Similarly, if you capture birth dates in your database do you ever send donors a birthday card? Craig's team once sent a card to all donors who were celebrating their ninetieth birthday (it was also the charity's ninetieth anniversary) and had a great response from donors who received the card. This included some sizeable gifts and a legacy pledge – a completely unintended, but pleasing consequence of doing it.

Treating donors with respect can also make you stand out. Damian O'Broin of Dublin-based fundraising agency Ask Direct reported on a form the Irish Hospice Foundation sent to all their regular donors in 2009. Rather than just ask donors for more money, it acknowledged the tough economic climate and gave donors the opportunity to cancel or reduce their gift. What happened? Four donors took the hospice up on their offer. A further 400 increased their gift and praised the hospice for giving them the option![21]

On the same theme, it can sometimes pay to change the ever-present donation amount boxes on donation forms. Adding an additional box with the words 'Surprise us' was found to boost donations by 15-20 per cent with no decrease in response rate.[22]

Craig has copied both of these ideas at charities he has worked for and seen similar (if not quite as spectacular) results.

Getting donor feedback is also crucial. Again we lag behind the commercial world in this respect. As Professor Adrian Sargeant explains:

> Corporates have known for over 30 years that the single biggest driver of customer loyalty is their satisfaction with the quality of service provided. This is why customer satisfaction surveys are now so ubiquitous. Managers are hungry for the data and want to use them to inform their strategy.[23]

Nearly every commercial transaction we've undertaken recently has had a request for feedback. From the incentivised survey on a till receipt, to the SMS after changing our phone contract, we are constantly being asked for feedback. Even Craig's local takeaway asked him to fill in a survey!

Why do they want this feedback? So they can fix problems, improve processes and improve customer satisfaction.

Again, we believe this is a huge area of opportunity for charities. Here are a few areas where you can ask for feedback to identify problems and improve processes:

- When a donor signs up on the street you can call later and ask about the experience. Was the fundraiser polite? Do you have any concerns? Do you know it is a long-term experience? How long do you think you will give for? What were you most interested in?

- After an online donation is made (or better still abandoned donations) you can ask donors to complete a survey to discover how they found the process. Any recurring problems can be identified as priorities for solving.

- Contact donors who don't respond to an appeal to discover if there was any particular reason why.

- Ask for feedback on your communications and see if donors have any preferences.

- Invite event participants to comment on the organisation, its communications and how likely they are to take part again.

There are numerous other opportunities. What we want to get across is that you should never miss a chance to get feedback from donors. This helps you with the following loyalty drivers:

1 The donor knows what to expect from your organisation with each interaction.
2 The donor receives opportunities to make his or her views known.

Closely related to soliciting feedback are complaints. Bill Gates famously said, 'Your most unhappy customers are your greatest source of learning.'

Unfortunately, most charities stick their head in the sand when it comes to dealing with complaints. This is a missed opportunity. Making it easy for donors to raise a concern can have a positive impact on retention.

In *Donor Churn*,[23] a discussion paper from experience and relationship company DonorVoice, the importance of encouraging and handling complaints is laid out.

Their research showed that you only retain 9 per cent of donors who have a complaint but do not tell you about it. You can double this retention by making it easy to complain, but not actually resolving the donor's problem.

If you can solve the problem then retention rockets to 81 per cent for problems that are immediately resolved.

That's why you should take a leaf out of Zappos's book. Publicise your donor care number and e-mail widely and encourage your donors to let you know when they have a problem. Solving it is one of the most powerful retention tools you have.

USING DATA TO IMPROVE LOYALTY AND COMMITMENT

As we stated in the first chapter, data is often the forgotten element of relationship fundraising. Yet data should be the base of your efforts that all the other elements are built on.

Many of the ideas we have already discussed in this chapter assume that you have the data available to implement them. If you don't then it is crucial that you find the expertise to help you do this. Sadly, very few charities are fully using the data they have available to provide insight and inform decision-making.

So what are some of the major mistakes that fundraisers make?

One of the major mistakes is the nature of the data we record on our donors. Try this quick exercise.

Write down all the information you record on donors. This could be when a donor makes a gift, when you call her or him, when she or he receives a communication.

Now, go through your list. Highlight every piece of data that is transactional in nature in one colour and every piece of relational data in another colour.

The list normally looks something like this:

Transactional	Relational
Name and address	Date of birth
E-mail	
Telephone number	
Amount, date and number of donations	
Bank details	
Communications sent	

Every time we have done this exercise the items of transactional data outweigh the relational items by three or four to one.

Why does this matter? Well, if you are only recording transactional data then how can you hope to provider a richer, more rewarding giving experience?

Some of the relational details that are often missed include:

- Reason for giving
- Area of work interested in
- Survey responses
- Commitment/loyalty scores
- Personal interests (subject to data protection laws)
- Conversational details
- Work details

So how could you use some of these details to improve your fundraising?

One of Craig's colleagues at Amnesty International in Turkey records notes on the conversations they have with donors during telephone calls. For example, if a donor says he is ill then the next time he is called the caller will open the conversation by saying something like 'Last time we spoke you weren't feeling well, I hope you're ok now'.

Simple, but showing genuine concern and sympathy for donors is a sure-fire way to earn trust and commitment from donors.

Taking this one step further, we know of some animal charities that ask donors for the name of their pet. Sean Triner, a fundraising consultant in Australia, describes how the Lost Dogs Home in Melbourne uses surveys to discover the name of a donor's dog.[25] They then use this information to personalise direct mail and telephone calls.

For example, look at this variable sentence from a direct mail piece:

> *Thank you. My very warmest wishes for the festive season to you and your family and an extra special cuddle for <PET NAME>*

The results? When the charity knew the name of a pet, donors were 43 per cent more likely to increase their regular gift.

Another missed opportunity to gather relational data is through direct dialogue fundraising. As you are having a face-to-face conversation then it is a great opportunity to find out more about the donor. You can then use the data you gather to provide a better donor experience and build loyalty. For example, do you brief your street fundraisers to record the part of your work the donor is most interested in? Do you record any hobbies the donor mentions? If they say running or sport you could approach them about doing a sponsored challenge for you. Do you find out what the donor does for a living? There are numerous possibilities.

When we think about data we need to be less robotic in our approach and more human. By thinking carefully about how you could gather and use additional data, you will be in a position to provide a more rewarding donor experience.

COMPLETING YOUR LOYALTY AND RELATIONSHIP FUNDRAISING MATRIX

We've presented a framework and a number of practical ideas for you to improve your fundraising programme. We thought it would be useful to share an example of a completed matrix. This is for reviewing how regular donors are treated in their first year of giving. The list isn't exhaustive, but gives you an idea of how you can systematically look at every part of your fundraising and develop a retention plan. You will see there are some gaps. This is deliberate. Not all combinations will be relevant to the problem you are addressing.

Once you have developed your matrix for one area of fundraising, it can be hard to know where to start implementing the ideas. That's why we want to help you develop an action plan to take forward the best ideas.

For each idea you have considered and included in your matrix you need to decide:

- How much time would it take to make the change? (1 – long time, 5 – quick.)
- How much money and resources would it take? (1 – expensive, 5 – cheap.)
- What difference would the change make to donors? (1 – not much, 5 – big difference.)

Loyalty and Relationship Fundraising Matrix	Why	Storytelling
Donor perceives your organisation to be effective in trying to achieve its mission	Remind donors about the charity vision and the donor's part in helping solve the problem	Use stories of the successes the donor has made happen.
Donor knows what to expect from your organisation with each interaction	Ensure every communication includes something about the 'why' the donor is helping to achieve. Set up a checklist to make sure this is done.	Send stories on donor interests.
Donor receives timely thank yous		Make sure all thank yous start with a relevant story.
Donor receives opportunities to make his or her views known		Use stories to explain why donor's views are important and feedback is appreciated.
Donor is given the feeling that he or she is part of an important cause	Describe what the world would look like without the donor's help.	Review all feedback communications to ensure that emotional storytelling outweighs use of statistics.
Donor feels his or her involvement is appreciated	Build an agenda for a donor event that reinforces the 'why' to the donor. Review telephone scripts to make sure the 'why' is always included in our calls.	Get a beneficiary to speak at a donor information event.
Donor receives information showing who is being helped	Offer prizes and incentives to colleagues who share examples of why the work we do is so important.	Work with services to gather more stories to use in communications – establish a monthly meeting with the head of services to do this.

Friends for life: welcoming and keeping your donors

Relationship building	Asking and thanking properly	Donor care/magic	Data
Give donors the chance to request the annual or impact report (online and offline).		Share any problems or setbacks with the donor.	Use data screening to make sure donor information is accurate. Conduct annual screening of database to identify deceased, gone away and wealthy donors.
Send initial e-mail from street fundraiser with photo and introduction on what happens next. Use a consistent name in communications – chief exec, frontline staff member, fundraising director, etc.	Ensure all subsequent thank yous sent within 48 hours. Publicise donor care phone number in all communications in case there are any problems or mistake	Take a photo of donor with street fundraiser to send in an e-mail to donor.	Review sign-up process and consider how we can gather more relational data. Ensure all data are entered accurately by conducting quarterly spot checks. Make sure we have a consistent message/experience through our online and offline communications. Set up a quarterly audit to assess.
Call all donors with phone numbers asap after sign-up to thank them for signing up.	Review process so first thank you sent within 48 hours. Test if sending an SMS between sign-up and first gift improves month three retention.	Handwrite a thank-you message on the welcome letter. Speak to trustees about getting involved with phone calls to donors once a year.	Record when thank yous are sent on the database so we can audit our response times
Ask for feedback on the sign-up process. Send donor survey after six months including commitment scores.	Test sending an SMS within 24 hours asking for feedback on sign-up experience. Measure if it improves 'no-show' rate.	Include a link in every e-mail asking for feedback.	Record survey results on database (use relational and transactional data).
Remind donor of need for continuing support. Brief copywriter to make sure we use 'you' in our copy. This demonstrates the donor is part of the solution.		Send donor a badge/certificate that makes them feel part of the cause. For every communication we send, plan how we can use relational data to make the donor feel important.	Train fundraisers on the importance of capturing phone number during sign-up process. Record who attended event, so you can remind them of it in future communications.
Invite to a donor information event.	Introduce anniversary thank yous to donors.	Follow up with all event attendees. Send handwritten Christmas cards to top 20 per cent of givers.	
Make sure donor has received feedback on her gift before we do an upgrade call or send an additional appeal.	Work with marketing team to produce a special thank-you video from a beneficiary.	Send a report to non-attendees on donor event.	Ensure suppressions are in place that make sure donor receives feedback before receiving an upgrade ask. Record which beneficiary stories and successes the donor has received.

This will give you a score out of 15. You should start by working on the highest scoring changes you have identified through this process.

In our example matrix, you might decide that asking fundraisers to gather more phone numbers in the sign-up process is easy to implement, cheap to do and would make a big difference to donors as you could call them soon after they sign up. You might score it five, four, four for a score of 13. This would make it a high priority.

In contrast, gathering the photos of the street fundraiser and donor may need a large investment in technology and so is too expensive in the short term. You might score it two on time, one on money, but four on difference to donors. This means you decide to keep the idea, but put it on hold for the time being.

It is also crucial to decide on how you will measure the difference made and the impact your change has on results. If you don't do this, then your work will be no more than a series of hunches and educated guesses. You need to do better than this and use data to help you understand which factors make the biggest difference to loyalty and your retention rate.

CONCLUSION

Current fundraising practice is often compared to a leaky bucket. Fundraisers keep filling the bucket with new donors rather than trying to repair the holes.

Approaching the problem from this way is expensive and increasingly unsustainable. As research from Adrian Sargeant has shown, it costs five times more to recruit a new donor than to keep a current one.

By using our loyalty and relationship fundraising matrix you can start fixing your holes one at a time, starting with the largest leaks.

This is much harder than simply filling the bucket with more donors, but we believe it is the only way forward in the medium and long term.

We urge fundraisers to take a structured and informed approach to solving the issue of donor retention. We hope this chapter will help you tackle the issue head on.

NOTES
1. Sargeant, Adrian (2001) Relationship fundraising: how to keep donors loyal *Nonprofit Management and Leadership* 12(2): 177-192.
2. Springer, T et al (2014), *Breaking the back of customer churn*. Available at: http://www.bain.com/Images/BAIN BRIEF Breaking the back of customer churn.pdf Last accessed 27 June 2015.
3. Ibid., p. 4.
4. Ibid., p. 2–8.
5. Craver, Roger (2014) *Retention Fundraising*, Emerson & Church, Medfield, MA, discussed in chapter 3.
6. Craver, Roger (2014) *Retention Fundraising*, Emerson & Church, Medfield, MA, Ibid., p.28-29.
7. Ibid., p. 67.

8. *Myths and dark legends: how old conventional 'truths' about fundraising are holding us back* Available on YouTube: https://www.youtube.com/watch?v=Tys6jD1CnA0 Last accessed 11 July 2015.
9. Manning, Harley, Bodine, Kerry (2012), *Outside In: the Power of Putting Customers at the Heart of your Business*, New Harvest, New York. (2012)
10. Longfield, Chuck (2011) *We can boost donor retention but only if we get smart*, SOFII website. Available at: http://sofii.org/article/we-can-boost-donor-retention.-but-only-if-we-get-smart Last accessed 12 July 2015.
11. Burk, Penelope (2003) *Donor Centred Fundraising.* Burk & Associates Publishing, Chicago.
12. Francis, Bethan (2012) *How to reduce attrition by a third in three minutes,* Pell & Bales' blogs. Available at: https://pellandbales.wordpress.com/2012/08/15/how-to-reduce-donor-attrition-by-a-third-in-3-minutes/ Last accessed 12 July 2015.
13. Ibid.
14. *Who sends your emails?* (November 2011) Queer Ideas blog. Available at: http://www.queerideas.co.uk/my_weblog/2011/11/who-sends-your-emails.html Last accessed 12 July 2015.
15. Smith, George (1996) *Asking Properly,* The White Lion Press, London, p. 66.
16. Hseih, Tony (2010) *Delivering Happiness: A Path to Profits, Passion, and Purpose*, Business Plus, New York, p. 142.
17. Ibid., p.145.
18. Ibid., p.146.
19. Ibid., p.147.
20. They even have a YouTube video channel dedicated to their thank-you videos. Check it out here: https://www.youtube.com/user/charitywaterthanks?feature=watch
21. *Have you asked your doors to cancel their direct debits yet*? (2009) Available at: http://www.askdirect.ie/2009/09/17/have-you-asked-your-donors-to-cancel-their-direct-debits-yet/ Last accessed 16 July 2015.
22. As reported on SOFII. Available: http://sofii.org/case-study/mcpherson-associates-wpbt2-the-surprise-us-tick-box Last accessed 16 July 2015.
23. Sargeant, Adrian (2010) *Tiny Essentials of Donor Loyalty,* The White Lion Press, London. P8.
24. *Donor churn: how to stop it before it starts and why current approaches prevent this from happening*, DonorVoice. Available at: http://www.thedonorvoice.com/publications/ Last accessed 18 July 2015.
25. Triner, Sean (2009) *The most powerful fundraising tool in the world*, Pareto Fundraising blog. Available at: http://paretofundraising.com/2009/07/the-most-powerful-fundraising-tool-in-the-world/ Last accessed 18 July 2015.

Community fundraising, mass participation events and peer-to-peer fundraising

Craig's first job in fundraising was as a community fundraising assistant at St Teresa's Hospice in Darlington, England. This job involved everything from counting collection boxes and getting prizes for raffles, to organising balls and dressing up in a variety of stupid costumes. It is a role he looks back on with much fondness and is an area of fundraising that doesn't always get the focus and attention it deserves.

This chapter will look at how you can build strong relationships in your community. We also look at how mass participation events, like Movember, and sponsored challenges, such as running and cycling, have grown exponentially over the last 20 years.

PART ONE: COMMUNITY FUNDRAISING
Community fundraising is often the first thing the general public think of when asked to describe fundraising. Collections, coffee mornings, cake sales, fetes, etc are all classic community fundraising activities.

They also happen to be big money raisers.

For example, in the US it is estimated that schools and nonprofits raise around $1.7 billion a year by selling popular consumer items, such as cakes and fortune cookies.[1] In the UK, there are no exact figures, but it is likely that a high proportion of the £3.8 billion given by individuals through 'fundraising' is from community fundraising and events.[2] For comparison, individual donations are approximately £7 billion and legacies are around £2 billion per year.

We are not going to explain how to organise a fete or a cake sale, but instead Craig is going to share some tips on how best to engage and encourage people who volunteer to undertake community fundraising on your behalf. You can then apply these to create a great community fundraising programme in your organisation.

Lesson one: small and local? Attend everything

One of the big lessons I learned in that first job was the importance of listening and spending time with supporters. At times I used to think my old boss was work shy as he was hardly ever in the office at his desk 'working'. Instead he was always popping in somewhere for a cup of tea or to say hello. I now realise this was what made him such a brilliant community fundraiser. Spending quality time with supporters built strong relationships (both with him personally and with the hospice) and it was why people supported the hospice year after year.

If you are a community fundraiser or manage a community fundraising team then one of the key objectives should be to have a high percentage of time out the office or to arrange a certain number of meetings per week.

I took this lesson forward in my next job and had a mantra of 'attend everything' and the aim to be the most visible charity in the community. It led to people complaining about how much we were in the local paper and that other causes didn't get a look in. However, it was always greatly appreciated by the people doing the fundraising.

It is a powerful motivator for someone to support your cause again if you are the only charity representative attending a cheque presentation at 9 p.m. on a Saturday evening. Although it might have been hard to justify on an immediate ROI (return on investment) calculation, it created lots of word-of-mouth and recommendations to other people to support our cause. If a staff member was unavailable then we recruited a team of volunteers to attend events on our behalf. This 'attend everything' strategy played a big part in us trebling income over a three-year period.

Larger charities neither had the resources or inclination to send people to community events so it became a real competitive advantage for us in our local area.

If you genuinely don't have the manpower to do this why not try and recruit volunteers to do this on your behalf? Recruiting motivated volunteer 'ambassadors' and providing great training can help share the workload.

Lesson two: large and national? Focus on the experience

If you are too far away to attend events supporters have organised on your behalf you need to think of other ways to keep people happy and willing to do events again in the future. This is where the bigger budgets of larger charities can help.

Many larger charities have now centralised their supporter services. This central body provides the administrative support for the frontline community fundraisers. This frees up the time that the fundraisers used to spend on admin for more money-raising activity in the community.

To make this work you need to make it easy for supporters to contact you and make sure you have people responding enthusiastically and quickly to enquiries. You should spend time on your website to make it easy for people to download or request materials and to tell you about their event.

You might not be able to attend, but you can send a good luck card or call the fundraiser before and after the event to see how it went. Make it personal and ask for photos and then share them (if appropriate) on your social media channels. Don't forget to record key information on the database so other departments will be aware of the activity if they need to contact the donor.

Finally, make sure you send an inspiring thank you and schedule a follow-up to see if the person would like to raise money again in the future.

Lesson three: make sure you get a return and maximise income
Super model Linda Evangelista famously said she didn't wake up for less than $10,000. That's my feeling about organising fundraising events too. If you are putting staff time into organising an event then make sure you have a minimum income target. You don't want to spend hours of staff time on something that won't raise a significant sum of money. It is a mistake we see many smaller charities make in their community fundraising when precious staff time is taken up on unsustainable events with minimal return.

Paul learned this when he was at Macmillan. He too was a community fundraising assistant and spent months organising a youth football tournament. Even with significant volunteer support, it took up an enormous amount of time and raised only about £5,000 net profit. It was something he really enjoyed doing. The local participants also gave great feedback. However, his time could have been far better used elsewhere.

Likewise, if volunteers are organising events you should guide them on how to maximise returns. Give them advice on tax efficiency, how to ask for donations from non-attendees, the best ways to run an auction or raffle, or suggest extra activities that will boost income.

Offer to help, but be clear on what you can and cannot do and agree it in advance of the event. It can be tricky to get the balance right between meeting supporters' expectations and making the most of the resources you have available. Put down in writing what you agree and learn how to manage the expectations your supporters have of you.

For example, if someone is organising a dinner and wants you to help sell tickets then this is usually very difficult. The person should be encouraged to use her or his own networks and contacts. If she can't sell to these areas you need to find a way to suggest she tries something else instead.

It is one of the saddest experiences as a fundraiser to see someone (or a group of people) put hundreds of hours of effort into organising an event that then only raises a minimal sum. It can be disconcerting all round. A good fundraiser will recognise when this is likely to happen and discuss alternatives with the organisers.

For example, I once worked with a family who were organising an auction. They'd done an amazing job at getting the prizes, but it was clear that they were unlikely to realise the full value at the event they had organised. Basically, there were around two prizes and auction items for every person attending. I sat down with the family and suggested some ideas to maximise the value and persuaded them to put reserve prices on the lots. We had another event a couple of months later where I knew many of the items would fetch a lot more money. The family still went ahead with their event and had a successful evening. However, we were able to keep back 10 to 15 items for the future event and this more than doubled the total the family raised, which they were delighted with.

Lesson four: think about the data

One of the big mistakes I've seen made is in the coding of income on the database from people who have raised money from community events. Often they are added in the same way as philanthropic donors, which can lead to problems. For example, if you don't distinguish between them you could send someone who has raised £750 from a cake sale (from lots of small donations) an appeal asking for a one-off gift of a similar amount. I have had this happen and had to apologise profusely for the offence caused. It isn't too difficult to get your coding right and to make sure that community fundraisers are excluded from appeal mailings (or at least asked at an appropriate level).

A big indicator of this is when you don't have round numbers. If someone has given £1,056.71 then double check where the money came from before inviting her to a major donor event or asking for a large personal donation.

In chapter 10 we talked about the importance of relational data. If you have two donors who both give £100 a year to appeals that doesn't tell you anything about their personal connections and ability to raise funds in the community.

However, what if you also knew that one of the donors was an active churchgoer, a member of the Women's Institute and used to be a respected local teacher? This person would seem to be a prime prospect for bringing people together and raising money from the community. She might not be able to give large sums of money herself, but can harness her connections to raise much more than her one-off gifts.

Capturing these data can be difficult, but you can be creative on how. Use local directories and websites to identify people who sit on boards, or have been the treasurer or secretary of local clubs. These are likely to be well-connected people in your community and people worth building a relationship with.

Lesson five: working with support groups and volunteers
In the UK, many charities have support groups that raise money on behalf of their cause. Run by volunteers these groups can raise huge sums of money, but also cause lots of problems if they are not well managed.

One of the first things I'd recommend when working with support groups is to agree a memorandum of understanding. This sets out what both sides can expect and the standards to adhere to. If the group is long established then this needs to be sensitively handled, so it is not seen as undermining their work. However, such an agreement should set out what support you can offer (designing and printing posters was always an area of contention in my experience) and also the standards expected when fundraising (such as following the law and best practice).

Similarly, it should set out the arrangements for banking money and handing it over to the charity in a timely manner. Also consider role descriptions (though ask your human resources team for assistance so you don't fall foul of employment law) for key volunteer roles such as chairperson or treasurer.

At their best, support groups will open up new opportunities for your fundraising, be self-reliant and a real asset to your organisation. At their worst, they can be a drain on time and morale and fail to raise much money.

As fundraising support groups often include some of your most loyal and passionate supporters you need to make them feel special. You should always acknowledge their fundraising efforts, provide praise when they reach certain milestones and provide 'inside' information on your work so they feel informed and an important part of your work. Invites to AGMs, to meet your chief executive, or other prestigious events can be hugely motivating for support group volunteers.

Lesson six: don't forget legacies and other cross-promotional opportunities
Finally, as I have just mentioned, volunteer fundraisers are often some of the most committed supporters a charity may have. They may not be able to give huge sums themselves, but are able to mobilise support from their networks. This means that volunteer community fundraisers can have a much higher lifetime value than those who support you via direct debit or giving to an appeal.

This commitment means that many would consider leaving a legacy to your cause if asked appropriately (see chapter 16 on how to do this). Our advice to create 'donors for life' is just as relevant for people fundraising through events as it is for all other donors. However, often not as much attention or time is put into nurturing these relationships and encouraging them to fundraise year after year.

It is not just legacies that volunteer fundraisers can help with. You should look for other ways they can help. They might be able to introduce you to major donors, recruit participants for challenge events, or help distribute promotional materials and posters.

PART TWO: MASS PARTICIPATION EVENTS AND PEER-TO-PEER FUNDRAISING
This is closely related to classic community fundraising, but is based more on securing sponsorship from friends, family and colleagues for a nonprofit. They can be effective as you don't have to organise a centralised event, you raise brand awareness, have the potential for data capture and, as we will show, they can be very lucrative. It is an area of fundraising that has seen a massive increase in activity and income over the last 20 years.

For example, the top 30 peer-to-peer fundraising events in the US (think walks, bike rides, etc) raised $1.62 billion in 2014. The top event – American Cancer Society's Relay for Life – raised $335 million alone.[3]

Although the sums are smaller, the top 25 mass participation events in the UK still raised an impressive £154 million in 2014. Nearly all large fundraising charities have at least one flagship mass participation event, or encourage supporters to take part in runs, cycle rides and so on.

As well as traditional charity organised events, there has also been a rise in fundraising memes and supporter-led campaigns: #NoMakeUpSelfie, the ice-bucket challenge and Stephen Sutton's fundraising campaign in the UK were all supporter led and harnessed social media to go viral and raise huge sums of money.

So how do you make the most of these opportunities? Here are some of the things we recommend you consider.

Communicate early and often

When someone signs up to do a sponsored event then having a clear communication plan is crucial. You need to build a close relationship with your participants and keep them inspired and motivated to exceed their fundraising target.

Probably the most intense relationship (in terms of frequency of contact) a fundraiser will have is when someone undertakes an event with a four-figure sponsorship target. There will be regular e-mails and phone calls, information packs to be sent, potential face-to-face meetings, attendance on the day of the event (where feasible) and then careful thanking and stewardship after the event. It wouldn't be unusual for a typical donor to receive 30 to 50 contacts from a charity ahead of an event such as the London Marathon.

When this is done properly it builds trust with the fundraisers and keeps them engaged and motivated to raise as much as they can. It can also lead to them becoming advocates and ambassadors for your cause. This word-of-mouth promotion can be very powerful and open up the personal networks of participants to engage with your charity. Make it easy to share content and think about how you can inspire people to be spokespeople for your cause. Ideas such as incentives or discount codes for people to share on Facebook and other social media can work well here.

Craig's first fundraising event was at Wetherby racecourse in the early 1980s. It was a fun run around the track and he remembers asking his parents, grandparents and other relatives for sponsorship (he can't remember the cause now).

This was all done on a paper sponsorship form, which is now close to extinction for most events in the UK – with schools being the noble exception in our experience.

Instead, the vast majority of sponsorship is now raised online, ether through online platforms such as JustGiving (FirstGiving in the USA), Virgin Money Giving and Network for Good or via charities' own websites and giving platforms.

In chapter 10 Paul described how World Jewish Relief had developed their own giving platform (myWJR) with impressive results. However, Craig has had the opposite experience and had to abandon a project to develop his organisation's own sponsorship pages, as there were too many problems with the software, making it hard for people to use. Whatever route you choose there are advantages and disadvantages of having your own sponsorship pages or using one of the generic providers. These are summarised in table 12.1.

Table 12.1: Having your own sponsorship platform versus generic sites for sponsorship

Your own charity platform or white-label product	Generic provider, such as JustGiving, Everyday Hero, or Network for Good
Able to capture more data on donors	Trusted by donors and many people already have accounts, which makes it easy for them to use.
Branding of pages/event to create a seamless experience for the supporter.	High investment in improving the technology (for example, making it work on tablets and mobile phones) and so making the user experience as easy as possible.
Generally slightly cheaper transaction fees.	No need for dedicated staff to update the software and free support.
Better lifetime value as you can follow up with all donors.	Many offer access to the application programming interface (API), which allows you to customise the experience and embed widgets on your website and social media platforms.

You need to balance sacrificing the potential loss of data for an easy donation experience that results in less abandoned transactions and higher average gifts. You can then work on capturing data in other ways.

Increasingly more and more donations are being made on smart phones and tablets rather than on PCs or laptops. Jon Waddingham, senior product manager at JustGiving, reports that 57 per cent of their website traffic is from mobile devices.[4] Facebook is responsible for 48 per cent of all visits, the majority of which come via mobile devices. Interestingly, in 2015 WhatsApp overtook Twitter as a source of sharing and referrals to the JustGiving site.[5]

What does this mean for fundraisers? Well, you need to be aware of the applications and technology your audience are using. You then need to build websites and processes that work seamlessly with the technology. If you don't make it easy for someone to donate on the device of their choice, you will be losing out on significant amounts of income.

Don't forget the automated response and thank-you messages

One of the big missed opportunities is the automated message that is sent after a donation is made. These are usually dull and thus mostly ignored by donors. We should never miss a chance to make a good impression and so we encourage you to test different ideas and update these messages regularly.

Here are a few ideas of things to include:

- Tell your best story about someone you've helped or a change that donations have helped to make in the world.

- Link to a short survey (and offer an incentive to do so) asking people to rate the giving experience and to ask if they'd like to learn more.

- Explain that most donations are anonymous and that this makes you sad as you can't say a proper thank you.

- Alternatively, link to a thank-you e-mail or share a picture.

- Ask people to like you on Facebook or follow you on Twitter.

- Give contact details of a real person and make it possible to respond to the e-mail.

Similarly, you can direct people to a specific page on your website after someone makes a gift. This is often neglected. However it is a great opportunity to thank the donor, share a story and attempt to capture more data.

Be ready to move quickly and follow trends

The #NoMakeUpSelfie didn't have a fundraising element when it first started. However, Cancer Research UK (CRUK) noticed that some participants were starting to donate and mentioning cancer charities. CRUK quickly provided a text number for people to donate to and became synonymous with the meme. By being the first to spot the opportunity CRUK raised millions of pounds for the charity.

A friend from Macmillan Cancer Support (another large UK-based cancer charity) told us that this led to an internal review of how Macmillan spot a trend and pick up on viral campaigns such as this in the future. They didn't want to miss out on such an opportunity again.

The results of this review were apparent when the ice-bucket challenge started to go viral. Macmillan moved quickly to establish themselves as a beneficiary in the UK instead of the Motor Neurone Disease Association (the UK equivalent of the US beneficiary ALS Association). The ethics of this were questionable and attracted criticism,[6] but it undoubtedly worked from a fundraising perspective.

None but the largest charities would be able to have a team dedicated to looking for such trends, but all staff should be trained to spot opportunities.

But don't try and create your own!
We're confident that many fundraisers were asked the question 'how do we create our own ice-bucket challenge or #NoMakeUpSelfie?' by colleagues. We're equally confident that lots of time and money have been spent on trying to come up with the next big viral-giving meme.

We'd urge you to respond to any such request with a polite 'no'. The simple truth is that no charity will be able to replicate these events, because by their very nature they are impossible to copy.

Even the largest, most successful fundraising events had humble beginnings and often didn't originate from charities, but from groups of supporters.

Movember was started by a group of friends in Australia in 2003 with just 30 people.[7] In the first year it didn't raise a penny. It was only in 2004 that the friends decided to raise money for a prostate cancer charity and the event has grown around the world since then.

An outside company[8] approached Imperial Cancer Research Fund (now CRUK) about organising the first Race for Life in 1994.

The Pan-Mass Challenge started in 1980 when Billy Starr and a bunch of friends raised money for a cancer charity through a bike-a-thon. It is now the largest mass participation event in the US and in 2014 raised $41 million for the Dana-Farber Cancer Institute.[9]

The annual London to Brighton bike ride for the British Heart Foundation was founded in 1975 and the first event only had 36 riders.[10] It didn't start raising money and become a fundraiser for BHF until 1980 but now has over 20,000 participants every year.

Use insight to look for new opportunities and to extend the life of your event
We are not saying you shouldn't create your own events, but you should avoid creating them in a vacuum and without proper research and insight.

Rather than trying to come up with an idea that will go viral, concentrate on knowing your donors, their lifestyle and look to design an event that fits with their values and passions.

You can then test on a small scale with a view to rolling out popular ideas to the wider community.

As an example, CRUK designed their successful Dryathlon event to appeal to young males, who were under-represented in the database. When CRUK were researching ideas and talking to young men they discovered two important points:[11]

1. Men are willing to support charity if it is low involvement, derives some personal benefit and is a talking point with friends.
2. It was important to piggyback existing behaviour and make the event something that would fit into men's lifestyle.

When looking closer at point two, CRUK's research found that 74 per cent of men had given up alcohol at some point and 50 per cent in January.

Hence, Dryathlon was born. It used very different language and design from more traditional CRUK events, but it understood its audience. By making the event easy to take part in, fun, healthy and a way to save money it was able to exceed all targets. In its first year it raised over £4.5 million and had 35,000 participants.

A number of new events in recent years have been based on targeting a group, studying their lifestyle and then designing an event that will fit in with them. We will discuss this ethnographic approach in chapter 19 on research methods.

Save the Children used similar research to launch Den Day in 2015. At a presentation at the Institute of Fundraising Insight Special Interest Group,[12] they explained how they developed the concept.

You would expect Save the Children to be well supported by parents of young children. However, their research discovered they weren't, so they set out to find out why. Was it because this demographic weren't interested or were there no fundraising products that appealed?

Save the Children used expert interviews, focus groups, diary entries and telephone conversations to test hypotheses and ideas. This revealed that traditional giving (regular gifts, donations) weren't appealing to this group. However, families would be willing to raise money together at an event.

From this they were able to create a fundraiser that fits with the lifestyle of young families, was easy to organise, but sufficiently different and that could create a link with the cause. The result was Den Day[12] – a chance for children to transform something into a fantastic den. The first year was a huge success and attracted over 500,000 participants.

One other thing to consider is the product life cycle of your event. Most products usually follow a pattern of growth, maturity and then decline over time. Looking for ways to keep your event fresh can extend its lifetime and keep participants coming back year after year. This could be something simple such as changing the route of a bike ride to organising offshoot events. For example, when CRUK saw a decline in Race for Life numbers they introduced Pretty Mudder (a five-kilometre muddy obstacle course) to give past participants a new challenge and something to return to.

Follow-up the money, keep in touch and integrate with other channels
Once the event is over you shouldn't stop talking to participants. You will need to thank them, chase any outstanding monies and plan how to engage the individual going forward. For example, one mistake is to put these fundraisers into the normal direct mail programme with no reference to how they raised money originally. Normally the profile of people doing peer-to-peer events is very different to those who respond to direct mail. You need to be more relevant than this and think how you can keep donors interested and involved.

At the end of the big event, consider holding a special get-together for participants. At this you can thank everyone who took part, let them know how the money raised will be spent and give out certificates or rewards to the top fundraisers.

It is also worth surveying participants. How did they find the event? How were the communications? Would they recommend it? What could be improved? As well as providing useful feedback for the future, it also keeps people engaged.

Often events donors are compartmentalised away from the rest of the organisation. This can be a mistake and a missed opportunity. Remember, from the donors' point of view there is only one charity and they won't necessarily see themselves as 'events' people.

When this goes wrong it can lead to a bad donor experience and destroy the relationship. Jonathon Cook, of data analysis company Insight-ful, describes an experience a friend had with a cancer charity: [14]

Two years ago, one of my close friends had cancer. One day, she thought she was fine. The next day, she was admitted to hospital for two months. While she was there, a cancer charity stepped in. Their research directly changed the course of her life. She went from near catastrophe to the possibility she would live.

Her husband felt eternally grateful; 40-years old and an avid cyclist, that summer, he signed up for Ride London, a 100-mile charity bike ride around the city. He raised several thousand pounds to support this charity that meant so much to his family.

The following year, his wife was officially in remission. In celebration and after his great experience the year before, six of his friends wanted to join him. In theory, that should have resulted in six times the amount he had raised the year before.

But a clerical error meant the charity didn't enter him into the race.

His friends were entered but he wasn't. He sent an email to the charity. They took weeks to respond. He replied to them, but didn't hear back so he phoned.

I need to stop here for a moment. He chased them. With his emotional connection, youth and years ahead of possible fundraising, why is he chasing anyone? Any charity should feel this kind of relationship is the foundation of their fundraising.

When he phoned, he was told there was nothing they could do. The person he spoke to seemed confused and didn't have any connection with the person sending emails. The lines of communication within the charity were not joined up.

He missed out on his place and the charity missed out on him.

Without my friend and the story of his wife, the fundraising momentum of the group fizzled out. The six friends raised a third of what he did alone the year before. Worse, there is a serious question over whether any of them will do it again next year. They talk about trying other charities, other events – the experience was a disappointment.

Sadly, we hear of similar stories from other charities. We look at silos and integration in chapter 10, but it is worth emphasising the point again here. No team should 'own' a donor, but instead should build a relationship where it becomes natural to ask the donor to do other actions such as take out a regular gift, volunteer, or sign up for another event.

CONCLUSION – PUTTING THE THEORY INTO ACTION

Relationships are the bedrock of a strong community and events fundraising programme. Yet it often feels that not as much time and attention is paid to this area of fundraising. We believe that this is a missed opportunity and there is huge potential in building strong relationships with supporters and encouraging them to fundraise from friends, family and colleagues.

When you get it right the rewards are impressive. Take Marie Curie.[15] In 2011 the charity was seeing static income in community fundraising and so implemented a new strategy. This was built around three goals:

1. To streamline the product portfolio to offer 'fewer but fuller' fundraising offers to supporters.
2. To grow their network of supporter groups by harnessing the enthusiasm of supporters and offering clearer direction and support.
3. To centralise fundraising administration to ensure consistency of experience for supporters and to free-up frontline fundraisers' time.

By switching from focusing on internal needs to the needs of fundraising volunteers' needs, Marie Curie was able to offer more useful support and direction to fundraising groups. This included revamping all fundraising materials, writing role descriptions for groups and setting clear objectives for their fundraising. This was combined with training and relationship building so supporters felt close to the charity and part of the team.

These changes have delivered massive increases in income, from £1.6 million in 2011 to a projected £5 million in 2015/16. The number of groups has grown from 261 to 609 and participation in core Marie Curie fundraising events, such as the Daffodil appeal and annual Swimathon, has greatly increased.

Charities of all sizes can follow Marie Curie's lead and put relationships at the heart of their community and peer-to-peer fundraising.

NOTES
1. As reported at http://www.maximillion.co.uk/event-management/which-fundraising-event-is-right-for-your-organization-3/ Last accessed 25 September 2015.
2. *UK Civil Society Almanac 2015* NCVO, London. Executive summary available at: http://data.ncvo.org.uk/a/almanac15/individuals/ Last accessed 25 September 2015.
3. *Peer to Peer 30 2014*, The Peer-to-Peer Professional Forum. Summary available at: https://www.peertopeerforum.com/run-walk-ride-resources/research/ Last accessed 25 September 2015.
4. This is for the three months until end of September 2015.
5. For a discussion on how JustGiving have developed tools for WhatsApp see: http://blog.justgiving.com/whats-up-with-

6. For example see: Macmillan Cancer accused of 'hijacking' ice bucket challenge. *The Independent*, 24 August 2014. Available at: http://www.independent.co.uk/news/uk/home-news/macmillan-cancer-accused-of-hijacking-the-ice-bucket-challenge-9688310.html. Also in this article a Macmillan spokesperson said they had changed their practices after missing out on #NoMakeUpSelfie.
7. For a history of Movember and the money raised visit: https://uk.movember.com/about/history Last accessed 27 September 2015.
8. See this letter from ICRF acknowledging the source of the idea and company responsible: https://cowanglobal.files.wordpress.com/2014/01/icrf-letter.jpg
9. For a history of the Pan-Mass Challenge visit http://www.pmc.org/about/pmc-history Last accessed 26 September 2015.
10. As stated in a BHF press release for the 2015 event: https://www.bhf.org.uk/news-from-the-bhf/news-archive/2015/january/pippa-middleton-launches-our-40th-london-to-brighton-bike-ride Last accessed 27 September 2015. This is Brighton says that the first event for the BHF was in 1980: http://www.thisbrighton.co.uk/cycling/bike-run.htm Last accessed 27 September 2015.
11. For further insight read *Cancer Research UK's Dryathlon* on SOFII. Available at: http://sofii.org/case-study/cancer-research-uks-dryathlon and *Two years of Dryathlon: an agency perspective* by digital agency Manifesto who worked on the campaign. Available at: http://manifesto.co.uk/two-years-dryathlon-agency/ Both accessed on 28 September 2015.
12. Presentation available from Insight SIG 2014 conference page at: http://insightsig.org/november-conference-2014/ Last accessed 1 October 2015.
13. You can read more about Den Day at: http://denday.savethechildren.org.uk/about/ Last accessed 1 October 2015.
14. *A fundraising relationship that went horribly wrong* Insight-ful blog, September 2015. Available at: http://www.insight-ful.co.uk/04092015-a-fundraising-story-that-went-drastically-wrong/ Last accessed 1 October 2015.
15. As presented by Mark Winton, head of regional fundraising (UK) Marie Curie at the Institute of Fundraising 2015 National Fundraising Convention.

Major donor fundraising: launching a twenty-first century programme

The opportunity to engage major donors can be extremely rewarding for a fundraiser. But it can also be incredibly intimidating.

As a young community fundraiser, Paul was allocated a portfolio of prospects to call with a view to building relationships and soliciting substantial gifts. He was quite terrified of the idea of contacting these influential and powerful people. Unfortunately, many had only a tenuous connection to the charity. Most had given in a 'transactional' manner via a donation made at an event or a silent auction bid and did not have a proper relationship with the charity. As a result, even when he did manage to get through, he was rebuffed by the vast majority; some of them responding in quite a forthright manner. It was a disappointing and sobering experience.

Fast forward a few years and his viewpoint was revolutionised. He began, gradually, to cultivate major donors effectively and secure significant donations. Indeed, when a cheque arrived in the post from one of these supporters, as a direct result of Paul's stewardship, he was exhilarated. It was for £50,000, six times more than the donor had ever previously given.

It was a supporter Paul had taken the opportunity to engage, build a relationship with and solicit successfully. Nothing had ever given him more pride in his relatively short career. At that moment, Paul realised the amazing transformative potential of major gift fundraising.

PHILANTHROPY – GLOBAL TRENDS

The potential for soliciting gifts of the highest value has never been greater.

Rapid wealth creation, coupled with uneven distribution, means the world now has a record 1,826 billionaires.[1] *The Coutts Million Dollar Donors Report*, which studies philanthropists' giving across the UK, USA, Russia, the Middle East, China and Hong Kong, found in 2014 that charities and organisations received a total of $26.3 billion in philanthropic gifts – an increase of $19 billion in just two years.² The USA leads the field, accounting for nearly $17 billion of these gifts, with higher education the preferred choice of philanthropists in most of the regions.

The growing trend seems to have arisen from a change in mind-set; a reaction against decline and austerity in the years leading up to this point. Matt Hermer, CEO of the Ignite Group, which sponsored the ARK (Absolute Return for Kids) Serpentine Party and the Love Ball in the UK, highlights the seismic shift:

> *[Since the recent economic downturn] ... there is a greater humility, an awareness of the value of money and desire to do the most you can with it. Philanthropy is definitely in vogue.*³

Symptomatic of this trend is the Giving Pledge, a philanthropic initiative launched by Warren Buffet and the Bill and Melinda Gates Foundation to encourage the super rich to pledge their fortunes early in their lives, so that they can have more control of how it's spent. Since it was launched in 2010, the pledge has recruited 193 billionaires, including Facebook founder Mark Zuckerberg and New York mayor Michael Bloomberg.⁴

Additionally, when Google went public the founders, Sergey Brin and Larry Page, announced that a slice of the search engine's equity and profits would be donated to Google.org, a philanthropic arm.

Underlying this growth in major giving is a complex and changing environment. Rather than inheriting their wealth, the majority of wealthy people are now self-made millionaires. Their attitudes have been shaped by their backgrounds. As Philip Beresford, compiler of the *Sunday Times Rich List* points out:

> *When the list started in 1989 only a quarter of the very wealthy were self-made millionaires. Now it is more like three quarters. The bulk of today's super rich are people with their feet on the ground, for whom poverty is not remote abstraction but something to be overcome.*⁵

With this in mind, for modern philanthropists, understanding the impact of their charitable giving is vital; it's not enough for them just to give, it's about leverage. They want, and expect, to know how their donation is going to make a difference.

Matthew Bishop, of *The Economist*, refers to these donors as philanthrocapitalists: wealthy entrepreneurs who are applying the same principles to philanthropy that made them successful business people:

> They make big bets, demand results, take risks, want some control over how their money is spent and so on. The quintessential philanthrocapitalist, of course, is Gates, but many others are now following his lead, trying to forge a new kind of activist philanthropy.[6]

As these donors seek greater impact from their giving, they are also investing in the services of professionals to advise them in this area. Private client advisors are emerging in the market offering a philanthropy guidance service to wealthy individuals. Organisations such as New Philanthropy Capital and Geneva Global, for example, provide tools that can help individuals measure the impact of their gift and optimise it.

Their use is becoming more widespread. As Dan Corry, NPC's chief executive, outlines:

> Since NPC's 2010 publication, The Business of Philanthropy, called for further, urgent development of the philanthropy advice market a lot has happened. Philanthropy advice has become much more common place – for instance, within the UK, private banks having an in-house philanthropy advisor has gone from being a differentiator to being essential.[7]

This charitable investment applies to time as well as money. The wealthy volunteer most in Ireland and India where 20 per cent of the population actively offers more than five hours per week (compared to just 10 per cent in the UK). Emma Turner, director of client philanthropy at Barclays Wealth, outlines the importance of these statistics:

> A new breed of wealthy philanthropists [is] evolving, who are more socially aware and motivated to give back to the communities they came from, as well as to global causes. These givers are increasingly engaging in 'go-giving' as they seek not just to support charities with monetary donations, but also by providing their time and expertise to benefit causes.
>
> The days of simply 'writing' a cheque and walking away' are fading fast... donors may start their philanthropic journey by giving up their time to support a charity but this may lead to financial giving as well. Equally this can work

the other way round, with financial donors going on to support charities with their time.[8]

LAUNCHING A MAJOR DONOR PROGRAMME

But how best to capitalise on these philanthropic trends and successfully engage the growing number of prospective major donors?

For those starting a high-value relationship fundraising programme, this can be a daunting task: where to start, who to target, what activities provide the greatest chances of success? Much has been written on this topic, assessing prospects' age, warmth and propensity to give. Giles Pegram CBE, who initiated the NSPCC's groundbreaking Full Stop appeal to end cruelty to children, noted that the Pareto Principle (stating that 80 per cent of your income will come from 20 per cent of your supporters) would apply to major givers too, so the focus would need to be on the elite within that group. This may be true, but it is certain that it is not a one-size-fits-all equation. It all depends on the charity: its size, its board, its track record in major giving to date, its networks and, all importantly, the makeup of its database.

Research

Your donors' giving records will tell you a great deal and should be properly analysed, not just for this purpose but to inform your fundraising activities across the board. Looking at supporter patterns, as outlined in chapter 11, as well as analysing attrition and acquisition rates, will tell you what is working and what is not; the challenges and opportunities that exist for your charity.

It is important to note that the donor pyramid will look very different for each charity. Some are broad based, requiring strong focus on intricate mass individual giving programmes. Others are more niche causes, relying on small networks of major donors and special events. The level at which a supporter should be classed as a major donor will depend on the organisation's structure and potential, as well as the number and capacity of the charity's major gift fundraisers.

Major donors require personalised and tailored donor care and so the team must only take on as many prospects as they can practically handle in terms of providing first-class support. The programme should be built accordingly, prioritising from the highest value donors downwards. For some organisations this will mean their programme comprises donors valued at £100,000+ per annum, for others £5,000+.

This should not just depend on gifts to date, but also giving potential. The analysis of your database, either in house or by a wealth-screening agency, will highlight warm prospects who might be suitable for the programme.

It's important, however, to consider a couple of notes of caution before embarking on such a process.

In the UK, the Information Commissioner's Office has recently outlined the need for charities to state clearly their intention to carry out research of this kind, even if prospects' details are all in the public domain. The approach should be overtly incorporated into privacy statements - failure to do so led to substantial fines for 13 UK charities in December 2016 and April 2017. It's an evolving debate and it's essential for major donor fundraisers to remain abreast of the latest developments in this area.

Additionally, it's important to highlight that screening will never prove to be comprehensive and will almost certainly over-estimate prospects' giving potential. Alison Montgomery, former head of research at NSPCC, rightly advises that it is liquid assets that count – your prospect may own a stately home on paper but if he or she has to maintain it and his or her wealth is tied up in it, then he has little to give away. Such research is a measure of wealth first and foremost, which does not always necessarily correlate with levels of charitable giving. It is, nonetheless, often a useful place to start when assessing the value of potential major donors in your database.

In order to ensure cost-efficiency, it is important to focus on warm supporters in the first instance, especially if the programme is in its infancy. As highlighted in chapter 11, it typically costs at least five times as much to recruit a new donor as it does to develop an existing supporter. However, it is advisable that the research process also includes colder prospects, especially those who have just come into wealth, have an obvious affinity with your cause and, or, have recently commenced their philanthropic activities.

The data screen will help you to prepare a shortlist of whom to reach out to, but additional manual checks and research systems need to be applied to supplement this and put your charity ahead of the field. For example, investigation of supporters' trusts and foundations, as well as simple internet searches to highlight other philanthropic activities, will help to prioritise those that are most likely to become benefactors.

New technologies are also enhancing the opportunities for prospect research. LinkedIn, for example, the professional social network, is a veritable goldmine, which has, as yet, not been recognised and utilised to its full potential. Linking with warm prospects allows modern high-value fundraisers to build up their virtual little black book of contacts. As it is dynamic, rather than static, it will always remain up-to-date and it can be accessed throughout their career.

It can also enable fundraisers to find routes of referral to second and third level contacts. In addition, information on existing donors can also be enhanced through the network, enabling you to better understand their professional expertise, their company, their alma mater, as well as areas of interest.

Moreover, colder prospects can also be sourced via this site, which, as of 2015, possesses more than 380 million members in over 200 countries and territories. If no warm introduction can be obtained a simple invitation to 'link in' can establish whether or not a donor is potentially open to a conversation. A request for advice can indeed be very effective in this process. The gaining of professional expertise from highly experienced marketers, business people and financial managers can be immensely useful in its own right and can also deliver the opening that will allow you to commence a professional relationship and build a personal rapport. After seeing a successful entrepreneur on *BBC News 24*, who had built a small business comparable in size to Paul's charity, he sent a LinkedIn request to meet for some advice. Not only did that person become a key advisor to the organisation, but also a significant donor and a member of the charity's volunteer fundraising board.

Motivations for giving and categories of major donors

The profile of these potential supporters will depend on the cause. For many, including Ken Burnett, the key cohort is the 50+ age group: there are more of them, they have more money (owning 76 per cent of all the financial wealth held by UK households) [9] and they often have more time. Even within this age bracket though, there are groups who will tend to support different types of charity. In 2009, Barclays Wealth commissioned Ledbury Research to conduct an in-depth quantitative study of 500 high net worth individuals in the USA and the UK on attitudes to philanthropy. A number of sub-groupings emerged:

Reactive donors – predominantly male, high-earning executives. They tend to be 'social givers' donating through peer expectation rather than through any moral or social conviction. They would rather spend the money on pleasures though, and see giving to charities as a way of offsetting increasing criticism of the wealthy. They tend to give to health and medical charities and are more likely to want public recognition for their donations.
Cultured inheritors – they tend to be in their late fifties and sixties often in

semi-retirement and with young grandchildren. They are successful in their own right but have inherited money too. Their motivation is social and moral rather than religious. They do have a culture of giving, but not necessarily the largest amounts, as they will be keen to bequeath money to their family. They will give time too and are one of the few groups still to support the arts, as well as children and local causes.

Professional philanthropists – high-earning executives and business earners who have reached the pinnacle of their careers or have sold their business interests. These are very large donors, demanding of charities and want to see impact and returns. Motivated by religious, political and social beliefs, they tend to give to education (especially universities) and religious causes, especially those that are local. They tend not, however, to be keen on global or environmental causes.

Whilst these core high net worth individuals are likely to be a priority for your charity (depending on the cause), they should not form the only target group, especially if your networks are limited. These prospects, particularly those that are long established in their philanthropic activities, are difficult to access. Many are likely to have already settled on preferred causes and will be approached on a regular basis by numerous charities. They tend to use standard brush-offs to protect their over-stretched resources.

Go-givers, however, are ambitious philanthropists with an entrepreneurial approach to charitable funding and could prove to be a fertile market. To date, they have demonstrated resilience to the effects of any downturn and they are keen to see the impact of their giving. Those under 45 have displayed the greatest responsibility to share their wealth in order to help charities survive during challenging economic environments. According to the research, nearly half of $10,000 donors in this age bracket said they plan to donate what they have earned in order to witness its impact.[10]

They divide into sub-groups:

Eco givers – the most likely of all groups to be female, they are predominantly successful businesswomen who are happy to organise events. As causes, they tend to favour environmental work and disaster relief, but also support children's charities and social welfare.

Altruistic entrepreneurs - typically middle-aged business owners with teenage children. They tend to give through duty and religious beliefs play a part in their desire to be philanthropic. Not social givers, they are driven by personal fulfilment. They will engage their family, in particular their children, in supporting the causes they serve. Their areas of interest are widespread. They give substantial donations and are happy to be active fundraisers.

Cultivation of individuals

Through these processes, donors can be sourced and prioritised but, in order for them to be managed and maintained effectively, a high-value communication strategy must be developed and a donor care system devised.

This should begin with the database coding of all major donors and prospects, whether they are individuals or organisations, to ensure they can be monitored and removed, where appropriate, from the general communication cycle. Instead, they should be placed on a dedicated major supporter journey.

For the reasons stated above, it is important that the potential of donors is taken into account when selecting these prospects. They should then be flagged on the database and, alongside the core major donor communications (e.g. tailored newsletter sent from account manager contact), action reminders should be set up for each of them, following discussions with trustees and those who know them best.

This was critical for Paul at World Jewish Relief. Previously donors had just been engaged when a board or staff member noticed that they had not given for some time; this does not help to build a long-term, successful and sustainable relationship. A series of reminders managed by administrators, or the major gift fundraiser, if the team is small, is essential to maintain meaningful conversations.

You would be surprised just how much money can be raised simply by plugging the holes in the system and ensuring that no major donor stops giving for the wrong reason. So often, at World Jewish Relief, supporters had ceased their support due to systemic failings rather than a conscious decision to end their engagement with the charity. The charity was able to generate an additional £100,000 per annum, simply by ensuring all warm lower level major donors were stewarded and asked for their annual gift at the appropriate time.

These prospects are likely to be extremely busy people and even your most loyal supporters are unlikely to be proactively seeking to converse with the charity. As fundraisers, we are unlikely to even appear on their list of reminders and we must respond accordingly, setting the agenda and ensuring we keep them informed and motivated, as well as soliciting them on a regular (but appropriate) basis.

Whilst there is certainly a degree of science involved, it's often tempting to over-complicate systems and processes. Long-term, detailed stewardship plans can help to crystallise thinking and a strategic approach, but can often be too complicated and inevitably inaccurate. While you should certainly have a goal and general direction in mind for each supporter, assumption is always a danger and it is highly unlikely that donors will follow your prophecies.

A few key touch points will be useful for planning purposes, but the engagement process itself will develop more organically, at a pace and in a direction unique to each supporter. Detailed notes on each stage of the journey are essential, however, so you can keep track of your progress. They also ensure a smooth transition to your successor, should you leave your organisation whilst cultivating a prospect.

Finally, no matter how powerful your cause, or how effective your proposals, this is about relationship fundraising after all, so most importantly, you must have the right professionals involved in your major giving programme. It is very much a speciality within the sector and the possession of exemplary interpersonal skills, gravitas and grounded confidence are essential. Additionally, fundraisers must be comfortable and keen to make these personal approaches for funding.

While Paul was at Macmillan Cancer Support major donor cultivation was delegated to local community fundraising teams. Not only did the substantial skills of the fundraisers lie elsewhere, but, more importantly, they were not motivated to carry out this work. Instead, they understandably preferred the core community tasks, for which they had been recruited in the first place. The results were unsurprisingly unimpressive and Macmillan have since centralised these activities. Now they have allocated this key account management to dedicated major gift fundraisers.

Sara Hertz, a trust and major gift specialist, now working at the Academy of Natural Sciences of Drexel University in Philadelphia, describes the rationale for this approach:

> *Relationship building with donors is like building a friendship in your personal life. It should flow naturally. You have to put yourself into it. When I worked in the US some donors sent me gifts on the birth of my son and some came to my leaving party. Of course donors must be committed to the cause, but it helps if they are also committed to you.*[11]

This is correct but perhaps does not go far enough: it isn't simply helpful that they are committed to you personally, it is essential and is of almost equal importance to the cause. In today's competitive world, where many worthy causes create a cacophony of noise to gain donors' attention and funds, in order to stand out from the crowd you must build a strong personal relationship with these prospects. Like any friendship, don't expect donors to come to your aid before they know and trust you. Patience is indeed a virtue; the relationship must be built gradually and in a genuine manner, so when it is time to make the 'ask', it feels natural and appropriate. Ken Burnett makes the point convincingly:

> *People give to people, not to organisations...[they] want to deal with people they like and trust... and want to believe the fundraiser is as committed as they are. Donors need to believe in the causes they are asked to give to and in the people who do the asking. Your enthusiasm and commitment need to shine through.*[12]

Consequently, it is of paramount importance that you ensure each key prospect, whether a trust, major donor, or corporate prospect, is allocated one contact inside your organisation and, when offering different options for engagement, you work collaboratively across your team. To the donor, the experience must appear seamless, so ensure you present a unified front.

Getting in front of the prospect is the first step. If she or he is a warm supporter, she will, more often than not, be pleased to see you, especially if she has not been involved. It is critical though that you make it clear from the outset that you are not coming to solicit further funds in the first instance. Reporting on the supporter's giving to date, sharing your charity's plans and gaining feedback is a much better place to start. It is also more likely to get you invited to a meeting. Indeed, who would give money to someone they barely know?

If the donor is not 'warm', an introduction from a mutual contact is essential too (LinkedIn, as highlighted above, is good option for sourcing the appropriate connection). Otherwise, you will most likely join the long queue of enthusiastic fundraisers attempting to engage the prospect in vain.

The initial meeting is an opportunity to gain vital feedback and perspectives on the organisation. Some open-ended questions will help to achieve this, allowing you to establish motivations for supporting your cause: what elements of your work appeal most, the donor's views on your communications, how she or he would like to engage in future. This will help to open a dialogue, which should be ongoing and genuinely bilateral.

Make sure you note everything relevant too, including family details and personal preferences. This will help to build the relationship and will place you in a far better position next time you meet.

The case for support – emotion, impact and demonstrating need

As you progress the relationship, it's important to have the right materials available for your meetings. At the most basic level, this includes well-branded, clearly presented and succinct literature. No major investor is going to donate to any organisation in which he or she has no faith and which fails to be professional in approach.

The centrepiece of this portfolio is the case for support, a compelling document that outlines exactly why a donor should invest in your cause. It should highlight clearly the impact their potential support will have. The document should also include details of your cost-efficiency and performance measurement, key concerns for most major philanthropists. More detailed responses to these inevitable questions must be also prepared in advance, as well as on other topics that may make your organisation seem controversial or unpalatable. Overheads and reserves will certainly need to be addressed in any dialogue with donors of this level and you must be confident, clear and fluent in your response.

Tom Ahern, in his book *Seeing Through a Donor's Eyes*, gives some detailed advice on the construction of your case for support. He summarises the key points for inclusion as follows:

> Why us? What is our group doing that is so extraordinary?
> Why now? 'The thing that makes your solicitation stand out is the urgency of doing something about the problem now', says Ahern.
> Why would prospective supporters invest specifically in your organisation? What is their motivation for doing so and what is their connection to your cause?

'Possibly the hardest question for charities to answer is the third one; this is where the issue of donor-centricity comes in', explains Ahern.[13]

It's important for an organisation to find that connection with the individual donor. Alumni, for example, give because of their loyalty to and compassion for their former school. So you need to establish the reason or reasons for your donor to lend their loyalty and compassion to your organisation. As you have been actively listening, the answers to your open-ended questions from earlier should help to establish these vital insights.

Alongside this key overview, as noted above, detailed, well-presented documentation on your individual projects are a must too. These should include a punchy executive summary, as well as a clear outline of the need, emotive but succinct case studies, the project's activities, an impact assessment, monitoring and evaluation plans and a clear table of costs, broken down into its constituent parts. Be prepared to answer additional questions on the project's viability, its long-term prospects and how you plan to find the remainder of funds.

Smaller gifts can be gained from most donors for projects that are being funded retrospectively or for general purposes. But for the largest gifts, especially when you are aiming for six or seven figures, the onus will be on the fundraiser to give an outline of the charity's plans and the projects it is hoping to initiate

It's not a problem if these programmes are simply conceptual at this stage. Indeed, if donors can advise and feel like they can have some input into their construction, then this can work to your benefit. Critically though, they must feel that without their support the project would not get off the ground. The more convincingly you can outline the potential impact of their gift, the more you are likely to receive in return.

Major donor 'products'

To meet the needs of major donors and adapt to the demands of a changing market, we must also create the correct structure and mechanisms for giving.

Some of the more traditional products have their limitations. 'Giving clubs' for example, where donors receive a specific level of recognition and communication in return for donating at a certain threshold, have their place, but only on a transactional basis. At World Jewish Relief, for example, the patrons programme was a useful mechanism by which to recruit and maintain donors at an annual giving level of £5,000. But it was a fairly cosmetic model that would engage reactive donors without necessarily increasing the depth of their involvement.

These techniques become more effective, though, when they incorporate the use of networks and relationship fundraising methodology. In the early 2000s, for example, St Cuthbert's College, in Auckland, New Zealand, initiated a fundraising vehicle to facilitate the giving of large donations (in excess of $2,000). They named it 'the Robertson circle', referencing a well-known name in the school. Donors become Robertson circle members for life.

The scheme consists of four giving levels: guardian (over $50,000), fellow

($25,000-$49,999), supporter ($10,000-$24,999) and friend ($2,000-$9,999). Additionally, donors have the choice of supporting six separate restricted funds: an endowment, a building, innovation, sport, arts and scholarships.

To help the director of development, Debbie Cook, maximise every opportunity to recruit Robertson circle donors they instigated a patron system comprising five prominent businessmen and women. They asked them to use their influence and their networks to help solicit donations.

The patrons also work closely with the trustees, with a board member chairing the Robertson circle, sharing policy and strategy in the process. Patrons are selected for their endorsement and support of the school, through recommendations from either board members or existing patrons and on the strength of their reputation in the community and, or, business world.

Patrons understand that they are endeavouring to encourage donations to the college and are happy to approach people within their sphere of influence. Engagement with these patrons on their terms is of paramount importance. Some will be the first to talk to class groups, hold fundraising drinks evenings in their house, or lead a fundraising event. Others, however, never make approaches and are just happy to share their knowledge, or networks and to encourage others.

Debbie and her team specifically do not make the expectation onerous for the group. The emphasis is on enjoyment, fulfilment and achieving great benefits for the school. Consequently, most patrons remain on the Robertson circle for about four years and so far the school has raised $12,750,000 during the course of its existence.

The programme is donor focused too. Those most likely to give are those that are warmest with the greatest vested interest, typically current parents who are highly committed and attached to the school. Cultivation and recognition also remain key factors. There is a robust stewardship programme in place, including the annual Robertson circle drinks evening, a cultivation event to which all members are invited. Here the principal gives a 'state of the nation' address informing donors about the health and achievements of the school.

Additionally, the patrons hold their own annual social event, where they celebrate the giving of their time and efforts. This has been modified over time based on donor feedback: time-poor supporters have requested more informal information breakfasts, or social drinks with their former classmates instead of a more formal dinner.

Through these functions the college has unearthed a number of committed volunteers and the vast majority of these have progressed to become significant donors. All because they have benefited from a gradual, engaging and personalised approach to relationship building, bringing them closer to the college and its vision for the future.

Other mechanisms, like endowment gifts, also give us the opportunity to meet the requirements of the newer breed of donors, by delivering return on investment. These funds, which are often earmarked for a specific project, produce ongoing income from their annual interest. Their use is growing, particularly in higher education. In the USA, for example, total giving to endowment funds was $4.288 billion in 1998 and $6.965 billion in 2006, an increase of 62 per cent over eight years.[14] It's important that we build the necessary infrastructure and proposals to take advantage of this growth area.

This is most pertinent for the younger generation. As noted earlier, these self-made philanthropists are looking to engage in the formation of the projects more than ever before, to participate in its implementation and to see clear impact and return on their investment. This is exemplified by the growth of seed-funding websites, such as Kiva and GlobalGiving. Here donors have the opportunity to invest in individuals and gain an insight into what has been achieved as a result of their generosity. They are then presented with the chance to be reimbursed, or to reinvest it in a new initiative.

To meet the needs of the go-giver philanthropists who invest in this manner, the onus will be on fundraisers to build closer relationships, sharing our plans and challenges in greater detail than ever before.

World Jewish Relief did just that as it sought to build new networks among the key 35 to 44-year-old target market: the next generation of major donors. They conducted focus groups with targeted prospects to build a feeling of engagement and ownership of the products created. The result was a flexible programme, WJR: The Network, which gave participants the opportunity to commit to donate and, or, raise £2,000 per year to sponsor the home repairs of one of the charity's beneficiaries. In return, they would be given tangible project feedback every six months, recognition and networking opportunities, and invitations to exclusive events at sought after venues. By fusing charity and supporter needs an exciting and effective new product was developed, and the results were impressive: in the first year, the vast majority of participants to focus groups signed up enthusiastically.

We could go further still. With donors wanting to generate impact and to engage more with charity professionals themselves, we should also give them the option to restrict their donation instead to a fundraising activity. If we are competent in our roles, these areas, rather than traditional charity programmes, could generate the greatest returns.

Dan Pallotta, an expert in nonprofit sector innovation and a pioneering social entrepreneur, puts it perfectly:

> *Leverage is the mantra of the times in philanthropy, and rightly so. The venture philanthropy movement, [however] only gets it only half right. Donors are strongly urged to seek out the organizations with the best, most innovative programs and fund those programs. But they're looking for them in the wrong places. They're missing the greatest leverage point of all: the multiplying effects of smart investments in fundraising. If you want to maximize the social effects of your donation, why would you buy, for example, $100,000 worth of great educational programming for inner city kids when the same $100,000 directed toward fundraising could generate enough money to buy $1 million worth of it? They're squandering the real and massive potential of their capital.*
>
> *Fundraising multiplies the potential of charitable gifts. There's nothing radical about this. It's only radical to those who have no experience with it. That lack of experience, endemic among donors, is a significant liability. That dream won't come to pass by funding programs, because program funding cannot multiply anything. The smart money is in multiplication.*[15]

This is a significant shift for charities and to achieve it we must rethink our approach to fundraising. We need to be asking ourselves how this new breed of entrepreneurial donors can invest in our income-generating activities and how we can best demonstrate impact. For example, donors may wish to fund additional telemarketing, face-to-face fundraising activities, new events, or perhaps even invest in posts for new members of staff who could generate additional revenue.

As with our programming requests, these proposals must stand up to scrutiny. They will need to clearly outline in detail the rationale, the projected returns, any risks and how the activity will be monitored, evaluated and reported. Creating these progressive opportunities will enable you to set yourself apart from your more traditional competitors and gain the support of a new generation of philanthropists. It may not be for every major investor, but if we are sufficiently adhering to relationship fundraising principles, then it should be a clear option, alongside more traditional alternatives.

Making the ask

The first important point on making a direct request for funds from major donors is that there are no set rules, especially with regard to the length of cultivation required. True, it is likely to take more time to solicit a six- or seven-figure gift, perhaps as long as 18 months or more. But that does not mean it is not possible to achieve such success in a shorter time. Donors are not uniform and what applies to one does not necessarily apply to another.

It is, however, critical to sense how the relationship is developing and whether the time is right to make the request for funds. As a general rule, if it feels too soon, it *is* too soon. Certainly, experience tells us that you can make a £5,000 request for funding in the first meeting, but this could quite likely be a token gift, in response to an overly direct ask. In the long term, it may well be very hard to get back through the door to that prospect and it could be at the cost of a far higher donation further down the line.

A one-to-one meeting offers the best environment to make a request for funding in a personal and appropriate manner. Asking face-to-face is more effective than the phone, which is in turn preferable to isolated written communication. As with the cultivation process though, it is important that the right person makes the approach. This will vary according to the prospect in question.

Generally, however, it should be the representative of the charity that has the closest relationship with the prospect. As we move into a new age of philanthropic giving, there is nothing to prevent the professional fundraiser making the ask if she or he feels most comfortable doing so. However, if the donor is of senior standing or is a social giver, for whom status is important, then a trustee or the CEO may well be preferable.

With this meeting, it is important to imagine journeying through a series of doors, checking the programme or proposal is suitable, that the donors can and are able to provide support and, of course, that the amount you are requesting is appropriate. Even though they are likely to be senior professionals, don't assume that your prospects won't need to know the difference this will make to the lives of your beneficiaries. They will appreciate a list of tangible, worthwhile benefits, not just the methods by which you will carry out this work. Conversely, you should highlight what would happen if this funding isn't secured. All of this forms part of *selling the clean, not the soap*. As Professor Theodore Levitt puts it:

> *When a customer buys a quarter inch drill, what he really wants is a quarter inch hole.*[16]

Once you have made the request for funding the most critical element is that you resist the temptation to fill the silence and to answer for them. If they are taking their time, it is likely it is because they are considering the request and it is important you give them the space to do so. It may feel awkward, but it is perhaps the defining moment of the whole cultivation period.

For some donors, this opportunity to engage once, or on an annual basis, may suffice. Giles Pegram, when he was at the NSPCC, found that one donor had been giving £5,000 annually for several years, having had minimal contact with the charity. Once he was added to the major giving programme, however, and his gift was acknowledged personally, he doubled his annual contribution.

Paul experienced the same thing with one supporter, Mr G, a few years ago. He had donated £5,000 to the charity's Asian tsunami emergency appeal back in 2004, but was neither personally thanked nor engaged thereafter. Paul came across him in a lapsed donor file on World Jewish Relief's database and called to set up a meeting. He was understandably rather perplexed as to why someone would want to give feedback on his support over three years after his gift! But, being a major donor fundraiser, Paul was persistent on the phone and he accepted.

The meeting went well and Mr G was pleased to hear more about the organisation. It transpired that he was moderately offended to have never been asked to one of the charity's special events. So Paul asked him to attend the annual dinner, World Jewish Relief's flagship event, as his personal guest, free of charge. He enjoyed the function, at London's prestigious Guildhall, and Paul felt the relationship had been furthered. It certainly did not feel right, however, to make an additional ask at this time, given the donor's previous experience, so Paul refrained from doing so.

A couple of months later, at the end of the year, Paul received a note from Mr G in the post. It thanked him for all the information and fed back very positively on his experience at the event. Enclosed with the letter was a cheque for £15,000, three times more than his previous single gift. He has since given over £75,000 to the organisation, all because someone bothered to engage him, feedback on what his giving had achieved, listen to what he had to say and spent the time to build a relationship: simple, really.

Stewardship and managing a caseload

Hunger, determination and curiosity are traits of successful high-level relationship builders. Richard Perry and Jeff Schreifels of the Veritus Group, a US agency, give the example of one inexperienced, but enormously effective fundraiser who they met:

> *In one year she has developed a caseload of over 100 donors and has helped bring in over $300,000. So how did she accomplish all this? By being curious. She asked questions – lots of questions. She started talking to donors, thanking them, making connections and reaching out to people in her community to help her. Whenever she came up against a barrier, she figured out a way to get around or move through it. The potential [in her] caseload is unbelievable – all cultivated by someone with no training in major gifts...but [who] was curious...and fearless.[17]*

Perseverance is key too. However, the greatest opportunity to build effective relationships and really bring your supporters closer to you and your organisation, is not during the solicitation, but immediately after they have donated.

Unlike our commercial counterparts, it is really the only time that charities have the opportunity to offer consumers anything in return, to make them feel special and valued. It will be at this stage that they will be most sensitive to the organisation's approach and its ability to deliver the highest levels of donor care. And actions here speak louder than words.

So the immediacy of the response is all-important and it must, of course, be personal, and tailored. A phone call for any major gift is a must, and it should come from a senior person within the organisation. Similarly, the thank-you letter must be issued immediately. It should clearly convey your genuine gratitude and should outline emotively the impact of the gift. Additionally, you should extend an invitation to see your work in action, if the donor hasn't had the opportunity to do so already.

Recognition, for some, may be essential too. As Ken Burnett points out, while Americans celebrate recognition it is not the norm in UK. For certain donors though, it's a key component of personalised cultivation. Sir Thomas Hughes-Hallett, former CEO of Marie Curie Cancer Care in the UK, shares this view:

> *In the UK it's still seen as vulgar to talk about money but we need a greater culture of celebration of giving at every level.[18]*

And it does not end here. A first major gift should be the springboard to many more, perhaps of greater value, if the donor is impressed by the use and recognition of their first donation. Penelope Burk, in her annual Canadian and

American survey, makes the point starkly. Should the initial gift be acknowledged promptly and in a meaningful way, and progress is reported on in measurable terms before an additional request for funding, 67 per cent of supporters said they would definitely or probably renew. Moreover, 52 per cent would make a larger gift and 67 per cent would continue to give indefinitely assuming they received these considerations each time they gave.[19] Gratitude and information lead to donor loyalty, the ultimate goal.

Essentially, the cultivation cycle should begin all over again, commencing with a comprehensive progress report on their last gift. The timing and format of this should be agreed with the donor as soon as they have given. Like the proposal, the update should include personal case studies, as well as detailed financial reporting. And, if anything has not gone to plan, do not try to hide it. Be transparent from the outset. Let donors know exactly what you have learned and what the solution is. They will be far more understanding than you think and will appreciate your candour.

Building their trust, in you and your organisation, is after all what this is all about.

CONCLUSION

There has undoubtedly been a seismic shift in major giving fundraising over the last few decades. We have moved into a new era of philanthropy, but as well as presenting numerous challenges, the opportunities are greater than ever.

By embracing this change, and involving this new generation of major donors in our work, more than ever before, the potential for growth is enormous. It will require absolute transparency and the highest levels of professionalism. Indeed, we must be prepared to let donors into the heart of our business and be ready for the highest levels of scrutiny.

And this should be welcomed. Anything that forces us to raise our standards and to be more commercially minded has to represent a positive step in the right direction. In essence, we are being tasked with earning our income rather than being granted it by default, or by gaining it through an anachronistic sense of benevolence. And this, in turn, places more emphasis on the skills of the modern major gift fundraiser.

Donors will be expecting us to convince them of the impact of their gift and of the effectiveness of our organisation. They will be giving us their time, their advice and their money, and we must be prepared to impress them at every turn. We are in the privileged position of being able to engage the most successful and influential people and to connect them with the causes about which we are most passionate. It is a challenge to which we must rise and we should be truly proud of what we achieve.

NOTES
1. *The World's Billionaires* (2015). Available at: http://www.forbes.com/billionaires/. Last accessed 29 August 2016.
2. *Coutts Million Dollar Donors Report Global Overview (2014)*. Available at: *http://philanthropy.coutts.com/content/dam/rbs-coutts/philantrhopy/documents/2014/general/Overview-2014.pdf*. Last accessed 29 August 2016.
3. Newman, Rebecca (2010) *Adventures in Philanthrophy*. The London Magazine, November 2010.
4. *Why billionaires find Gates, Buffet's giving pledge so easy to sign* (2015). Crain's Chicago Business. Available at: http://www.chicagobusiness.com/article/20150604/NEWS01/150609876/why-billionaires-find-gates-buffetts-giving-pledge-so-easy-to-sign. Last accessed 29 August 2016.
5. Newman, Adventures in Philanthropy, op. cit.
6. Nocera, Joe (2008) *Self-made philanthropists*. New York Times Magazine, March 2008.
7. *Engaged Philanthropy,* Christian Aid, December 2009.
8. *Global Giving: The Culture of Philanthropy* (2010*)*. Barclays Wealth in cooperation with Ledbury Research, p.13.
9. Solomon, D & Corfe, S (2014). *The Wealth of the Over 50s*, Cebr, London, January 2014, p.4.
10. *Tomorrow's* Philanthropist (2009. Barclays Wealth in co-operation with Ledbury Research, p.14.
11. Burnett, Ken (1996) *Friends for Life: Relationship Fundraising in Practice*, The White Lion Press, London, p. 229.
12. Ibid., pp. 99-103.
13. *Show a Little Donor-Love in Your Case for Support* (2013). Available at: http://www.afpnet.org/ResourceCenter/ARticleDetail.cfm?ItemNumber=14937 Last accessed 3 September 2016.
14. Rogers, F (2007). *Strategies for Increasing Endowment Giving at Colleges and Universities.* Available at: http://docplayer.net/4531697-Strategies-for-increasing-endowment-giving-at-colleges-and-universities.html. Last accessed 3 September 2016.
15. Pallotta, Dan (2012), *Multiplication Philanthropy*, Harvard Business Review. Available at https://hbr.org/2012/02/multiplication-philanthropy.html Last accessed 3 September 2016
16. Clayton Christensen, Clayton, Cook, Scott & Hal, Taddy. *What Customers Want from Your Products,* Working Knowledge, Harvard Business School, January 2006. Available at: http://hbswk.hbs.edu/item/what-customers-want-from-your-products. Last accessed 3 September 2016.
17. Schreifels, Jeff (2012) *The Six Secrets to Becoming an Extraordinary Major Gift Officer*, *Secret #5.* Available at: https://veritusgroup.wordpress.com/2012/06/22/the-six-secrets-to-becoming-an-extraordinary-major-gift-officer-secret-5-you-don't-have-all-the=answers/ Last accessed 3 September 2016.
18. *Barriers to Giving* (2010). Barclays Wealth in co-operation with Ledbury Research, p. 20.
19. Burk, Penelope (2014). *The Burk Donor Survey, Where Philanthropy is Headed in 2014* Cygnus Applied Research Inc, Chicago, p.12.

Transformative appeals: achieving your charity's visionary goals

In his 15 years as a fundraiser Paul has sat in on numerous interviews to recruit new talent into his team. He would often ask candidates why they wanted to work for the charity. Nine times out of ten, the question would receive the following response: 'because I want to make a difference', or some derivative thereof.

While this is an admirable motivation, it is not something that fundraisers can necessarily achieve in isolation. On their own people can, of course, play a central role, but a number of elements across the charity have to align successfully if we are to have real impact and bring about genuine magic and change.

REALISING OUR HIGHEST GOALS

If an organisation is prepared to stretch its ambition, take some risks and effectively coordinate key activities across all its constituent parts, then it may be possible to achieve unprecedented levels of success. These groundbreaking developments are typically fuelled by visionary special appeals, which are characterised by an evident and motivational need, high aspiration, strong leadership, advanced planning and appropriate investment. They constitute a set of fundraising and outreach activities focused on raising money for a specific, defined cause or project, usually over a set period of time.

Surprisingly, it doesn't necessarily have to be possible to achieve such an appeal. Ending child cruelty, no child born to die and eradicating cancer have all been used as themes for successful major transformational appeals; it's even been said that the higher and more out of reach the ambition the more successful the appeal will be. Donors like ambition and react well to the highest of aspirations – provided of course that the leadership is trustworthy and the appeal is backed by a short but solid case for support.

REQUIREMENTS FOR SUCCESS

Often a major appeal of this type will include a substantial *public* phase, incorporating broad mass-market income generation techniques. But gifts from major donors – the *private* phase – will almost always generate the lion's share of the revenue. For this reason, the private funding stage usually precedes the public component. This provides the appeal with solid foundations and the required momentum; by the time the public are invited to lend their support most of the capital has already been raised or pledged.

To ensure their success, these often complex appeals require clear goals, meticulous planning, effective integration across all departments, calculated risk-taking, the full endorsement of trustees and senior management, adequate investment and, perhaps most importantly, an iron will to succeed.

In the UK, the gold standard in this area was set a few decades ago by both the NSPCC and Great Ormond Street Hospital (GOSH).

Today, the NSPCC is one of the largest and most respected charities in the UK, annually raising in excess of £130 million. Back in 1980, though, its finances were in a parlous state. Annual income was just £3 million and there were less than two weeks' operating costs in reserve.

With the significant anniversary of their hundredth birthday just four years away, the fundraising team, inspired by their newly appointed director of appeals and publicity, Giles Pegram, energised the organisation into creating a new vision and reason for supporters to give. The charity resolved to create a step change in its service delivery by establishing a network of 60 new childcare teams across the country. They substantially restructured their fundraising activities and plans to meet this goal.

Four years of careful preparation led to the launch of the NSPCC Centenary appeal, for which they set a £12 million target to fund their childcare teams. This was a huge sum then, the largest public charity appeal ever in Britain and it was a massive uplift on their level of annual income. Careful recruitment of wealthy and influential figures during the private phase, such as the Duke of Westminster, who chaired the initiative, was a critical factor in achieving their goals – and eventually exceeding them. The tangible target and strategic co-ordination of all their activities under this umbrella campaign were also central to its success. Before the campaign ended the NSPCC had raised in excess of £15 million and transformed the future of the charity.

Sixteen years later – this time to mark the turn of a new millennium – the NSPCC launched another groundbreaking initiative: their Full Stop appeal, to end child cruelty. When it drew to its close in 2009 it had comfortably exceeded its £250 million target, raising more than any other charity in UK fundraising history. In both cases these transformative appeals not only exceeded their seemingly impossible targets, they also boosted the regular non-appeal income of the charity substantially, lifting general income to levels substantially higher than before the appeal, levels from which the charity never fell back.

These large-scale appeals are often most closely associated with capital project fundraising. For example, back in 1987, Great Ormond Street Hospital urgently needed extensive redevelopment. At that time the total cost of properly housing and equipping the hospital was estimated to be £72 million. The UK government had promised £30 million of this huge sum, provided that the hospital itself raised the remaining £42 million. A carefully assembled team of professional fundraisers and volunteers, led by Marion Allford, was recruited to meet this goal.

Building the team from scratch, GOSH was able to launch the astoundingly successful Wishing Well appeal. Using a range of techniques and employing a business-like approach, they coordinated their activities to great effect. Unifying behind a common goal, they raised £54 million in just four years. The NSPCC and GOSH campaigns are both featured in detail on SOFII.org.

In the higher education sector, the most significant appeals have also centred on capital projects, such as building construction, refurbishment or tangible product improvements. But the parameters of these campaigns have broadened in the last few years. The lucrative possibilities they present are now not necessarily restricted to charities focused on bricks and mortar programmes.

In fact, most of the ingredients that make capital campaigns so successful are replicable across other, potentially transformational, appeals. For example, Leah Leto, vice president for advancement and external affairs at Saint Peter's University, in New Jersey, USA, recently concluded an extremely successful $65 million capital funding project to build a new student centre. She recognises the intrinsic value of a campaign, where all activities are fully integrated and both staff and donors alike are united behind one vision and goal:

> *It will be the norm in future to always be focused on a campaign. Having tangible targets, something that donors can more easily wrap their arms around, is central to this. And being part of a collective – seeing other people make these gifts, is extremely motivating. Internally too, fundraisers inspire others in the team with their successes. It's about being part of something really big, something urgent and dramatic, and sweeping others into that dynamic narrative.*

While the potential is great, the work and preparation involved in a successful campaign should not be underestimated. The execution of transformational appeals relies on the effective navigation of five key stages.

IDENTIFYING THE NEED

The starting point for any appeal should always be a clear case of need. As ever, this is central to all fundraising, but when seeking to generate significant sums of money, longer term, detailed project goals are of paramount importance.

This necessitates close working with senior leaders, as well as with finance and service delivery staff. Essentially, a transformational campaign requires full buy-in from your board of trustees, who ultimately will need to approve the vision and the required investment.

Also in the USA, the VMI Foundation, established to raise funds for the Virginia Military Institute, launched an extremely ambitious multi-purpose campaign in 2009. Entitled, An Uncommon Purpose: A Glorious Past, A Brilliant Future: The Campaign for VMI, they set out to raise $225 million to transform a range of services in advance of the Institute's bi-centennial anniversary in 2039.

Their starting point was to conduct a needs assessment, coordinating closely with the Institute's strategic plan: Vision 2039. Some game-changing goals emerged, which built upon the rich traditions and history of VMI, while radically broadening the remit and quality of its programmes. They aimed to expand their capacity by 20 per cent to support the annual development of 1,500 cadets and to invest heavily across the board to enable this step change. This included improvements in their educational activities, facilities, scholarships, military infrastructure and athletics, as well as the preservation and upgrading of their battlefields and museums.

Identifying and defining this compelling need was central to the approval of these plans. If they are to form the basis of a transformational appeal, these needs have to be big enough and bold enough to capture the imagination of major investors and the public as a whole. The Institute, the VMI Foundation and the campaign cabinet, comprising eight former graduates tasked with coordinating all the activities, believed this to be the case. They ratified the campaign goals with enthusiasm and ambitious targets in advance of the launch of the private phase.

Integration and collaboration are vital when attempting plans on this scale. The Institute and VMI Foundation developed a memorandum of understanding regarding responsibilities, cooperation and, most importantly, the roles to which the parties needed to adhere in order to ensure the success of this pioneering project. There was a lot at stake: if successful, the campaign would, in effect, enable the VMI to fulfil its mission and to build a leadership plan that would would result in it becoming one of the premier undergraduate colleges in America.

BUILDING THE APPEAL INFRASTRUCTURE
Complex transformational appeals require in-depth planning and preparation to achieve their ambitious aims.

As the stakes are so high, it's important to begin with an assessment of the viability of the proposed campaign. Once the parameters have been agreed and finalised, the onus will be on the fundraisers to generate the required income, so it's essential to check that the targets proposed are realistic and can be achieved. Cancer Research UK (CRUK) conducted such a feasibility study when preparing for their £100 million Create The Change appeal, to help fund the Francis Crick Institute, an interdisciplinary medical research institution in central London. This unique initiative arose out of the collaboration of a number of leading research bodies who sought to inspire a new generation of leading scientists to bring tangible health benefits to future generations.

To ensure the viability of the project, CRUK interviewed existing donors and potential supporters to establish their appetite for supporting such a campaign. This was also an opportunity to help identify those willing and able to lead the initiative, as well as those who might wish to donate. Additionally, they canvassed the opinions of senior staff and carried out research into other bodies that had conducted similar appeals. Conversations with leading global institutions, such as the Universities of Cambridge and Oxford, the London School of Economics, Dana-Farber Cancer Institute, MD Anderson Cancer Center and Rockefeller University, enabled CRUK to gain valuable insights and advice on how to conduct the campaign and the pitfalls to avoid.

Similarly, before embarking on the appeal to support their ambitious strategy, the VMI Foundation carried out over 60 face-to-face meetings with top campaign prospects and two focus groups (39 participants) including their board and alumni representatives. They sent an e-mail survey to more than 800 previous donors as well as to a segment of alumni who had not previously supported them. Additionally, they carried out dedicated wealth screening of their database and analysed warm donors' support of other charities and political causes.

This research should feed into the construction of a giving pyramid, or gift table, which outlines the number of gifts the campaign should aim to solicit from each level of donor. It is important to check the feasibility of your income targets, line by line, based on what you actually know about your prospects. This will prevent the setting of an arbitrary round figure that is in practice unachievable. If your giving table total falls short of your target, you will need to fundamentally restructure the campaign, or consider calling it off. Committing to an overly ambitious initiative with an unrealistic fundraising target could pose too great a risk to the financial security and reputation of your charity.

Figure 14.1: Sample £20 million appeal giving table

Donation level	Number of donations	Engaged prospects required (4:1)	Donations total
£2,000,000	1	4	£2,000,000
£1,000,000	5	20	£5,000,000
£100,000	50	200	£5,000,000
£10,000	500	2000	£5,000,000
Smaller gifts/Public appeal	n/a	n/a	£3,000,000
Total	556+	2220+	£20,000,000

Tips for completing your giving table

- Work from the top down. Based on your research, identify the highest level 'lead' gift that will be made to the campaign. Be realistic. As you can see from figure 14.1, it should be around 10 per cent of the target as a whole. The higher bands should account for approximately 60 per cent of income. Having a base that is any broader would require many more gifts at a lower level, which would be extremely difficult to resource.

- People give in round numbers. Build your table accordingly, around sums such as £1 million, £100,000 and £10,000.

- For each gift, you will need around four interested prospective donors. Many will not be prepared to meet with you or a campaign representative. Of those who do respond, some will not donate, even if you are able to involve them personally.

- Remember to phase your income. Just because a donor pledges at the required level does not mean that you will receive the gift in the same year. Larger gifts, in particular, are likely to come in over a longer timeframe.

- Monitor your progress; as Giles Pegram advises, it's useful to make a comparison between the table and actual gifts pledged in order to indicate where you need to focus your attention.

- Use your giving table, as appropriate, to help you secure major gifts. The next time you meet with a potential major donor, bring the chart with you. It engages potential donors in the campaign and provides a visual tool to identify need. It also demonstrates to donors how they might be part of the solution.

Figure 14.2: NSPCC Full Stop Appeal gift table

Donation level	Number of donations	Engaged prospects required (4:1)	Donations total
£50,000,000	1	4	£50,000,000
£25,000,000	2	8	£50,000,000
£10,000,000	3	12	£30,000,000
£5,000,000	5	20	£25,000,000
£2,000,000	10	40	£20,000,000
£1,000,000	15	60	£15,000,000
£100,000	100	400	£10,000,000
£10,000	1000	4000	£10,000,000
Smaller gifts/Public appeal	n/a	n/a	£40,000,000
Total	**1136+**	**4544+**	**£250,000,000**

Like fundraising as a whole, giving tables are not an exact science. It is possible to adapt your approach to meet the needs of an individual campaign. Figure 14.2, for example, is a gift chart used by the NSPCC for the Full Stop appeal. In this instance the top gift was as much as 20 per cent of the total. And 7 per cent of the target, £190 million, was planned from 36 gifts.

Traditionally, donations on that scale had been limited to the arts and education institutions. Given the scale of the NSPCC's appeal, however, such weighting was necessary to achieve their goals. Giles and his colleagues at the NSPCC rightly saw no reason why gifts of this magnitude should not be successfully solicited by a conventional charity. They set their ambition high and duly broke the mould.

TAILORING TRANSFORMATIONAL APPEALS

Many of the major giving processes outlined in the previous chapter apply to the private phase of transformational appeal fundraising too, though they may need to be tailored and developed further. A case for support, for example, should be constructed and used consistently. This should compellingly outline the need, outputs, potential impact, costs and key stages of the campaign. Recognition options should be prepared as well. For capital projects these can be centred on specific products or projects, or parts of a building.

The right staff will also be required to achieve the necessary impact internally and externally. Saint Peter's, for example, recruited carefully and invested in training their new capital fundraisers to ensure they were methodical in their approach and would follow best practice. And they were proactive, aiming for 12–15 prospect visits per month, with transparent metrics in place to ensure accountability.

Similarly, Cancer Research UK (CRUK) recruited a specialist team of seven fundraisers specifically for their Create The Change Campaign, including a head, Antonia Newman, to lead on all of their activities. In addition, they were well supported by an operations team, which included the following key functions:

- A dedicated project manager with responsibility for board papers, agendas for fortnightly leadership meetings (with chair of campaign, CEO of CRUK and wider project management).

- Prospect research.

- Stewardship and marketing – production of brochures, updates, videos and bespoke thank-you communications. Early in the campaign they drafted a number of recognition opportunities but updated the materials as they went along. Some options were positively received and gifts were recognised as planned. Less popular categories were modified, where possible, in order to meet donors' requirements.

- Philanthropy communications – focusing on the creation of bespoke proposals for major asks.

- Additional support from the science communications team who led on the case for support, development and delivery.

The most successful transformational appeals have also benefited from the recruitment of wealthy and influential volunteers to support the campaign. You may choose to formalise this arrangement and replicate the 'development board' model, which has been effectively employed in America and elsewhere for a number of years. This board consists of a small team – eight to 12 people maximum – who are each recruited not just for their giving potential but also for their networks and areas of influence, as well as their willingness to help you achieve your goals. The benefits and recognition of such exclusive association with the charity are major opportunities to engage prospects that would otherwise be beyond your reach.

Such a board needs to be built upon solid foundations. Start with the recruitment of the chair, the most important member of the group. Often he or she will prove to be the defining factor in determining the success or otherwise of your fundraising activities.

The chair should be sufficiently well networked and influential to solicit gifts from the most prominent prospects. Additionally, the chair needs to be fully committed and must possess the energy and drive, when necessary, to shepherd the development board and ensure all members are pulling their weight. For CRUK, Charles Manby, a senior partner at Goldman Sachs, was the ideal choice. Antonia Newman highlights his influential role: 'He has been fantastic – dedicated, networked and has really driven the campaign.'

For the Create The Change campaign, Manby was central in recruiting his fellow development board members. Most of the 18 members were found through the chair and his networks, or through the contacts of others in the leadership group.

From the outset it's important that all development board members are clear about what's expected of them in terms of time and fundraising. A simple description of the role will aid this process and help to focus the discussion with any potential recruit. The VMI Foundation utilised further checks. All board members were nominated, vetted by their nominating and awards committee and then recommended to the full board. After approval, members were asked to serve based on criteria that underline the mission of the VMI Foundation.

It's not unusual to get this part of the process wrong. Leah Leto reflected on this as a key lesson learned for the Saint Peter's development board:

> *We should have educated them better as to what was expected, especially at the point of recruitment. Some didn't clearly understand what they were needed to do. Some didn't want to do the fundraising. Different people have different perceptions of what is required.*

EXECUTING THE PRIVATE PHASE

With the board in place, cultivation and stewardship of your prospects will allow you to maximise your returns during the private phase of the campaign. This is important: you should be aiming to generate between half and two thirds of the target before you go public with your appeal. The level will vary depending on the funds available for mass-market promotion and the extent to which your cause is likely to resonate with a wider audience.

Adhering to major giving and relationship fundraising techniques will prove to be most effective. A combination of face-to-face meetings and cultivation events are central to this process. This could include a launch party as well as more intimate affairs, including small cocktail parties, or briefings hosted by board members.

Additionally, you can run cultivation events that focus more on the programme in question. If it's a capital project it could include a tour of the site to inspire prospective donors. Or it could consist of a talk by one of your service delivery colleagues, or an opportunity to meet a celebrity who is endorsing your work.

To reap maximum long-term rewards, special or cultivation events must appear as exclusive as possible and feature a blend of facts and emotion to satisfy both the head and heart. You should use these occasions to share the excitement and transmit the tangible benefits that your transformational appeal will bring. These events present a wonderful opportunity to share your passion for the cause and envelop your guests in the spirit of the campaign. And even if donors cannot attend the event, they very much appreciate being asked. This certainly has been the case in Paul's experience, and is supported by Amber Nathan's research on mid-value donors, outlined in chapter 15.

The most effective cultivation opportunity, however, is often a personalised tour of your proposed project or site and the opportunity to meet those who will benefit directly if the appeal proves to be success. This is a great opportunity as it will give you time to build your relationship with the prospective donor, giving him or her the chance to see your work first hand and, if applicable, to engage your clients. This meeting gives you the opportunity to create a friend for life.

Paul found this to be the case during his time at World Jewish Relief. Three-day tours of their programmes in Ukraine and Moldova led directly to a substantial increase in the commitment and generosity of donors. Those who attended were moved and inspired by the work of the charity.

Don't be afraid to look for the pledge, or to ask for further support whilst you and the donor are still on the trip, or on site. It's best to strike whilst the iron is hot, as your prospects will never be more emotionally connected. Involve them before they return to their regular routines and while the emotion and personal connection is still fresh in their minds.

The VMI Foundation conducted a systematic approach in its donor cultivation, defining, planning and tracking the progress of 1,800 prospective supporters. They had a clear focus on increasing the number of face-to-face engagements and building a strong relationship that would result in a solicitation. In terms of then asking for the gift, the opportunities were planned strategically with desired outcomes and the constant discipline of always asking, 'do we have the right people, asking the right person for the right gift, at the right time?'

This was also an important consideration for both CRUK and for Saint Peter's University. For each donor they would select the appropriate combination of people to build the relationship and ask for the funds. Typically, partnering a board member with a fundraiser, or a member of the senior leadership team, proved to be most effective.

Of course, after the gifts are received, the stewardship continues. Leah Leto highlights the importance of acknowledging major donations in a warm and personalised manner:

> *Thanking is the first step in the cultivation cycle of a new gift – never forget how important it is. Everything is about making things less mechanical and more personal; handwritten notes on the highest quality stationery, and above a certain threshold the president will call. In addition, we will phone on the donor's birthday or on any special occasion, such as a child getting married. We do everything we can to make our supporters feel like they are part of our community.*

Brian Scott Crockett, CEO of the VMI Foundation, has a similar perspective, emphasising the importance of relationship fundraising in their ambitious and highly successful appeal:

> *The greatest factor of success is building relationships. These relationships begin internally – and spread outward to external relationships – with the understanding that those external relationships will then circle back to feel like they are the 'internal relationships'. Consistent and meaningful 'touches' through a well thought-out, and well-executed plan are essential. This takes 'buy-in' from all internal sources so that communication efforts and events have a 'best possible outcome' that engages constituents in the life of the Institute. If prospects do not feel as if they are part of the Institute then the chance of them giving to the campaign is nil.*

ROLLING OUT THE PUBLIC APPEAL

Once you have achieved sufficient levels of income from your major donors, you are ready to engage the general public with your appeal. The planning for this stage though, including contingency options, will need to have been carried out far in advance. Co-ordinating different departments, or teams, in support of a single goal is challenging. It will take time, diplomacy and patience.

Additionally, the financial risks of this phase are higher. Major gift fundraising tends to have a cost-to-income ratio of about 10 per cent, whilst public phase fundraising is much more expensive – nearer 25 to 30 per cent. If you are seeking to acquire new supporters in the process it can be even more costly.

As outlined in chapter 10, there are a number of channels available to promote your cause in the public phase, including social media, direct mail, telemarketing, face-to-face, door-to-door, as well as corporate partnerships, advertising and PR opportunities.

A number of factors influence the channels you will choose, including your budget, capacity and the strategic aims of your appeal. Are you, for example, looking solely to generate income? Or are you also seeking to use this unique opportunity to raise awareness of your cause and acquire new supporters? If it's the former, then you will look to utilise the most cost-effective fundraising channels, such as direct mail. If you wish to move beyond your existing audiences, then it's worth considering the use of other channels, such as door-to-door, or face-to-face fundraising. As we outline in greater detail in chapters 8 and 9, these will be less cost-effective in the short term, often taking several years to yield a surplus for your charity.

Either way, you should certainly be engaging your warm supporters in this campaign, as they will be most receptive to your requests for support. Additionally, keeping your most committed donors fully updated and interested, perhaps by sharing the latest news about your appeal in advance of your updates to the wider public, will help to make them feel special and bring them closer to your cause.

Effective integration, which involves the application of consistent brand messaging across all marketing channels, is a key component of the public phase. Co-ordinating all your colleagues and media to ensure that you present a uniform message during designated periods is not easy. But the rewards, if you are able to do it successfully, are worth the effort.

If effectively synchronised, the promotional activities will reinforce one another. The more your prospective supporters are engaged by your appeal through an assortment of channels, the more likely they are to respond. Recent research carried out by Gartner, a leading information technology and research company in the USA, shows that integrating four or more digital channels will outperform single or dual-channel campaigns by as much 300 per cent.[1]

Great Ormond Street Hospital used a range of fundraising methods to great effect back in the 1980s, including major advertising on radio, television, in cinemas, on posters, buses and the underground, sustaining these campaigns throughout the public phase of the appeal.

They also succeeded in establishing a number of major corporate partnerships, which included widespread employee fundraising activities, as well as cause-related marketing. In their first joint promotion, 40 million Mars bar wrappers carried the 'teardrop' logo and Tesco raised £2 million by involving their customers, suppliers and staff in their fundraising activities. A substantial trading operation was linked to the appeal, with a wide range of products for sale, some through outlets such as Harrods and Allders.

Both GOSH and the NSPCC also succeeded in mobilising and empowering their grassroots support too. The Wishing Well appeal office set up 90 regional groups in the six months before the public launch by consulting the Lord Lieutenant (the Queen's representative) in each of the counties that benefited from the services offered by Great Ormond Street. The Lord Lieutenants' involvement ensured that the appeal was able to recruit strong leadership for each group and that their plans were well prepared before their fundraising started. The appeal office supplied the regional groups with all the necessary marketing materials and guidance.

Similarly, the NSPCC engaged its volunteers in the placement of collection tins at every railway station in the country. Their regional supporter groups also organised a year-long calendar of events, helping to generate vital income and raise awareness of the campaign.

CONSOLIDATION AND CONCLUSION OF THE APPEAL

The end of the transformational appeal is typically marked by a consolidation phase. This is an opportunity to ask for final gifts, celebrate achievements and – most importantly – to thank all concerned appropriately.

Saint Peter's, for example, exceeded their target by nearly $3 million and took the opportunity to publicly acknowledge their donors' efforts with a spectacular event to conclude their campaign. They invested a huge amount of time and effort in order to highlight their successes and demonstrate the magnificent progress they had been able to make as a result of their transformative appeal. Leah Leto outlines its impact:

> *It was spectacular and made people feel amazing. We had students thanking attendees for their support. Their stories captured the hearts and minds of the attendees, giving the impression of a thriving university made possible by the generosity of our supporters.*

Like all fundraising initiatives, no matter what their size, it's important to fully evaluate the appeal at its conclusion. Lessons must be captured at this stage while they are fresh in the mind. Staff turnover is high in the charity sector, so failure to do so may mean that you run the risk of losing vital institutional knowledge.

This applies particularly to large-scale, multi-year appeals, where significant investment has been made. The more activity you have carried out, the more potential there is to gain a real insight into what media, messaging and audiences are most effective for your organisation. At its most basic level, for each channel or activity, this should include net income and return on investment. These should incorporate short- and longer-term projections, as well account for staff time and levels of supporter acquisition. For further details of the quantitative assessment of mass-market activities, see chapter 19.

Additionally, it's worth evaluating the appeal internally, in a qualitative manner. Did your systems and processes for managing the appeal prove to be effective? Could you have done more to integrate your activities? If you ran another major transformational appeal, what would you do differently? These are just a few questions that you can pose to capture some of the most important lessons and lay solid foundations for future growth.

THE POWER AND PITFALLS OF TRANSFORMATIONAL APPEALS

Major integrated appeals, if properly executed, can be incredibly powerful tools for nonprofits. Their income, their prestige and impact can reach unprecedented levels.

Saint Peter's raised $65 million through their campaign in seven-and-half years, representing nearly 50 per cent of the total the university had raised in its entire history. Similarly, CRUK moved from having a single £1 million gift and an average major donor income of £3 million per annum, to securing 18 £1 million+ gifts and average income of £15 million – £20 million per annum, mostly driven by the Create The Change campaign. They secured three gifts each over £10 million, including CRUK's largest ever donation of £17 million. Most importantly, both of these campaigns achieved their aims for the programmes, transforming the lives of countless individuals as a result.

The systems that have been created to facilitate these outstanding achievements and the relationships that have been formed can also act as a springboard. They can help to build long-term, sustainable income. VMI's Brian Crockett sums up:

> *… many of the practices that were put in place during the campaign will remain in place under normal operations. The importance of relationship fundraising, prospect management, solicitation tracking, face-to-face meetings, principle gift fundraising, as well as new energy from non-alumni, corporations, foundations and parent fundraising – have become a priority for the Foundation, the Institute, boards, and other volunteers. I believe a campaign has a well-defined and well-executed plan that brings everyone together to play a role in meeting one common goal. A campaign unites.*

It is worth noting, however, that there is always the chance of a post appeal hangover, as it can be difficult to maintain the momentum that you have generated. Giles Pegram noted that the NSPCC lost a number of good employees after its Centenary appeal in the mid-1980s. Feeling that the excitement of recent years had come to an end, they imagined their future career prospects would be better elsewhere. Similarly, NSPCC saw a small dip in income following the centenary year but, as figure 14.3 shows, the effect of this major activity was entirely benign. Instead of regressing, the Society's income reached new levels and it continued to grow for several years. This same effect was experienced years later with the Full Stop appeal.

Figure 14.3: Impact of the NSPCC's Centenary Appeal on core income

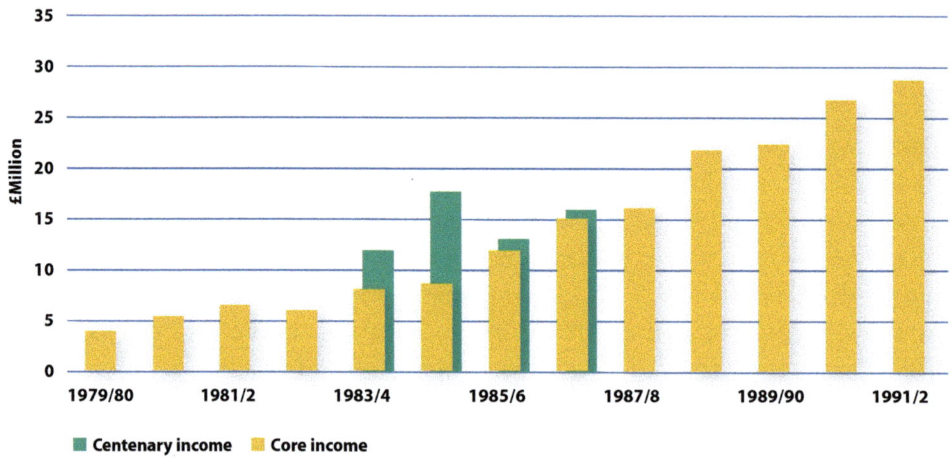

As Ken Burnett explains:

> *There were huge satisfactions from the big appeal. It had galvanised and revitalised the organisation, giving it a new impetus and momentum. And the benefits for children were considerable. Thanks to the Centenary Appeal the NSPCC was able to totally reorganise, modernise and re-equip its new childcare teams. There was no looking back.*[2]

It's important that the level of success of these appeals is matched by a similar scale of planning and investment. The constituent parts, in terms of staff, volunteers, materials, prospects and events, are high in number and require immense coordination and time, in order to deliver the returns. Indeed, transformational appeals can be extremely expensive. So you will need to gain a concrete commitment from your board that this is a level of ambition and investment at which they will not baulk.

Additionally, the flagship programme, or collection of projects for which you are raising money must be clearly identified. This is necessary in order to bring the whole organisation together, working towards one collective goal. At World Jewish Relief, for example, Paul found that a lack of holistic planning around their development board led to only moderate levels of success. The charity had been very successful at soliciting £5,000 to £10,000 donations, but it was not gaining access to larger prospects and it needed to expand its networks. Paul started by recruiting a development board chair, a successful early retired businessman and key supporter who had visited the charity's projects in the field. The charity then set about approaching prospects to join the group, known as the Ambassadors. These included warm supporters who it was felt had more potential, either personally, or through their networks. Prospects were shown a role description and were asked to commit to generating a sum of £25,000 per annum, for three years, through any combination of personal gifts, referrals and sponsored fundraising. Eight supporters signed up to participate.

In terms of the programme goal, rather than supporting a particular project in the field the Ambassadors chose instead to obtain leverage on their investment to multiply the effects of their contribution beyond its face value. In order to achieve this they universally opted to directly fund World Jewish Relief's awareness and fundraising acquisition programmes. They saw this as an opportunity to make their contribution work harder, by generating additional funds for the organisation. The textbook theory of the go-givers, outlined in chapter 13, was being realised in practice.

The results were positive. A few months in, by the time Paul left the charity to take on his next post, £132,000 had been raised through individual gifts and donations from the Ambassadors' contacts. Most of these referrals had been invited to attend the charity's regular special events, especially their annual dinner. As a nice by-product of this process the regular event portfolio was enhanced by a substantial increase in attendees. In addition, the organisation broadened its networks considerably.

While the results were encouraging, in hindsight Paul failed to connect the group to the wider organisation and to imbue its members with a cohesive focus of an inspiring programme and vision. A more organised, longer-term plan for the board and what they were setting out to achieve would have helped enormously and would likely have led to better results. Additionally, the team could have been more selective in whom they asked to join the group. Some members' contributions improved dramatically, but others were less responsive, either due to lack of time or connections, or both.

So you get back what you put in. Ambitious, well-executed plans will yield the highest rewards. But remember, at the heart of all of this remains the individual donor and your ability to implement relationship fundraising best practice. Brian

Crockett led the VMI Foundation to outstanding levels of success, exceeding their original $180 million goal by over $50 million. Despite this, he remains grounded in his views:

> *I strongly recommend that you spend a little time thinking outside the box; however, don't ever lose focus on the target. Major gift fundraising, cultivation and solicitation are definitely the top targets in putting dollars on the table. We don't take a novel approach in many of our activities. Staying current on best practices is critical. We define best practices as those practices that have worked and been proven at other institutions and we all should implement them at our school as appropriate.*

This should give hope to us all as fundraisers that transformational change is within our reach. We simply need to stretch our ambition and embrace the risk. If we are visionary in our aims, and adhere closely to relationship fundraising principles, then anything might just be possible. It genuinely gives us the opportunity to make a difference, to change the world. It's a privilege that we as fundraisers must always aspire to achieve.

NOTES
1. *The benefits of having an integrated campaign*, Winbox, May 2015. Available at: http://www.winbox.co/blog-articles/2015/5/25/the-benefits-of-having-an-integrated-marketing-campaign
2. Burnett, Ken, *The gold standard in fundaising, Part 2: exceeding expectations*, SOFII, April 2010. Available at: http://sofii.org/article/the-gold-standard-in-fundraising-part-2-exceeding-expectations

Techniques for specialist areas of fundraising: trusts and foundations, corporate engagement and mid-value donors

In his book *Face Time: Relationship Philanthropy*, Canadian fundraiser, Robert Ian Peacock outlined the need to be adaptable in higher-value fundraising:

> *There are various sources of support for philanthropic organisations to achieve the success necessary for their development. The greater the number of opportunities for funding within an organisation's donor base, the more room there will be for increased growth. Given the variety of sources, fundraisers need to be adaptable. They will require innovative approaches tailored to maximise philanthropic engagement.*[1]

The greatest potential often lies in the development of individual donor relationships. These still account for the largest proportion of charitable giving, representing nearly three quarters of all donations in the USA and similar amounts in other countries.[2]

However, decisions about the sources of fundraising must be strategic. They should be based on the type of charity, its capacity and the maturity of its relationship fundraising portfolio. Smaller, newer nonprofits, or more niche causes, for example, with a paucity of major donor networks and, or a limited capacity, will need to focus on areas that are most likely to yield returns. They may be best advised to seek donations from grant-making bodies, such as trusts and foundations.

Those seeking to diversify their fundraising, to prevent over-reliance on one income stream, or simply to grow may well look to expand into corporate or mid-value donor fundraising. These activities can both present a significant opportunity to bolster revenue.

As Peacock outlines, however, each of these supporter groups will require a tailored approach to maximise returns. They each have a unique set of behavioural characteristics and requirements, which are worthy of more detailed analysis. Relationship fundraising principles still apply, of course, but specialist techniques must be utilised to ensure the highest levels of success.

TRUSTS AND FOUNDATIONS

The principles of relationship fundraising apply to trusts and foundations, and other grant-making bodies, just as they do to individuals.

As a result, it's also equally important to build personal relationships with trustees and key decision makers. Like the individual donor, they are far more likely to support you if you strike up a rapport and if they have faith in you and your charity. Face-to-face and personalised engagement is central to achieving this goal.

As trusts and foundations are in the public domain, they will be receiving numerous enquiries and applications for support. Consequently, they are likely to operate at more of a distance than individual major donors. In order to achieve the best possible results, though, it's still essential that you offer the highest prospects, especially, tailored, first-class supporter care.

Research and selection criteria

A systematic approach, to establish the trusts and foundations on which you will focus your efforts, will prove to be most effective.

Trusts generally will fall into one of two categories. The first – private trusts – are set up to manage an individual's charitable giving in the most tax efficient manner. They should be treated as individual donors and a more traditional major donor approach should be implemented (as outlined in chapter 13). The second category, which we'll cover here, is managed by a group of trustees who disburse gifts on a more formal basis, usually involving a set application process.

Trusts and foundations that require a formal funding application will be open about the types of causes they support. In the UK, search engines like Trust Funding, GuideStar and the Charity Commission's website, as well as *The Directory of Grant Making Trusts* (Directory of Social Change, UK) will help you to find the required information.

There are a number of criteria that you should use to help you narrow your search and prioritise your engagement:

- Annual distribution levels – strategically, it's preferable to assess the largest trusts first, usually those that distribute in excess of £1 million per annum. Then work downwards, dividing your research into donation bands as you go. It's advisable to employ a bespoke approach for all trusts that disburse annually around £100,000 or more.

- If your capacity is limited though, it's best to focus on the highest-level prospects, as funding potential is heavily weighted towards the largest trusts, particularly in the UK. Although there are roughly 10,000 foundations, the top 300 account for 90 per cent of the total of their charitable giving.[3]

- Alignment with your charitable objectives – carry out the necessary research to establish whether or not your charity's aims fit with those of the trust. And if you're not sure, ask. As ever, it's best to pick up the phone; it's a great opportunity to engage with their administrators and begin to build relationships.

- Access – as with individual major donors, a personal introduction will provide an opening to engage the trust, especially if your cause is not an obvious fit for their work. It's best to start with your database, cross-referencing which grant-making bodies have supported your charity before and also which trustees may have donated in an individual capacity. It's also worthwhile circulating a list of the trustees to your own board and volunteer fundraising networks to establish any connections.

Cultivation

The basic principles of relationship fundraising still very much apply to trusts and foundations. Make your contacts feel special and personally engaged and you will reap the rewards. Start with conversations with trustees or the administrators to gain an understanding of their communication preferences and their areas of interest.

Allocate a single point of contact in your charity to co-ordinate the relationship with each prospect. People give to people, so establishing familiarity and trust will provide solid foundations on which to build. Personalised updates, invitations to intimate cultivation events, opportunities to see your work first hand, the chance to meet senior personnel in your organisation are really important and are likely to be received positively. Even if they do not act or respond to every opportunity, your efforts will be noted and the relationship will be enhanced significantly.

Solicitation

Most sizeable trusts will require a formal application for funding. This is your chance to outline how your organisation and proposed area of activity meet their charitable goals. Typically, major foundations will prefer to donate to specific projects, though some may be open to supporting running costs or general funds.

Before submitting your proposal, make sure you spend sufficient time gaining an understanding of their aims and requirements. A tailored approach will be received more positively. In order to optimise the effectiveness of your application, ensure you incorporate the following elements:

- Clear identification of need – it may sound obvious, but you should clearly demonstrate the need for funding. Use detailed case studies to bring the proposal to life and make it more emotive. If appropriate, describe your project as if its future literally hangs in the balance.

- Build a partnership – take the reader on a journey. Describe the outcome of a scenario where no funding is secured and the impact this would have on your beneficiaries. Put that in stark contrast to what can be achieved with their investment. The trust must feel that it is their support that will make your work possible and help to bring about real and lasting change. It's important to make them feel part of the organisation in the process. Outline how you would recognise their investment and, if possible, involve them in the programme in future.

- Ensure impact – donors now are taking their giving more seriously than ever before and are becoming more selective in the process. You must demonstrate professionalism as well as your charity's credentials in the proposal. It's also vital to outline exactly what you are planning to fund and what it will cost. Include a detailed budget for the programme in question. You will also need to demonstrate that the money is spent effectively and that its impact is maximised. Outline your credentials as programme managers, your background, results to date and the expertise within your professional team.

- Describe how you will monitor and evaluate the project in question and how you will measure its impact both in the short and long term. Additionally, to cement their confidence in your charity, highlight what other funds have already been committed to the programme and outline your plans to approach other potential funders.

Stewardship

If you are successful in your request for funds, the key to establishing a long-term relationship with the trust is to ensure they are kept fully updated and informed on your progress. Account accurately for all expenditure and let them know exactly how their support has made a difference. Timely, personalised and detailed reporting, meeting any specific requirements of the trust in the process, will reassure them that you are a trusted recipient of their funds. It will also stand you in good stead for any future applications.

CORPORATE DONORS

Corporate donors, like trusts, foundations and major donors, also require a high level of bespoke, personalised supporter care. They have the potential to provide significant levels of funding and resources to their charitable partners. A strategic approach is required to access these opportunities and manage what can be highly valuable relationships.

Research and selection criteria

Like trusts and foundations, search engines exist for corporate giving, including the *Guide to Corporate Giving* (Directory of Social Change, UK) in the UK. But how do you decide which companies to engage? Unlike trusts and foundations, partnerships with these prospects rely on a more mutually beneficial arrangement. The crucial question here is what you can offer them.

The introduction of corporate social responsibility (integrating social and environmental development into everyday activities) in the 1960s and 1970s resulted in companies becoming more amenable to charitable support. But since then it's become far more about engagement rather than responsibility. It requires a quid pro quo relationship, as Ken Burnett outlines:

> *It's not about responsibility, it's about engagement. It's not about them giving and us taking. It's not about what you need or want, it's more about what you give. It's about what you can bring to the boardroom table, in a two-way*

> *partnership, to show the remarkable difference both parties can make when cause and company combine to motivate staff, management and customers as, together, they deliver a powerful amount of good.*[4]

A major annual survey of 129 leading UK-based companies and NGOs showed that the primary motivation for corporate donors to engage in charitable partnerships was to enhance their brand or corporate reputation. Ninety-six per cent of those surveyed cited this as the key driver in embarking on these activities.[5]

Many companies will have a dedicated charitable arm. But philanthropic support, for companies, is not the only, or even primary prerequisite, for successful engagement. It's important to think about the following when seeking the most effective corporate partnerships:

- Brand alignment – is there a clear link between the goals and aims of your charity and the companies with which you wish to partner? For example, if your cause specifically supports children, you might want to seek out a commercial partner that has a similar target market. Pampers and UNICEF have worked together in such a manner since 2006; this leading producer of nappies enhanced its own brand through promoting and funding the international children's charity's vaccination programme against tetanus.

- Also, of course, you must consider any reputational risks that could arise from controversial brand partnerships. A cancer charity, for example, will be understandably reluctant to be involved with a tobacco company. Relationships with the charity's core supporters must be placed above all others.

- Cost-effectiveness – as well as assessing which companies donate the highest sums to charity, consider whether or not your charity can adequately service their corporate needs. Many of the bigger companies may seek extensive employee engagement activities, such as community fundraising or challenge events, as a central feature of any partnership. If you're a smaller charity or don't have the capacity or ambition to staff these requirements you need to consider whether these are the right opportunities to pursue. Less labour intensive partnerships or applications for corporate donations may be preferable.

- Strategic goals – what are your objectives for engaging with corporate partners? There are many benefits to be gained, including income, access to major donor networks, supporter acquisition and brand awareness. But, don't jump into a partnership for the sake of it; your charity's stage of development and long-term aims should determine where you should focus your efforts.

- Selection process – some potential corporate partners may be very democratic in the selection of their charities, or may only support very specific causes (focused on benefiting their local area, for example). If your cause is niche, or does not obviously fulfil their selection criteria, an application is unlikely to be successful.

Like individual donors, and trusts and foundations, gaining access to those with influence in the short-listing or decision-making process is important. Dedicated corporate social responsibility or engagement contacts can prove to be accessible points of entry.

But often companies will have set agendas and their activities may be limited to volunteer activity. Unless this is something that might be of particular value to your charity, it may well be preferable to seek support from alternative partners that are explicit in their provision of financial support. Developing relationships with key decision makers, either senior personnel, or those with particular responsibility for charitable partnerships, is a more efficient way of increasing your chances of success. Like trusts and foundations, you should cross-reference these targets with your database, in order to identify any corporate contacts who may be supporters in an individual capacity. Additionally, as outlined in chapter 13, LinkedIn provides a valuable search engine as it can highlight otherwise unknown connections as you invest time in building up your business networks.

When it comes to convincing potential corporate partners to support your cause, as with most individuals, it comes down to satisfying the needs of both the head and the heart. Kate Jacques, former head of corporate partnerships at Diabetes UK, understood the importance of this when constructing their successful pitch for the lucrative Tesco Charity of the Year partnership, in 2013:

> We gave the Tesco team confidence that their staff and customers would be inspired to match their already impressive fundraising records. Equally as important, the pitch supported Tesco's corporate responsibility objective to use

their scale and reach to help colleagues and customers adopt a healthier diet and lifestyle.[6]

Just as individuals are becoming more strategic in their fundraising, so too are corporate donors. Where previously bilateral partnerships were the most common model for collaboration, corporate donors are now leading the way in promoting consortia as relationships with more impact and which are more cost-effective.

Sixty-seven per cent of companies are actively involving more than one partner in their efforts to address specific issues.[7] In 2015, a consortium – the Tesco/Diabetes UK/British Heart Foundation collaboration – broke into the top three in the poll of most admired corporate – NGO partnerships. So targeting and relationship building may well have to extend beyond commercial bodies to incorporate strategic alliances with other nonprofits too.

Stewardship

Once you've successfully gained the support of a corporate partner the process of building the relationship should begin in earnest. Establish an open dialogue to ensure you are delivering the required added value and, if necessary, adapt your approach. It is likely that they will be seeking brand exposure, positive PR, possibly staff involvement and, most certainly, a clear idea of their return on their investment. To develop long-term, meaningful partnerships, you must consistently provide updates on their specified areas of interest.

Breast Cancer Care did exactly that when revitalising its 18-year collaboration with British Home Stores (BHS). They employed an exemplary relationship fundraising approach, tailoring their approaches to ensure mutual benefit for their corporate partners. Critically, they opened up an effective and genuine two-way dialogue to understand fully how they could best meet BHS's needs. Their account manager, Hannah Sanders, and Sara Rees, head of corporate partnerships, outlined their proactive efforts:

> *We held face-to-face meetings to get under the skin of their objectives, challenges and culture. It was important to have an honest conversation to evaluate what was working and what could be improved. We asked for feedback about everything from the look and feel of fundraising packs to whether we were communicating in a way that suited their structure and culture… While we were intent on listening, we shared too; by explaining our vision and strategy,*

giving insight into upcoming campaigns, we made it clear that BHS was a valued partner.[8]

Breast Cancer Care adopted a genuinely personal approach too, setting up closer links between employees at all levels of both organisations. This included discussions and brainstorms, as well as taking the time to have lunches together. The informal conversations they established generated some of the best ideas. And they adapted their communications to meet BHS's requirements, including e-mails instead of phone calls and top line information in place of heavy detail.

The personal touch was at the centre of these relationship-building activities:

We started to build into our account management ideas as to how we could let them know that we appreciated them. It takes no time at all to schedule a reminder for someone's birthday, make a quick phone call after a tough week, or to pop a card in the post. But it makes all the difference as to how they perceive your relationship.[9]

It proved to be an exceptionally effective approach. The Breast Cancer Care team were now able to work far more closely with BHS's retail operations personnel, developing ideas that were more tailored to the partnership than ever before. It prompted, for example, the launch of BHS's first post–surgery lingerie, as well as participation in Breast Cancer Care's flagship event, the Fashion Show. The results were highly impressive. More money was generated during the first month of activity in 2014 than had been raised in the entire year that preceded it.

More significant though were the long-term benefits gained as a result of a fresh injection of energy and strategic direction. The charity's efforts to build relationships throughout the organisation were particularly beneficial. Corporate relationships can be transient, as staff and trustees often move on. So it's imperative to invest time in building links with more than one key contact. This will help to ensure that your connection with the company remains as secure as possible.

As Breast Cancer Care demonstrated to great effect, employing relationship fundraising techniques in a strategic and focused manner will generate the highest return on investment. Placing your corporate supporters at the centre of your planning and development will result in meaningful and lucrative partnerships that will benefit both parties for years to come.

MID-VALUE DONORS

The opportunity

Another potential group of supporters that requires specialist fundraising techniques is mid-value donors. It's not as easy as you might think, though, to define these individuals. Support bases differ from one charity to another and therefore the lines that delineate major, mid- and low-value supporters will inevitably be drawn at different levels.

Sitting just below the major donor category, typically the upper boundary for mid-value donors will be placed at around £5,000 per annum. It could, though, be as high as £25,000, depending on the scope, ambition and capacity of your major donor programme. The lower threshold is typically set at around £250-£500, the minimum level at which a tailored approach is likely still to achieve a significant return on investment.

The fundraising community as a whole has been slow to adapt its approach and realise the potential of these supporters, many of whom, if engaged in the right manner, could comfortably donate four-figure sums. They commonly slip through the net and fail to receive the tailored supporter care that would yield the greatest returns. As Alia McKee and Mark Rovner note in their study *The Missing Middle* a lack of integration and unnecessary silos are often to blame:

> *In short, major donor fundraisers are chasing the big score while direct marketers chase short-term gains.*[10]

Given their ability and propensity to give, it's worthwhile spending time engaging these prospects. Whilst McKee and Rovner's study set their upper bar at $10,000 per annum they found that this group critically represented roughly 1 per cent of the donor population, but were giving more than a third of the total donations.

All too often, however, they are receiving the same standardised appeals as lower-value supporters, ensuring their substantial potential remains unfulfilled. Fundraising expert Roger Craver comments:

> *Frankly, when you see the amount of money that is left on the table by these organizations – I mean tens of millions of dollars—sooner or later they are going to have to deal with [this neglect] because they can't squeeze any more blood out of the particular business-as-usual stone they are currently working.*[11]

This was certainly the case at one major charity in the UK, Marie Curie Cancer Care. Millie Perrett, who set up their mid-value programme in 2013, describes the chasm that existed:

> Mid-value was not something that was defined at Marie Cure prior to the actual active decision to develop a tailored initiative. We had very strong direct mail and major giving programmes, but nothing in between. The most significant issue was in the missed potential of people who were giving significantly despite only being asked for small value gifts.

External consultants who were helping to analyse their database brought this shortcoming into focus. Their findings and recommendations led directly to Millie's appointment and a move to set up a distinct offering for mid-value prospects. It was a decision they would not regret.

Characteristics

In 2007, Amber Nathan from Bluefrog co-ordinated an extensive survey of mid-value donors to find out more about their motivations and behaviour. She conducted 100 in-depth interviews of supporters who had made multiple cash gifts of between £100 and £1,000 in the preceding two years. They included donors to a number of leading UK charities.[12]

Amber's key findings were as follows:

- They think they are special – mid-value donors all claim that they don't see themselves as particularly generous and that they're just giving according to their means, so they don't need special treatment. But almost without exception, they soon contradict themselves, describing themselves as key contributors to the charity.

- Engagement generates gifts – the more personally a charity engages and provides attention to a donor the more the organisation becomes front of mind and will receive the lion's share of their giving. And even though they say they don't want thanks, they do, very much.

- Pitching at the correct level – most mid-value donors have a high opinion of their own intelligence. They need to believe that you think they're clever too. If issues are watered down, or simplified too much, it can be seen as an insult to their intelligence. Consequently, they don't respond as well as they could to standard, emotive direct mail.

- Their 'own' projects – this is where real engagement lies. Ownership makes them feel instrumental not incidental. It's a reward for their generosity. Buying specific items or projects allows them to feel like a hero and gives them a tangible outcome from their donations.

Identifying your mid-value donors

The starting point for your mid-value programme is to select which donors will be part of this group. You'll need to define what 'mid-value' means for your organisation.

In order to do this, you'll need to review your donor pyramid and see where and at what levels it would be most practical to distinguish between major, mid- and low-value donors. During this process make sure you take into account the cumulative value of an individual's cash gifts over the course of a year, rather than single contributions. Additionally, consider supporters' potential and their giving history, rather than just their current donation levels.

Millie Perrett at Marie Curie embraced this approach:

> *When I started, the first thing I did was spend a lot of time thinking about who should be a part of the programme – this was particularly important because I wanted to look at potential mid-value donors as well as current and lapsed supporters. We went with a really broad approach that incorporated people who had made a cash gift of £100 or more at some point within the last three years. We kept all of these people (it was about 8000) in for the first year of the programme, with the intention of examining the responders after this period to see what we could learn to further refine and inform our selections.*

By mapping the characteristics and behaviours of your existing mid-value donors you can begin to identify which supporters are most likely to develop and reach this level. You could, for example, assess how many years typical mid-level donors contributed before reaching or exceeding the lower giving threshold. Or establish the average age at which mid-level giving generally commences.

With this insight you can cultivate new donors in the two or three years preceding that point, increasing the likelihood of their progression into this giving band. Or you could focus your efforts further still, placing more emphasis on individuals with a steeper ascending trajectory in their levels of giving. Indeed, it is possible to combine all this information into statistical models that highlight not only those who are likely to become mid-value donors, but also those most likely to transition into your major giving programme.

Additionally, there are many external data sources that you can use to gain further insight into your existing supporters and help identify potential mid-value prospects. Cluster data, for example, available through products including Experian's Mosaic in the UK, Equifax's Niches, Acxiom's Personicx, or Nielsen's Prizm in the USA, essentially group households by commonly held behavioural and marketing statistics. These denote patterns such as likely buying behaviour, household composition, hobbies and recreational interests.

Overlaying this information onto details of existing mid-value donors, as well as Amber Nathan's insights above, will enable you to identify your best prospects. These clusters also help to build more detailed donor profiles, allowing you to craft targeted communications which will make supporters feel as if you are talking to them personally.

Preparing your programme

A successful mid-value programme is all about the quality of communications with the donor, rather than the quantity.

To ensure these standards can be met practically and cost-efficiently it's advisable to carry out an audit of all existing touch points with these supporters. Create a simple table with mid-value segments down the y axis and all the current communications across the x axis. Remember to include all the messaging they will be exposed to across the full range of channels. This should incorporate appeals, newsletters, e-bulletins and committed-gift conversions and upgrades by telephone, as well as invitations to participate in your charity's portfolio of challenge, mass participation and cultivation events. It is likely to include more contacts and activities than you initially expected!

Now you should look to streamline these approaches. In their paper on cultivating lifelong donors the database specialists Blackbaud describes this process:

> Look for communications that overlap in purpose and in timing, then consolidate and eliminate. In doing so, you will be freeing budget resources for higher touch cultivation and reducing the intrusion in the lives of your donors and prospects, and that is exactly your intent.[13]

The emphasis for mid-level prospects should be on fewer, higher-level touch points with a strong bias towards cultivation over solicitation. To remain cost effective, when building your plans see if you can piggyback on existing cultivation events, or use budget allocated elsewhere.

A mid-value donor programme will, though, require a hybrid of direct marketing and major donor techniques, using the best methods from each. McKee and Rovner highlight this point:

> *It draws on major gifts by keeping the focus on the donor. It provides a sense of exclusivity, access and special status. And it draws on the richer and more sophisticated content that major gifts departments produce. From direct marketing comes a passion for efficiency and employment of analytics so the program can scale. It is possible to add a personal touch to the donor experience of thousands of mid-level donors and still reap enormous returns, but it requires the analytic discipline of a direct marketer.*[14]

Having said this, the balance should definitely be in favour of a major donor approach. That means fewer mailings per year and more personalised communication, with a single point of contact and greater emphasis on cultivation.

In particular, make sure that prospects stop receiving any generic direct mail or telemarketing communications. You need to be thinking about how to deliver far more bespoke and personalised messaging. One untimely request for a low-level gift or small monthly increase on a direct debit could ruin all your hard work. As Roger Craver puts it:

> *If the telephone people are doing one thing, the internet people are doing another thing and the mail people still another thing, the one certainty is that you'll lose those donors.*[15]

In order to address Nathan's point of perceived intellect and ownership, it is necessary to make sure there is real substance in your communications with these supporters. Personalised cultivation and the inclusion of genuinely relevant, erudite material will generate the greatest long-term results.

Cathy Grams, deputy vice president of strategic services at the US Wilderness Society, has adopted this approach to great effect with her mid-value donors:

> *We've got quarterly scheduled cultivation mailings and there are a couple of additional ad hoc things they'll get if it is needed. There was a great New York Times editorial in February, which we just reprinted and sent with a little note. The New York Times thing didn't reference us. It was just all about our issues. We did a quick reprint and said 'you may or may not have seen this but this is why our work is important'. That brought in $26,000 just on its own.*[16]

And when it comes to direct funding requests, they should be more akin to the major giving or trust proposals, outlined above and in chapter 13.

In the USA, Jamal Harris, who runs the Nature Conservancy's mid-level programme, certainly takes this view:

> *One of the things that we try to work on is less of a direct mail spiel, less of an aggressive ask. What I try to do is have it be as much about explaining or showing examples of how their money works. We treat the donor as if they were investors. They are investing in an organization and we want to make them feel like this is what your investment returned.*[17]

Disappointingly, not all charities who have embarked on a dedicated mid-value programmes have heeded this sound advice. Paul was recently shocked to come across a well-presented but poorly planned mailing to mid-value donors from a long-established major UK charity. It was immaculately laid-out, using high-quality materials. Additionally, it was formatted much like any typical major donor proposal, seemingly tailored towards its intended recipient, who was a long-term committed giver.

But it lacked any meaningful content. The funding request, for £500 (more than double what the supporter had previously given in a whole year), was not for any particular project or initiative, but instead was superficially focused on the opportunity to join a fairly meaningless giving circle. Unsurprisingly, it did not have the desired impact and it actually only irritated the recipient, who was a loyal donor. She was concerned about the cost of the mailing and was annoyed to be asked for further funds as, in her opinion, the charity had not demonstrated a good reason to do so.

Finally, like all supporters and major donors in particular, mid-level donors welcome the opportunity to engage, give feedback and select the manner in which they wish to be updated. That's why at The Nature Conservancy, as Jamal Harris outlines, mid-level donors receive a short survey as part of their welcome process:

> *When they join, as a part of the acknowledgement we send them a survey. It is four or five questions basically asking them how they want to be communicated with, what their interests are, what their motivation was.*[18]

Acting on your supporter preferences is likely to generate an increase in engagement and support. And compiling a report of the survey findings will serve to demonstrate your interest in their participation and your commitment to ongoing institutional learning.

It is also advisable to develop a solid infrastructure for your mid-value programme. An ambitious and fully integrated initiative will, for example, require dedicated staff to account manage prospects. They will need to take responsibility for following up mailings through phone and e-mail, engaging donors at cultivation events and thanking them when they have donated. You will either need to recruit fundraisers for this purpose, or negotiate with existing teams to include this as part of their current roles.

At Marie Curie, this was a challenge for Millie Perrett:

> *Mid-value occupies an often awkward position across two or more teams, which means that balancing different perspectives and priorities is a challenge. Another issue is that the budget for the mid-value programme had been set up before we'd decided what we actually wanted to do with the programme and what we wanted it to deliver – this was an internal challenge to do with managing expectations and sourcing additional resources. But there's a message in there about making things easier for yourself by either working hard on a budget that reflects the programme you're setting up, or ensuring that other members of staff (often more senior) are happy to be a bit flexible as tests develop and the programme is refined.*

Service delivery staff also need to be involved in a mid-value programme. The funding proposals will require a higher level of programmatic detail and will result in a larger proportion of restricted gifts too. Make sure that you identify the right areas for funding and that you are firmly on message with your description and budgeting of these projects.

Mid-value programmes in practice

These findings were widely capitalised on by Paul's team at World Jewish Relief. Detailed data analysis of its supporter file established that the organisation had a large number of mid-value supporters, around 500 individuals (nearly 4 per cent of their active database) with an annual value of £485,000.

Their individual level of giving, however, was below the charity's major donor threshold (£5,000 per annum). Like the vast majority of World Jewish Relief's donors they were solicited via standard direct mail, so it was highly unlikely that their potential was being realised. Consequently, these supporters were removed from the regular communication cycle.

A new, fully integrated mid-value supporter journey was constructed. In line with Amber Nathan's recommendations, it was far more personalised and involving. Activities included invitations to twice-yearly stewardship events based around specific projects in the field. If no reply was received, the invitations were followed up with a call (if the charity didn't have the donor's telephone number a personal e-mail was sent instead). Supporters were asked if they had received the mailing and if they could attend.

Following the event, a customised funding request, similar to a major donor proposal, was sent to them. The covering letter was tailored to whether or not they had attended the cultivation event. A further donor care call was then made to see if the proposal had been received. Additionally, for those who donated to the project, two, again tailored, project updates were sent out six months apart. The process was repeated for two specific programmes during the course of a year.

The combination of phone, e-mail, proposal and face-to-face communication through this method was extremely effective. The £485,000 supporter file income for 2011/12 increased to £624,000 within two years, an uplift of 28 per cent, with only a marginal increase in cost.

Significantly, the number of donors did not increase greatly, but the value of average gifts and response rates grew instead. One festival appeal resulted in as many as 22 per cent of supporters making a donation. The improved cultivation approach resulted in one donor increasing his giving substantially. Having never donated more than £5,000 previously, he graduated onto the major donor programme, making a £50,000 pledge (not included in the above income totals).

Emma Burns, World Jewish Relief's deputy director of philanthropy, summarises the underlying approach:

> *The key to success is to think like a mid-value donor – constantly bearing in mind that they want to make an informed decision. We created the mailings to appear, as much as possible, like they had come from the office and were*

> *personal to that donor, always referring to our 'major donor' proposals. And test, test, test – we tested different segments and changed our approach accordingly based on what we learned.*

Millie Perrett implemented a similar process at Marie Curie, reducing the quantity, but improving the quality of mid-value communications. They replaced traditional direct mail with a far more personalised and detailed proposal format. The charity retained the emotional case-study element, but placed more emphasis on a rational proposition that explained why support was required at such a significant level. The mailings were purposefully more tailored and given an 'inside track' feel, appearing more like they had come from the desk of a Marie Curie employee, rather than being mass produced. All communications also contained a single named point of contact.

Millie also segmented the programme to provide an even more customised offering for the highest-level donors and prospects within the mid-value category. Around 200 people benefited from increased personalisation and, as a result, Millie was able to form strong relationships with a proportion of these donors.

After an 18-month cultivation and solicitation period, the charity reaped the benefits, generating just over £1 million in gross income from their direct appeals alone (excluding any additional income from other sources such as newsletters or committed gifts). This compared very favourably with the £794,264 income donated in the year and a half preceding the new initiative – an increase of 26 per cent even in the earliest test stages of the programme.

These arose directly from the enhanced mid-value cultivation and engagement programme. Indeed, Marie Curie effectively ring-fenced these supporters, soliciting them less frequently. Like Paul's charity, this was more than offset by the change in average gift, which increased from £102 to £150. One donor increased his giving from £1,045 in the period leading up to the change, to a total of £40,000 following its implementation.

The charity' prospecting activities were also effective, resulting in a number of mid- and high-value gifts from donors who had previously only given at a lower level. Following this success, Marie Curie also overlaid an additional wealth screen, utilising a dedicated agency, as outlined in chapter 13, to help expand their prospect pool.

To optimise impact, they also carefully tracked their results, adapting their approach according to the insights gained. In the first year, for example, they established that committed givers tend to only respond to higher cash asks at key points in the calendar, such as Christmas. So for this segment they focused their requests for funding on these critical periods.

Following Amber Nathan's research, Marie Curie had also established that their supporters greatly appreciated being invited to cultivation events, even if they didn't attend. So they planned to increase the number that were being engaged in this manner, piggybacking on major gift cultivation events that were already a fixture in the calendar.

CONCLUSION

There is clear potential in the mid-value market, but generally it is unfulfilled. One agency, Factary, estimates the UK market value to be between £16 million and £25 million per annum.[19], which is small relative to other donor groups. They highlight a number of likely reasons:

- Few are asking – the number of specialist mid-value donor fundraisers is limited.

- Few are providing suitable recognition – outside education and the arts, a limited number of organisations are naming their mid-value donors in annual reports and on their websites.

- The focus is on the top and the bottom of the donor pyramid – major donors and small value cash givers receive the majority of the attention from fundraising teams, while mid-value donors are often neglected.

Similarly, while their markets are more developed than the mid-value segment, trusts and corporate donors still present real opportunities for growth.

The consultancy Good Values and the Institute of Fundraising's 2015 report into corporate fundraising highlights the sector's potential. Over the last three financial years there has been a consistent annual increase of 12 per cent in the average amount raised by UK companies through their charitable activities.[19]

There has been a similar increase in the funds raised from trusts and foundations, in both the USA and UK. In real terms, growth in 2014 was at 4 per cent in the USA and nearly 10 per cent in the UK. [20]Additionally, trusts and foundations remain one of the most cost-effective forms of fundraising (£9.56 per £1 spent), second only to legacies in terms of their return on investment.[21]

The evidence demonstrates the potential impact of specialist fundraising techniques. There are huge possibilities for what can be achieved with these valuable supporters if we are able to give them the attention they deserve and effectively implement relationship fundraising practices.

The returns could be significant and could help to relieve pressure on other, more saturated markets. Reducing the emphasis and burden on over-serviced individual donors at the base of the pyramid, in particular, could feasibly lead to an increase in retention and giving levels. In short, a robust, a relationship fundraising approach to trusts, mid-value and corporate supporters could result in long-term gains for our sector across the board.

NOTES
1. Peacock, Robert Ian (2007). *Face Time: Relationship Philanthropy.* Civil Sector Press, Toronto, p.30.
2. *Charitable giving statistics*, National Philanthropic Trust. Available at: http://www.nptrust.org/philantrhopic-resources/charitable-giving-statistics/
3. Pharaoh, C, Jenkins, R and Goddard, K (2014). *Giving Trends Top 300 Foundations Report.* Association of Charitable Foundations, London, p. 20.
4. Burnett, Ken (2015). *Some keys to fresh fundraising success. Three mega-opportunities for all fundraisers.* Available at: http://www.kenburnett.com/Blog53Threemega-opportunities.html Last accessed 3 September 2016.
5. *Consortia-Based Partnerships: A New Paradigm?,* Corporate-NGO Partnerships Barometer, 2015.
6. Jacques, Kate (2013) How Diabetes UK won the Tesco Charity of the Year partnership. *Fundraising, September 2013.*
7. *Consortia-Based Partnerships,* op. cit.
8. Rees, Sara and Sanders, Hannah (2015). Let's get personal. *Fundraising,* October 2015.
9. Ibid.
10. McKee, Alia and Rovner, Mark (2014). *The Missing Middle, Neglecting Middle Donors is Costing you Millions,* Sea Change Strategies, Takoma Park, MD, p. 11.
11. Ibid., p.4.
12. Nathan, Amber and Phillips, Mark (2007). *The Fundraiser's Guide to Mid-Value Donors,* Bluefrog, London.
13. Barry, Frank, Henze, Lawrence, Lamb, David and Swank, Katherine (2010). *Cultivating Lifelong Donors: Stewardship and the Fundraising Pyramid,* Blackbaud, Charleston, p.33.
14. McKee and Rovner, *The Missing Middle,* op. cit., p. 12.
15. Ibid., p. 17.
16. Ibid., p. 17.
17. Ibid., pp. 16-17.
18. Ibid., p. 21.
19. Ibid., p. 21.
20. *Corporate Fundraising, A Snapshot of Current UK Practice in the UK Non-Profit Sector* (2015). Institute of Fundraising & Good Values, July 2015.
21. *Fundratios* (2014). Centre for Interfirm Comparison

Legacy fundraising

Legacy fundraising can be a very humbling experience. It's incredible that so many amazing people want their favourite causes to benefit after their death. Craig has had the privilege of meeting and listening to many legacy pledgers and donors over the years. These donors may all have had different lifestyles and backgrounds but all believed passionately in the work of the charity he was representing.

From the childless couple who were so touched by watching a concert given by vision impaired children they wanted to leave their entire estate to the charity, to the millionaire who wanted to honour the care given to his son in a hospice by funding a bed in his name – every legacy pledger has his or her own unique story for wanting to leave such a gift.

This chapter is all about giving you the tools to become your donor's favourite charity so that leaving a legacy gift is a natural final step in the relationship. As we'll show, there are some well-established techniques underpinned by academic research that will help you to inspire donors to leave you the ultimate relationship fundraising gift.

LEGACY FUNDRAISING – THE GLOBAL CONTEXT

Every country has its own culture, traditions and legal systems, which can encourage or hinder legacy giving. The Anglo-Saxon world has been a leader in planned giving/bequest/legacy fundraising, but there are signs that other countries and regions of the world are awakening to the potential of legacy fundraising.

According to *Giving USA*,[2] bequest giving was around $28 billion in 2014 and the *UK Civil Society Almanac 2015*[3] calculated that around £2 billion per year is donated to charities in the UK, via legacies.

In *An Overview of Philanthropy in Europe*, a report from the Observatoire de la Fondation de France and Centre d'Etudes et de Recherce sur la Philanthropie,[4] it is noted that Germany, Switzerland, the Netherlands, Belgium and Italy have all seen big increases in legacy giving in recent years. Figures from the Belgian tax authorities show a 40 per cent increase in charity legacies between 2006 and 2010.

In South America forward thinking charities such as Fundación Alejandra Forlán in Uruguay have started promoting legacies[5] and in South East Asia many educational institutes benefit from bequests. The Beautiful Foundation in South Korea is currently campaigning to improve tax incentives for legacy giving.

KEY CONCEPTS

Asking for a legacy requires a different fundraising proposition to donor recruitment and general on-going requests for funds. It is likely to be the largest, most significant gift a donor ever makes so you need to change your approach accordingly. As we'll show, a strong legacy offer is less about urgency and more about the donor's values and vision for the future.

Professor Adrian Sargeant and fellow academic Professor Jen Shang published groundbreaking research in 2008 on how a donor's identity and life values are key drivers of deciding to leave a charitable bequest.

The report, *Identification, Death and Bequest Giving*,[6] identified some important findings on the language to use when talking about bequests. First of all was the need to be more abstract than you would normally be in fundraising:

> *When taking decisions about the future, however, individuals prefer to think in the abstract and would thus pay more attention to what these things might mean in the continuation of organizational values. Talking with passion about the quality of care, the relief of suffering, the dignity afforded to clients etc. would be more effectual in this future context.*[6]

Secondly, the *why* is crucial in communications about bequests:

> *It may be more effective to talk about what the successful achievement of the mission will deliver. Promotional messages stressing the organization's ability to improve the community, open up life experiences and to make a difference in the lives of local people, would be more appropriate. 'Why' is more important in the future than 'how'.*

Thirdly, you need to talk about the wider society context than the here and now:

> *For bequests the organization should give consideration to illustrating why the work of the organization is of broader social significance. For example, 'society has a duty to provide the best terminal care that it can', our loved ones might one day benefit from their work', 'no one should be allowed to suffer unnecessarily', etc. Rather than talk about the immediate impact on beneficiaries, the benefit to the local community and/or wider society should be emphasized.*

Fourthly, the promotion of values that will appeal to the donor's view of the world is important:

> *To stimulate bequests nonprofits should promote organizational values that appeal to a donor's long-term life goals and their sense of individual identity. For example, an organizational value, which states 'we're here to make sure that people who are not going to get better can still enjoy a good quality of life in the time that remains', can appeal well to a hospice donor's sense of ideal moral identity.*

Finally, you need to articulate the vision of your cause:

> *While annual appeals can be undertaken in a relatively unstructured way, focusing on the most immediate and pressing of needs, appeals for bequests need to articulate a longer term and coherent plan for what the organization is trying to achieve.*

The other major finding in the report was around identity. People often identified themselves as being part of a community, which they wanted to see live on after their death and so left a bequest.

This affiliation could be with a city, a university, or any other group sharing some common traits.

The second form of identity is with the values of the nonprofit and a desire to see it continue over time. In their conclusions Sargeant and Shang say:

> *…organizations need to consider planning the supporter journeys on which they will take different categories of donor. The prompting of a bequest should be an integral part of every journey. More importantly, however, the organization must also consider the various identities that are (or might be) important to its supporters and develop a plan to introduce supporters to these over time.*

Selected identities should be consistently reinforced over time. This is not just about maximizing the income for the organization it also maximizes the utility for the donor that accrues from their giving. Organizations can make donors feel good about themselves by priming identities that reinforce their desired sense of self.[8]

We will look at how organisations can do this in the next section. Before doing that we also want to discuss the work of Professor Russell James of Texas Tech University, who has built and expanded on the findings of Sargeant and Shang.[9]

Professor James and his team use neuro-imaging in their research to look at the different reactions in the brain when discussing legacies with people. The aim is to try and understand the huge discrepancy between people who give to charities in their lifetime, but don't include a bequest gift to a charity in their estate.

According to the research, when thinking about charitable bequests two parts of the brain light up on MRI scans of people. These are different parts to when people talk about other types of giving. One of the areas is a part of the brain that deals with visualisation. The other part of the brain is the one we use when we take an outside perspective back on ourselves. These together equate to a concept Professor James classifies as 'visualised autobiography'.

This means that when thinking of legacies the donor is thinking about the last chapter of their autobiography and considering whether a charity fits into their life story.

The research was tested in the real world and produced two major findings about the best ways to speak about legacies. First, it was found that storytelling was the best way to get people to think about legacies. And the best stories featured donors who wrote about why they had left a gift in their will to a charity. These 'living donor stories' were more effective than stories about deceased people who had left a gift. To see this in action, compare the following two paragraphs:

Dog owner Norma Jones died in 2013. Her gift in her will has provided food, shelter and love to hundreds of abandoned dogs.

Dog owner Norma Jones made her will today. One day her legacy gift will help provide food, shelter and love to hundreds of abandoned dogs.

The second paragraph would be much more effective in getting people thinking about leaving a legacy gift to your cause. This is because it features a 'living donor story'.

Secondly, the researchers looked at charitable legacy giving compared to gifts to friends and family. Decisions to leave gifts to family were more strongly linked with memory and emotion than gifts to charity. This is not a shock. However, it was interesting that people who spoke about leaving a gift to charities often did this in the context of a person or thing close to them, e.g. 'my father had cancer, so I have included a cancer charity', or 'I loved my cat, so I've included an animal charity'.

This is not surprising and explains why medical and animal charities get such a large percentage of legacy giving. The practical applications of this are important. If you can get people to think about leaving a legacy in the context of honouring someone important to them, the numbers of people making a bequest increases dramatically.

Further research by Routley and Sargeant[10] (using interviews with legacy pledgers) reinforced what had been found in the lab and earlier research:

- People leave legacy gifts to family and friends to manage the memories they leave behind. Charities need to recognise this and work with this desire.

- Charities could do more to show the loved ones of legators (people who leave a gift in their will) the impact the gift has made.

- Connections to causes are developed throughout the life of donors. It is a desire to reflect this life history that influenced the selection of charities.

- Donors were interested in leaving a lasting impact. Charities need to demonstrate how previous legacies have been used and to paint a picture for the future.

- Community is important to many donors. Therefore charities should look at how they can create a sense of belonging. This could be through bequest clubs or highlighting the collective impact that legacies make.

BARRIERS TO LEAVING A LEGACY

However, inspiring a donor to leave a legacy requires more than just using the language and concepts described above. There are also a number of barriers that need to be addressed and overcome in the donor's mind.

In the report *Unlocking the Pot of Gold in Legacy Giving*,[11] Joe Saxton of UK research consultancy nfpSynergy identified five barriers to people leaving a legacy, as shown in figure 16.1.

Let's take a closer look at each one in turn.

Own mortality

Many people don't like to think about their own death. Therefore donors switch off when they hear about legacies as it's something they don't want to discuss.

Figure 16.1: The five barriers to legacy giving

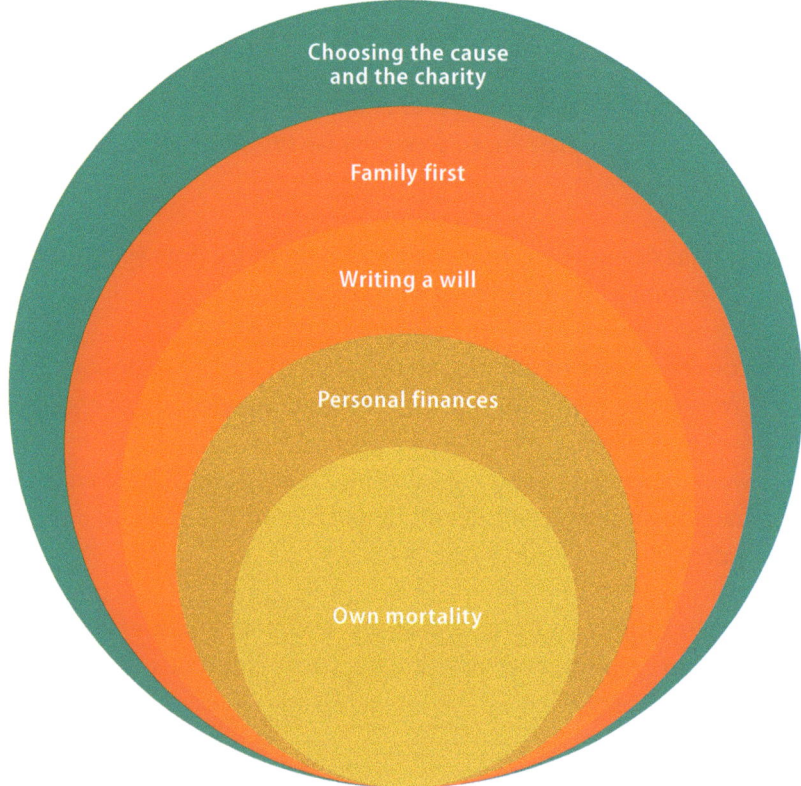

Professor Russell James of Texas Tech University shares five common reasons people give for not discussing death or making a will:

- Distract: I'm too busy to think about that right now.
- Differentiate: it doesn't apply to me now because I (exercise, have good cholesterol, don't smoke…).
- Deny: these worries are overstated.
- Delay: I definitely plan to talk about this…later.
- Depart: I am going to stay away from that reminder.[12]

To get around these avoidance tactics we can use stories and provide reassurance to make it a less scary experience for donors to talk about death and dying. We can 'sugar coat the pill' and discuss making a will in more subtle and integrated ways. For example, rather than advertising a seminar to donors on estate planning, promote a seminar on your cause and how it is funded. Of course, it might be just a coincidence that one of the funding methods discussed at the seminar is about wonderful, generous donors who leave a legacy! This avoidance and worry about your own mortality is why the drip, drip, drip legacy promotion we will discuss in the next section is effective.

Personal finance and writing a will

Many people don't believe they are rich enough to leave a legacy to a charity and worry, amongst other things, about the costs of care in old age. Also, many people often don't want to discuss money and how it will be distributed after death. It is viewed as a private matter and if charities don't ask in a sensitive, polite and respectful way, donors may be discouraged from leaving a legacy gift.

Many people put off writing a will until a significant milestone in life, such as marriage, having children, or retirement. Legacy communications should be targeted at the over 55s, as making a will increases rapidly in this age group. The nfpSynergy research shows that 40 per cent of 45 to 54-year-olds have a will, compared with 69 per cent for the 55 to 64 and 82 per cent for over 65s. Gentle reminders about how important it is to make a will and the dangers of leaving a mess behind if you die without one should be a part of your legacy communications mix.

It is important to emphasise how all legacies, large and small, make a difference to your cause. Again, this can be done in subtle ways. One charity Craig worked for talked about some of the unusual gifts that had been left to the charity – the contents of a handbag and a cuckoo clock being two of the more unconventional ones – to demonstrate that all gifts were appreciated.

Both Dr James's research and the nfpSynergy report show that the number of people who would like/intend to leave a charitable legacy is much higher than the actual numbers who do. This is a huge missed opportunity. It emphasises again why charities need to inform and engage people on the process and how it is easier than many people think to remember your favourite cause in this way. Case studies on donors can be very useful here.

Family first

Of course, when we are encouraging people to leave a charitable legacy it is not meant to be instead of taking care of their loved ones. Family and friends first is an important mantra and one that donors appreciate. Macmillan Cancer Support in the UK tackled this head on with the following headline and caption on a legacy poster:

> *Family.*
> *Friends.*
> *Macmillan?*
> *Is there a place for us in your will?*

Of course, there are some donors who deliberately cut families out of their will after a falling out or disagreement and many charities have benefited in this way.

When talking about legacies to donors with families, giving examples of how you can support your family and still leave a charitable legacy or how small sums can make a big difference are good tactics.

Many of the largest legacies come from individuals without children or close relatives, which is not surprising. If they have been charitable in their lifetime, leaving the bulk of their estate to causes they care about is a natural option and a way for donors to continue to help after death.

If handled with sensitivity and tact, trying to capture information on whether donors are married, have children and their ages can help you identify potential legacy prospects.

Choosing the cause and the charity

Of course, even if donors have overcome all the barriers and are ready to include a charitable bequest in their estate, there is no guarantee they will choose your cause.

That's why applying the research findings in your communications will be a big help. It is also why we urge charities to become friends with donors and to create life-long relationships. When a donor sits down to write her or his will and a solicitor asks whether there are any charities she would like to remember, who is that donor going to choose? The charity that got her name wrong, didn't listen and never thanked her, or the charity that was always respectful, listened and made the donor feel special and valued?

Ultimately, everything in this book is about building the life-long story for donors to want to remember you in their will – just like they would with a family member or friend. It is the best realisation of relationship fundraising and creating donors for life.

PROMOTING AND ASKING FOR LEACIES

As we acknowledged at the start, every country in the world has different traditions when it comes to legacy giving. However, that does not mean that in your country you should not promote giving in this way.

It is interesting to look at how legacy promotion has evolved in the Anglo-Saxon world. The first stage was to raise awareness and to grow the market. The second stage has then been to focus on the individual. If you don't have a culture of bequest giving in your country, then targeting individuals may be hard until you have grown the general market by raising awareness of how to make a charitable legacy.

Stage one: growing the market

In the 1980s mass marketing of charitable legacies to people was in its infancy and there were no agreed best practices. Then, in the middle of the decade, WWF[13] and YMCA[14] both launched transformational adverts that changed the fundraising landscape. These campaigns are both featured on SOFII (www.sofii.org).

Both approaches focused on sharing information and educating donors by offering a free guide to people who wanted to make a will. At the same time, they also asked if the donor would consider leaving a gift to their respective causes.

Both campaigns were hugely effective and have led to many copycat versions.

Perhaps the more memorable ads came from the WWF. They used the hard-hitting headlines below to emphasise how important making a will was and to promote their free guide:

More men are guilty of intestacy than adultery.
More women are victims of intestacy than divorce.

The YMCA used a celebrity, World War II forces sweetheart Dame Vera Lynn, who would be trusted and appeal to the target audience, to promote their guide.

Both campaigns were hugely effective and resulted in tens of thousands of requests for the booklets. This in turn led to hundreds of legacies and millions of pounds being left to the respective causes.

Similar tactics are still used today (though with much smaller returns) and if your country does not have a culture of bequest giving then starting with promoting a similar booklet would be a good approach.

Following on from the free guides came offers for free wills. The Imperial Cancer Research Fund and Cancer Research Campaign (who merged to form Cancer Research UK in 2002) are perhaps the biggest users of this technique. However, hundreds of charities take part in the UK's annual Make a Will Week and offer discounted or free wills at other times of the year. Of course, this seeming generosity needs to be sensibly handled, as any suggestion of undue influence would not go down well in a court of law.

Fortunately for us, CRUK have tracked income from their scheme since its inception in 1993. The long-term returns have been amazing. By the end of 2012 the scheme had raised nearly £70 million at a cumulative cost of £20 million. In total, over 91,000 pledges have been received with an estimated cumulative value of around £426 million – staggering sums of money. And all this has been achieved by offering a free service to a defined audience (55s and older) with a simple ask to help fight cancer.[15]

The next major development in the UK came in 2000, when a consortium of charities set up Remember a Charity to promote legacy giving among the general public. The consortium runs an annual high-profile promotional week and has commissioned research on gifts in wills. It now has over 140 charity members. Similar consortia have also been established in the USA, Canada, Germany and Belgium.

Stage two: talking to individuals

Once leaving a charitable legacy is established as a reasonable thing to do and has wide acceptance in society, you can look at how to promote legacies to individual supporters.

Passive promotion
This is the 'drip, drip, drip' method that we mentioned earlier in the chapter. As we don't know when donors will be making a will, we need to gently drop in mentions of the importance of legacies in our communications. By constantly promoting legacies in this way, hopefully, you will be in donors' minds when their circumstances mean they are going to make or update their will.

Here are some of the passive ways to promote legacies in your organisation:

- Regular articles in your supporter newsletter. Ideas include practical tips on making a will, case studies on legacy pledgers, information on the impact legacies have made to your services and interesting facts on legacies. One of our favourites is that people who leave a charitable legacy in the UK tend to live for three years longer than people who don't.[16]

- Legacy leaflets available in your public areas and at events.

- Supporter surveys, which include a question on whether a donor would consider leaving a legacy.

- Tick boxes on response forms, back of thank-you letters, envelopes asking if people would like to know more about leaving a bequest.

- Posters in charity shops. One charity Craig worked for took this further and included a free bookmark with a legacy message in every book their shops sold.

- Easily available information on your website. This could include downloads of leaflets, testimonials, videos of service users saying how important legacies are, ways to encourage people to let you know they have left a bequest to your cause and anything that gives donors a real sense of what can be achieved through legacies.

- Mentions in your annual report and at an annual general meeting.

Active promotion
An active approach to promoting legacies to your supporters needs to be handled sensitively and with tact. Some donors will find it intrusive and a private matter

that they'd prefer not to discuss with you. However, others will be delighted to share their story and personal reasons for supporting your charity in this way.

Your job as a fundraiser is to make it easy for the former to opt out and to concentrate on inspiring the latter supporters.

One of the most effective ways we have used is the integrated approach that telephone fundraising expert Rich Fox from the USA advocates. He first used the technique in the 1990s and shared his method on SOFII.[17]

This takes the following six-step approach:

1   Identify donors who may be interested in making a legacy gift. Good indicators include length of giving, age, marriage status and number of children.

2   A letter explaining the campaign, the importance of legacies and giving donors the option of opting out of receiving a telephone call to follow up. This includes a response form for donors to send back.

3   A phone call asking donors if they received the letter to look out for an important piece of mail that will be arriving soon.

4   An immediate and personal thank you to all those people who request further information or indicate they have made, or would be willing to make, a legacy gift.

5   A gentle reminder mailing and phone call to those people who gave a positive response on the phone but haven't returned the form.

6   A follow-up phone call to positive responses to thank the donors for requesting the information and considering a legacy. This call can also ask if they have any concerns, if the information was useful and if they have included the charity in their will.

Steps two and three give supporters the opportunity to ask for more information, indicate they intend to leave, or have already left, a legacy, or to let you know that they don't wish to be contacted further on the matter.

UK fundraising agency Bluefrog have run similar legacy campaigns for numerous charities in recent years (including a charity Craig has worked for).

According to Bluefrog's legacy and in-memory expert Hugh Stockhill,[17] the three-stage approach is over four times more effective than a two-stage approach (a two-stage approach will get just over 1 per cent of people enquiring or pledging and a three-stage approach will produce closer to 5 per cent).

Stockhill recommends this approach in conjunction with the drip, drip, drip approach we discussed earlier in the chapter. Bluefrog's method takes a highly personalised approach. The mail pack is typically an inspirational long letter (at least four pages) and signed by a respected senior figure such as a CEO or chair of the board. Variants are used to personalise and make the letter relevant to the donor's giving history and the letter is referenced in the subsequent phone calls.

Typical response rates for the mail are:
1.25 per cent pledgers
0.2 per cent intenders
0.3 per cent enquirers

The follow-up phone call then generates:
5 per cent pledgers
4 per cent intenders
8 per cent enquirers

This sounds great, but how many donors actually leave a legacy? Bluefrog's research shows it is surprisingly high: 70 per cent of pledgers, 30 per cent of intenders and 3 per cent of enquirers follow through and leave a gift in their will.

This means a mailing to 20,000 supporters would produce around 345 actual legacies and millions of pounds in long-term income.

Special events are also a great way to discuss legacies with loyal supporters. These can take many forms. Here are a few reasons to invite supporters to a special event:

- Celebrating an anniversary.
- Achieving a significant milestone.
- Holding open days to give an authentic look at the workings of your charity.
- Meeting experts and specialists.
- To launch a new service.
- To share information.

There are no hard and fast rules to organising events, but in our experience you need to make donors feel special (without being extravagant), be willing to listen, record relevant information and follow up as appropriate. During the course of the event a prominent person – the chief executive, chair of the board, frontline staff, or service users can all work well – should make the donors feel inspired by what their donations achieve, set out plans for the future and remind donors the difference that legacies make.

Mind your language!

We talked at the start of the chapter about the language you should use when discussing legacies with donors. There are some additional tips that we want to share with you if you are writing to donors about legacies.

First of all is to avoid puns on the word 'will'. Certainly in the English language there is a huge temptation to use phrases such as 'where there is a will there is a way' to promote legacies. These have been massively over-used by charities and are likely to be ignored and to be ineffective.

That's not to say humour does not have its place. UK-based legacy expert Richard Radcliffe has spoken to thousands of donors over many years and believes that humour can help break down some of the barriers people have about discussing death.

He gives the example of PETA (People for the Ethical Treatment of Animals) who combine hard-hitting facts and stories about animal cruelty with playful puns from animals rescued by the charity. The animals address concerns donors may have about leaving a legacy in a humorous way.

Take this 'quote' from a pig!

> *Some people think a will is a pig of a document. Personally I think they are great (pigs and wills!). A legacy to PETA in your will can help save my skin (and lots of other animals)!*

In the same leaflet a rabbit reminds donors they are part of a community:

> *I have hundreds of children and can't leave them anything! PETA's family really need help though. Don't just rabbit on about getting a will – do it now!*

These light-hearted quotes are combined with hard-hitting stories such as this:

Rose and her son Teddy (donkeys) were destined for the glue factory when a PETA member bought them at an auction.

Using language that will appeal to your supporters is also important. Christian Aid use a passage from the Bible, Ecclesiastes 3:1-8, King James Version, which begins 'To every thing there is a season, and a time to every purpose under the heaven: A time to be born, and a time to die', to talk about their work, the role of donors and the importance of legacies. Using a biblical passage in this creative way will appeal to their Christian audience. Overall, the brochure[19] makes a compelling case for why donors should leave a bequest.

Nostalgia can also be powerful in legacy fundraising. This ties into the concept of visualised autobiography discussed earlier. By reminding donors of the past and how the charity fits with their life experiences you can increase the likelihood of donors leaving you a legacy. Many universities and colleges use this in their legacy promotion. By getting people to remember their time studying (hopefully with fond memories) and combining it with a vision for future plans, a powerful case can be made for legacy gifts.

Similarly, charities that have been around for a long time can also look back and link their work and donors' lives. When Craig worked at Sue Ryder Care (now Sue Ryder) they used the story of the founder (who many older donors had a strong connection with) to ask supporters for their memories of supporting the charity and to ask them to leave a legacy to continue the founder's crucial work. Sue Ryder Care were overwhelmed with the stories they received back and many donors re-connected with the charity and wanted to know more about leaving a legacy gift.

You should also consider whether you can develop a strong offer to encourage donors to leave a legacy. One of our favourite legacy offers is from The Dogs Trust. They make a simple, but compelling offer to supporters. Pledge to leave a gift in your will and we promise to look after your dog after your death. The charity sends a canine care card[20] to donors (much like organ donation cards) that gives the contact details of the charity and says they will look after the pet after death. This offer works for a number of reasons. It provides peace of mind for the donor, it reflects the values of the donor and the charity and makes sure no animals are abandoned after the death of the owner.

Another legacy offer we like comes from France. Here some charities offer to tend the graves of supporters who leave a legacy. Again, this gives peace of mind to donors and offers a tangible benefit – even if they aren't around to see it come to fruition.

A final word of warning about language. In his book *How to Love Your Donors (to Death)*, fundraising consultant Stephen Pidgeon emphasises the importance of grammar and how older people in the UK can be 'picky'. He warns:

> *And if they spot bad English, they will stop reading the content and start looking for the grammatical howlers. People currently over 60 were taught grammar in their English lessons and remain proud to get it right ...If poor grammar is preventing your target audience from getting your message, and it will, then get your grammar right!* [21]

Don't forget the solicitors and professional will writers

In 2013, the Remember a Charity consortium teamed up with the Cabinet Office Behavioural Insights Team, Charities Aid Foundation and Co-Operative Legal Services to conduct a fascinating piece of research.[22]

They wanted to see if they could increase the number of people leaving a charitable legacy by using behavioural economic insights to ask solicitors to change the language they use when writing a will.

The control group proceeded as normal. One group of will writers were asked to include the question, 'Would you like to leave any money to charity in your will?' A second group included the question, 'Many of our customers like to leave money to charity in their will. Are there any causes you're passionate about?'

The results were astounding. In the control group 4.9 per cent of individuals left a gift in their will to a charity. This percentage jumped to 10.8 per cent for those asked the first question and a staggering 15.4 per cent for those asked the second question. A huge 200 per cent increase from the control group.

Perhaps even more interesting is that the average gift for the last group was nearly double that of the other two groups. If every solicitor (lawyer) in the UK was persuaded to ask the second question then it would raise billions for good causes.

For smaller charities based in a specific community, then, it can be worth investing time in building relationships with local solicitors. From working with solicitors we know that many people want to leave something to charity, but are unsure which charity to choose. If the potential donor ask questions along the lines of 'who should I support?' or 'do you know any good local charities?' to the solicitor, then having a good relationship and reputation with solicitors means they may recommend your cause.

PLEDGER CARE

It is no good spending time on securing legacy pledges if you don't then maintain a good relationship with the donor and keep her inspired to give. Perhaps the most powerful tool donors have is the ability to change their mind at any time.

We've heard of many charities removing legacy pledgers from the general mailing list with the intention of providing special communications for this important group. However, for many reasons, this doesn't happen and charities lose touch with some of their most passionate and committed supporters.

In *Identification, Death and Bequest Giving*, Sargeant and Shang also looked at the impact of charity communications on bequest giving. They quoted research from Susanne DameGreen in 2003 that studied records of a million donors at a national charity over 15 years. This concluded:

> *a) Donors who received a letter directly asking them for a bequest were 17 times more likely to give a bequest than donors who were not asked.*
>
> *b) Donors who were asked and thanked gave twice as much as those who were not thanked.*
>
> *c) Those who were cultivated (notes, letters, visits, etc) after the thank you gave three to four times as much.*
>
> *d) Fewer than one donor in 14 had informed the charity that they had named them as a beneficiary in their will.*[23]

Sargeant and Shang go on to say:

> *Despite the critical importance of communication, data from the NCPG (2001) reveals that only 25% of donors who had informed a charity of their bequest intention experienced being treated any differently as a consequence. As Sargeant et al (2006) conclude that bequest pledgers place a greater emphasis on the quality of service they receive, this would seem to be a critical deficiency.*

Craig has seen at first hand the difference outstanding care of pledgers can make. The legacy manager at one of the charities he worked for was dedicated to providing personal and outstanding care to legacy pledgers. She did this not because it would raise more money, but she believed it was the right thing to do.

This included sending handwritten Christmas cards to pledgers, sending covering notes with newsletters, speaking on the phone with donors whenever they wished and generally treating pledgers with respect. This was not just extended to pledgers, but also to families and friends of people who died and left a gift. Perhaps the biggest vindication of this personal approach came with the charities largest ever legacy gift of over £1 million. The personal communications, invites to events and phone calls were all logged over a 15-year period. It is no surprise that the charity remained in the will to the end and was the joint beneficiary of nearly the entire estate.

Finally, a reminder about age, keeping in touch and fundraising ethics.

It goes without saying that legacy donors tend to be elderly. It is worth considering just how old legacy donors are. In the US, over half of all bequests came from people 88 or over. In Australia it was age 90. In fact, only 13 per cent of the total value of bequests came from under 70s in Australia.

Given that most realised charitable legacies are made within five years of death, it means we need to be talking to donors in their 70s and 80s about legacy giving.[24]

This has to be handled sensitively. As a profession we cannot be seen to be applying undue pressure when communicating with donors, particularly the vulnerable or infirm. That's why whatever plan you undertake to promote legacies needs safeguards in place to make sure it is ethical, uses appropriate language and makes donors feel inspired by the possibilities of what a legacy can achieve.

It is also important that charities don't stop communicating with older donors even if they have stopped giving. This often happens due to the costs of care and low disposable income. We have received many letters from older donors who have got to the point where they can no longer afford to support our charity. Often these letters are sent with an apology and sense of guilt from the donors. We believe it is crucial to go back and thank these donors for their support, ask if they'd like to be kept updated (but not asked for money) and let them know what a difference their support has made over the years. It's not only polite and the right thing to do, it shows friendship and an empathy for donors and their current situation.

Finally, we'd recommend sending an update mailing (with no financial ask, but a soft legacy message) at least once a year to donors over the age of 70 who have supported your cause for five or more years, but are no longer giving. This mailing should acknowledge that they haven't donated for a while, thank them for their past support, share plans for the future and show how a legacy could help achieve something wonderful.

CONCLUSION

Legacy fundraising can seem a bit of a dark art and mysterious to many fundraisers. Yet it remains one of the greatest opportunities available to our profession.

Charities who have taken a long-term view and invested in promoting legacies have reaped millions of pounds in extra income. As the results are not immediate, legacy promotion can often be sidelined and not given the prominence it deserves. This is a mistake.

The best fundraisers will do all they can to promote legacies at every appropriate moment. They may not be working at the charity to see the results, but it will be one of the most cost-effective uses of their time.

There is now a body of research to help develop compelling legacy messages and campaigns. We ignore this at our peril. It may seem hard to talk to people about death and what happens to their money. But, as the best legacy fundraisers will tell you, legacy fundraising is not about dying, but about a donor's values, dreams and hopes for the future.

NOTES
1. We have used terms legacy and bequest interchangeably throughout the chapter.
2. The Giving Institute, *Giving USA 2015*, press release, 2015. Available at: http://www.givinginstitute.org/?page=GUSA2015Release Last accessed 7 August 2015.
3. NCVO (2015) *UK Civil Society Almanac 2015*. NCVO, London. Available for download at: https://data.ncvo.org.uk/almanac15 Last accessed 15 August 2016.
4. *An Overview of Philanthropy in Europe*, Observatoire de la Fondation de France, 2015. Available at: http://www.fondationdefrance.org/Outils/Mediatheque/Etudes-de-l-Observatoire?id theme-5028. Last accessed 7 August 2015.
5. You can see their brief legacy message at: http://www.fundacionalejandraforlan.org/como-colaborar/ Last accessed 5 September 2015.
6. Sargeant, Adrian and Shang, Jen (2008) *Identification, Death and Bequest Giving*, Association of Fundraising Professionals, Arlington, VA. Available at: http://www.afpnet.org/files/contentdocuments/sargeant_final_report.pdf Last accessed August 2015.
7. Ibid., p. 44.
8. Ibid., pp. 58-59.
9. *Russell James: The neuroscience of philanthropy podcast*, The Philanthropy Hour. Available at: http://www.philanthropyhour.com/blog/russel-james-the-neuroscience-of-philanthropy Last accessed 15 August 2015. See also *Inside the mind of the bequest donor: research findings from experimental psychology and neuroimaging*, presentation on Slideshare. Available at: http://www.slideshare.net/rnja8c/inside-the-mind-of-the-bequest-donor-40549539 Last accessed 15 August 2015.
10. Routley, Claire and Sargeant, Adrian (2014). Leaving a bequest: living on through charitable gifts. *Nonprofit and Voluntary Sector Quarterly* 1-17, at p. 14.
11. Saxton, Joe (2012) *Unlocking the Pot of Gold in Legacy Giving*, nfpSynergy, London.
12. Op cit, Slideshare, slide 54/105.

13. WWF integrated legacy campaign, SOFII. Available at: http://sofii.org/case-study/wwf-integrated-legacy-marketing-campaign Last accessed 18 August 2015.
16. YMCA: 'soft sell' legacy advertising. SOFII. Available at : http://sofii.org/case-study/ymca-soft-sell-legacy-advertising Last accessed 13 August 2016.
17. All facts from a presentation made at the Institute of Fundraising legacy conference in 2012. *Free Wills, What's the Catch?* Presented by Jack Visser and Pauline Mayer of CRUK. Available on Slideshare at: http://www.slideshare.net/iof_events/free-wills-whats-the-catch-pauline-mayer-jack-visser-cancer-research-uk Last accessed 18 August 2015.
18. Radcliffe, Richard, at many seminars! Available, at for example: http://ahern.comm.com/ss_plugins/content/content.php?content.3006
19. Fox, Rich (2012) *Is this the best way to develop bequests?* SOFII. Available at: http://sofii.org/article/is-this-the-best-way-to-develop-bequests Last accessed 5 September 2015.
20. All the facts are from an interview with Hugh Stockhill and a presentation he shares with prospective clients.
21. Available at: http://www.christianaid.org.uk/images/will-writing-guide.pdf Last accessed 5 September 2015.
22. You can read more about the Canine Care Card on the Dogs Trust website: https://www.dogstrust.org.uk/get-involved/wills-legacies/canine-care-card/ Last accessed 6 September 2015.
23. Pidgeon, Stephen (2014) *How to Love Your Donors (to Death)*, Directory of Social Change, London, p. 99.
24. Cabinet Office Behavioural Insights Team and Charities Aid Foundaiton (2013) *Applying Behavioural Insights to Charitable Giving*. Available at: https://www.gov.uk/government/uploads/system/uploads/attachment_data/file/203286/BIT_Charitable_Giving_Paper.pdf
25. Sargeant and Shang, *Identification, Death and Bequest Giving, op. cit.*, p.22.
26. James, Russell (2014) *Charitable bequest demographics*, Available at Slideshare: http://www.slideshare.net/rnja8c/charitable-bequest-demographics-33283226_at_slide_58

17

How do people really make decisions?
By Rob Woods

Here we present a guest chapter prepared and written by award-winning trainer Rob Woods, who we asked to apply insights from behavioural economics principles to relationship fundraising. Rob was asked as he regularly runs training on the subject. His 2015 book, The Fundraiser Who Wanted More, *tells the story of someone who uses the principles of persuasion to become better at fundraising.*

In late October 2012 Hurricane Sandy ripped through the Caribbean and parts of north-eastern United States and Canada. Thousands of homes and businesses were destroyed and more than 180 people died.

Following the event, fundraising appeals were launched to help those affected by the disaster. When the psychologist Jesse Chandler analysed the donations he discovered something intriguing.[1]

He found that people were more likely to donate to a Hurricane Sandy appeal if their first name began with an S. Similarly he found that people whose names began with the letter R, such as Rachel or Richard, were 260 per cent more likely to give to the Hurricane Rita appeal than people whose names began with a different letter. In fact the same effect has been found following every hurricane that he studied, going back several decades.

If you were asked to predict the factors likely to affect the chances of someone giving to a hurricane relief appeal would you have suggested the first letter of their name?

Another astonishing example is the story of an unintended consequence when NASA landed a space probe on Mars. Apparently news coverage of the event led to an increase in the sale of Mars bars.

Just think about that for a minute. People heard the word 'Mars' more often than normal, in the sense of the planet, and some of them had so little conscious control of their decision-making that they bought more of that particular chocolate bar.

Confronted with examples like these, we find it hard not to be a little sceptical about the rationality of human decision-making.

Yet most traditional economics textbooks are written as though people make decisions like *Star Trek*'s Dr Spock, by carefully weighing costs against benefits. In their book *Nudge*, Richard Thaler and Cass Sunstein suggest this 'rational choice theory' is not the way most real people think and make decisions. But they point out that many people (and we would argue, many charities) 'seem committed to the notion that each of us thinks and chooses unfailingly well'.

Why does this matter for relationship fundraising? Because unless we acknowledge it, we will prepare our communications full of clearly laid out logic and statistics, as if all human decision-making derives solely from rational thought. We will fail to inspire our donors because we will ignore many of the less obvious factors that could have made all the difference in helping them take action.

BEHAVIOURAL INSIGHTS CAN HELP

In recent years the field of behavioural economics has explored the social, cognitive and emotional factors that affect the way decisions are made. In 2002 Daniel Kahneman was awarded a Nobel Prize for his groundbreaking studies of human thinking and decision-making. His best-selling book, *Thinking Fast and Slow*, suggests there are two ways our thinking operates. The fast, automatic one he calls system 1 and the slow one he calls system 2.[2]

Kahneman explains that when we are asked 'what is two times two?' or 'what is the capital of France?', the answers occur to us automatically and with no effort, accessing our associative memory. These are examples of system 1 thinking at work.

When we are asked 'what is 24 times 17?' most people need to laboriously work out the answer. This is system 2 thinking. It requires effort and is tiring.

Most people would assume that the decision to donate money to help people after Hurricane Sandy would be governed by the rational, conscious thought processes of system 2 thinking. But the fact that some people were in part swayed to do this because their name begins with the letter S suggests that the automatic pilot system 1 thinking was also involved. And some people were nudged to choose Mars bars ahead of other available chocolate bars because the word 'Mars' was top of mind in system 1 thinking.

There are many insights from *Thinking Fast and Slow* that have implications for successful fundraising, but two of the key ones are:

- Because system 2 thinking requires deliberate effort, people often try to avoid using it. So fundraisers must work hard to make it as easy as possible for donors to do what they want to do.

- Because system 1 thinking is largely automatic, the means by which it makes decisions tend to involve mental shortcuts, or rules of thumb. Understanding how these mental shortcuts work, and a respect for how powerful they are, enables fundraisers to enlist the support of system 1 thinking as well as system 2 thinking when donors make decisions.

In this chapter I will explore six principles derived from research into how people make decisions. Where it is useful I include research from outside fundraising in order to demonstrate how the principles work. I will then give examples of how the ideas have been used by charities and make suggestions for ways you might apply them in your own fundraising.

PRINCIPLE ONE: SIMPLE
A key idea that recurs in the behavioural science literature is that when you make something easier to do it increases the chances that people will do it. Using Kahneman's language, when behaviours require much mental effort (that is, they require system 2) they are less likely to happen.

Make it easier – opt in versus opt out
For example, a key problem for charities is that the actual value of donations decreases with inflation. The behavioural insights team at the Cabinet Office in the UK report that a £10 donation begun in 2005 would be worth just £7.50 by 2015. Charities can proactively address this by explaining the issue to donors when they sign up to make regular donations and invite them to set their donations to increase over time without the need for further decisions.

In one study, the behavioural insights team joined with the Charities Trust and the Home Retail Group to explore the impact of changes to how people were invited to sign up to inflation-proof their donations.[3]

At the Home Retail Group there was already a scheme that people could join called the Xtra factor, whereby an automatic escalation increases donations by 3 per cent per year. Though the payroll-giving scheme itself is very successful (25 per cent of all employees take part), take up of the Xtra factor scheme had been low.

The study found that when inviting people to enrol in payroll giving positioned the Xtra factor as something people needed to opt in to, 6 per cent of people opted in. As you might expect, deciding to opt in to something takes more mental effort than leaving it as it is. When the process was changed so that the Xtra factor was the default, but which people could opt out of if they wished, 49 per cent of people opted for their gift to increase annually.

Making it easier – simplifying mobile landing pages
It's easy to under-estimate the amount of time and mental energy it takes to fill in an on-line form. We believe that many charities are unaware of how many donations they are losing because filling in these forms is too much hassle for the would-be donor's weary system 2 brain.

In 2014 the Norwegian individual giving expert Beate Sorum examined the cost of not taking action in this area, by comparing the results of two charities.[4] The first charity had a landing page and form that was optimised for mobile visitors, whereas the other had a rather complicated form, which also asked unnecessary questions like 'what prompted you to make this gift?' One had made the giving process much easier than the other. Both charities conducted Christmas appeals, using a clear, direct request for a donation, with traffic coming from similar sources. In theory, this means that the same percentage of visitors should have left a donation.

On Charity A's landing page, which was optimised for mobile phones, the information requested in order for people to make a donation was kept to a minimum (for example, it did not ask for their address) and the form was designed to make the process as simple and intuitive as possible.

Charity B had not yet optimised their landing page (they were working on it), so it was more difficult to read on a mobile phone and the process of completing the form was harder work.

What happened? With charity A – the optimised one – 8 per cent of visitors on a mobile phone donated. With charity B – the one that had not optimised its landing page for mobile, just 2.5 per cent of the visitors using a mobile ended up donating.

Beate explains that by far the most likely explanation for the results for charity B being much lower than for A is that many of their mobile phone visitors simply gave up.

If charity B had optimised its landing page for mobile users as charity A had done, she calculated it would have raised at least an extra €36,000 through their Christmas appeal alone.

Make it easier – fewer options

The behavioural scientist Sheena Iyengar, author of *The Art of Choosing* and professor at Columbia Business School, found that offering a lot of choice often reduces the likelihood of people making any choice at all.[5] For example, in an experiment in a supermarket, researchers set up a table at which customers could taste different flavours of jam and varied the number of flavours available. When 24 flavours of jam were available only 3 per cent of customers actually bought any jam, whereas when there were only six flavours available to try 30 per cent of customers ended up buying a jar of jam.

Beate Sorum has pointed out that many charities would do well to apply the underlying message from these experiments in the way they design their websites. The would-be donor visiting the website is often faced with far too many options. For example, would they like to find out about legacies, or volunteer, or sign a petition, or become a member (or a family member), or give £2 a month, or a one-off £10 donation, etc.

The result is that just like would-be jam buyers, their system 2 thinking is paralysed from the effort of trying to decide and they end up taking no action at all.

There are two challenges that make this problem harder to solve than you might expect. Firstly, one prevailing rule of thumb is that all donors have different motivations and we should try to cater for this by providing a variety of ways for them to help our causes. We would agree that providing options is important, but the truth is that one or two options are far more realistic for most website visitors than the rest. Using the layout of the webpage to make those options far more obvious helps visitors take some action.

Another challenge is that you may need to make tough decisions within the charity about which option is strategically most important to prioritise. This can be difficult, but if you don't find a way to solve it you are leaving the decision to the donor instead. This will probably require a lot of effort from their system 2 thinking, so you run the risk that they will fail to make any decision at all.

In one charity where Beate worked, she reduced confusion for visitors to the website by making a donation form the primary element on the 'support us' page; all other donation offers were made less prominent as links further down the page. In this prioritised form (next page), both regular donations and one-time donations were possible, with a regular gift as the default option. Prioritising this, removing ambiguity and using the default setting resulted in a massive increase in the annual value of regular givers signing up online. From 2011 to 2014 the increase was 847 per cent.

Reducing options on your website can increase donations

Member!	Donate!	Regular gift!
Facebook!	Instagram!	Twitter!
Legacy!	Volunteer!	Sponsor!
Fundraise!	Give stuff!	Holiday cards!
Webshop!	App!	Newsletter!

Donate!

Member!		Regular gift!
Facebook!	Instagram!	Twitter!
Legacy!	Volunteer!	Sponsor!
Fundraise!	Give stuff!	Holiday cards!
Webshop!	App!	Newsletter!

PRINCIPLE TWO: SOCIAL PROOF
We are strongly influenced by the behaviour of those around us, especially when we feel they are similar to ourselves.

For example, in *Influence: The Psychology of Persuasion*, Professor Robert Cialdini[6] describes an experiment involving a street musician in which one of the researchers walked past every two minutes, putting money in the hat. Most people predict this example would lead more passers-by to give. But we have found that few people would predict the extent of the increase. It turns out that passers-by were now eight times more likely to put money in the hat.

Encouraging payroll giving – what details make a difference?
It seems clear that, where possible, it is helpful to show potential supporters that other people like them are giving. But what kind of information is it most important to include?

The behavioural insights team at the UK Cabinet Office explored this question in the context of a campaign to increase payroll giving among staff at the HMRC office in Southend, Essex.[7]

In December 2013 employees received winter greetings e-cards with messages from their HMRC colleagues. The cards were from people who were already giving to charity. They explained why they give and invited the reader to do the same. Half the cards contained only the message and half also included a photo of the person who had sent it.

They found that including a picture of the existing donor made a big difference to the results. When people only received the message, 2.9 per cent signed up, but this more than doubled, to 6.4 per cent, when the photo was included.

Corporate fundraising – using examples when talking to potential partners
A key principle in building corporate partnerships is that the partnership will help the company achieve some business benefit, in addition to helping the charity with its goals.

But a big challenge is that few company employees, especially those working in the marketing department (which is often important for a genuinely strategic partnership), have much experience of working with charities in a way that brings strategic benefit. So many companies you talk to will be sceptical that what you propose is realistic. And if they're sceptical it can be hard to persuade them to even meet you, or indeed to encourage them to discuss what their business challenges really are. But if you don't know what business challenges they face, it's very hard to create proposals that would actually help them solve those challenges.

How can we help these potential partners grasp just how great this opportunity would be, if they have not experienced proof that it is even possible? One solution, according to the NSPCC fundraiser Ben Swart, is to provide social proof that other companies have benefited by doing the same.[8]

His approach is to proactively help potential partners believe and want strategic partnerships by giving them examples of other companies that have derived business benefit from partnering with charities.

For example, in an initial meeting with a company (or on the phone to secure an initial meeting) he is able to mention that NSPCC's partnership with The Garden Centre helped that company increase revenue by nearly £1 million; or that the NSPCC's partnership with one large business-to-business insurance provider helped the company achieve prompt payment of clients' invoices to the value of more than £1 million.

Note that in these examples, he does three things that many corporate fundraisers fail to do:

- He is able to summarise the story in a single sentence – given that the examples are not about the company you are talking to, they may not pay attention if you go into too much detail.

- He often does so in terms of benefit to companies, rather than to the children the NSPCC serves (though obviously when the primary interest of the listener is likely to be the NSPCC's cause, he is able to give the example in terms of the children the partnership has helped).

- He is specific about the level of benefit to the company. He works hard at finding these numbers, because he knows such details make a difference to the impact of what he is saying.

Corporate fundraisers who do not currently know examples of benefit to their partners will find it harder to help companies believe they are genuinely interested in partnership. If you would like to make use of the power of social proof in this way, but don't currently have examples to use, then the two following tactics will help.

Call or meet existing partners to find out just how much benefit they are receiving from the partnership; study examples of how much benefit companies have generated from partnering with other charities. Even if it's not about you, it's still powerful social proof that can help them believe that partnership brings huge value to the company as well as the charity.

Major donor and trust fundraising – three ways to use social influence

One UK charity that has recently achieved extraordinary growth in major donor and trust fundraising is the cancer care charity Marie Curie. Between 2009 and 2015, annual income from major donors and trusts increased from £1 million to more than £5 million.[9] According to Lucy Sargent, who led the team that achieved this growth, the improvement was achieved through several strategic choices. The mind-set that under-pins the strategy is that all trusts are run by people, so the charity endeavours to build relationships with them in the same way that they would any individual supporter.

Since trusts are run by people, social proof is an invaluable tool that can help you build these relationships. Here are three ways it has been used to achieve this huge growth:

- One of the key performance indicators (KPIs) used to monitor activity is the number of proposals submitted which included an endorsement from someone external to the charity. This KPI helps the team keep track of how well they were doing at finding and using social proof.

- Since 2009, there has been a deliberate strategy of recruiting senior volunteers into ambassador-type roles. The purpose of these roles is to influence on behalf of the charity. The strategy requires time and effort, but having a large group of influential people who support the charities' aims is immensely helpful.

- Lucy's team regularly circulated a 'peer review' list of trustees they would like to meet. This list continues to be sent to the ambassadors and other networks of people who already support the charity, such as volunteers on other committees. Often this enables the fundraiser to start a conversation with a trust that had otherwise seemed impossible to reach. As a result, Marie Curie fundraisers were extremely successful in securing initial meetings with influential people at trusts. Obviously, they still needed to make an excellent case for an important need that meets the trust's criteria, but their chances of doing this well were vastly increased because they knew what to aim for.

PRINCIPLE THREE: LIKING

It should come as no great surprise that when you like someone you are more likely to be influenced by her or him. What can be surprising is the power of certain factors to make us like something in the first place.

Names

Remember the finding from the start of this chapter that people are more likely to give to a hurricane relief appeal if their initial matched that of the hurricane?

It seems that this is not the only example of how our names make us more likely to respond in surprising ways. The truth is, our names are very important to us and, indeed, we like the letters in our names. Martin, Goldstein and Cialdini, in their book *The Small BIG*, report that when people are asked to write down their five favourite letters of the alphabet, the letters they write bear an uncanny resemblance to the letters in their own names.[10]

An example of how our system 1 thinking is attuned to our names is the so-called cocktail party phenomenon. This describes what happens if you are at a party, engrossed in a conversation with a friend until you suddenly hear someone else in the room mention your name. Your attention is immediately diverted. It seems that all the while some part of you had been alert and scanning for things that matter to you, even if your conscious thinking had been fully focused on your friend.

Campaign to donate a day's salary – using names

The UK Cabinet Office's behavioural insights team was interested in options for encouraging employees to donate a day of their salary.[11] They worked with the fundraising team in the London offices of Deutsche Bank as part of a fundraising campaign in support of Help a Capital Child and Meningitis Research UK. The existing scheme asked employees to give a day's salary, once a year.

On the day of the campaign, all of Deutsche Bank's employees received an e-mail from their chief executive. It was either addressed to 'Dear colleague' or was personalised by using their name. And everyone received one more nudge: they were greeted either by posters advertising the campaign, by volunteers with flyers, or volunteers with sweets. The sweets included the campaign strap line:

There is an easier way to donate to one day – take the easyway.com.

In the control group (who were met by the volunteers with flyers) roughly 5 per cent of people decided to donate, whereas in the group that received the sweets, 11 per cent donated. Cialdini would describe this as the principle of reciprocation at work. What about the different kinds of e-mail? It turned out that receiving a personalised email from the chief executive ('Dear Sarah' rather than 'Dear colleague') made even more difference than the sweets, as 12 per cent of this group gave a day's salary.

The most powerful intervention of all was when the three nudges were combined. In the group that received sweets (reciprocation) and a personalised message (liking) from the chief executive (authority), 17 per cent of employees donated, which is more than three times as many as those who received none of these nudges.

Actions speak louder than words

In *Influence: The Psychology of Persuasion* Professor Cialdini describes compelling studies that show the power of compliments to both make people like you more and be more likely to say yes when you ask for help.[12] It seems that sincerely complimenting someone verbally is an extremely effective influencing tool.

Several years ago a UK retailer set about choosing a new partner to be their charity of the year.[13] The partnership would be worth a quarter of a million pounds to the charity. The process for choosing the partner was initially for five charities to pitch. Based on the pitches, the best three would be put forward to a staff vote to choose the winner.

All five pitched on the Monday morning. They were told that a decision would be reached on Wednesday, at which point they would be informed whether they had got through or not.

Except that as it turned out, the members of the panel at the retailer changed their minds. At 2.30 on the Monday afternoon, less than two hours after the last pitch had been made, the chair of the panel telephoned one of the five charities, the NSPCC. They said they were so keen to select NSPCC as their partner, they had decided to cancel the planned staff vote altogether. The pitch alone had been enough for them to make their decision.

The fundraiser who took that unexpected call was Tori Griffiths, who had led the NSPCC's pitch.

When I asked Tori why she thought the pitch had been so successful, she said that in addition to making a clear and logical case, the team had worked hard to make their presentation extremely likeable. Two of the ways they did this were to pay the company two unusual compliments.

The first part of the NSPCC's presentation focused on how the partnership would help the retailer. This may sound obvious but, in fact, nearly all charity pitches to companies start with an introduction to the charity: who it serves, when it was founded, etc. And although this explanation is often intended to last one minute, in practice it usually takes two or three, by which time the attention of most members of the panel has started to wander.

The logic behind this kind of opening seems reasonable, in that if a company is to partner with us, they're going to need to know who we are and who the funds would help. But in practice, for most corporate pitch opportunities, it is the least persuasive way to open, because it means you address your needs (however noble they are) ahead of the company's.

The first sentence of Tori's pitch was different. It went something like this: 'We're here to encourage you to choose the NSPCC to go through to the staff vote because doing so will help position you as the most family-friendly department store in this city...' She went on to paint a picture of the difference the money would make to vulnerable children, but only after she had brought to life the impact the partnership would have for the company.

Tori had surmised that although everyone on the panel was serious about the charity of the year partnership making a difference for a good cause, most of them would not be able to ignore the commercial, brand-enhancing reasons for partnership. Although many corporate fundraisers say they want to help their corporate partners achieve business benefits, the signal that is sent to the pitch panel's system 1 thinking tends not to back this up, if they start out by talking about themselves.

To set up the second compliment, Tori told a true story from her childhood. She explained that as a child she had precious memories of being taken to this shop as a treat and, in particular, she clearly remembered the day she was taken there for a haircut. In fact, after the happy visit her mother had kept the certificate and lock of hair they had received at the end. At this moment in the pitch, Tori produced the certificate and lock of brown hair which she'd found in her mother's keepsake box the previous weekend.

To say the pitch panel were surprised to see the 30-year-old keepsake is an understatement. Actually there may have been a number of reasons, some of them highly rational, why the panel liked the NSPCC's pitch. But when someone doesn't just talk the talk and actually goes the extra mile in order to pay us a compliment through her actions, it is very hard not to like her, or indeed infer that she is the sort of person to go the extra mile for us if we were to enter a partnership with her organisation.

PRINCIPLE FOUR: AUTHORITY

Early in this chapter we mentioned that Daniel Kahneman had won a Nobel Prize for economics. In the split second that it took you read this, the various associative memories that you have for Nobel Prize winners are likely to have affected your attitude to Kahneman's ideas.

One of the influence principles that Robert Cialdini describes in *Influence: The Psychology of Persuasion* is authority. He cites many studies which show that when we perceive someone to be an expert or with high status, such as a doctor or university professor, we are far more likely to give credence to what he or she is saying.

If you have used Wikipedia you may remember reading a message from the site's founder, Jimmy Wales, asking for a donation. In tests, Wikipedia found that when the request came from Jimmy more people donated.[14]

Reassuring donors about impact

One of the most important questions that we need to be able to answer for donors, whether or not they ask it explicitly, is 'if I make a donation, will it make an impact?'

There are several ways we can reassure donors, including a numerical measure of something that improves for our beneficiaries thanks to our charity's intervention and stories about particular people it has helped.

In addition to these more obvious tactics, another way to build credibility is to use the authority principle. If you are preparing to talk or write to a donor about a particular project area that needs funding, ask yourself which source of authority you could mention that would reassure them of its high quality.

For example, when describing their innovative Skylight Centres, the UK charity Crisis has found it helpful to mention that the Centres' effectiveness has been independently evaluated by the University of York's Centre for Housing Policy.

Apply for and proactively mention awards

If your charity has ever won an award for some aspect of its service, or for a particular corporate partnership, are your fundraisers proactively mentioning and displaying this? This is not a new idea, but I have found that many fundraisers underestimate the impact it can have and so they never get round to finding out and practising it. Reading Kahneman's work helps me justify the effort needed, because even if the potential partner's system 2 thinking is uninterested, their system 1 thinking will nevertheless receive a signal that will positively affect their attitude to your charity.

If you haven't won an award, knowing how helpful this can be in winning future partnerships or trust bids can help you find the time to apply for one. Note, even if you get short-listed for an award but don't win this fact can still act as a powerful endorsement. Film promoters make good use of this authority frame when they describe the star of their new film as an 'academy award nominee'.

If you organise an event, either to thank existing donors, or as an introduction to prospective ones, which expert or authority figure could you invite to speak on your behalf?

PRINCIPLE FIVE: COMMITMENT AND CONSISTENCY

A key problem for health services is the money that is wasted when people fail to turn up for their doctor's appointments. UK health economists have estimated the total cost of people failing to show up for health appointments is £800 million per year.

In *The Small BIG*, psychologists Martin, Goldstein and Cialdini describe studies into how health services could reduce the number of 'no-shows'.[15] The decision-making principle they used was what Robert Cialdini labelled commitment and consistency.

This principle describes a deep motivation that most of us have to behave consistently with the previous commitments we have willingly made. It is especially strong when those commitments require effort on our part and are made public to other people.

They found that when patients initially called up to make their appointment, simply asking them to read back the date and time of the appointment led to a small but significant reduction in 'no shows'. And they found the effect was even stronger when the receptionist asked patients to write down the date and time of the appointment on a card themselves. In this study, this simple change to what happened when appointments were made led to an 18 per cent reduction in appointments being missed, equating to a saving of around £144 million. This is an extraordinary amount for a tactic that takes just a few seconds to implement each time someone books an appointment.

Each step builds commitment

I once heard that on a first date, even if you really like someone, it can be counter-productive to start talking about what you would want the first dance to be if the two of you were to get married. If you really have high hopes for this relationship, the best strategy is to focus on making the first date a success and build from there.

And the crucial lesson I take from the research into the principle of commitment and consistency is the importance of building relationships with donors one step at a time. When planning communication in high-value and corporate fundraising, an early thing to be really clear about is what would be the best next step that this communication could achieve in this relationship.

This seems obvious and yet, in talking to thousands of fundraisers on training courses, I have found that doing it in practice is harder than it looks. For example, when fundraisers are asked what they would like this letter, or pitch, or phone call to achieve the answer they very often give is 'for them to agree to a gift', or 'to get them to agree to a partnership with us'.

Whereas when you think carefully about it, it is very unlikely that a pitch, letter or proposal, in isolation, can achieve these big results. This is because major gifts and corporate partnerships are complex and can only be made with significant exchange of information and building of trust.

So in most high-value fundraising situations, a useful answer to the question 'what would you like this piece of communication to achieve?' is likely to focus only on the next step in this journey, such as 'for the donor to agree to meet us', or 'to put us through to the staff vote', or 'to decide to put a proposal forward for discussion at the next board meeting'. Once someone has agreed to and taken any of these steps the chances of the relationship leading to a gift or partnership clearly increase.

Why is this principle so important when we are seeking to influence? Because it is easier to ask someone to write down the date of their doctor's appointment than it is to actually get them to turn up, yet if they do write it down they are more likely to show up. So in fundraising, each step donors willingly take builds their commitment and so increases the chances that they will act consistently with that commitment.

Seeking feedback builds commitment

As I mentioned earlier, it is unlikely that examples of companies getting value from their relationship with you will fall into your lap. To build up a bank of social proof stories that help other companies believe you are serious about adding value you are probably going to need to search these stories out, which means calling existing partners to seek feedback. Or better still, you could include this item on the agenda when you next meet them.

According to the principle of commitment and consistency, a second benefit to doing this is that anyone who tells you examples of how much value the partnership has added is likely to become a more loyal supporter of your charity.

I recently attended a conference session about how to help corporate partners extend their partnership over the long term. During the presentation, the speaker showed us short video clips from senior people from five of her most long-standing corporate partners in which they explained why they found the partnership so rewarding.

Asking those busy, senior corporate executives to be filmed would not have been remotely easy. And yet it was well worth the effort because quite apart from the way their insights improved the conference presentation, the act of making such public commitments about the value of the partnership can only have made those senior corporate executives even more loyal to their charity partner.

PRINCIPLE SIX: CONTRAST

Some time ago I was at the beach with my children and while we were walking to the sea they splashed through several cold puddles. After a 20-minute swim in the bracing North Atlantic, they walked back up the beach and discovered that the puddles seemed to have warmed up considerably.

Even though my rational brain knew that the puddles could not possibly have changed temperature in objective terms (it was a cloudy day), they undeniably *felt* far warmer after spending time in the much colder sea.

The extraordinary impact of contrast on how we perceive reality is one of the many fascinating ideas that Phil Barden brings to life in his book, *Decoded: The Science Behind Why We Buy*. He explains that 'we need comparisons to make decisions'. We do not perceive things in terms of absolutes. In order to tell whether something is cold or warm, expensive or cheap, light or dark we cannot help but look at how it compares to the things around it.

This stems from the fundamentals of how our brains work. Barden explains that:

> *...if we look at single neurons in the sensory brain, they all have one thing in common: they respond only to differences and changes. If there is no difference*

or contrast, the receptors stay inactive.[16]

Wise communicators understand the importance of contrast. There is a good reason why adverts for slimming clubs or other weight loss products invariably include a before and an after picture. They have found that only showing the inspiring, slimmed down person is less effective because without contrast there is no story and, therefore, less interest.

Framing how much people give
In 2012, Smith, Windmeijer and Wright were interested in the online giving pages for people running the London Marathon.[17] They found that the size of gifts that had already been left and that were therefore visible to subsequent givers affected the amount that was pledged. A £10 increase in the mean of past donations increased subsequent giving by £2.50.

So if you plan on being sponsored to do a run or trek for charity, encouraging your richest and most generous friends to give first is a shrewd move because setting this 'frame' will help uplift subsequent pledges.

In a study of gifts made to National Public Radio in the USA, Professor Adrian Sargeant was interested in whether mentioning how much other callers give would make a difference to the average size of people's telephone pledges.[18]

One group of people answering the calls from would-be donors shared social information about another caller who had pledged a donation to the radio station. What they said was along the lines of 'we had another member who contributed $300'. Care was taken to only refer to real past donations. When callers included social proof in this way the average gift increased by 25 per cent. The average gift size was $86.58 when other donors' gifts were not mentioned and rose to $111.91 when they were.

Furthermore, as Katya Andresen and Alia McKee explain in their e-book, *Homer Simpson for Nonprofits*, human beings are often prone to choose the middle option.[19] They relate the example of the bread machine maker, Williams-Sonoma, whose $279 machine didn't sell well until they introduced a bigger model for $429. When it was not the most expensive, the mid-range model for $279 felt like a bargain and sales of that increased dramatically.

The ethics of using these principles
Given how powerful these principles can be, it is important that fundraisers should think through the ethical implications.

Is it possible to use these ideas to manipulate, to make people do things that are not in their best interests? Absolutely. Cialdini's books include many examples of how unscrupulous people in many professions take advantage of these insights.

However, I believe that there is a place for tactics informed by behavioural economics in ethical fundraising. As long as there are nonprofits with the means to alleviate suffering and solve problems, it is inevitable that some people will want to donate money to enable this to happen. Giving is good for people.

As Andresen and McKee point out, the challenge is that, even though people want to help, barriers often arise which reduce the chances that donors will act on their desire to donate, campaign, or volunteer. I think that behavioural insights can be a helpful tool to remove the barriers. This enables donors to take an action that is helpful to both the beneficiaries and themselves.

You may have heard of the phenomenon of 'bystander apathy'. Research has shown that someone who is badly in need of assistance, for example if he has been taken seriously ill on the street, is less likely to receive help from other people if the street is crowded; help is more likely if fewer people are around. When a situation is ambiguous, a common response is to work out the appropriate way to respond by observing what everyone else is doing. Unfortunately for the person in need of help, when the street is crowded people are often apathetic because there is so much social proof that the appropriate response is to walk on by.

The phenomenon demonstrates that, whether or not we fundraisers decide to use the kind of behavioural insights described in this chapter, people will be influenced by these mental shortcuts anyway, and not necessarily for good.

When someone is presented with the opportunity to sign up to payroll giving through his or her company, he will take into account whether this is a normal behaviour. So if you do not share some social proof of a colleague who gives in this way and finds it rewarding, he won't see any evidence of payroll giving as normal and so wrongly conclude that this is not an appropriate behaviour.

To be aware of insights such as those discussed in this chapter, and not to use them, is naïve. Used appropriately they can make a big difference.

The key to using these ideas ethically is to make sure they are helping donors do things that they want to do, that is things that on reflection they would agree are in their interests. My view is that for people to give money to solve a problem they care about is absolutely in their best interests.

NOTES
1. Martin, Steve, Goldstein, Noah and Cialdini, Rober (2014) *The Small BIG: Small Changes that Spark Big* Influence, Profile Books, London.
2. Kahneman, Daniel (2012) *Thinking Fast and Slow*, Penguin Books, London.
3. Cabinet Office Behavioural Insights Team (2015) *Applying Behavioural Insights to Charitable Giving*, pp. 17-18. https://www.gov.uk/government/uploads/system/uploads/attachment_data/file/203286/BIT_Charitable_Giving_Paper.pdf
4. Sorum, Beate (11 February 2015) How much money are you leaving on the table? A lot. Beate thinks out loud blog. Available at: https://beateinenglish.wordpress.com
5. Thaler, Richard and Sunstein, Cass (2009) *Nudge: Improving Decisions and Health, Wealth and Happiness*, Penguin Books, London.
6. Cialdini, Robert 1993 *Influence: The Psychology of Persuasion*, Quill, New York.
7. Cabinet Office Behavioural Insights Team, *Applying Behavioural Insights*, op. cit., pp. 18-19.
8. Woods, Rob (2015) Four techniques to help you win more corporate partnerships. *The Fundraiser* online magazine. http://www.charitychoice.co.uk/the-fundraiser/how-to-win-more-corporate-partnerships/508
9. Woods, Rob (2014) *Treating trusts as major donors*. Bright Spot Fundraising blog. Available at: www.brightspotfundraising.co.uk
10. Martin et al., *The Small BIG*, op. cit.
11. Cabinet Office Behavioural Insights Team, *Applying Behavioural Insights*, op. cit., pp. 20-21.
12. Cialdini, *Influence*, op. cit.
13. Woods, Rob (May 2015) *Three tips to win more partners by finding the smoking gun*. 101 Fundraising blog. URL http://101fundraising.org/2015/05/3-tips-to-win-more-partners-by-finding-the-smoking-gun/
14. Cabinet Office Behavioural Insights Team, *Applying Behavioural Insights*, op. cit., p.11.
15. Martin et al., *The Small BIG*, op. cit.
16. Barden, Phil (2013) *Decoded: The Science Behind Why We Buy*. John Wiley, Chichester,
17. Smith, S, Windmeijer, F and Wright, E (2012) *Peer Effects in Charitable Giving: Evidence from the (Running) Field*, The Centre for Market and Public Organisation, University of Bristol.
18. Sargeant, Adrian (2012) *Philanthropic psychology – Using donor identity to grow giving*, Fundraising Institute Australia Conference, Gold Coast Convention Centre, February.
19. Andresen, Katya and McKee, Alia (2010) *Homer Simpson for Nonprofits – The Truth about How People Really Think and What it Means for Your Cause*, e-book. Available at: http:www.fundraising123.org/homer Last accessed 16 December 2015.
20. Thaler & Sunstein, *Nudge*, op. cit.

Rekindling friendships

Even if you implement all the ideas in this book, it is impossible to retain 100 per cent of donors. Death and change in circumstances (such as unemployment) are beyond the control of even the best fundraisers. Your aim is to reduce the loss of donors from preventable reasons, such as apathy, lack of appreciation and poor customer service, down to a minimum.

Despite having the best stewardship programme in the world, it is still inevitable that some donors will stop giving to you, or you might move to a role where there is a large file of past supporters, so what can you do to re-ignite the passion that led to their previous support? This chapter will talk you through some of your options.

RENEWING AND SAYING GOODBYE TO YOUR REGULAR GIVERS

We'll start by looking at those donors who you will know have stopped giving relatively quickly – monthly givers. Your bank statement allows you to identify (usually within a couple of days) any monthly givers who haven't paid in a particular month.

So what should you do?

Speed is of the essence here. You want to contact these donors as soon as you realise there is a problem with the gift. This shows the donors that they are important and that you will miss their donation.

The best way to do this is by phone. This allows you to have a conversation with them and dig a bit deeper about the their reasons for stopping and to see if you can do anything to persuade them not to stop.

From careful listening you may discover the donor doesn't really want to stop, but can no longer afford to give a regular gift. You could offer to lower the monthly gift amount or ask if she wants to go on to your mailing list for ad hoc appeals.

The donor might be between jobs and so is short of cash in the meantime.

Rather than cancelling you could ask her to take a payment holiday and to re-start in the future. Many charities offer payment holidays of up to six months, which donors appreciate and then continue to give for a long time.

We find on the phone that a good caller will retain up to 33 per cent of the donors who were planning to cancel, but every week of delay reduces this and if you leave it more than a year your response is likely to dip under 10 per cent. Quick reactivation adds up to a significant amount of money saved in donor recruitment and ensures your attrition remains as low as possible.

The other important reason to call is that it gives you a chance to thank donors for their support and to let them know that they will be missed. You can feedback on what their gift has helped to achieve and leave them with a positive experience, which should make them pre-disposed to re-start supporting your cause if their circumstances change.

Whatever the outcome of the call we recommend following up your conversation with a thank-you letter. For those who re-start the gift this makes them feel appreciated and needed. For those who have stopped, it reinforces the fact that they will be missed, makes them feel good about their past support. And you should also mention other ways they could help, i.e. through volunteering or campaigning.

HOW LISTENING TO DONORS INCREASED REACTIVATIONS BY 33 PER CENT

Charlie Hulme, former creative director at Pell & Bales and now director of DonorVoice in the UK, shares one of his favourite telephone campaigns which used the above technique with stunning results:

For many years Pell & Bales and a major UK charity have run campaigns designed to reactivate supporters whose regular gift had lapsed. Depending on when the donor last made a gift the sign-up rates vary between 12 and 33 per cent.

We wanted to find ways to raise this response rate, and so started looking into what the key challenges were.

One theme came up time and again. People would say 'I'd love to help but I can't afford to do anything now'.

Supporters weren't telling us they didn't want to support; they were telling us that they did, but not right now. For this campaign we wanted to take those principles even further by designing a campaign based on the premise 'if not now, how about 6 months from now?'

This campaign, and its subsequent success, is a testament to the power of true collaboration. Supporters spoke, fundraisers listened and a response was designed.

Our aim was to give donors the chance to opt in to a communications stream that fit with their life rather than shoe horning them in to one that 'worked' for us organisationally. (After all if it doesn't work for them then how can it work for us?)

The entire conversational tone and fundraising approach had to change. Instead of trying to appeal to supporters by talking about the organisation's need, we instead appealed to their moral identity as someone who clearly cared about children. With that primed we made our ask at a time that worked better for them.

The follow up call was positioned as a natural next step from their last conversation. Supporters were very happy to take the call as in our last conversation they had opted in for us to get in touch at a better time.

Logistically this meant we needed to change the way donors' information was stored. In the past campaigns were set up with very specific timelines based on organisational need. Here a special flag was created on the charity's database to create a whole new subsection of people who said they couldn't help now but would willingly do so in the future.

We set ourselves two kinds of target; 'hard' targets based on response and return, and 'soft' targets based on supporter experience.

The first of our 'hard' targets was to see an improvement in response rate for this group. Based on previous results we hoped that by changing our approach we could raise this to from 12 per cent to 15 per cent. The second 'hard' target was based on return on investment for the campaign, which again based on past experience we set at 1.74.

Our 'soft' targets were based on providing supporters with a better conversational experience. Regardless of the call's outcome we wanted them to put the phone down feeling much closer to the cause than they had when they picked it up. Our intention was to re-engage this group of supporters; to show them that we valued them not just for their financial support, but also for the emotional commitment they continued to show.

Gauging the 'hard' targets was a simple question of monitoring the numbers. Results against target far exceeded expectations. Our target response rate was 15 per cent; the actual result was 22.88 per cent! Our return on investment was projected at 1.39, the actual ROI was 2.03!

Assessing the 'softer' targets was done through regular call listening as well as anecdotally through our fundraisers. We were delighted with what we heard; supporters were clearly engaged with what we had to say and responded enthusiastically to our new approach.

To validate our learning and approach we ran a test and control group over one quarter. The test group comprised a number of supporters going through the new process; the control an equal number of supporters going through the previous approach. The results were in stark contrast. 24.5 per cent of the test group re-joined us with a monthly direct compared with just 15.10 per cent in the control group. The test group's return on investment was 2.28 compared with 1.7 for the control.

These figures speak for themselves, but what really delighted us was the incredible level of supporter engagement we heard during conversations. Our aim throughout had always been to make sure supporters knew that we valued them for what they had done, and to show them that we were listening to their concerns. We heard countless deeply moving conversations with supporters who thanked us for getting back in touch, and making it easy for them to come back as well as inspiring us with their own reasons for supporting the work of the charity.

So what about those donors you are unable to reach by the telephone?

A well-composed letter can achieve many of the same objectives as a phone call, although you will need to lower your expected response rate to less than 5 per cent.

We've used a short survey and response form with the letter to ask for feedback on why the donor has stopped giving and to see if we could have improved our communications. We also want to let the donor know that he or she will be genuinely missed and how much his support meant to our organisation.

The majority of the time donors tell us they have stopped due to a change in financial circumstances, but occasionally it is because we have not met expectations or have made a mistake. Once we know this we can go back to the donor with an explanation and an apology. It is surprising how often these donors come back to the fold. On one occasion successfully resolving an issue for a supporter had resulted in her doubling her gift. This fits with the evidence we presented in chapter 11 about resolving complaints. Another comment we've received regularly from such mailings is, 'your letter made me realise I'm more than a number on a database, so I'm going to continue to give'.

Those donors who say 'no' on the phone or do not reply to your letter should not be ignored. Keep in touch with them on a regular basis (we'd suggest once a year as a minimum) and evaluate your results. You should keep doing this as long as your returns exceed the costs of recruiting a new donor. Some basic modelling should help. For example, you might find it is only cost effective to try and reactivate donors who gave for over a certain length of time, or who were recruited by a specific appeal or campaign. As ever, testing is key here, as every organisation will be different, but we would encourage you to find a reactivation model that works for your donor base and implement it.

DIRECT MAIL DONORS

It is much harder to know when someone who gives ad hoc cash gifts through direct mail has stopped giving. Is it after a certain length of time? The number of appeals they haven't responded to?

Most charities tend to class donors who haven't given for two to three years as 'lapsed'. Yet donors may still consider themselves a supporter even if they haven't given for a longer period than that.

Whatever measure you use, there will come a point when you will need to take a different approach for these donors compared to your warmest donors. So what should you do?

Before sending another letter, take some time to understand those donors who haven't given for a long period of time and try to group them together. Potential data to look at includes:

- Total amount given
- Average gift size
- Largest gift
- Number of gifts
- First appeal given to
- Categories of appeal given to
- Length of support

You might find some interesting things. For example, you may have a group of donors who only ever give to one aspect of your work. Your last five appeals might have focused on other aspects of what you do, so getting those donors to give again could be as simple as sending them an update and donation request based on the work they have previously supported.

It is important to say that the level of analysis you conduct on your past donors is relative to the potential returns you might get. You don't want to create micro-segments that will be inefficient to cater for. However, you should be able to use laser printing to insert variables such as total given, length of support and numbers of gifts without too much trouble.

SHOWING THE VALUE OF SEGMENTING OUR LAPSED DONORS

Research from database company Blackbaud[1] showed how taking a more sophisticated look at segmenting your lapsed donors can pay big dividends. They analysed a combination of a donor's loyalty and overall philanthropic behaviour and proposed six segments for lapsed donors (table 18.1).

These segments were then applied to the lapsed file of a major international relief organisation who were about to undertake a reactivation mailing. The results are shown in table 18.2.

As you can see, three segments accounted for 74 per cent of the file, but 95 per cent of the income.

Table 18.1: Loyalty/philanthropy segments for lapsed donors

Missed connection	Donors who at the time of their lapsing had shown engagement to your organisation beyond what they typically showed other organisations – and are still active donors to other organisations
Absent allies	Donors who at the time of their lapsing had shown engagement to your organisation beyond what they typically showed to other organisations – but are not actively giving to other organisations
Higher dollar	Donors who have lapsed with your organisation – but after lapsing have been identified as consistently giving high-dollar gifts to other organisations
Giving stalwarts	Donors who showed little engagement to your organisation prior to lapsing – but are currently philanthropic to other organisations
Constant low dollar	Donors who are unlikely to give anything but a low dollar gift, based on their previous giving to your organisation and current giving to other organisations
Long shots	Donors who are unlikely to give an additional gift to you based on their overall giving history to all organisations and relationship with you

Table 18.2: Analysis of lapsed donor file by loyalty segmen

Segment	% of lapsed donor file	Campaign Response	Average Gift	Amount raised per mailed prospect	% of total amount raised in campaign
Missed connection	14%	6.7%	$55.39	$6.01	15%
Absent allies	2%	0.8%	$83.79	$0.83	0%
Higher dollar	21%	6.5%	$128.36	$12.70	49%
Giving stalwarts	39%	6.2%	$48.83	$4.46	31%
Constant low dollar	3%	2.1%	$12.89	$0.35	0%
Long shots	21%	1.0%	$70.77	$1.00	4%

> By isolating those givers most likely to give again, the organisation could save significant mailing costs and increase the net income raised by future reactivation campaigns.

Most of the best reactivation letters we've seen keep things relatively simple. They acknowledge past support, update the donor on the need and results that have been achieved and ask if they'd consider supporting the charity again.

The following letter from Cancer Research UK is a textbook example of a reactivation letter done well. When it was first sent in 2013 it beat CRUK's existing banker reactivation pack, which had been in place for a decade.

CRUK's reactivation letter
Here is what we like about it:

- It starts with thank you and highlights past support.
- Acknowledges that there are lots of worthy causes.
- Makes donor feel part of a team.
- Says what donations have helped achieve previously.
- Equates gift to outcome and emphasises any support is appreciated
- Reiterates that the donor is part of the solution.

The accompanying leaflet emphasises all those points and includes poignant case studies of people who are alive thanks to research, as well as some key facts.

A B Sample
12 Sample Street
Sample Town
Sample Place
Sampleshire
ABC 123

Cancer Research UK
PO Box 1561
Oxford
OX4 9GZ
United Kingdom
T 0300 123 1861
supporter.services@cancer.org.uk
cruk.org

EVERY TIME YOU CHOOSE TO HELP US, YOU'RE HELPING THOUSANDS OF OTHER PEOPLE TOO

Dear <personalised>,

I've got a couple of things I'd like to share with you today. But before I start, I'd like to say thank you.

I'm aware that there are many worthy causes out there all asking for your help. It must be incredibly hard to choose between them, which makes us particularly grateful that you've decided to support Cancer Research UK in the past.

So as well as writing to thank you for thinking of us in this way, I'd like to use this letter to show you how important you are to us. I hope you don't mind if I also ask you to help us again, with a gift of £x.

You're a crucial part of our team

The thing is, when you give a gift to us, you're not just giving money. You're giving our scientists the tools they need to carry out their life-saving research; giving our doctors and nurses the ability to carry out clinical trials to find new treatments; and each day, together we are creating more tomorrows. You're very much part of our team: a dedicated team of people all over the UK, in the relentless fight against all cancers.

What's more, as you may already know, we do not receive any government funding for our research. So we are totally reliant on our supporters, and without them, our work would simply stop. More than one in three of us will develop cancer at some point in our lives but each year our scientists are getting closer to finding cures for cancer.

Gifts like yours can help us make breakthroughs like these

Let me give you an example of one fantastic thing that we've achieved, within the last 4 months. It's the best way I can think of to show you how important your support really is.

Our scientists have recently identified markers which can highlight individuals who have an increased risk of developing breast, prostate and ovarian cancers. This opens up new opportunities for targeted

continued overleaf...

13MMW3LET4

I WANT TO HELP CANCER RESEARCH UK FIND BETTER WAYS OF DELIVERING CANCER TREATMENTS

If your name or address details are incorrect, please amend them so we can keep in touch with you.

A B Sample
12 Sample Street
Sample Town
Sample Place
Sampleshire
ABC 123

Promotion code
supporter number

If you're happy for us to contact you by email, please write your address below.

Email

☐ I am a UK taxpayer. Please treat all donations I make or have made to Cancer Research UK for the past four years as Gift Aid donations until further notice. For further information on Gift Aid please see overleaf

Please send us your completed donation form in the envelope provided to:
Freepost RRAL-TRSC-TTEL, Cancer Research UK, Halifax Road, Melksham, SN12 6YY

Please accept my gift to Cancer Research UK of
£X ☐ £XX ☐ £XX ☐
Or my preferred amount of £ _____

I enclose my cheque/postal order made payable to Cancer Research UK or please debit my Maestro/MasterCard/Visa/American Express/Charity Card
(please delete as appropriate)

| | | | | | | | | | | | | | | | |

Maestro Only | Expiry Date | Issue No. (Maestro)

Signature(s) | Date

Your generous gift will be used to fund our life-saving work wherever it is needed most.

screening and prevention and takes us closer to a time when people could take a cheap and efficient test which could give a personalised risk profile for these devastating cancers. That's the kind of project that simply wouldn't be possible without our supporters.

Every gift, large or small, will help us work to save more lives

The fact is we're seeing more and more outstanding research projects that we have to turn down simply through lack of funds. We're doing everything we can with the money we have, but we know we've got to do even more if we're to stop cancer tearing more lives apart.

In the UK alone, there are around 890 people diagnosed with the disease every single day who are relying on us to do just that. 890 people, and their families and friends; all pinning their hopes on our life-saving research. By giving a gift today, you can help us keep working until we have beaten this disease, for good.

I know from talking to supporters that it can be hard to relate individual gifts to huge projects like these. But the point is that when all our donations are added together, we become a collective force working to save more lives, by preventing, controlling and curing cancer.

We always make your money work as hard as possible, too. 80p from every £1 you give goes directly to our life-saving research: funding our pioneering scientific projects, information services and campaigning work, such as championing the smoking ban and more recently campaigning for cigarettes to be packaged in plain packaging.

The remaining 20p is reinvested into our fundraising activities – such as writing to you today – and for every £1 we spend we raise a further £4. So nothing is wasted; everything you give helps us work to save more lives, or raise even more funds to fight cancer.

Now, more than ever, we really need your help

I hope this letter has shown you how important you are to us, and how much we have been able to achieve thanks to your generosity in the past. I strongly believe that one day; all cancers will be cured so that for future generations, instead of being their greatest fear, it'll be just another disease that can be prevented detected and treated successfully. Help us beat cancer sooner.

Yours sincerely

Nick Georgiadis
Fundraising Manager

YOU CAN NOW DONATE:

By telephone:
call 0300 123 1861
and quote 'RESEARCH'

By mail:
return the donation form in the FREEPOST envelope provided

Online at
cruk.org/cures

THANK YOU

Patron Her Majesty The Queen
Presidents HRH The Duke of Gloucester KG GCVO and HRH Princess Alexandra, the Hon. Lady Ogilvy KG GCVO
Chief Executive Dr Harpal S. Kumar
Registered Charity in England and Wales (1089464), Scotland (SC041666) and the Isle of Man (1103)
Registered Company limited by guarantee in England and Wales (4325234) and registered in the Isle of Man (5713F)
Registered Address Angel Building, 407 St John Street, London EC1V 4AD

GIFT AID INFORMATION

In order to qualify for Gift Aid you must have paid an amount of income and/or capital gains tax at least equal to the amount of tax reclaimed by all charities and Community Amateur Sports Clubs on all your donations in the tax year (6th April to the 5th April). We can currently receive an extra 25p for every £1 you donate. Other taxes such as VAT and Council Tax do not qualify. Please let us know if your circumstances change. If you are unsure whether you can Gift Aid your donations please phone our Supporter Contact Team on 0300 123 1861 Monday – Friday from 8am–6pm.

Cancer Research UK is a registered charity in England and Wales (1089464) and Scotland (SC041666) and the Isle of Man (1103)

CRUK's leaflet accompanying reactivation letter

Another great lapsed campaign comes from Ontario Nature in Canada via fundraising blogger and consultant Pamela Grow:[2]

Ontario Nature's reactivation pack
What makes this letter great?

- It hooks you by painting a vivid picture of a local wetland trail.
- It says 'we miss you' and that you are important.
- It gives specific examples of what your previous giving achieved.
- It asks for the donor's opinion.
- It gives choice.
- The response form uses personalisation and an incentive to encourage giving.
- There is space for donors to leave a comment about what it would take for a donor to give again.
- It asks for contact details and the best time to get in touch if the donor wants to discuss the feedback.

November 18, 2013

Ms. Pamela Grow

Dear Ms. Grow,

Just this morning as I was walking on our local wetland trail, I was surrounded by tamaracks – glowing gold in a final fall blaze just as the first snowflakes are flying. They took my breath away! I didn't fumble for my phone to take a grainy and forgettable picture. I didn't reach for a pencil to jot down the date in my notebook.

Actually, I thought of you.

For over 80 years, and because of members like you, Ontario Nature has been a voice for nature. Our members include people of all ages and backgrounds who share a love of nature – in our backyards, our boreal forest and beyond.

I'm writing to you because we miss you. We haven't heard from you in some time so I'm reaching out to connect with you. Our members are the heart and soul of Ontario Nature. We only succeed in our mission to protect Ontario's wild species and wild spaces because of people like you. We want you back!

This is your Ontario Nature. As naturalists, we are active people. Probably every week, you get out and enjoy nature. Or at least you wish you did! Ontario Nature is an active organization, and our members take action every single day to save nature in Ontario.

I'm going to share with you some specific examples of recent accomplishments made possible because of our members. Please, take a moment to reflect on the impact you can have if you come back to Ontario Nature.

We are taking action to save species you love.

Our laws to protect nature are under fire. Last spring, our government almost gutted the Endangered Species Act. Our members wrote letters, called their MPPs and we raised our voices. Together, we convinced the government to remove the most damaging changes. Today, this issue is back and this fight is not over. We must

---

These are two simple packs from very different charities that are sincere and warm. There is no reason why you could not adapt a similar format for your own reactivation mailing. (Unfortunately, the first line on the second page of Ontario Nature's letter is missing.)

you and other members have fought for and won.

We are taking action to protect wild spaces you explore.

Hand-in-hand with saving vulnerable species is protecting their habitat. Ontario Nature has the largest system of member-owned nature reserves in Ontario. That's right – these are YOUR nature reserves! Together, we've protected 24 reserves, and our 2 newest are the Reilly Bird Nature Reserve in the Upper Ottawa Valley and the Sauble Falls Nature Reserve on Lake Huron.

We are taking action to connect kids (of all ages) to nature.

Connecting people to nature has been at the heart of Ontario Nature since we were founded in the 1930s. We are actively inspiring and encouraging all Ontarians to get out and explore our reserves and to grow a love of nature. Through our Nature Guardians program for kids, more than 700 kids are getting out to explore nature and last year they planted more than 500 trees!

These are just some of the ways we take action for nature. But we can't do any of these things without our members. Without you. Will you come back to Ontario Nature?

As I said earlier in my letter, this is your Ontario Nature. I want you to choose to support us again. I want you to feel invigorated by your decision to renew your membership. And I want to hear about what matters to you. You'll see on the enclosed form that there is a space for you to tell us what you think and feel.

Thank you for reading my letter today. I hope you will consider coming back to us. As you'll see on the form we haven't suggested how much to give to renew your membership. That's up to you. You can define exactly how you want to hear from us and connect with us. There are many different paths leading to Ontario Nature – I hope you will choose to join us once again.

Yours for nature,

Caroline Schultz

Caroline Schultz
Executive Director

SUPPORTERS WHO CAN NO LONGER AFFORD TO GIVE – DON'T NEGLECT LEGACIES

Some donors become cash poor as they get older. Their pension might be insufficient or they need their hard-earned savings to pay for medical care. They may have supported your charity for years, but sadly there comes a point when they simply can no longer afford to give.

One of the biggest mistakes you can make is to exile these donors to the desert

Ms. Pamela Grow

Ontario Nature

Welcome Back to your Ontario Nature, Ms. Grow!

Your renewed membership today helps save wild species you love and protect wild spaces you explore.

I'll renew my membership with my gift of $_____

☐ I have enclosed a cheque payable to Ontario Nature OR
☐ I prefer to pay by credit card. Please charge my:

VISA ☐   MasterCard ☐   AMEX ☐

Cardholder's Name: _____
Card Number: _____
Expiry: _____
Signature: _____

45620717   Fall1314WHYFU   LM10

(If you renew your membership with a gift of $50 or more you will receive our award-winning ON Nature magazine, exclusive to Ontario Nature members!)

We would be happy to give you a call or send you an email if you prefer. You tell us! We want to hear what it will take to bring you back to Ontario Nature.

☐ Please give me a call to discuss my support of Ontario Nature.

My phone number is: _____

and the best time to reach me is _____

☐ Please send me an e-mail. My email address is: _____

continued on back...

I will renew my support of Ontario Nature if/when:

---

of apathy and stop communicating with them. Often these donors are your best legacy prospects and many remain asset rich, mainly through property.

They shouldn't be classed as lapsed donors, but more as friends for life who have fallen on hard times. Just as you wouldn't ignore a friend in need, you shouldn't cut off contact with these donors. Doing so could seriously jeopardise your chances of being left a legacy.

_____
_____
_____

What matters to you? This is your space to tell us what you think and feel about Ontario Nature and you. We promise to listen to you and follow up with you if you wish.

_____
_____
_____

☐ Yes, please contact me about this feedback.

My phone number is: _____

and the best time to reach me is _____

My email address is: _____

Thank you!

CANADA POST
Postage paid if mailed in Canada
Business Reply Mail
3371441

1000067171-M5H3S6-BR01

ONTARIO NATURE
612-214 KING ST W
TORONTO ON M5H 9Z9

As we said in the chapter on legacies, we'd suggest anyone who has supported you for over five years and/or has made over 10 cash gifts should be kept on a long-term lapsed file (provided your opt in/opt out consents policy permits). You might also want to add a field to your database that highlights donors who indicated to you (normally through a survey or appeal response form) that they can no longer afford to give but are still interested in your work.

Instead of sending these donors appeals, send them a simple update once or twice a year that shares recent news and highlights of your work and includes a soft legacy message.

Not only will the donors be pleased that you remember them and keep in touch, you are also likely to be at the forefront of their mind to be left a gift in their will.

OTHER WAYS OF KEEPING IN TOUCH WITH PAST DONORS

Although we recommend the telephone and mail for communicating with past donors you shouldn't ignore the potential of e-mail and SMS to keep in touch regularly in a cost-effective manner.

These should be considered 'nudges' to remind donors of their previous support rather than a constant stream of asking.

To use a boxing analogy, if you constantly go for the knockout blow with your communications you will likely have more misses than hits and will put people off, which in turn will lead to people unsubscribing. Instead if you constantly jab away and engage your previous supporter with interesting and relevant content, when you have a knockout ask to deliver (via any medium) they will be much more predisposed to give to you again.

Here is an e-mail 'jab' from American Red Cross that gives feedback to donors on the Haiti earthquake appeal and shows what has been achieved in the last four years.

This Easter Seals 'jab' tells an inspiring story and offers an easy way to engage (by signing the congratulations card):

One thing we've seen few charities achieve in their e-mail is to recognise when a donor has stopped being a regular donor and to use different language in their communications. For example, one charity Craig stopped giving to five years ago still sends him e-mails thanking him for his continued support. Make sure you don't make this mistake and try and update your e-mail and SMS marketing lists to distinguish between types of donors.

Another thing to consider is natural opportunities to go back to past supporters and update them with a relevant piece of news. This could be a new service or research breakthrough that has been made, or another development that might appeal to their values, emotions and previous reasons for giving.

Finally, update events can be a great way to invite past donors back to your

Rekindling friendships

Figure 18.1 American Red Cross – Haiti infograph and update[3]

Figure 18.2 Easter Seals

cause. You could organise site visits, talks from beneficiaries or a Q&A with the chief executive to try and get past supporters to re-engage. As long as you make the events authentic and inspiring, these can be great opportunities to get lapsed donors to give again.

BRINGING IT ALL TOGETHER – SAVE THE CHILDREN'S INTEGRATED APPROACH

We've already spoken about the importance of integration in donor acquisition and the same applies to donors who have stopped giving. Save the Children have seen some impressive results by combining e-mail, phone and mail asks, as Kris Ilic, their senior supporter retention manager explains:

> Save the Children have 380,000 regular givers and it's my team's job to ask people who have stopped giving to consider starting again. Traditionally we've done this by telephone. However in the last year we have started to test a multi-channel programme. We took a three-step approach. First of all we sent an email to 45,000 supporters. We started with this because it is the cheapest method. Anyone who reactivated a regular gift was removed from the following communications. We then mailed those who we had a mailing address for. Finally, we telephoned those who hadn't responded to mail or email.
>
> The aim was to pull out those most likely to respond by the cheapest methods and use the telephone (the most expensive method) for those harder-to-reach donors.
>
> In terms of creative, we used one of our most powerful stories. We told donors about baby Priya, born in Bangladesh and how past gifts had meant there was a midwife on hand to save her life. We used the same story across all channels.
>
> We were delighted with the results. The initial email was over twice as successful as previous re-activation e-mails. Those who received an email and mail responded three times higher than those who only received mail. Similarly, phone only response rates were half of those who received all three communications.

Sample reactivation e-mail from Save the Children:

You can save a baby's life, every month.   No pictures? Click here.

Save the Children

Right now, in the poorest parts of the world, thousands of babies are dying within hours of being born.

Please restart your regular gift today: for just £3 a month you could save a baby's life, every month.

In those crucial first hours, simple things can mean the difference between life and death: a sterile knife to cut the umbilical cord, a warm blanket, an experienced pair of hands.

Baby Priya is lucky. She was born at a clinic run by Save the Children in Bangladesh, with expert midwives there to ensure a safe delivery.

Thanks to people like you, they were trained and equipped to listen to Priya's heartbeat, look for signs of distress, and help her take her first few breaths.

Start giving to Save the Children again today and you could help pay for a midwife to be there when it matters.

Every year, 3.1 million newborn babies die around the world – their lives cut short before they're even four weeks old. Many are born at home, with no medical help.

Together, we can stop this happening.

Please restart your regular gift today. We just can't do it without you.

http://savethechildren.org.uk/start-your-gift

With a gift of just £3, you could welcome a baby like Priya safely into the world every single month.

Thank you,

Supporter Care Manager
Save the Children

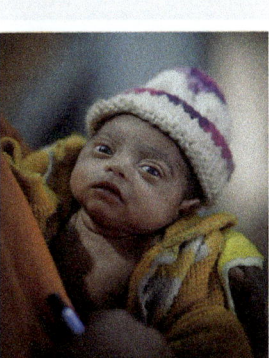

A monthly donation could help welcome more babies like Priya safely into the world.

GIVE NOW

WHERE YOUR MONEY GOES

 From every £1 you give us we spend 88p to benefit children – 11p to raise the next £1, and the other 1p goes on governance and other costs. Find out more about our finances.

NO CHILD **BORN** TO DIE

If you wish to no longer receive these updates you can unsubscribe here.

Save the Children works in more than 120 countries. We save children's lives. We fight for their rights. We help them fulfil their potential.

This email was sent from Save the Children, registered charity England and Wales (213890), Scotland (SC039570) and registered in England and Wales under company number (178170), or from Save the Children (Sales) Ltd, registered company in London (875945). For legal information go to savethechildren.org.uk/privacy.

FundRaising Standards Board

The key learnings were that a lower £3 per month ask worked best, the reactivation ask needs to have strong emotional element and the more channels we contacted the donor through, the higher the overall response rate.

A FINAL WARNING: BE CAREFUL OF THE LANGUAGE YOU USE

'Lapsed' is a horrible word. Who wants to be known to have lapsed or to be inactive? These aren't great labels so, if you must use them, make sure that you don't use them outside the four walls of your office. This might seem obvious advice, but we have seen reactivation letters that have used language such as 'we are sorry your support has lapsed'.

You wouldn't address a friend who forgot your birthday or you hadn't heard from for a couple of years as a lapsed friend, so make sure you don't allow your internal labels and jargon to creep into your actual communications.

NOTES
1. Becker, Richard (2013) *Reactivating lapsed donors: how to use loyalty and philanthropic segmentation to optimize donor reactivation*, Blackbaud. Available at: https://www.blackbaud.com/files/resources/downloads/ReactivatingLapsedDonors.Whitepaper.pdf Last accessed 26 January 2014.
2. Grow, Pamela (2013) *Loving lapsed donors back into the fold*. Available at: http://www.pamelagrow.com/3878/loving-lapsed-donors-back-fold-simple-brilliant-oh-swipe-able. Last accessed 26 January 2014.
3. Examples from Mike Snusz at NPEngage: http:www.npengage.com/online-fundraising/9-underutilized-emails-improve-donor-retention-2/ Last accessed 26 January 2014.

Measurement of performance, innovation and the planning cycle

'What gets measured, gets done', remarked Peter Drucker, the renowned American management consultant, in his seminal work, *The Practice of Management*.[1] Accordingly you need to know how you are performing across all your fundraising activities. Without this information, you can't understand and be in control of your direction and your work. It is surprising to find that the charity sector lies so far behind its commercial counterparts in these areas of monitoring and evaluation.

Though many set key performance indicators, KPIs, they are not as comprehensive as they ought to be and we are not assessed against them as stringently as possible. Indeed, in an era of supposed increased transparency, where donors, especially higher-value supporters, demand accountability, we need to be setting and checking progress against a range of metrics that cover the most important areas of our work.

The first point to make is that the targets should not be hypothetical. They should be consistent, measurable and achievable. The measurement you plan to use should be a part of any fundraising strategy, which itself should stem directly from a charity's wider corporate strategy. And, in turn a *golden thread* should flow right through to individual objectives, giving clear responsibility to you and your team, if you have one. This will ensure that planned activity does in fact take place and all involved remain accountable for their actions. Should there be any disconnect between these metrics your strategy is in danger of becoming simply theoretical. Indeed, all fundraisers should adhere closely to their set objectives and be aware of exactly how these fit into the wider goals of the charity.

BENCHMARKING

Before setting any strategy and wider objectives, it is advisable to first benchmark and set your results to date in the context of the wider sector. There are three principal reasons for doing so:

- Achievability: a central tenet of setting objectives is that they must be challenging, but achievable. Creating targets that are beyond the reach of you and your team will raise expectations unnecessarily and likely to lead to disappointment amongst your trustees and loss of morale throughout your team. By first checking the performance of others in the sector, we can see what has been achieved to date and safely stretch ourselves to surpass these results.

- Accuracy: only by directly comparing ourselves with our competitors can we measure our true progress, given the climate as a whole. If one area, such as average gift in an economic downturn, for example, is showing a sector-wide decline, progress could still be made if the median donation is reducing to your charity, but at a slower rate of decline than your competitors.

- Best practice: similarly, comparison with other charities can help to predict future trends and gain a better understanding of what is working in the sector and which areas may not warrant further investment. There are a number of such reports and studies, in which it is possible to participate and compare. These include the US-centred *Donor Trends* and the *Fundraising Effectiveness Report*, produced by the Association of Fundraising Professionals. Additionally, the UK-focused *Fundratios*, produced by the Centre for Interfirm Comparison since 1995, involves data collected from over 80 charities, both large and small.

And by participating and sharing, you can network more effectively and learn from other fundraisers. In a complex and multi-faceted environment, it is highly likely they have gained experience in areas with which you are not yet fully acquainted.

Taking into account some of the topics and themes in this book the following are some suggestions for KPIs that can be used to measure your ongoing progress as an individual or as a team. These are divided into two categories: quantitative metrics, which define your top-line progress, and more qualitative measurements, which relate to your supporters' assessment of your relationship fundraising performance.

QUANTITATIVE METRICS

- Gross income: it goes without saying, perhaps, that this is the most important metric of all. Whilst we can (we hope) safely assume that most fundraisers will know how much money they have raised in any given year, it is of greater importance that they monitor it on a regular basis, at least once a month, hopefully more regularly. And they should know the source of this income, by activity or on a departmental basis.

- Net income: funds raised, no matter how impressive, should be placed in the context of how much it has cost us to achieve our results. So, net income (gross income above, minus expenditure) should be monitored as a KPI too. Ideally this should include salaries and proportionate overhead costs, as well as regular direct expenditure. Time is a precious commodity and to not incorporate it into your calculations may well warp your results and prevent the elimination of the least efficient activities.

- Cost-to-income ratio: a clearer indication of how your income is performing in relation to your expenditure. It can either be displayed as a per cent figure (cost divided by income) in which case the lower the figure the better. Or as ratio 1:x, where x is income divided by cost and a higher number is clearly preferable. Cost-to-income can be particularly useful when tracking historical progress and projecting future trends, especially when you are investing in acquisition or other long-term income-generating activity. It can drop quite substantially during periods of investment. So, returning the cost-to-income ratio to its original levels, or to even more favourable proportions, can be critical in persuading senior management or trustees to sign off on the investment.

Trustees, who are often cautious, might well look to the cost-to-income ratio as their primary measurement of fundraising success within an organisation. Professional fundraisers may well challenge this, however, and they are right to do so. Whilst cost should never be overlooked, it's growth in net income, or profit, and the additional funds that are produced for charity beneficiaries, which should be dominant metric. Dan Pallotta makes a cogent case for this strategic approach:

> *The cutting edge is investment in fundraising. Yet everyone tries to suppress*

> it, invoking a flawed theory of social change that says the less you spend on fundraising, the more you have for programs. That's true if it's a zero sum game. But it's not. Imagine a $10 million pie with $8 million going to programs and with the 20 percent fundraising slice taking $2 million away from programs. The last thing we want to do is make that a $3 million slice, leaving only $7 million for programs. But that's not how it works. If done correctly, the extra million enlarges the pie — substantially. A $10 million pie becomes a $15 million pie, and the $7 million available for programs grows to $12 million.

He continues:

> ... charitable giving has remained constant in the US at 2 percent of GDP ever since we have been measuring it, and has not budged...But imagine, if we could move that 2 percent to 2.5 percent or 3 percent, we could put our dreams on steroids...[2]

That is not to say that we as fundraisers should spend donors' money as freely as we wish. Indeed, we need to invest smartly and responsibly in the areas of greatest return. Activities that have little chance of making a profit, or those that are conducted at the expense of more lucrative methods should not be undertaken. But if we wish to test new activities that may be more costly to begin with, or are presented with one-off opportunities to raise additional funds that may be less efficient than our usual portfolio (for example, supporting a third party event organiser), we should embrace the chance to increase our net income.

- Active supporters: there are a number of ways of expressing the amount of current activity on your database, but if we are to practise integrated relationship fundraising, this must not be expressed in departmental or income source silos. Instead, it should highlight gifts (usually within the last year, though some express it in two-year cycles) of any type. In fact, if we are to recognise that there is a direct correlation between volunteering, campaigning and donations, then it should include any action in support of the charity. And if we are to stretch theory to its logical conclusion, it should also include any supporter that endorsed, or followed, the charity through social media too. Though an integrated database would be required to ensure this could be calculated effectively.

- Retention rate: essentially the percentage of donors that give in one year and make at least another single gift in the next. As above, it can be calculated in one- or two-year cycles (one is preferable as it highlights more immediately any concerns or upturns). Again, it would effectively reflect the progress of the organisation if it related to supporter retention rather than simply donor retention.

- Attrition rate: the converse of retention rate – the number of supporters that lapse in any given cycle. Together with the retention rate, it should equal 100 per cent.

- Acquisition: the measurement of new recruits to your cause. Purposely placed below retention, but nevertheless essential as attrition, sadly, can never fully be eliminated. As Nancy Schwartz of *Getting Attention* states:

If an organization stops acquisition for a year, losing 20 to 40 percent of its 0 to 12 month donors due to attrition with no plan to replace them, it's tough to come in and turn that ship around. It is a reminder of the art and science of direct mail, knowing that the one year with no acquisition will take at least three years to recoup.[3]

Once more, this should relate to new supporters acquired in any given year, rather than just donors.

- Current net cost per new donor, by acquisition media: it is acceptable for most charities to subsidise prospecting, to guarantee longer-term income, but a careful eye should be kept on the cost and the recruitment methods utilised. By monitoring and evaluating carefully, the most lucrative long-term supporters, found through the most cost-effective media, can be recruited. Sadly, there is no formula; it will differ for every charity and a fair degree of investigation and testing will need to be carried out to establish which methods are the most effective.

- First-year retention rate for new donors, by acquisition media: a donor is three times more likely to become a long-term supporter once they have given a second time.

- Net lifetime value of donor: it's important to know how many of your supporters remain on board but, as highlighted in chapter 3, it is income that counts and it matters most that you are retaining the most valuable prospects. This can be calculated by analysing the average income between three and five years of supporters retained, again grouped by the source of acquisition. By subtracting the cost of acquisition per donor you are left with the basic theoretical lifetime value. This is another indication of what media are worth investing in and which is best avoided.

Table 19.1: Example year one face-to-face fundraising acquisition value

Month	1	2	3	4	5	6	7	8	9	10	11	12
Monthly donors	1000	800	720	684	650	617	599	581	563	547	530	514
Monthly attrition(%)		20	10	5	5	5	3	3	3	3	3	3
Income (donors x average gift of £8)	£8,000	£6,400	£5,700	£5,472	£5,198	£4,938	£4,790	£4,647	£4,507	£4,372	£4,241	£4,114
Expenditure												
Cost of recruitment	£100,000											
Welcome pack	£1,000											
Thank you phone call			£3,600									
Newsletter						£308.66						£257.10

Planning assumptions

Cost per donor = £100
Cost per newsletter = £1
Cost per phone call = £5
Year one income: £62,439
Year one expenditure: £104,815
Year one ROI: 0.60

This simple model doesn't take into account things such as tax relief, any gifts that the newsletter might produce, the cost of a reactivation programme, etc. You can quickly see how these models can get complicated.

However, it is only by building these models and then monitoring your results over a period of time (we'd say the three to five years is a minimum) that you can build an accurate picture of the success of your fundraising programme.

Here are some of the other variables that you might need to take into account into your lifetime value calculations:

Acquisition
- Cost per acquisition – how much each donor costs to recruit.

Maintenance
- Attrition by year – how many acquired donors stop giving every year?
- Cost of reactivations – the cost of getting someone to re-commence their giving.
- Cost of upgrades – expenses associated with convincing a supporter to increase their gift.
- Costs of maintaining the relationship – the cost of keeping in touch. This could be via the post, e-mail, telephone, etc.

Value
- Year one value – the total value of a donor's support in the first year of giving.
- Average gift – the average gift per year.
- Percentage of donors making a second gift.
- Percentage of donors responding to cash appeals.
- Percentage of donors upgrading their gift – either an increased second donation or committed gift.
- Value of cross-selling other organisational and fundraising asks – what is it worth if someone participates in a challenge event for your organisation or takes part in a campaign by signing a petition?
- Is the value of an increased donation? This could be monthly or yearly.

Putting together income models and understanding the key variables and drivers of fundraising success is vitally important. Only looking at short-term results could mean that you abandon recruitment methods that produce the best long-term income in favour of quick, but insubstantial, gains.

One of Craig's favourite studies on lifetime value comes from the MS Society. In 2006 he attended a presentation that looked at what had happened to a group of donors who were recruited in 1985. The results were fascinating and demonstrate the importance of the relationship fundraiser taking a long-term view on giving:

- In 1985 the MS Society spent £125,000 on acquisition and recruited 7,085 donors.
- By 2005, 50 per cent had gone missing, 39 per cent were lapsed and 11 per cent were active.
- 11 per cent of the donors only gave once.
- 1,500 of the donors had given over 10 times.
- Over the 20-year period the 7,000 donors had cumulatively given £2.1 million.
- Allowing for mailing costs, discounted cash flow (what the acquisition money would have been worth if it had been put in a bank) and the initial investment, then the campaign returned 300 per cent.
- Taking into account legacies and the continued giving of the active file, the final value of the £125,000 investment will be in excess of £5 million and will return over 700 per cent (in real terms) of the initial investment.

Committed givers

In terms of cost efficiency and the sustainability of your organisation, repeat, predictable income is of paramount importance. Consequently, paying close attention to planned giving, in all its forms, even it is just once a year, is highly recommended. This should be expressed in terms of numbers of those signed up as committed givers, their annual value and as a percentage of your total supporter file. The latter figure will highlight the effectiveness of your cash to committed giving conversion rates, as well as giving an indication, alongside legacy pledgers, of the long-term security of your organisation.

Supporter progression – a measure of the effectiveness of your segmentation and supporter journeys

If your stewardship is working well, supporters will be increasing their engagement with your charity. If you are contacting them in an inappropriate manner – whether too much, too little, or with irrelevant asks – their levels of participation are likely to move in the opposite direction. For this metric to be generated effectively, it is necessary to analyse your database and create engagement tiers, with cumulative annual donation bands highlighting the number of donors and total value in each category.

Demonstrating the movement of donors between categories from one year to the next, in terms of a per cent of each band progressing up or down, will provide a rough measure of progress. Once more, it may be sensible to include all engagement options in this equation, if you are to demonstrate a full picture of what is occurring. You might, for example, like to add in two tiers below your lowest donation band, formed of those who have supported your charity in another manner (e.g. campaigning or volunteering) with another below that of those who have simply provided you with their contact details but have not yet engaged in any meaningful way.

Digital footprint

This is a newer, longer-term KPI, but one that should be given premier value given that is it is a measure of potential support. It can be broken down into component parts:

- Unique website visitors – this is one of the few, cost-effective measures of awareness and interest in your cause. Bearing in mind that very few prospects are ever going to make a donation unless they have actually heard of you, it's an important metric on which you should keep an eye. Again, monthly measurement is best. And, as inevitably there will be seasonal variation, it should always be held in direct comparison with the same point in the previous year or years.

- Digital 'reach' – in recent years this would have included just the number of e-mail addresses for active supporters but, as above, it should, if at all possible, now also include a combined figure for social media followers. The ability to contact freely with your supporters, as long as you are segmenting and tailoring effectively, is of great benefit to the modern fundraiser and allows you to keep your supporters fully up-to-date and engaged. And, given its importance as a vital ingredient in the mix, it is certainly worth placing it at the heart of your activity with its own dedicated KPI.

Legacies

The metrics here should be centred not simply on money received from bequests, but the results of any direct promotion to potential profiled legacy prospects. Even though your charity is most likely to receive financial reward after you have long since departed the organisation, your contribution is no less important and should be targeted and monitored.

RELATIONSHIP FUNDRAISING METRICS

Whilst the above are top-line indicators, if we are to build truly meaningful relationships with our supporters and seek to immerse them truly in our cause, we should aim even higher and monitor yet deeper. We should endeavour to measure the strength of their engagement and empathy for our work through ever more meaningful metrics.

Sargeant and Schulman suggest the following:

> *We know from research that multiple factors are at work, notably how satisfied donors might be with the quality of service provided by the fundraising team. Organizations must therefore unpack the dimensions of their service and ascertain the extent to which donors are satisfied with each. To obtain managerially useful information, however, data must also be gathered in respect to perceptions of importance. Then, those aspects of the service scoring high on importance and low in terms of satisfaction would be clear candidates for investment. Extant research also equally tells us that satisfaction is not in itself enough. Learning from the commercial world has taught us that sometimes even very satisfied customers will defect, doing so because although they may be very satisfied with their treatment, they lack commitment to the organization.*
>
> *In our world, donors who are committed to the organization, cause and/or brand will be substantively more loyal than those that are not. We also understand much about the implications of trust on giving. In this context, most donors (unless they are major donors) will not be able to see for themselves exactly how their gift of $20 or $50 was applied to the cause. Instead, they must trust the organization to do what it promised to do in its communications. Donors with higher levels of trust in a focal organization will donate a higher proportion of their philanthropic 'pot' than those with lower levels of trust. They will also have a longer lifetime of support and consequent LTV.*
>
> *Finally, to take other learning from the commercial world, attitudes are one of the best predictors of subsequent loyalty. Specifically, if I indicate in a survey that I will continue to be a loyal donor, by and large I will continue to be a loyal donor. If I indicate that I intend to give again next year, equally, I very likely will. Re-purchase intention, as it would be labelled in the commercial world, is a very good indicator of subsequent behaviour.*[4]

Accordingly, one of the best ways of establishing supporter commitment and satisfaction is to ask to them directly through a simple survey containing questions with fixed option responses. If you do need to do your own research then we recommend you employ a range of quantitative (gathering numerical data) and qualitative (useful for gathering data on people's attitudes and motives) methods. Here are some of the methods you can use for your own research, both in terms of measuring impact, as well as gaining advice on how you can improve your supporter engagement:

Focus groups
These take the form of an in-depth, face-to-face discussion amongst a group of supporters or prospective supporters on a designated research topic. Usually led by an external facilitator (though if money is tight you can do it yourself, but be aware that this is a skilled task), focus groups can be a fantastic way to gather information and feedback from supporters and allow you to discuss a topic in great detail.

Focus groups, however, are not without their own flaws. One session that Craig ran a while ago concluded that fundraisers shouldn't contact donors for at least a year after. This completely conflicted with their previous experience and quantitative data. The services team, though, wanted to take the research at face value and issue a blanket ban on communication during this period. It was only when they reviewed the tape and transcript of the group that they were able to establish that it was the opinion of one domineering and outspoken individual, who didn't allow other participants a chance to speak. When we were able to demonstrate that this wasn't the case for most donors (through an additional survey) their services colleagues relented and they avoided making an erroneous decision that could have potentially cost the charity millions of pounds.

Whilst this is certainly a danger of which fundraisers should be acutely aware, Paul experienced some more positive aspects of focus groups. Based on the theory that engagement leads to increased financial support, Paul established that focus groups are a great opportunity to meet donors, hear their views and build affinity to your cause. One such opportunity arose around the generation X major donor target audience outlined in chapter 13. World Jewish Relief were looking at how they could engage this target audience (high net worth individuals aged 35–44), as well as a network that would participate in the initiative. Three focus groups were held, attended by 20 supporters and potential donors of that age group; the request, which was just for advice in this instance, proved very effective with some donors, who had previously proved elusive.

The group also demonstrated some clear and consistent feedback, which was instrumental in assessing the effectiveness of previous activities as well forging the content of the new offering. A few months later, when it came to running the finalised product past those that participated, the request for signing up also came far more naturally. They had been engaged from the start, felt ownership of the programme and it was certainly harder for them to turn down the opportunity to engage after the charity had listened to them and built the initiative around their feedback. Most of the 20 members signed up and the programme was firmly on target to raise its first £50,000 in its inaugural year. This included £15,000 of corporate sponsorship from a major City bank, who were suitably impressed by the depth and preparation involved in the development of the new supporter product.

Supporter surveys

We've always been great proponents of supporter surveys. They can give a snapshot of how donors feel and how engaged they are with your cause, as well as providing information on communication preferences. They can also be conducted relatively quickly and cheaply via post, telephone, or e-mail.

They do have limitations though. By default, the supporters who respond to surveys are likely to be those most highly engaged, or who have an issue they want to raise. This self-selection can lead you to ignore the thoughts of those indifferent to your communications and messages.

Much of fundraising is led by emotion. Asking donors to take the time to consider the reasons for their support and give rational answers can mean that, unintentionally, they might give wrong answers, as they don't actually know the truth. For example, it might be the compelling photo and headline in a direct mail letter that caused donors to first give, but they may be unlikely to admit that in a survey.

Here are some sample questions that we've used in surveys to donors to help inform our fundraising:

Why did you first give to x charity?
Do you know anyone who has been affected by x?
How can we improve our communications to you?
Which of our programmes are you most inspired by?
Which of the following reasons best describes why you stopped giving?

And some quantitative examples will enable you to benchmark and measure your performance and the effectiveness of your proposition. On a scale of one to five, five being the highest rating and one the lowest:

- How would you rate our efforts to keep you updated on our work?
- How suitable are the fundraising opportunities we present to you?
- How closely do you think we are adhering to our charitable objectives?

Additionally, here are 10 tips for designing a survey to measure performance and develop improvements:

1. Don't make your survey too long. People will quickly get bored if your survey extends to more than two pages, or requires an hour phone call to complete. This is especially pertinent for digital surveys, where attention spans will prove to be even shorter.

2. Use a mix of closed and open-ended questions. As above, closed questions are great for providing data that can be analysed statistically i.e. on a scale of one to five please rate x. However, they only give you figures. Open-ended questions provide qualitative data that can give a richer picture of your donors' thoughts. However, they do take more analysis and work. Craig discovered this when he started giving donors the choice of how often they wanted to hear from his charity. He started by using a closed question that gave four options: currently, once a year, twice a year, or quarterly. A high number of people ticked one of the once, twice, quarterly boxes. He abided by this, but subsequent analysis showed that these donors gave less and tended to lapse when they only heard from the charity once a year.

   When he switched to an open question 'how can we improve our communications to you?' only a small number felt strongly enough to specify a preference. He then found this small number ended up giving more as the charity respected their opinion. In contrast, the closed question didn't really involve much thought on the donors' part (they quickly ticked a box) and so they didn't buy into the implied contract, i.e. 'you respect my decision to only receive mail once a year and I will reciprocate by donating'.

3. Use a robust sampling technique. If you are using a tranche of donors for

your research, you need to ensure that you use a large enough sample to have confidence in the statistical value of your results. A quick Google search gives a number of free, online calculators that help you work out the size of sample you need.

4   Make every question clear and unambiguous. One common mistake we see made in surveys is questions that try and answer two things at once. For example, the following question wouldn't be appropriate:
Do you agree with the following statement: this charity has high standards and their appeals are always excellent?

A donor might think the charity has high standards, but think the appeals are poor, as they don't explain the difference they can make. You can't answer two questions in one.

5   On a related note, you should avoid leading questions. A question such as: *Do you have any problems with our communications?* is likely to lead people to list a string of complaints. A more considered question would be: *What do you think about our communications?* This would produce both positive and negative comments and more balanced feedback on your engagement with supporters.

6   Order your questions in a logical sequence. You want to make the respondents feel comfortable whilst completing the survey and not confuse them by flitting about topics, which may make them abandon it.

7   Keep personal questions to the end. If you ask these first, the respondents might assume that the whole survey will probe for personal data. When supporters have already spent time completing the survey, they are more likely to provide such data, as they don't want to have wasted time and not conclude the questionnaire.

8   Test your survey. Gain feedback on the questions and the order from a pilot sample or colleagues before rolling out the questionnaire. This can identify any problems in advance.

9   Use scaling techniques to gather data. The two most common are Likert

scales and semantic differential scales. A Likert scale is a list of statements with a range (usually five or seven) of possible choices which has a range from negative to positive, i.e. agree to disagree, or unimportant to important. A semantic differential scale is designed to measure differences between words. These generally use a five- or seven-point scale again, but compare opposite constructs, such as amateur/professional, listens/ignores, to build a picture of an organisation.

10. Feedback on the results. We think it is common courtesy to offer to share the results of any survey you undertake with the participants. You can include this option as part of the survey. Simply add a tick box with the option. In our experience not many people will take up the offer but, like small focus groups, those that do opt in will appreciate the involvement and trust your faith in them. Don't do what one large charity did, which asked donors for comments and then said 'We're really sorry, but we are unable to respond to all the comments we receive'. The survey was just a gimmick to boost response rather than a genuine effort to listen and engage supporters. We hope donors were as dismayed as we were to read such a disingenuous statement.

Ethnographic research

This is an under-used research method in fundraising, but one that has huge potential. Ethnography has its roots in anthropology and is simply the practice of observing your donors' behaviour in their natural setting. This can be achieved through diary studies, in-home observation and one-to-one interviews. These can be used to design experiences that fit with your donor's actual personal or professional life.

As an example, every Christmas Craig's mum gathers all the appeals she's received in November and December, puts them into a pile and randomly selects two or three to which to send donations. Similarly, Paul's dad does exactly the same for a couple of key Jewish festivals during the year, allocating a set sum of money across appeals he has accumulated during recent months. As an aside, we've spoken to other donors who use exactly the same method, which can be a bit of a blow to the fundraiser's ego – this would be unlikely to come out in a survey or focus group, but using ethnography we would discover the actual reasons for how and why donors make decisions. This type of research can be expensive, which is probably why it hasn't been adopted too widely, but there are some cheaper ways that any charity can use it. For example, you can use websites like usertesting.com or whatusersdo.com to watch how donors do specific tasks online, such as making a donation or signing up for an event. This can be done for a couple of hundred pounds and can give real insight into how donors actually use your own web-pages to find information.

Unsolicited feedback

This isn't a research method as such, but it can provide incredibly useful supporter insight and you should try and find a way to collate unsolicited feedback from across your organisation. This can be short handwritten notes on a response form, comments made on phone calls from a donor, posts on social media and verbal feedback at events. Often these details are lost, but by systematically recording this information you can start to notice trends in this unsolicited feedback and then act on the information. For example, on response forms one of Craig's team noticed an increase in comments asking why the charity kept asking for gift aid as the donor had already signed a declaration. This led the team to use personalisation on the forms so that they could acknowledge and thank people who had already made a gift aid declaration and only asked them to get in touch if their circumstances had changed. A small thing, but one that sends the message to donors that we know them and acknowledge the past information they have given us.

Complaints and compliments

It is certainly good practice to log all complaints and to set up a transparent and effective procedure for responding promptly and appropriately. Additionally though, they can also be a good measure of supporter satisfaction, in terms of the number received in a financial year and whether or not they resulted in a positive resolution. Complaints concentrated around a particular department or activity can also highlight specific areas of your supporter care that are falling below the required relationship fundraising standards. You shouldn't just focus on the negative though. Keep a log of any compliments you receive during the year as well. Hopefully this number will outweigh the level of your complaints!

Feedback from your front-line staff and stakeholders

How often do you speak to your street fundraisers, telephone callers, or receptionist? How do you get continuous feedback from them on what your donors are telling them in the conversations? By engaging with your colleagues and incentivising them to share their thoughts and to give you feedback you can probably save some of your research budget and quickly identify issues that matter to donors and which you can improve.

Most importantly, we would recommend that every fundraiser gets out of the office and meets supporters regularly, specifically to engage and listen to their feedback. It's this regular contact that helps inform your decision-making and strategy and ensures you build a true picture of what your donors think about your organisation.

INNOVATION

Whilst fundraising can be very formulaic and in some respects scientific and process driven, we must work hard to inject free thinking and inspiration into our work. Otherwise we run the risk of becoming detached from the cause, losing our passion and sacrificing longer-term progress by becoming slaves to the here and now.

When caught up in the budget and planning cycle, coupled with the analysis of existing activities, we may well find ourselves unable to find the time and head space to consider new ideas and different ways of doing things. This can be hugely detrimental. It may prevent us operating effectively.

Much of what we do is in the public domain, so a failure to investigate the best practice of others is nothing short of negligence. Quite often the best ideas are those that have already been implemented by others, perhaps even in other fields and industries, and just require a little bit of adaptation. Never should you feel that you have to recreate the wheel, searching for the 'next big idea' to be a success.

Likewise, we are at our most effective when we step back from our everyday challenges and think both creatively and strategically. An hour away from our desk may feel like 60 minutes of lost endeavour but, in truth, investment here in top-line analysis is far more lucrative in the long term than run-of-the-mill activity.

It is perhaps helpful first to clarify exactly what innovation is, starting with some of the myths around it. Respected author and speaker Scott Berkun wrote *The Myths of Innovation* as he believed:

> The word innovation has fallen on hard times. There is no innovation super hero, flying around at innovative speeds, using innovative ninja moves to prevent abuse of the word. Simply saying something is great doesn't make it

so, yet as the success of marketing and advertising demonstrates, this doesn't stop people from trying. The i-word is thrown around so frequently it no longer means anything.[5]

He summarises the 10 myths of innovation in this excellent book as follows:

- The myth of epiphany – few mention the millions of 'epiphanies' people have had that ended in years of failure. We love stories of flashes of insight and they dominate how creativity is reported. Epiphany stories project illusions of certainty since they're always about successful ideas. Epiphanies are a consequence of effort, not just the inspiration for it. When you hear a story about a flash of insight, the useful questions to ask are **(1)** how much time the creator spent working before the flash happened and **(2)** how much work they did after to make the idea successful. An epiphany doesn't find investors, make prototypes, sacrifice free time, or persist in the face of rejection: only you can do that and you'll have to do it without a guarantee of success.

- The myth that we know history – we romanticise the past to fit the present, creating traps for creatives who don't know the true history of their own field. Inspiring lies are often more popular than complex truths. History is not a straight line of progress, which means the present isn't either. Innovation is old and the tactics for trying to change the present are ancient. Why did America succeed when 90+ per cent of revolutions fail? Was there anything really special about the Rosetta Stone? Dominant ideas aren't necessarily good ones. Find the biggest idea in your field and dig in: you'll be surprised at what you find beneath the surface that helps your work in the present (see myth: the best idea wins).

- The myth of a method – the challenge with creative work, especially in a marketplace, is the many factors beyond your control. You can do everything right and still fail. Most books on creativity make big promises based on history: they cherry pick examples from the past and claim they are predictive. Methods can be useful but they deny that the present is different from the past. There are too many variables in the present to have certainty. This is why terms like innovation system or innovation pipeline are absurd. The idea of an innovation portfolio, where a range of risk is assumed, is more honest. Many books on creativity are surprisingly uncreative (light bulbs should be banned from creativity book covers) and unreal.

- The myth that we love new ideas – we are a conservative species, try something as simple as standing, rather than sitting, in your next group meeting. How accepting were your peers? Conformity is deep in our biology. Whilst talking about creativity is very popular, actually being creative puts your social status at risk. All great ideas were rejected, often for years or decades, yet we bury this in our history (see myths one and two). The history of breakthroughs is a tale of persistence against rejection. Much of what makes successful innovators is their ability to persuade and convince conservative people of the merits of their ideas, a very different skill from creativity itself. Your problem is likely not your ideas, but your skills in pitching ideas to others. Ideas are rarely rejected on their merits; they're rejected because of how they make people feel. The bigger the idea, the harder the challenge of persuasion.

- The myth of the lone inventor – it's easier to worship heroes if they are portrayed as superhuman. But even people worthy of the title genius or prodigy, like Mozart, Picasso and Einstein, had family and teachers who taught them. Many of Edison's patents are shared with co-workers, as despite his huge ego he knew collaboration was critical (his Menlo Park office was one of the first research labs). Stories of mad geniuses who worked completely alone are rare. Pick any master who you think worked alone and read some of their history: you'll be surprised how many people influenced their work. Learning to collaborate, and give and receive feedback, may matter more than your brilliance.

- The myth that good ideas are rare – if you watch any six-year-old child she or he will invent dozens of things in an hour. We are built for creativity. The problem is the conventions of adult life demand conformity and we sacrifice our creative instincts in favour of social status. Unlike a child, adults are supremely and instantly judgemental, killing ideas before they've had even a moment to prove their worth. It's easy to rediscover creativity, which is why brainstorming rarely helps much. We're already creative. The challenge is *ideas don't come with the courage to invest in them*. Good ideas are everywhere; what's uncommon is people with the conviction to put their reputation behind ideas.

- The myth your boss knows more than you – a fallacy of workplaces is that senior staff are better at everything than the people who work for them. This is false in many ways, but creative intuition might be the most false. To rise in power demands good political judgement, yet innovation requires a willingness to defy convention. Those who defy convention are harder to promote in most organisations, yet essential for progress. To assume that senior staff are the best at leading change is a mistake.

- The myth the best idea wins – we lionise winners and history blames losers for their fate. Marketing, politics and timing have tremendous influence on why one idea or its competitors wins, yet these details are more complex than we want to hear. It's satisfying to believe the best idea has won in the past, because it's something we want to believe about the present too. But to be successful with ideas demands studying why some lousy ideas have triumphed (why doesn't the USA use the metric system?) and some great ones are still on the sidelines. The world of ideas is not a pure meritocracy and you need to act accordingly.

- The myth that problems are less interesting than solutions – Einstein said, 'If I had 20 days to solve a problem I would take 19 to define it.' There are many creative ways to think about a problem and different ways to look at a situation. The impatient run at full speed into solving things, speeding right past the insights needed to find a great solution. If you listen to how successful creators talk about their daily work, they spend more time thinking about the problem than epiphany-obsessed media would have us believe.

- The myth innovation is always good – how would you feel about an invention that ends your profession? What impact will an idea have one, five, 10, 100 years from now? All innovation is change and all change helps some people and hurts others. Many horrible inventions were created with the best intentions (and some horrible intentions led to some good consequences). Benz and Ford never imagined automobiles would kill 40,000 people annually in the USA. And the Wright brothers never imagined Predator drones. Any successful idea has a multitude of consequences that are impossible to predict and difficult to even measure.

So, if those are the myths of innovation, then what does it actually mean for fundraisers? We subscribe to the view in *Innovation (still) Rules.*[6] that there are three types of innovation that are important to the nonprofit sector:

- Incremental innovation – also described as operational or tactical, is about making small changes to processes or services to make a big difference to impact or outputs.

- New product development innovation – is about strategic development of products and services, or adapting and developing current ones to new or existing audiences.

- Radical innovation – also referred to as disruptive or transformational, is developing something so different that it will change the not-for-profit world as we know it.

When most people say 'we need to innovate!' they are thinking about radical innovation, yet most of the time the solutions to the problem you face are likely to have been solved elsewhere, can be solved through incremental innovation, or new product development innovation.

We can't think of any truly radical innovation in fundraising in the last 50 years. Don't believe us? Then let us take a look at face-to-face fundraising, which is often hailed as a radical innovation.

When you break it down, the innovation comes from building on existing sound practices and bringing them together:

- Years of major donor fundraising had taught fundraisers that face-to-face asks work best.
- For many years it was too expensive to do this for smaller gift amounts.
- Direct bank payments gave the ability to take regular payments and reduced the costs of doing mass market face-to-face asks.
- The best place to talk face to face with someone is in public.
- Put that all together and street fundraising is born.

This is not to downplay the brains and foresight that developed face-to-face fundraising. Direct bank payments had been around since the 1950, but took over 40 years before the idea was developed.

The point we want to make is that street fundraising was not truly radical, rather a combination of clever insight, hard work and lateral thinking that produced a great new way to raise money.

Innovation works best when it is part of a continuous drive to improve standards and the quality of your fundraising. Yes, you should undoubtedly try new things and develop new products. But do not do this at the expense of good quality fundraising practices that have stood the test of time. Do all you can to make sure you and your colleagues do not fall for one of Berkun's myths listed earlier.

Consultant and author Lucy Gower shares 10 steps to enhance your innovation skills in her book *The Innovation Workout*.[7]

1. Pinpoint your purpose – pick areas for innovation that have the potential to make the most impact to your fundraising. Be clear why your innovation is important and communicate this in a way that inspires others to get involved. Make sure you describe the problem you want to solve (or the unmet need you are addressing) in a way that other people can easily understand.

2. Know and understand your donors – you need to understand who your donors are and what motivates them. Use some of the research tactics described earlier in this chapter to turn your knowledge into insight that you can use for your innovation.

3. Your market today and predicting the trends of tomorrow – you need to understand the marketplace that your customers operate in and what your competitors/other charities are doing. Identify what they are succeeding at and failing at. Use this information to spot trends and to help you develop ideas for the future.

4. Build your creative capacity – think about how you can broaden your own and colleagues' capacity for having ideas. Expand your experiences to help

broaden your thinking skills. Learn how to collect and record ideas and practise connecting new ideas.

5   Creative superstardom and lots of ideas – see if anything is inhibiting your creativity. Use a range of techniques to help generate lots of ideas. Develop multiple solutions to problems and don't stop at your first idea.

6   Don't expect anyone else to like your idea – you need to be able to influence others and gain support for your ideas. Consider other people's motivations and try and create win-win situations.

7   Filter and choose the best ideas – you need to filter your ideas and choose those that have the greatest chance of success. Don't be afraid to say 'no' to weaker ideas and only progress an idea that you believe can work.

8   Prototype, fail fast and refine – use prototyping to sample or model your idea so you can get immediate feedback. This can save many problems later on in the process. By doing this quickly and cheaply you gain feedback to evaluate your ideas and refine your solution.

9   Pilot, adapt and invest – use pilot testing to see if your idea works in the real world. This will give you an idea if your innovation is ready to launch, or if it still needs further refinement.

10 Take your ideas to market – the final stage is to fully launch your innovation. Make sure you have a strong business case for investing in the innovation and have monitoring tools in place so you can develop (or stop) with the innovation depending on results.

Innovation is a much-used buzzword and seen as something you should be doing. Whilst we agree it is important that you set aside time to develop new ideas, don't forget to get the basics right as well.

Whatever process for innovation you follow, make sure you save all your lessons – what steps have been taken to create and protect your nonprofit's institutional memory? When a long-serving, key member of staff moves on, what will your organisation know about what's worked – and what hasn't?

SYSTEM EXECUTION

All of these endeavours need integration into your organisation's culture and practice. The following cycle is important:

- Benchmarking
- KPI setting
- Innovation and testing
- Execution, monitoring and evaluation
- Integration of lessons learned into the next phase of planning and target setting

And it needs to come from the top down. It should form a central part of your organisation's corporate strategy and be given due attention in your fundraising planning. Additionally, fundraisers should have relevant individual objectives in these areas. And finally, the infrastructure of planning, monitoring and evaluation needs to be created too. This should include templates for recording KPIs and briefing and evaluation documents. Record and assess everything you need to inform your decision-making.

But finally, a note of warning: don't overstretch yourself and overcomplicate the analysis. Reporting forms and analysis documents should be clearly laid out and only the relevant information recorded. Less can be more, if it is insightful. The whole process must be manageable. Only produce data that you can comfortably evaluate and ensure the queries do not have to be run more regularly than you can handle. You will otherwise become overwhelmed and the whole process risks being undermined. Given your undoubted commitment to sector best practice, this would be a calamitous outcome.

NOTES
1. Drucker, Peter (1955). *The Practice of Manager*, Butterworth-Heinemann.
2. Pallotta, Dan (2012). Multiplication philanthropy. *Harvard Business Review*. Available at: https://hbr.org/2012/02/multiplication-philanthropy. Last accessed 10 June 2017.
3. Schwartz, Nancy (2012). *The Non-Profit Marketing Wisdom Guide*. Available to download at: http://gettingattention.org/nonprofit-marketing/nonprofit-marketing-wisdom-guide.html Last accessed 26 October 2016.
4. Schulman, Kevin and Sargeant, Adrian (2013). *How to Measure Donor Loyalty* DonorVoice, page 5. Available to download at: http://www.thedonorvoice/com/downloads/how-to-measure-donor-loyalty-an-article-by-kevin-schulman-and-adrian-sargeant/ Last accessed 15 August 2016.
5. Berkun, Scott (2010) *The Myths of Innovation* (paperback edition), O'Reily Media, New York.
6. nfpSynergy (2013). *Innovation (still) Rules* Online report. Available for download at: http//:nfpsynergy.net/innovation-still-rules. Last accessed 15 August 2016.
7. Gower, Lucy (2015) *The Innovation Workout*, Pearson, London.

Final thoughts and further reading

Well done for reaching the final chapter, although if you are one of those people who read the last chapter first – welcome!

Over the last 19 chapters we have outlined our thoughts on the state of fundraising, our hopes for the future and practical advice on how to be a successful relationship fundraiser. We hope you have found it useful and that the book has given you some ideas you can implement in your organisation and career.

We have both spent the majority of our careers working in the UK. It pains us to see the backlash fundraising has received in recent times from a hostile media and weary public. However, we feel stronger than ever that fundraising is a force for good and we hope this book will convince colleagues that there is a way to inspire donors, keep them happy and raise lots of money.

We want to end with a short summary and reminder of some of the key themes and messages from this book.

Relationship fundraising and supporter experience is more important than ever
In some ways the word 'relationship' can be misleading. As we explained in chapter 3, the view we take is that 'relationship' should be used in its widest sense – how two things relate. As such, our version of relationship fundraising (building very much on Ken's definition) is one that is about all aspects of the supporter experience. How you communicate with donors, understanding your 'why', asking properly for money and delivering fabulous supporter care and feedback.

We believe the transactional model of fundraising, which has been dominant in the UK and US over the last 20 years is untenable. Relationship fundraising is no longer a 'nice to do'. It is an absolute necessity.

We have a duty to beneficiaries to ask for money
That being said, the needs of our beneficiaries should not be ignored. We have a duty to ask for money and must do so in ethical, emotional ways. This duty to ask has to be balanced with the donors right to say 'no' in a way that leaves both parties open to future communication and donation requests.

We are often frightened to treat our donors as adults who can be trusted to keep giving in the face of being offered the chance to say no. If you are doing fundraising well, then people will find giving to your organisation a joy and an important part of who they are. Treating them with respect and giving control to how they interact with you will not lead to mass cancellations and less money raised. We firmly believe the opposite.

In the opening plenary of the 2016 International Fundraising Congress, singer/songwriter and successful crowdfunder Amanda Palmer reminded the audience of fundraisers:

> *A real relationship is never a trick…good asking is an act that fundamentally leaves space for a 'no'.*

We are in complete agreement.

Fundraising can, and must, change
Fundraising ignores the social and technological changes the digital era has brought at its peril. Donors can give increasingly to causes and people in need directly and definitions of charity are changing. Don't believe us? See the rise in popularity of crowd funding, Kiva and Donors Choose.

Of course, there is still room for traditional charities and fundraising to operate and thrive. However, the old fundraising business model will come under increasing pressure and those who won't or can't change could see declining income and relevance.

The era of fundraising based on values and beliefs is here
If the last 20 years of individual giving fundraising could be defined as the transactional and product era, then we hope the next 20 years will be known as the era of supporter-based fundraising driven by deep understanding of someone's values and beliefs.

One of our favourite fundraising thinkers, Richard Turner (formerly of Solar Aid and ActionAid) describes supporters as channels and that fundraisers' should use the power of networks to connect people and raise money. You can only do this when you clearly articulate your 'why' and mission, then allow supporters to share your story in their own way, to their own networks. This is a big shift from traditional approaches based solely on fundraising products and RFM analysis.

One of our favourite quotes comes from artist and author Hugh Macleod. He says 'the market for something to believe in is infinite.' Nowhere is this truer than in our profession.

Make your donors believe, share your values and watch the money follow.

Silos must be demolished: integration across media channels is crucial to success
The result of these changes is that our internal ways of organising our teams need to evolve. Departments shouldn't 'own' segments of donors. You shouldn't be fighting internally about who sends what to donors. They don't care about your internal silos, they care about the problem you are trying to solve.

Looking at how you organise your team to provide the best supporter experience and integrate other departments, such as marketing, campaigning or services is a challenge. Shifting your organisational culture from one that focuses on transactions and products to push is hard to do. However, you need to adapt your team structures accordingly if you mindset is one of partnership, shared values and great experiences.

This is not easy, but is essential for relationship fundraising to flourish.

Further reading and resources
Of course, there is only so much any book can cover and we had to leave out as much as we put in. Therefore, we wanted to share some of our favourite fundraising books and websites for you to delve deeper.

We think all fundraisers have an obligation to keep up to date with the latest thinking and research on our profession. Here are some places to start.

Great fundraising websites and blogs
There is a plethora of fundraising blogs and websites. Craig maintains a list of over 200 on his own blog, *Fundraising Detective*. Over the last decade, some excellent fundraising websites blogs have come and gone. We've listed a small number of our favourites with a focus on those who are long established and cover a wide range of subjects. Apologies in advance to some of the great websites and blogs we have had to leave out.

The Showcase of Fundraising Innovation and Inspiration (www.sofii.org):

We've used a number of stories and examples from SOFII throughout the book. It is a resource the fundraising profession should treasure and contribute to (either financially or with case studies).

The Agitator (www.theagitator.net – subscription required, but we can highly recommend it): daily insights from Roger Craver and Tom Belford. The Agitators never shirk from controversial subjects and telling fundraisers how and why they can do better. They also share some great research and insight.

101fundraising (www.101fundraising.org) – recently taken over by the Resource Alliance, this crowd-sourced blog gives fundraiser's around the world the chance to share their ideas and thinking.

For the latest UK fundraising news we'd recommend, Fundraising UK (www.fundraising.co.uk), *Third Sector* (www.thirdsector.co.uk – registration required) and *Fundraising Magazine* (www.civilsociety.co.uk/fundraising - registration required). In the US the *Chronicle of Philanthropy* (www.philanthropy.com) posts regular updates and news.

We first came across many of the case studies and examples in this book from websites and blogs. These are listed in the references and are worth checking out.

Our favourite fundraising books

Again, it has been hard choosing our favourite fundraising books to share with you. However, we've both picked a small selection that have influenced our thinking and improved our fundraising. We've cheated slightly by not including Ken Burnett's books, or his blog at www.kenburnett.com, as we thought that was a given.

We've borrowed extensively from much of the research in *Retention Fundraising* (Emerson & Church, Publishers, 2014, USA) by Roger Craver. It is a must-read if you are interested in improving your retention.

Jeff Brooks' advice on copywriting and crafting fundraising offers is essential reading. He has a number of books, but the *Fundraiser's Guide to Irresistible Communications* (Emerson & Church, Publishers, 2013, USA) is the one we'd recommend.

Tom Ahern is another amazing copywriter who has written numerous books on fundraising. If you have any responsibility for newsletters then his *Raising More Money With Newsletters Than You Ever Thought Possible* (Emerson & Church, Publishers, 2005, USA) is indispensable. Indispensability also applies to his book on writing a good case for support *Seeing through a Donor's Eyes* (Emerson & Church, Publishers 2009, USA).

Craig's final choice is *It's Not Just About the Money* by Jeff Schriefels and Richard Perry of Veritus Group (Veritus Group, 2014, USA). The Veritus Group blog is an excellent resource for major donor fundraisers and this book encapsulates Schriefels' and Perry's years of experience in the field.

Paul has learned a great deal from Stephen Pidgeon over the years and thoroughly endorses his latest work, *How to Love Your Donors (to Death)* (Directory of Social Change, 2015, UK). *Revolution in the Mailbox*, by Mal Warwick (Jossey-Bass, 2011, USA), also provides a good overarching guide to direct marketing practice.

Finally, Terry Axelrod's *Raising More Money* (Raising More Money Publications, 2004, USA) series on special event and high-value fundraising is also a particularly informative and enjoyable read.

Get involved in the future of fundraising

Craig and Paul have both contributed to the Commission on the Donor Experience, which was established in the wake of fundraising controversies in the UK. The Commission has an ambitious plan across 28 projects and has begun to publish recommendations and research.

We are also on the advisory panel of fundraising think tank Rogare. Based at the University of Plymouth, Rogare is the home of critical fundraising – evaluating what fundraisers know, or think they know, about their profession. There is a rolling process to join their advisory panel and to contribute to their research.

Authors' note

As this book was passing for press there was considerable interest – and, indeed, anxiety – across the UK fundraising fraternity about new fundraising regulation that is about to be introduced. Of course, fundraisers must always follow the law and strive constantly to be not just legal but also decent, honest and truthful in their dealings with donors and the public, pursuing their craft, as this book has consistently stressed, with integrity and commitment to providing an exemplary donor experience at all times. The implications and practical impact of much of this imminent regulation are still to be seen, so readers should take care to familiarise themselves with their duties and obligations under these changes, which may in some places influence or affect the advice given in this book. That said, the donor-based approach to the business of raising money that underpins relationship fundraising is clearly entirely in step with the spirit and intention of these regulatory changes.

For further information please contact the Institute of Fundraising: http://www.institute-of-fundraising.org.uk/home.

Get in touch

Finally, we'd love to hear your thoughts on the book. What parts were most useful? Did you disagree with anything? Have you done anything differently after reading it? Do you have any experiences or stories you'd like to share? You can contact craig@fundraisingdetective.org or paulstein66@hotmail.com

Thanks again for reading and best of luck with your fundraising.

Final thoughts and further reading

Craig Linton

Craig loves helping charities improve their individual giving results. He provides consultancy and hands on support to deliver improved results and donor satisfaction. His clients include the Royal Society for Blind Children, Doctors of the World, CARE International and the Commission on the Donor Experience.

He has been fundraising since 2000 at organisations including Sue Ryder and Amnesty International and held a variety of senior positions.

He blogs at fundraisingdetective.com and has written numerous articles on fundraising. He is a trustee at Thames Hospice, Windsor and on the advisory panel at Rogare - the fundraising think tank based at Plymouth University.

Outside of work he is a foster carer, season-ticket holder at Everton, avid reader and occasional golfer and gardener.

Paul Stein

Paul began his career as a community fundraiser at Macmillan Cancer Support in 2001. He moved to World Jewish Relief six years later, where he became their first director of fundraising, marketing and communications.

In that role, he oversaw a broad-ranging portfolio and, following the implementation of a new strategy, the charity's profile and voluntary income increased substantially, reaching over £5m per annum.

In 2014, Paul joined MQ: Transforming Mental Health; a major new national research charity, seed-funded by the Wellcome Trust. There he has overseen a doubling of voluntary income year on year and was recently acknowledged in a list of the UK's 50 most influential fundraisers.

He is also a regular journal contributor and speaker on the fundraising and marketing conference circuit, where he outlines his commitment to best practice and innovation throughout the sector.

In his spare time, Paul enjoys an eclectic mix of hobbies, including military history, cats, exercise as well as the travails of supporting his two largely unsuccessful football teams: Everton and Barnet FC.